STRATEGIC HUMAN RESOURCE MANAGEMENT

Theory and Practice

Second Edition

Edited by
Graeme Salaman, John Storey and Jon Billsberry

The Open
University

⑤SAGE Publications

in association with

London ● Thousand Oaks ● New Delhi

First published 1998

Second edition published 2005

SAGE Publications Ltd
1 Oliver's Yard
55 City Road
London EC1Y 1SP

SAGE Publications Inc.
2455 Teller Road
Thousand Oaks, California 91320

SAGE Publications India Pvt Ltd
B-42, Panchsheel Enclave
Post Box 4109
New Delhi 110 017

British Library Cataloguing in Publication data

A catalogue record for this book is available from the
British Library

ISBN 1-4129-1900-2
ISBN 1-4129-1901-0 (pbk)

Library of Congress Control Number: 2005926178

Typeset by C&M Digitals (P) Ltd., Chennai, India
Printed and bound in Great Britain by The Cromwell Press Ltd, Trowbridge, Wiltshire
Printed on paper from sustainable resources

Contents

Acknowledgements   vii

**Strategic Human Resource Management:
Defining the Field**   1
Graeme Salaman, John Storey and Jon Billsberry

**Part 1   Strategic Human Resource Management
and Knowledge**   13

1   Human Resources and the Resource Based View of the Firm   17
Patrick M. Wright, Benjamin B. Dunford and Scott A. Snell

2   The Conduct of Management and the Management of Conduct:
Contemporary Managerial Discourse and the Constitution
of the 'Competent' Manager   40
Paul du Gay, Graeme Salaman and Bronwen Rees

3   Foucault, Power/Knowledge, and its Relevance for
Human Resource Management   58
Barbara Townley

4   The Cognitive Perspective on Strategic Decision-making   78
Charles R. Schwenk

5   Achieving 'Fit': Managers' Theories of How to Manage Innovation   91
Graeme Salaman and John Storey

**Part 2   Strategic Human Resource Management
and Business Performance**   117

6   The Impact of Human Resource Management Practices on Turnover,
Productivity, and Corporate Financial Performance   121
Mark A. Huselid

7   A Critical Assessment of the High-performance Paradigm   147
John Godard

8   Performance-related Pay   177
John Storey and Keith Sisson

**Part 3   The Emergence of New Organizational
Forms and Relationships**   185

9   New Organizational Forms and Their Links with HR   189
John Storey

10 Changing Organizational Forms and the Employment Relationship   208
*Jill Rubery, Jill Earnshaw, Mick Marchington,
Fang Lee Cooke and Steven Vincent*

Contents

11 Human Resource Management, Trade Unions and Industrial Relations   237
    David E. Guest

12 Missionary Management   251
    Madeleine Bunting

**Part 4   Strategic Human Resource Management
           in Practice**   271

13 Managing to be Ethical: Debunking Five Business Ethics Myths   273
    Linda Klebe Treviño and Michael E. Brown

14 The Myth of Managing Change   295
    George Binney and Colin Williams

15 Performance Management Strategies   318
    Greg Clark

    Index   342

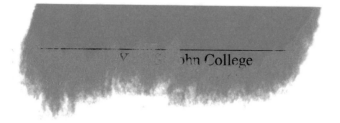
STRATEGIC HUMAN RESOURCE MANAGEMENT

The Open University Business School

The Open University Business School offers a three-tier ladder of opportunity for managers at different stages of their careers: the Professional Certificate in Management; the Professional Diploma in Management; and the Master of Business Administration.

This Reader is the prescribed MBA Course Reader for the Managing Human Resources Module (B824) at The Open University Business School. Opinions expressed in this Reader are not necessarily those of the Course Team or of The Open University.

Further information on Open University Business School courses and qualifications may be obtained from Open University Business School, PO Box 197, Walton Hall, Milton Keynes, MK7 6BJ, United Kingdom; OU Business School Information Line: tel: +44 (0) 8700 100311.

Alternatively, much useful course information can be obtained from the Open University Business School's website at http://www.oubs.open.ac.uk.

Acknowledgements

The editors would like to acknowledge and thank Mark Fenton-O'Creevy, Paul Gooderham and Jenny Lewis for their work sourcing and editing several of the articles. In addition, the editors would like to thank Kiren Shoman, Gill Gowans, Jean Attenborough, Jean Kennedy and Karen McCafferty. Without their considerable help, this book would not have been possible.

Grateful acknowledgement is made to the following sources for permission to reproduce material in this book.

1   *Human Resources and the Resource Based View of the Firm*
    Patrick M. Wright, Benjamin B. Dunford and Scott A. Snell (2001) *Journal of Management*, 27: 701–21. © 2001, with permission from Elsevier Science Inc.

2   *The Conduct of Management and the Management of Conduct: Contemporary Managerial Discourse and the Constitution of the 'Competent' Manager*
    Paul du Gay, Graeme Salaman and Bronwen Rees (1996) *Journal of Management Studies*, 33(3): 263–82. Reproduced by permission of Blackwell Publishers Ltd.

3   *Foucault, Power/Knowledge, and its Relevance for Human Resource Management*
    Barbara Townley (1993) *The Academy of Management Review*, 18(3): 518–45. © 1993; permission conveyed through Copyright Clearance Center, Inc.

4   *The Cognitive Perspective on Strategic Decision-making*
    Charles R. Schwenk (2002) in G. Salaman (ed.), *Decision Making for Business: A Reader*. London: SAGE/The Open University. Originally published as C. Schwenk (1988) 'The cognitive perspective on strategic decision-making', *Journal of Management Studies*, 25(1): 41–55. Reproduced by permission of Blackwell Publishers Ltd.

6   *The Impact of Human Resource Management Practices on Turnover, Productivity, and Corporate Financial Performance*
    Mark A. Huselid (1995) *Academy of Management Journal*, 38(3): 635–72. Republished with permission of The Academy of Management © 1995; permission conveyed through Copyright Clearance Center Inc.

7   *A Critical Assessment of the High-performance Paradigm*
    John Godard (2004) *British Journal of Industrial Relations*, 42(2): 349–78. Reproduced by permission of Blackwell Publishing Ltd.

10 *Changing Organizational Forms and the Employment Relationship*
    Jill Rubery, Jill Earnshaw, Mick Marchington, Fang Lee Cooke and Steven Vincent (2002) *Journal of Management Studies*, 39(5): 645–72. Reproduced by permission of Blackwell Publishers Ltd.

11   *Human Resource Management, Trade Unions and Industrial Relations*
     David E. Guest (1995) in J. Storey (ed.), *HRM: A Critical Text*. London: Thomson.
     Reproduced by permission of the publisher.

12   *Missionary Management*
     Madeleine Bunting (2004) *Willing Slaves: How the Overwork Culture is Ruling
     our Lives*. London: HarperCollins Publishers. Reprinted by permission of
     A.P. Watt Ltd on behalf of Madeleine Bunting and HarperCollins Publishers
     Ltd. © Madeleine Bunting 2004.

13   *Managing to be Ethical: Debunking Five Business Ethics Myths*
     Linda Klebe Treviño and Michael E. Brown (2004) *Academy of Management
     Executive*, 18(2): 69–81. Republished with permission of The Academy of
     Management © 2004; permission conveyed through Copyright Clearance
     Center Inc.

14   *The Myth of Managing Change*
     Chapters 2 and 3 in G. Binney and C. Williams (1995) *Leaning into the Future:
     Changing the Way People Change Organisations*. London: Nicholas Brealey
     Publishing Ltd. Reprinted by kind permission of Nicholas Brealey Publishing.

15   *Performance Management Strategies*
     Greg Clark (1998) in C. Mabey, G. Salaman and J. Storey (eds), *Human Resource
     Management: A Strategic Introduction*, pp. 123–52. Reproduced by permission
     of Blackwell Publishers Ltd.

Strategic Human Resource Management: Defining the Field

Graeme Salaman, John Storey and Jon Billsberry

The significance of Strategic Human Resource Management

Strategic Human Resource Management (SHRM) has been, and remains, one of the most powerful and influential ideas to have emerged in the field of business and management during the past twenty-five years. Policy makers at government level have drawn upon the idea in order to promote 'high performance workplaces' and 'human capital management'. Within business corporations, the idea that the way in which people are managed could be one of, if not *the* most crucial factor in the whole array of competitiveness-inducing variables, has become a widely accepted proposition during this period. Many management consultancy firms – both large and small – have built substantial businesses by translating the concept into frameworks, methodologies and prescriptions. And, not least, academics have analysed, at considerable length, the meaning, significance and the evidence base for the ideas associated with SHRM.

The central idea – broadly stated – is that while for much of the industrial age, 'labour' was treated as an unfortunate 'cost', it became possible to view it in an entirely different light; as an 'asset'. Economists and accountants routinely classified labour as one the main 'variable costs'. Accordingly, procedures and managerial systems were aligned with this view. Labour was seen as plentiful and dispensable.

Little thought was given to its recruitment, little investment was made in its development, and the modes of 'industrial discipline' were based on direct command and control mixed occasionally with the strictures of performance related pay. 'Hire and fire' was a common term. In these circumstances, conflict was expected and industrial relations officers were employed in order to negotiate 'temporary truces' (otherwise known as collective agreements). These were considered successful if they delivered compliance with managerially-prescribed rules.

Progressive labour management in the decades before SHRM was based on productivity bargaining (Flanders, 1964) which periodically 'bought-out' accumulated customs and practices which impeded productivity. Government industrial relations policy in the mid-twentieth century was built around the idea of joint regulation: the accommodation of interests between the 'two-sides' through mutual respect and collective bargaining.

But, in the 1980s, a number of large companies began to change the rules of the game. New concepts, new logics and new aspirations emerged and many of the previous ones fell out of favour. Employers such as British Airways began to talk in terms of wanting not simply compliance but 'commitment'. Faced with severe competition they were prepared to dispense with employees who were not prepared to 'commit' to the new agenda of customer service. They spent unusual sums on staff training, staff development and 'culture change'. At the same time, Jaguar, the luxury car maker introduced its programme for 'winning hearts and minds'. General managers, rather than industrial relations officers and personnel managers, began to set the agenda. They started to drop the language of compromise and of customary practices and instead talk about 'customers first' and the 'needs of the business'.

The wider economic and political contexts, of course, also played a part though they were by no means deterministic. Heightened competition from Japan and other Far-Eastern economies resulted in factory closures and huge job losses in the USA and in other western economies. Reagonomics and Thatcherism established a free-market climate; de-regulation and privatization were making a difference to patterns of thinking.

Taken together, there occurred a wholesale shift in thinking and in practice relating to people-management over a period of some twenty-plus years. Perhaps not surprisingly, while some observers expected rapid transformation, others were sceptical and academics frequently detected as much 'continuity' as change. Many expected HRM and SHRM to be transient.

Depending how one interprets the contours it is still possible to construct images of rather different landscapes. One stance would be to note that the past two to three decades have been as marked by subcontracting and the loosening of employment contracts as they have moved towards human asset-management. In recent months, the 'gangmasters' who buy, sell and deploy labour, much of it comprised of workers not legally-entitled to work, and under conditions reminiscent of the nineteenth century let alone the twentieth, have captured the headlines more than HR Directors. Short-term contracts, temporary work, call-centre employment, off-shoring and the like have all challenged the simple idea of an unproblematic transition and progression to a more sophisticated, high-value-added, high-performance workforce, high-commitment management, employment nirvana.

Yet on the other hand, it can also be argued that while the contingent workforce has grown, this evidences the 'hard' version of SHRM (the willingness to treat human resources as other resources and not to be fettered by long-standing practices). Alongside this, employment management in the core (and it has also been noted that short-term contract labour has remained at around 7 per cent of the workforce) is now routinely conceptualized in terms of SHRM assumptions, frameworks and logics rather more so than in terms of the erstwhile industrial relations paradigm of the 1960s–1980s. The intervening period has seen a whole series of movements (in theory and practices) which are easily interpreted as expressive of, or even re-workings of, the SHRM framework. Key examples include: the learning organization, the resource-based view of the firm, the celebration of the importance of 'knowledge workers', investment in people, high performance work systems and so on. Perhaps most important of all, whether fully realized in practice or not, the idea that it is sensible for an organization in the public or private sector to view its people management in a *strategic way* is nowadays conventional wisdom.

So, given this pattern and climate of change at multiple levels, how should strategic human resource management be defined?

A definition of SHRM?

There is a fundamental paradox at the heart of any attempt to define or otherwise engage with SHRM. Despite, or possibly directly because of, the important role SHRM plays in theories of, and attempts to describe, understand, critique and change organizations and theories of organizational structures and functioning, it is virtually impossible to define SHRM. There is no such thing as SHRM because SHRM is not a unitary phenomenon but a collection of phenomena. It consists of very diverse phenomena: prescriptions, models, theories and critiques.

Categories of SHRM

Broadly speaking, the SHRM literature can be divided into two categories.

The first consists of work which is concerned with identifying and seeking to understand the features of organization that are regarded as determinants of organizational performance. The task is to identify key causal connections and to assess their impact on the capability of the organization and on the behaviour, attitudes, and skills of staff. This line of work can itself be further differentiated into two forms. On the one hand, there are the academic, research-based analyses and assessments of the factors which may influence levels of performance (selection processes, competences, types of training, changing structural forms, various employment strategies, the resource-based view and so on). And on the other hand, there is the consultancy literature which advocates particular 'solutions' and seeks to sell their merits to managers.

The standard academic literature seeks to identify and understand the role and impact of the organizational measures (structures, processes and so on) that are installed as a result of consultant recommendation or as a result of other influences. Singularly and together, these measures are claimed to impact positively on organizational performance. Therefore they merit attention.

The second type of SHRM literature, which is less well developed than the first but of equal importance, is directly related to, but stands apart from, this prescriptive literature. Rather than focusing directly on how organizational performance can be improved through capacity-building or staff management processes, it focuses on the *ideas underpinning* prevalent practices.

Moreover, difficulties of definition arise because SHRM changes over time; it is a moving target. Authoritative and dominant views of what constitutes sensible and effective programmes of organizational change, are themselves highly changeable. Conceptions of the organizational factors or processes, which are seen to determine high levels of organizational success, vary over time: for example, culture change, process re-engineering, management competences, knowledge management, and transformational leadership. That said, a good case could be made that these changes are more apparent than real, and that underlying the shifting interest in culture change, competences, leadership and so on is a set of unchanging and probably unresolvable core organizational and management issues and problems.

None the less, the above difficulties notwithstanding, it is possible to say something about the underlying ideas that have caught people's imagination. Moreover, statements have to be made because those managers who seek to mobilize others (including other managers) need to be able to articulate the big idea. It has been noted that the idea of strategic human resource management can be regarded as a 'discursive formation' and that when exponents talk about SHRM, they are broadly referring to an understood set of interconnecting propositions. Within the confines of this approach, SHRM has been defined as follows:

> A distinctive approach to employment management which seeks to achieve competitive advantage through the strategic deployment of a highly committed and capable workforce using an array of cultural, structural and personnel techniques. (Storey, 2001: 6)

It should be noted that this is not *our* definition but rather the encapsulation of the meaning-making of strategic actors. That point has not always been understood.

Another approach to 'defining' SHRM is to treat the task as the demarcation of an academic field of enquiry and/or a general field of practical activity. This is essentially what Boxall and Purcell (2003) do when they describe how their definition 'allows for a wide variety of management styles' (p. 3). They go on to state 'Human resource management (alternatively employee relations or labour management) includes the firm's work systems and its models of employment. It embraces both individual and collective aspects of people management. It is not restricted to any one style or ideology' (p. 23).

Both approaches are legitimate. It is a reasonable ambition to seek to construct an analytical framework with hypothesized causal connections and with an open-model which allows for multiple and variegated choices about how to manage work (and often, indeed, multiple choices are made for different groups within the same firm). This endeavour is in effect designed to define the field. But it is equally legitimate, albeit a different ambition, to seek to explore the meaning and implications of a more specific mode of approach to managing labour – of the kind that came to prominence in the 1980s. Boxall and Purcell acknowledge this point, but this distinction between the generic and the particular meanings of SHRM, which has been noted from the very outset of the debate, seems periodically to trigger misunderstanding.

Underlying forces

How and why the content of SHRM is so diverse and why it changes over time are themselves important issues. If SHRM is a repository of the ways in which academics, consultants, senior managers and other authorities think about and attempt to change organizations – and how some of them at least think about and evaluate these theories and prescriptions – then an understanding of how and why SHRM changes is important because these changing ideas are highly significant. They affect how organizations are changed, and how they perform; they affect how employees are treated, they affect security of employment and they affect the nature of employment. They also affect us as individuals, influencing how we see ourselves and our relationships. SHRM prescriptions, theories and practices mediate between the public and the private, defining the relationship between biography and history. Although SHRM initiatives are frequently presented by their proponents as simply technical matters – means of improving organizational performance – they frequently owe their appeal and influence to their affinities with larger political ideological forces.

Since SHRM ideas are so influential in defining and constituting both organizations and individuals, and the relationship between the two, these ideas require searching, critical, attention. One of the curiosities of the SHRM field – at least as defined by some critical academic contributors – is the propensity of those with responsibility for organizational efficiency (managers, civil servants, governments) enthusiastically to embrace ideas about and prescriptions for organizations and management whose appeal seems to be based more on the attractiveness of their promises than the quality of their logic, assumptions or any basis in research. It is crucial that those interested in these ideas, as HR practitioners or managers or academics, thoroughly evaluate and understand them. Central to this evaluation is the exploration of their appeal.

Sometimes this conviction of the obvious and inherent good sense of a popular and appealing approach to organizational change arises from extra-organizational factors – from wider societal and political ways of thinking or ideologies, or from societal values and established ways of thinking. A number of examples can be cited ranging from the rise to prominence of ideas of 'excellence' in the early 1980s (Peters and Waterman, 1982) which represented a 'discovery' of a home-grown American formula for management, ideas of 'enterprise' and ideas around the importance of 'leadership'. For instance, Guest (1992) charted how the appeal of 'excellence' owed its success and appeal to, among other factors, the ways it resonated with basic American values. The success of Peters and Waterman's book which advocates management's exploitation of values within the corporation itself rests on the authors' ability to exploit the values held by the book's reader.

Similar analyses have been conducted into a range of recent popular management fashions and fads. These include studies of management gurus (Clark and Salaman, 1998); Business Process Re-engineering (BPR) (Grint, 1994); corporate culture (Jeffcutt, 1994); the management of innovation (Storey and Salaman, 2005); and individual management inspirationalists such as Steven Covey (Jackson, 1996). An example of how the advocates of new approaches to organization seek to position the proposals in terms consistent with the values of the audience can be taken from the writing of Hammer and Champy, who are the most well-known and most influential advocates of Business Process Re-engineering. For example, they argue quite explicitly that 'reengineering capitalises on the same characteristics that traditionally made Americans such great business innovators: individualism, self-reliance, a willingness to take risks, and a propensity for change' (Hammer and Champy, 1993: 3).

Peters and Waterman's (1982) book on excellence launched a huge number of programmes aimed at culture change within organizations; that is, organizational change programmes and training and development initiatives aimed at changing employees' attitudes. The appeal to management was obvious and strong: that culture change could solve the primary organizational problem – the problem for which Henry Ford ninety years ago devised his particular brand of paternalism with the $5 a day promise for committed workers: the problem of worker attitude. Enormous sums were spent by organizations on culture change initiatives because managers were persuaded of the sense and value of Peters and Waterman's recommendation, regardless of the many and manifest deficiencies of the research on which the book was based and the coherence and strength of the argument they advanced.

Integral to the appeal of culture change programmes was their claim to be able to solve one of the most basic management problems: how to ensure that employees are committed to the objectives of the organization as set by senior management. Currently, the favoured solution advocated to help deal with this problem is 'leadership'. The amount of attention paid to and money invested in, leadership over the past decade is extraordinary. As Storey has noted, the literature and the courses on leadership have grown exponentially (Storey, 2004: 3–7). He observes:

> more telling than the absolute numbers (of publications on leadership)
> is the apparent increase in attention to the theme over recent time.
> A search of the Ebsco site which indexes and abstracts published
> articles on business and management, reveals a phenomenal trend.
> During the two-year period from January 1970 to the end of
> December 1971 there were just 136 published articles, according to a
> search using the defaults field. During the equivalent period ten years later
> (1980–1) the number had doubled to 258. But in the two-year period 1990–1
> the number mushroomed to 1,105 articles, and even more remarkable was
> that the result for the equivalent two-year period a decade later (2001–2),
> which revealed an astonishing 10,062 published articles – an average of
> 419 per month. (2004: 4)

Meanwhile, organizational expenditure on leadership development in the USA is estimated at £45 billion in 1997. In the UK and Europe, leadership is central to the European Foundation For Quality (EFQM) management framework and other quality assurance models. Central government has launched the National College of School Leadership, the health service has a leadership programme, and the Department of Trade and Industry and other government departments launched a heavy-weight report on 'Leadership: The Challenge For All'.

Then there are the omnipresent ideas about 'managing change'. Management thinking and decisions about the management of change are influenced by the ideas and practices about necessary and desirable organizational change and training and development that are popular, prevalent and pervasive at the time. This is an important area for research. Too little is known – although much is assumed and asserted – about the models and assumptions underlying managers' decisions on and choices of, organizational structures and logics. Two researchers have argued, for example, that in reality a great deal of organizational change is driven not in fact by rational analysis of organizational problems, but by the availability of attractive 'solutions' for which managers then find the problems (Brunsson and Olsen, 1993). Frequently, the appeal of SHRM ideas at the organizational level arises from their connections with higher level societal and political ways of thinking which supply authoritative support. The apparent 'truth' of the recommended SHRM proposals arises from the power of these higher-order ideas, which supply legitimacy and make normal, proposals for change at the organizational level and in due course at the individual level as well.

A good example of this is supplied by the notion of 'enterprise'. Enterprise is central to many of the most important forms of organizational change (and is significant as a rationalizing authority in a number of chapters in this collection). It is central to the assault on bureaucracy; it legitimizes de-regulation and privatization of public services and it underpins policies of empowerment and teamwork. Enterprise is an idea which operates on three levels: economic/political, organizational/institutional, and technologies of the self or individual (Rose, 1990a; b). Originally a term applied to economies and to organizations, it emerged as a dominant theme of Conservative Government ideology in the 1980s and 1990s as a key component of the advocacy of economic liberalism and the advocacy of market forces, and remains fundamental to the Labour Government of today (Keat and Abercrombie, 1991). It is one of the attractions of the notion of enterprise that it allows connections between these individual, institutional and political levels: 'enterprise links up a seductive ethics of the self, a powerful critique of contemporary institutional and political reality and an apparently coherent design for the radical transformation of contemporary social arrangements' (Rose, 1990a: 6).

So, enterprise exemplifies a number of key features of SHRM thinking and practice. First, it shows how ideas that are dominant at a societal/political level are also highly influential at the organizational and ultimately individual levels. For example, the chapter by Storey (in this volume) reveals how notions of 'enterprise' (and neo-liberal conceptions of market forces) are powerful determinants of organizational restructuring. And the chapters by du Gay et al. and Townley show how the notion of enterprise as an organizational value impacts on the individual.

The second feature of SHRM illustrated by the emphasis on enterprise is the way in which this dominant value becomes not only associated with, and supportive of, a series of projects at various levels (restructuring, decentralization, the move to SBUs, the installation of PRP, of management competences and so on), but also associated with and supportive of, the critique or assault on organizational forms and processes which are defined as un-enterprising. Hence, enterprise 'rules-in' and makes normal and acceptable some organizational forms, processes, relationships and logics, while it 'rules-out' others. Enterprise is inherently associated with, and required and legitimated by, reference to the pervasive and dominant critique of bureaucracy at the organizational and societal levels. The much-maligned bureaucracy is framed in opposition with virtuous enterprise which permits only one outcome. Bureaucracy 'is reduced to a simple and abstract set of negativities contrasted with an equally simple and abstracted, but positively coded, set of entrepreneurial principles' (du Gay, 2004: 44). Within this enforced polarity, the stronger and more pervasive the critique of bureaucracy, the greater the acceptance of the importance of enterprise at organizational and at individual levels.

The field of SHRM in our view is therefore constituted by a series of diverse influences: overarching societal/political discourses within which certain sorts of organizational initiatives appear natural and sensible; consultants' prescriptions which appeal because of their affinities with pervasive values and ideologies; and managers' underlying models and assumptions.

The role of the discipline of SHRM – and therefore of this volume – is to identify these influences and assess their impact; it is to evaluate and assess. In a way that parallels the recent emergence of interest in the cognitive aspects of organizations – especially the cognitive aspects of strategy development and environmental analysis – this approach to SHRM focuses on the nature and origin and influence of the ideas underpinning SHRM initiatives. Furthermore, students of SHRM must not only avoid merely accepting passively the recommendations and prescriptions of those authorities who advocate SHRM initiatives, they must assess their provenance and assumptions and evaluate them in practice. Students of SHRM must also explore and evaluate how these work in practice and with what consequences, which is a major feature of this volume.

Receptors and interpreters

But there is another crucial stage in this sequence of the design (or advocacy) of SHRM initiatives and their application and evaluation: it is also important to understand the processes whereby available and dominant SHRM proposals are understood, translated and assessed by senior decision-makers within organizations. This key step is often overlooked. Much SHRM literature simply assumes that senior managers understand and accept the proposals for organizational change advocated by the various authorities who propound them. But this is to ignore the crucial role of *managers' own theorizing* about organizations – the way they seek to understand the relationship between proposals for change and organizational effects – and their models of organization. These issues are explored in some depth by two chapters in this collection: those by Schwenk (Chapter 4), and by Salaman and Storey (Chapter 5).

Against this backcloth, as students of SHRM we have two main tasks – both of which are represented in this volume. We must identify and understand the processes whereby the field of SHRM is defined and constituted (and the processes whereby senior managers make sense of these propositions); and we must address the specific proposals and projects which in our view are the more interesting, important, and possibly, effective. Of course in executing this second task we too are defining the field: neglecting some areas of activity, emphasizing others. This collection does not represent the whole field of SHRM: it represents our view of it and our assessment of some of its most important issues and areas.

Much of this volume is dedicated to presenting and assessing the various diverse projects which constitute SHRM initiatives or the theory underpinning SHRM initiatives. These chapters represent the ways in which those who study SHRM initiatives and theories attempt to make sense of and assess these initiatives.

This volume is organized into four main parts. The first of these is a collection of chapters which illustrate the critically detached assessment of SHRM; that is, the approach which we described above as focusing on the ideas underpinning the theory and the practice. The second part addresses the subject from the point of view which has been predominant in recent years; namely the evaluation of the impact of SHRM on performance. The third part then turns to another major theme; the newly emerging forms of organization and of relationships. The standard assumption in much discourse of a singular employer with a directly employed workforce is coming under increasing challenge. The SHRM implications of the changes are explored in this part of the book. Finally, in the final part of the volume we attend to three key sub-themes of contemporary practice: ethics, change management and performance management.

In summary, we suggest that SHRM can best be understood in relation to wider political, economic and social movements; in relation to major shifts in ideas and their underlying cultural contexts; and in relation to daily experimentation by managers and workers as they seek to try-out the theories of 'professional theorists' and of practitioner-theorists. It is in these multiple ways that knowledge of the field of SHRM slowly emerges.

References

Boxall, P. and Purcell, J. (2003) *Strategy and Human Resource Management*, Basingstoke: Palgrave Macmillan.

Brunsson, N. and Olsen, J.P. (1993) *The Reforming Organisation*, London: Routledge.

Clark, T. and Salaman, G. (1998) Telling tales: Management gurus' narratives and the construction of managerial identity, *Journal of Management Studies*, 35(2): 137–61.

du Gay, P. (2004) 'Against Enterprise (but not against enterprise)', *Organization*, 11(1): 37–59.

Flanders, A. (1964) The Fawley Productivity Agreements.

Grint, K. (1994) Re-engineering history: Social resonances and business process re-engineering, *Organisation*, 1: 179–201.

Guest, D. (1992) Right enough to be dangerously wrong, in Salaman, G. (ed.), *Human Resource Strategies*, London: Sage, pp. 5–19.

Hammer, M. and Champy, J. (1993) *Reengineering the Corporation*, London: Nicholas Brealey.

Jackson, B. (1996) Re-engineering the sense of self: The manager and the management guru, *Journal of Management Studies*, 33: 571–90.

Jeffcutt, P. (1994) The interpretation of organisation: A contemporary analysis and critique, *Journal of Management Studies*, 31: 225–50.

Keat, R. and Abercrombie, N. (1991) *Enterprise Culture*, London: Routledge.

Peters, T. and Waterman, R. (1982) *In Search of Excellence*. New York: Harper & Row.

Rose, N. (1990a) *Governing the Soul*, London: Routledge.

Rose, N. (1990b) Governing the enterprising self, in Heelas, P. and Morris, P. (eds), *The Values of the Enterprise Culture – The Moral Debate*, London: Unwin Hyman.

Storey, J. (2001) 'Human resource management today: an assessment', in Storey, J. (ed.), *Human Resource Management: A Critical Text*, London: Thomson Learning.

Storey, J. (ed.) (2004) *Leadership in Organizations: Current Issues and Key Trends*, London: Routledge.

Storey, J. and Salaman, G. (2005) *Managers of Innovation*, Oxford: Blackwell.

Part 1

Strategic Human Resource Management and Knowledge

The strategic management of human resources consists of a number of different – even opposed – things at the same time. For example, it is an actual role, or position within organizations; a position with responsibilities and associated expertise, a role which is itself subject to change. It is also a set of practices or processes associated with this role. It is a distinctive approach – or approaches, for there is more than one – to the development of organizational capability, supplying recommendations for ways to improve organizational effectiveness and efficiency. Since it consists of practices and prescriptions about what should be done, it is also a theory since it argues that certain actions will produce certain effects, which is what theories do. And finally, because it contains so many promises and assumes so much, it has attracted the attention of those who study or advise organizations or who have an interest in understanding the nature, origin and implications of what happens within organizations. It has attracted commentary, critique and analysis. This collection includes materials relevant to all of these elements. But it starts with work from the final two categories.

The writers, from whose work the selection in Part 1 is drawn, focus on the nature and validity of the theoretical underpinnings of SHRM, or on the critical assumptions or implications of the claims and practices of SHRM. This doesn't mean that they are not interested in the practical outcomes of SHRM; but it may mean that the practical outcomes they identify and address may be different from those stressed by the more practically minded SHRM advocates.

For example, they may explore the unintended consequences of SHRM proposals, or evaluate the bases of the claims made by SHRM writers. Or they may unpick the mechanisms involved in common-place SHRM processes and structures – competences, appraisal, development – and show that these pervasive and widely accepted processes are not as simple as they seem or that they carry significant, but overlooked, implications for the individuals involved. Nor does an interest in the nature and validity of the theories and assumptions employed (however implicitly) by those who advocate initiatives to improve organizational performance, lack practical consequences. Poor theories produce poor consequences: all SHRM prescriptions need to be thoroughly evaluated, however appealing they may be – especially when they are appealing and appear to be obviously sensible – for that is when we may be tempted to drop our critical guard.

The theme which unites and gives coherence to all the chapters in this first part is the theme of knowledge; the nature, origins and implications of the various types of knowledge that are involved in SHRM. Chapter 1 is about the knowledge involved in theories of SHRM. It plots the relationship between theories of the resource-based view of the firm and theories of SHRM. It is about academics' knowledge and helps to make sense of two related but distinct sets of theoretical and conceptual knowledge. Chapter 2 is about a certain sort of HR knowledge: organizational knowledge of managers in terms of competence frameworks, its nature and implications. Chapter 3 is about the nature of knowledge itself and the power significance of HR knowledge. Chapter 4 is about the process whereby people come to think they know: it is about the processes of organizational cognition (about strategy or HR strategy or the links between the two). The final chapter is about the crucial linkage between strategies and structures. If SHRM in at least one of its versions is about achieving a 'fit' between objectives and organizational capacity, the achievement of this fit is dependent on how managers and their HR advisers understand or theorize the relationship between strategies and the design of organizations. But this link has been relatively unstudied.

The first chapter in Part 1 is a mapping exercise. It offers a useful and comprehensive overview of the many and various connections between the resource-based view of the firm (RBV) and the theoretical and practical elements of SHRM. As we noted earlier, one aspect of SHRM is concerned with the ways in which organizational capability to achieve strategic objectives can be enhanced. However, there is more than one way of improving organizational capability. The usual ways are either by installing 'high performance' measures, or by adapting organizational elements to the requirements of organizations' strategies – what is known as improving 'fit'. Both argue that organizations must be adapted to support existing strategies. RBV reverses the causal connection between organizational capabilities or strengths and strategy by arguing in essence that strategies can be built on existing organizational capacities – variously defined. In principle, the RBV places considerable practical and strategic emphasis on the role of organizational and human factors in determining organizational performance – and thus supports the contribution of SHRM and of HR professionals since these are directly concerned with the management of these factors.

Chapter 2 represents another tradition within the critical analysis of organizational structure and dynamics and thus of SHRM initiatives: how senior management attempts to control and direct the organization and to ensure the commitment and compliance of staff through attempts to define the character, conduct and identity of the manager. Here, as in a number of other chapters in this section, the focus is on the origin and implications of current SHRM initiatives; in this case, management competence frameworks and architectures. The chapter defines 'implications' in distinctive ways; an approach Chapter 2 shares with the following chapter by Townley. Implications are defined here not in terms of the objectives of senior managers and their HR advisers; but for those who are caught up in competence initiatives. Chapters 2 and 3 continue a long tradition of research into and discussion about organizations: the impact of organizational structures and processes on the individual employee. Organizations and senior managers are understandably more interested in what individual employees can do for the organization than what organizations do to individuals. And this is responsible for the importance of decisions about how they are managed – not least through HR initiatives designed and implemented by HR professionals – in order to maximize their contribution to the organization. Chapter 2 explores the ways in which efforts to ensure the maximum contribution of managers to their employing organization increasingly occur through initiatives which stipulate what is expected of the manager and, in effect, seek to redefine the individual's view of herself as a person. This chapter raises a possibility which deserves serious attention from HR professionals and those concerned with understanding the nature and significance of HR activities: that attempts to control how people think and behave at work (for this is essentially the focus of HR and management activity) also have significance for how people see themselves; for the sort of people they become; and, how they understand and make sense of themselves in their narratives of themselves.

Drawing on the work of Michel Foucault, Townley argues that power and knowledge are inextricably inter-linked: knowing something involves power and power is exercised through knowledge. The ramifications of this for SHRM and those who study or practise it are fundamental and important. One implication concerns the status of knowledge, including the sort of knowledge that HR develops of individuals. If knowledge and power are indistinguishable, each supporting the other, knowledge makes the thing or person that is known, subject to the play of power. Thus knowledge does not describe the person; as du Gay et al. in Chapter 2 argued, it 'makes up' the individual, constitutes or invents her. It also means that knowledge – including the expert or professional knowledge of the HR function, or the knowledge gathered by HR staff creates the world (and the individuals) it describes, and is not powerful because it is true, but is regarded as true because it is powerful.

Chapter 4 continues this interest in the knowledge that is central to SHRM and its relationship to power. Schwenk addresses important features of knowledge: the knowledge and ways of thinking which underpin the development of strategy. SHRM focuses on the ways in which organizations can improve their capacity to achieve their strategic objectives. But what if their capacity to develop strategies is itself flawed? Schwenk explores the different ways in which the strategic thinking and decision-making of decision-makers can be distorted in a number of ways. SHRM not only involves knowledge – as earlier chapters have shown – it also relies on knowledge; about strategy and HR strategy, and how these could be linked. SHRM relies on cognitive processes. The nature of, and possible distortions to, these processes are critically important, not only when they influence the strategies that are developed, but also if they impact on the thinking that surrounds the selection of HR strategies to support selected business strategies.

Finally, Chapter 5 completes our analysis of the knowledge inherent in SHRM through an exploration of how senior managers think about the relationship between strategic objectives and necessary organizational arrangements. SHRM is based on the assumption that organizational structures and processes vary and can be chosen. The 'fit' version of SHRM argues that the nature of this choice – and thus the degree of fit – is a major determinant of organizational performance. But how managers make this choice and what views or theories determine the choices they make has been under-studied. Chapter 5 reports the results of a study which explored these issues; managers' views on the sort of organization that is required to achieve the specified strategic objective. The strategic priority in question was innovation. But the chapter is not simply about innovation; its wider significance is that it reveals the ways in which managers understand the connections between types of strategy and types of organization. The first chapter in this section of the reader was an attempt to map and make sense of two related forms of academic thinking about organizational performance and SHRM. The concluding chapter explores managers' theories of the relationship between strategy capability and performance. If SHRM is to achieve its full potential it must be informed by a more thorough understanding of how those with the capacity to influence organizational design decisions 'know' and understand the linkage between strategy and capacity. This chapter contributes to this goal.

Human Resources and the Resource Based View of the Firm

Patrick M. Wright, Benjamin B. Dunford and Scott A. Snell

Introduction

The human resource function has consistently faced a battle in justifying its position in organizations (Drucker, 1954; Stewart, 1996). In times of plenty, firms easily justify expenditures on training, staffing, reward, and employee involvement systems, but when faced with financial difficulties, such HR systems fall prey to the earliest cutbacks.

The advent of the sub field of strategic human resource management (SHRM), devoted to exploring HR's role in supporting business strategy, provided one avenue for demonstrating its value to the firm. Walker's (1978) call for a link between strategic planning and human resource planning signified the conception of the field of SHRM, but its birth came in the early 1980s with Devanna, Fombrum and Tichy's (1984) article devoted to extensively exploring the link between business strategy and HR. Since then, SHRM's evolution has consistently followed (by a few years) developments within the field of strategic management. For example, Miles and Snow's (1978) organizational types were later expanded to include their associated HR systems (Miles and Snow, 1984). Porter's (1980) model of generic strategies was later used by SHRM researchers to delineate the specific HR strategies that one would expect to observe under each of them (Jackson and Schuler, 1987; Wright and Snell, 1991).

Though the field of SHRM was not directly born of the resource-based view (RBV), it has clearly been instrumental to its development. This was largely

Source: Patrick M. Wright, Benjamin B. Dunford and Scott A. Snell (2001) 'Human resources and the resource based view of the firm', *Journal of Management*, 27: 701–21. Edited version.

because of the RBV shifting emphasis in the strategy literature away from external factors (such as industry position) toward internal firm resources as sources of competitive advantage (Hoskisson, Hitt, Wan and Yiu, 1999). Growing acceptance of internal resources as sources of competitive advantage brought legitimacy to HR's assertion that people are strategically important to firm success. Thus, given both the need to conceptually justify the value of HR and the propensity for the SHRM field to borrow concepts and theories from the broader strategy literature, the integration of the RBV of the firm into the SHRM literature should surprise no one.

However, two developments not as easily predicted have emerged over the past 10 years. First, the popularity of the RBV within the SHRM literature as a foundation for both theoretical and empirical examinations has probably far surpassed what anyone expected (McMahan, Virick and Wright, 1999). Second, the applications and implications of the RBV within the strategy literature have led to an increasing convergence between the fields of strategic management and SHRM (Snell, Shadur and Wright, 2001). Within the strategic literature, the RBV has helped to put 'people' (or a firm's human resources) on the radar screen. Concepts such as knowledge (Argote and Ingram, 2000; Grant, 1996; Leibeskind, 1996), dynamic capability (Eisenhardt and Martin, 2000; Teece et al., 1997), learning organizations (Fiol and Lyles, 1985; Fisher and White, 2000), and leadership (Finkelstein and Hambrick, 1996; Norburn and Birley, 1988; Thomas, 1988) as sources of competitive advantage turn attention toward the intersection of strategy and HR issues.

The purpose of this paper is to examine how the RBV has been applied to the theoretical and empirical research base of SHRM, and to explore how it has provided an accessible bridge between the fields of strategy and HR. To accomplish this, we will first review the specific benchmark articles that have applied the RBV to theoretical development of SHRM. We will then discuss some of the empirical SHRM studies that have used the RBV as the basis for exploring the relationship between HR and firm performance. Finally, we will identify some of the major topic areas that illustrate the convergence of the fields of strategy and HR, and propose some future directions for how such a convergence can provide mutual benefits.

■ Applying the RBV to SHRM

While based in the work of Penrose (1959) and others, Wernerfelt's (1984) articulation of the resource based view of the firm certainly signified the first coherent statement of the theory. This initial statement of the theory served as the foundation that was extended by others such as Rumelt (1984), Barney (1996), and Dierickx and Cool (1989). However, Barney's (1991) specification of the characteristics necessary for a sustainable competitive advantage seemed to be a seminal article in popularizing the theory within the strategy and other literatures. In this article he noted that resources which are rare, valuable, inimitable, and nonsubstitutable can provide sources of sustainable competitive advantages.

Although debates about the RBV continue to wage (e.g., whether the RBV is a theory, whether it is tautological, etc. Priem and Butler, 2001a, b; Barney, 2001) even its critics have acknowledged the 'breadth of its diffusion' in numerous strategic research programs (Priem and Butler, 2001a, p. 25–26). With its emphasis on internal firm resources as sources of competitive advantage, the popularity of the RBV in the SHRM literature has been no exception. Since Barney's (1991) article outlining the basic theoretical model and criteria for sources of sustainable competitive advantage, the RBV has become by far, the theory most often used within SHRM, both in the development of theory and the rationale for empirical research (McMahan, Virick and Wright, 1999).

RBV and SHRM theory

As part of *Journal of Management*'s Yearly Review of Management issue, Wright and McMahan (1992) reviewed the theoretical perspectives that had been applied to SHRM. They presented the RBV as one perspective that provided a rationale for how a firm's human resources could provide a potential source of sustainable competitive advantage. This was based largely on what was, at the time a working paper, but later became the Wright, McMahan and McWilliams (1994) paper described later.

Almost simultaneously, Cappelli and Singh (1992), within the industrial relations literature, provided an examination of the implications of the RBV on SHRM. Specifically, they noted that most models of SHRM based on fit assume that (1) a certain business strategy demands a unique set of behaviors and attitudes from employees and (2) certain human resource policies produce a unique set of responses from employees. They further argued that many within strategy have implicitly assumed that it is easier to rearrange complementary assets/resources given a choice of strategy than it is to rearrange strategy given a set of assets/resources, even though empirical research seems to imply the opposite. Thus, they proposed that the resource-based view might provide a theoretical rationale for why HR could have implications for strategy formulation as well as implementation.

Shortly thereafter, two articles came out arguing almost completely opposite implications of the potential for HR practices to constitute a source of sustainable competitive advantage. Wright et al. (1994), mentioned above, distinguished between the firm's human resources (i.e., the human capital pool) and HR practices (those HR tools used to manage the human capital pool). In applying the concepts of value, rareness, inimitability, and substitutability, they argued the HR practices could not form the basis for sustainable competitive advantage since any individual HR practice could be easily copied by competitors. Rather, they proposed that the human capital pool (a highly skilled and highly motivated workforce) had greater potential to constitute a source of sustainable competitive advantage. These authors noted that to constitute a source of competitive advantage, the human capital pool must have both high levels of skill and a willingness (i.e., motivation) to exhibit productive behavior. This skill/behavior distinction appears as a rather consistent theme within this literature.

In contrast, Lado and Wilson (1994) proposed that a firm's HR practices could provide a source of sustainable competitive advantage. Coming from the perspective of exploring the role of HR in influencing the competencies of the firm, they suggested that HR systems (as opposed to individual practices) can be unique, causally ambiguous and synergistic in how they enhance firm competencies, and thus could be inimitable. Thus, whereas Wright et al. (1994) argued for imitability of individual practices, Lado and Wilson noted that the system of HR practices, with all the complementarities and interdependencies among the set of practices, would be impossible to imitate. This point of view seems well accepted within the current SHRM paradigm (Snell, Youndt and Wright, 1996).

Boxall (1996) further built upon the RBV/SHRM paradigm, suggesting that human resource advantage (i.e., the superiority of one firm's HRM over another) consists of two parts. First, human capital advantage refers to the potential to capture a stock of exceptional human talent 'latent with productive possibilities' (p. 67). Human process advantage can be understood as a 'function of causally ambiguous, socially complex, historically evolved processes such as learning, cooperation, and innovation.' (p. 67). Boxall (1998) then expanded upon this basic model presenting a more comprehensive model of strategic HRM. He argued that one major task of organizations is the management of mutuality (i.e., alignment of interests) to create a talented and committed workforce. It is the successful accomplishment of this task that results in a human capital advantage. A second task is to develop employees and teams in such a way as to create an organization capable of learning within and across industry cycles. Successful accomplishment of this task results in the organizational process advantage.

Most recently, Lepak and Snell (1999) presented an architectural approach to SHRM based at least partly in the RBV. They proposed that within organizations, considerable variance exists with regard to both the uniqueness and value of skills. Juxtaposing these two dimensions, they built a 2 × 2 matrix describing different combinations with their corresponding employment relationships and HR systems. The major implication of that model was that some employee groups are more instrumental to competitive advantage than others. As a consequence, they are likely to be managed differently. While the premise of an architectural perspective is rooted in extant research in HR (cf., Baron et al., 1986; Osterman, 1987; Tsui, Pearce, Porter and Tripoli, 1997)

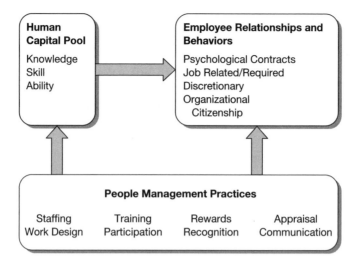

Figure 1.1 *A model of the basic strategic HRM components*

and strategy (cf., Matusik and Hill, 1998), Lepak and Snell (1999) helped SHRM researchers recognize that real and valid variance exists in HR practices within the organization, and looking for one HR strategy may mask important differences in the types of human capital available to firms. (cf. Truss and Gratton, 1994).

In essence, the conceptual development within the field of SHRM has leveraged the RBV to achieve some consensus on the areas within the human resource architecture in which sustainable competitive advantage might be achieved. Figure 1.1 depicts these components.

First, the human capital pool refers to the stock of employee skills that exist within a firm at any given point in time. Theorists focus on the need to develop a pool of human capital that has either higher levels of skills (general and/or firm specific), or achieving a better alignment between the skills represented in the firm and those required by its strategic intent. The actual stock of human capital can and does change overtime, and must constantly be monitored for its match with the strategic needs of the firm.

Second, an increasing consensus is emerging among researchers that employee behavior is an important independent component of SHRM. Distinct from skills of the human capital pool, employee behavior recognizes individuals as cognitive and emotional beings who possess free will. This free will enables them to make decisions regarding the behaviors in which they will engage. This is an important, if subtle, distinction. A basic premise of human capital theory is that firms do not own it; individuals do. Firms may have access to valuable human capital, but either through the poor design of work or the mismanagement of people, may not adequately deploy it to achieve strategic impact. For example, MacDuffie (1995) focuses on the concept of discretionary behavior. Discretionary behavior recognizes that even within prescribed organizational roles, employees exhibit discretion that may have either positive or negative consequences to the firm. Thus, a machine operator who hears a 'pinging' has discretion to simply run the machine until something breaks or to fix the problem immediately, and thus save significant downtime. Similar to March and Simon's (1958) concept of 'the decision to contribute' SHRM's focus on discretionary behavior recognizes that competitive advantage can only be achieved if the members of the human capital pool individually and collectively choose to engage in behavior that benefits the firm.

Finally, while many authors describe HR practice or High Performance Work Systems, a broader conceptualization might simply be the people management system. By using the term *system*, we turn focus to the importance of understanding the multiple practices that impact employees (Wright and Boswell, in press) rather than single practices. By using the term *people*, rather than HR, we expand the relevant practices to those beyond the control of the HR function, such as communication (both upward and downward), work design, culture, leadership, and a host of others that impact employees and shape their competencies, cognitions, and attitudes. Effective systems for managing people evolve through unique historical paths and maintain interdependence among the components that competitors cannot easily imitate (Becker and Huselid, 1998). The important aspect of these systems is that they are the means through which the firm continues to generate advantage over time as the actual employees flow in and out and the required behaviors change because of changing environmental and strategic contingencies. It is through the people management system that the firm influences the human capital pool and elicits the desired employee behavior. This dynamic process, while not depicted in the figure, will be taken up later in the paper.

The implications of our figure and this model are that while a firm might achieve a superior position in any one of the three, sustainable competitive advantage requires superior positions on all three.

This is because of three reasons. First, the value that skills and behaviors can generate requires that they be paired together (i.e., without skills, certain behaviors cannot be exhibited, and that the value of skills can only be realized through exhibited behavior). Second, it is difficult to conceive of a firm's human capital pool containing both the highest levels of skills and exhibiting optimal behaviors in the absence of an aligned people management system. Finally, the effects of the people management systems are subject to time compression diseconomies (Dierickx and Cool, 1989). While these systems might be immediately imitated, a significant time lag will occur before their impact is realized, thus making it costly or difficult for competitors to imitate the value generated by the human capital pool. We will later build upon this model to explore how this fits within the larger organization.

Summary of RBV based conceptual literature

In summary, the RBV has proven to be integral to the conceptual and theoretical development of the SHRM literature. Our brief review demonstrates
how the RBV based SHRM research has evolved in the last decade. This evolution began when HR researchers recognized that the RBV provided a compelling explanation for why HR practices lead to competitive advantage.
Ensuing scholarly debate about the specific mechanics of this relationship
advanced the SHRM literature to its current state. The net effect has been a
deeper understanding of the interplay between HRM and competitive advantage. The model depicted in Figure 1.1 demonstrates that sustained competitive advantage is not just a function of single or isolated components, but
rather a combination of human capital elements such as the development of
stocks of skills, strategically relevant behaviors, and supporting people management systems. Although there is yet much room for progress it is fair to
say that the theoretical application of the RBV has been successful in stimu-
lating a substantial amount of activity in the SHRM arena. Having summarized the conceptual development, we now turn to the empirical research.

▌ RBV and empirical SHRM research

In addition to the many applications of the RBV to theoretical developments
within SHRM, this perspective also has emerged as one of the more popular
foundations for exploring empirical relationships within SHRM. In fact, one
is hard pressed to find any SHRM empirical studies conducted over the past
few years that do not at least pay lip service to the RBV. In the interest of
brevity, we will cover a sample of such studies that illustrate the application
of RBV concepts to empirical SHRM research. We chose these studies either
because they specifically attempt to build on resource-based theory or because
they tend to be most frequently cited within the SHRM literature and at least
tangentially rely on resource-based logic.

In an early application, Huselid (1995) argued at a general level that HR
practices could help create a source of competitive advantage, particularly if
they are aligned with the firm's competitive strategy. His study revealed a relationship between HR practices (or High Performance Work Systems) and
employee turnover, gross rate of return on assets, and Tobin's Q. That study
received considerable attention because it demonstrated that HR practices
could have a profound impact on both accounting and market based measures
of performance.

Koch and McGrath (1996) took a similar logic in their study of the
relationship between HR planning, recruitment, and staffing practices and
labor productivity. They argued that '... a highly productive workforce is

likely to have attributes that make it a particularly valuable strategic asset,' (p. 335). They suggested firms that develop effective routines for acquiring human assets develop a stock of talent that cannot be easily imitated. They found that these HR practices were related to labor productivity in a sample of business units, and that this relationship was stronger in capital intensive organizations.

Boxall and Steeneveld (1999) conducted a longitudinal case study of participants in the New Zealand engineering consultancy industry. They suggested that one of the firms in the industry had achieved a superior competitive position because of its human resource advantage in 1994, but that by 1997 two of the competitors had caught up in the competitive marketplace. They posited that this could mean that either the two competitors had been able to successfully imitate the former leaders' human resource advantage, or that the former leader has developed an advantage about which there is presently uncertainty, but which will be exploited in the future.

Diverging from the focus on HR practices, Wright, Smart and McMahan (1995) studied NCAA Men's basketball teams using an RBV framework. They focused on the skills of the team members and experience of the coach, and examined how a fit between skills and strategy impacted the team's performance. They found that the relationship between certain skills and team performance depended upon the strategy in which the team was engaged. In addition, their results indicated that teams whose coaches who were using a strategy different from their preferred strategy performed lower than teams where the coach was able to use his preferred strategy.

Recent empirical studies using the RBV build on Lepak and Snell's (1999) architectural framework discussed above. Lepak and Snell (in press) asked executives to describe the HR systems that existed for jobs that represented particular quadrants of their model. They found considerable support for the idea that the value and uniqueness of skills are associated with different types of HR systems within the same organization. These results were mostly consistent with the Lepak and Snell (1999) model, and supported the basic proposition that diverse HR strategies exist within firms. A follow up study (Lepak, Takeuchi and Snell, 2001) indicated that a combination of knowledge work and contract labor was associated with higher firm performance. This finding not only raises some interesting ideas about the development of valuable human resources, but also highlights the importance of combinations of various types used in conjunction with one another.

In another example of examining the human capital pool, Richard (2001) used resource-based logic to examine the impact of racial diversity on firm performance. He argued that diversity provides value through ensuring a variety of perspectives, that it is rare in that very few firms have achieved significant levels of diversity, and that the socially complex dynamics inherent in diversity lead to its inimitability. He found in a sample of banks that diversity was positively related to productivity, return on equity, and market performance for firms engaged in a growth strategy, but negatively related for firms downsizing.

In an effort to look beyond human capital pool alone, Youndt and Snell (2001) studied the differential effects of HR practices on human capital, social capital, and organizational capital. They found that intensive/extensive staffing, competitive pay, intensive/extensive training and promotion from within policies were most important for distinguishing high levels of human capital in organizations. In contrast, broad banding, compressed wages, team structures, socialization, mentoring, and group incentives distinguished those with high social capital (i.e., relationships that engender knowledge exchange) but had very little effect on human capital itself. Finally, organizational capital (i.e., knowledge embedded in the organization's systems and processes) was established most through lessons learned databases and HR policies that reinforced knowledge capture and access.

Summary of RBV based empirical research: limitations and future directions

Recent debate about the usefulness of the RBV provides an interesting commentary about the current state of SHRM research (Barney, 2001; Priem and Butler, 2001a). In response to claims that the RBV is tautological and does not generate testable hypotheses, Barney recognizes that most research applying the RBV has failed to test its fundamental concepts. Rather, he notes that much of the existing research has used the RBV to 'establish the context of some empirical research – for example that the focus is on the performance implications of some internal attribute of a firm – and *are not really direct tests of the theory developed in the 1991 article.*' (Barney, 2001, p. 46, emphasis added).

Much of the existing SHRM research falls into this category. Although the empirical application of the RBV has taken a variety of forms, ranging in focus from High Performance Work Systems and stocks of talent, to the fit between employee skills and strategy it has employed a common underlying logic: Human resource activities are thought to lead to the development of a skilled workforce and one that engages in functional behavior for the firm, thus forming a source of competitive advantage. This results in higher operating performance, which translates into increased profitability, and consequently results in higher stock prices (or market values) (Becker and Huselid, 1998). While this theoretical story is appealing, it is important to note that ultimately, most of the empirical studies assess only two variables: HR practices and performance.

While establishing such a relationship provides empirical evidence for the potential value of HR to firms, it fails to adequately test the RBV in two important ways. First, no attempt has yet been made to empirically assess the validity of the proposition that HR practices (or HPWS) are path dependent or causally ambiguous, nor whether they are actually difficult to imitate. While intuitively obvious and possibly supported by anecdotal data, the field lacks verifiable quantitative data to support these assertions. In fact, Boxall and Steeneveld's (1999) findings might suggest that HR systems are more easily imitated (or at least substitutable) than SHRM researchers previously believed. Certainly, efforts such as King and Zeithaml's (2001) study assessing causal ambiguity of competencies could be replicated with regard to SHRM issues. These authors asked managers to evaluate their firms competencies and then generated measures of causal ambiguity based on these responses. While ambiguity was negatively related to firm performance in their study, they provide an example of how one might attempt to measure some of the variables within the RBV.

Second, few attempts have been made to demonstrate that the HR practices actually impact the skills or behaviors of the workforce, nor that these skills or behaviors are related to any performance measures. Arthur (1994) and Huselid (1995) did find a relationship between HR practices and turnover. Wright, McCormick, Sherman and McMahan (1999) found that appraisal and training practices were related to executives' assessment of the skills and that compensation practices were related to their assessments of workforce motivation. However, as yet no study has demonstrated anything close to a full causal model through which HR practices are purported to impact firm performance.

In short, a major step forward for the SHRM literature will be to move beyond simply the application of RBV logic to HR issues toward research that directly tests the RBV's core concepts. In fairness, this state of affairs does not differ from attempts to study competitive advantage within the strategy literature. As noted by Godfrey and Hill (1995), it is impossible to assess the degree of unobservability of an unobservable, and inimitable resources are often purported to be unobservable. Thus, strategy researchers are often left to using proxy variables that may not be valid for measuring the underlying constructs (Hoskisson, Hitt, Wan and Yiu, 1999).

However, given the single respondent, cross sectional, survey designs inherent in much of this research, one cannot rule out alternative explanations for the findings of empirical relationships. For example, Gerhart, Wright, McMahan and Snell (2000) and Wright, Gardner, Moynihan, Park, Gerhart and Delery (in press) both found that single respondent measures of HR practices may contain significant amounts of measurement error. Gardner, Wright and Gerhart (2000) also found evidence of implicit performance theories suggesting that respondents to HR surveys might base their descriptions of the HR practices on their assessments of the organization's performance. This raises the possibility that research purporting to support the RBV through demonstrating a relationship between HR and performance may result from spurious relationships, or even reverse causation (Wright and Gardner, in press). The point is not to discount the significant research that has been conducted to date, but rather to highlight the importance of more rigorous and longitudinal studies of HR from a RBV perspective.

Taking a deeper understanding the resource-based view of the firm into empirical SHRM research entails focusing primarily on the competencies and capabilities of firms and the role that people management systems play in developing these. It requires recognizing that the inimitability of these competencies may stem from unobservability (e.g., causal ambiguity), complexity (e.g., social complexity), and/or time compression diseconomies (e.g., path dependence). This implies that rather than simply positing a relationship between HR practices and sustainable competitive advantage, one must realize that people management systems might impact this advantage in a variety of ways.

For instance, these systems might play a role in creating cultures or mindsets that enable the maintenance of unique competencies (e.g., the safety record of DuPont). Or, these systems may promote and maintain socially complex relationships characterized by trust, knowledge sharing, and teamwork (e.g., Southwest Airlines' unique culture). Finally, these systems might have resulted in the creation of a high quality human capital pool that cannot be easily imitated because of time compression diseconomies (e.g., Merck's R&D capability). Whichever the case, it certainly calls for a more complex view of the relationship between HR and performance than is usually demonstrated within the empirical literature.

In addition to a more complex view, such grounding would imply different strategies for studying HR and competitive advantage. For instance, recognizing time compression diseconomies implies more longitudinal or at least historical approaches to examining competitive advantage as opposed to the more popular cross-sectional studies. Focusing on causal ambiguity and social complexity might suggest more qualitative approaches than simply asking subjects to report via survey about the HR practices that exist. In sum, strategic HRM research more strongly anchored in the RBV of the firm would look significantly different than what currently exists. However, such research would shed light on both HR and strategy issues.

Extending this further, strategists who embrace the RBV point out that competitive advantage (vis core competence) comes from aligning skills, motives, and so forth with *organizational systems, structures, and processes* that achieve capabilities at the organizational level (Hamel and Prahalad, 1994; Peteraf, 1993; Teece et al., 1997). Too frequently, HR researchers have acted as if organizational performance derives solely from the (aggregated) actions of individuals. But the RBV suggests that strategic resources are more complex than that, and more interesting. Companies that are good at product development and innovation, for example, don't simply have the most creative people who continually generate new ideas. Product development capabilities are imbedded in the organizational systems and processes. People execute those systems, but they are not independent from them. So while core competencies are knowledge-based, they are not solely human. They are comprised of human capital, social capital (i.e., internal/external relationships and exchanges), and organizational capital (i.e., processes, technologies, databases) (Snell, Youndt and Wright, 1996).

That doesn't negate the importance of HR; it amplifies it and extends it. The RBV provides a broader foundation for exploring the impact of HR on strategic resources. In this context, HR is not limited to its direct effects on employee skills and behavior. Its effects are more encompassing in that they help weave those skills and behaviors within the broader fabric of organizational processes, systems and, ultimately, competencies.

Notwithstanding a great deal of room for development, it is clear from the preceding review that the conceptual and empirical application of the RBV has led to considerable advancement of the SHRM literature. In a broader sense, the RBV has impacted the field of HRM in two important ways. First, the RBV's influence has been instrumental in establishing a macro perspective in the field of HRM research (Snell et al., in press). This macro view has provided complimentary depth to a historically micro discipline rooted in psychology. Relatedly, a second major contribution of the RBV has been the theoretical and contextual grounding that it has provided to a field that has often been criticized for being atheoretical and excessively applied in nature (Snell et al., 2001).

The convergence of RBV and SHRM: potential mutual contributions

Thus far, we have discussed how the RBV has contributed to the field of SHRM. As noted before, however, that the RBV has also effectively put 'people' on the strategy radar screen (Snell et al., in press). In the search for competitive advantage, strategy researchers increasingly acknowledge human capital (Hitt, Bierman, Shimizu and Kochar, 2001), intellectual capital (Edvinsson and Malone, 1997) and knowledge (Grant, 1996; Leibeskind, 1996; Matusik and Hill, 1998) as critical components. In so doing, the RBV has provided an excellent platform for highlighting the importance of people to competitive advantage, and thus, the inescapable fact that RBV strategy researchers must bump up against people and/or HR issues.

In fact, recent developments within the field of strategy seem to evidence a converging of that field and SHRM (Snell et al., in press). It seems that these areas present unique opportunities for interdisciplinary research streams that provide significant leaps forward in the knowledge base. We will discuss the concept of core competencies, the focus on dynamic capabilities, and knowledge-based views of the firm as potential bridges between the HR and strategy literatures. We choose these concepts because of both their popularity within the strategy literature and their heavy reliance on HR related issues.

Core competencies

Prahalad and Hamel (1990) certainly popularized the core competency concept within the strategy literature. They stated that core competencies are '… the collective learning in the organization, especially how to coordinate diverse production skills and integrate multiple streams of technologies,' (p. 64), and that they involve 'many levels of people and all functions,' (p. 64). While the distinctions between core competencies and capabilities (Stalk, Evans and Schulman, 1992) seems blurred, one can hardly conceptualize a firm capability or competency absent the people who comprise them nor the systems that maintain them.

For example, competencies or capabilities refer to organizational processes, engaged in by people, resulting in superior products, and generally these must endure over time as employees flow in, through and out of the firm. Numerous researchers within the strategy field focus on firm competencies (e.g., King and Zeithaml, 2001; Leonard-Barton, 1992, 1995). These researchers universally recognize the inseparability of the competence and the skills of the employees who comprise the competence. In addition, some (e.g., Leonard-Barton, 1992) specifically also recognize the behavioral aspect of these employees (i.e., their need to engage in behaviors that execute the competency) and the supportive nature of people management systems to the development/ maintenance of the competency. However, often these treatments begin quite specifically when examining the competency and its competitive potential within the marketplace. However, they then sometimes become more generic and ambiguous as they delve into the more specific people-related concepts such as knowledges, skills, abilities, behaviors, and HR practices.

This illustrates the potential synergy that might result from deeper integration of the strategy and strategic HRM literatures. To deeply understand the competency one must examine (in addition to the systems and processes that underlie them) the people who engage in the process, the skills they individually and collectively must possess, and the behavior they must engage in (individually and interactively) to implement the process. In addition, to understand how such a competency can be developed or maintained requires at least in part examining the people management systems that ensure that the competency remains as specific employees leave and new employees must be brought in to replace them. This again exemplifies the interaction of people and processes as they comprise competencies.

Focusing on the people-related elements of a core competency provides a linking pin between the strategy and HR literatures. Traditional HR researchers refer to a 'competence' as being a work related knowledge, skill, or ability (Nordhaug, 1993) held by an individual. This is not the same as the core competencies to which strategy researchers refer. Nordhaug and Gronhaug (1994) argue that firms possess individuals with different competences that they refer to as a portfolio of competences. They further propose that a core (or distinctive) competence exists when a firm is able to collaboratively blend the many competences in the portfolio, through a shared mindset, to better perform something than their competitors. For SHRM researchers, this implies a need to develop an understanding of firms, the activities in their value chains, and the relative superiority in value creation for each of these activities. For strategy researchers, it suggests a need to more deeply delve into the issues of the individuals and groups who comprise the competency, and the systems that develop and engage them to exhibit and maintain the competency. Lepak and Snell's (1999) model provides one tool for making this link between the firm's competency, the people that comprise it, and the systems that maintain it.

▌Dynamic capabilities

The RBV has frequently focused on resources or competencies as a stable concept that can be identified at a point in time and will endure over time. The argument goes that when firms have bundles of resources that are valuable, rare, inimitable, and nonsubstitutable, they can implement value creating strategies not easily duplicated by competing firms (Barney, 1991; Conner and Prahalad, 1996; Peteraf, 1993; Wernerfelt, 1984, 1995).

However, recent attention has focused on the need for many organizations to constantly develop new capabilities or competencies in a dynamic environment (Teece et al., 1997). Such capabilities have been referred to as 'dynamic capabilities' which have been defined as:

> The firm's processes that use resources – specifically the processes to
> integrate, reconfigure, gain, and release resources – to match and even create
> market change. Dynamic capabilities thus are the organizational and strategic
> routines by which firms achieve new resource reconfigurations as markets
> emerge, collide, split, evolve, and die. (Eisenhardt and Martin, 2000)

Such dynamic capabilities require that organizations establish processes that enable them to change their routines, services, products, and even markets over time. While in theory, one can easily posit how organizations must adapt to changing environmental contingencies, in reality changes of this magnitude are quite difficult to achieve, and the difficulty stems almost entirely from the human architecture of the firm. The firm may require different skill sets implying a release of some existing employees and acquisition of new employees. The change entails different organizational processes implying new networks and new behavioral repertoires of employees. The new skills and new behaviors theoretically must be driven by new administrative, (i.e., HR) systems (Wright and Snell, 1998).

This implies the centrality of HR issues to the understanding and development of dynamic capabilities. This centrality is well articulated by Teece et al. (1997) who note:

> Indeed if control over scarce resources is the source of economic profits, then it follows that such issues as skill acquisition, the management of knowledge and know how and learning become fundamental strategic issues. It is in this second dimension, encompassing skill acquisition, learning and accumulation of organizational and intangible or invisible assets that we believe lies the greatest potential for contributions to strategy. (pp. 514–515)

Knowledge-based theories of the firm

Unarguably, significant attention in the strategy literature within the RBV paradigm has focused on knowledge. Efforts to understand how firms generate, leverage, transfer, integrate and protect knowledge has moved to the forefront of the field (Hansen, 1999; Hedlund, 1994; Nonaka, 1991; Svieby, 1997; Szulanski, 1996). In fact, Grant (1996) argues for a knowledge-based theory of the firm, positing that firms exist because they better integrate and apply specialized knowledge than do markets. Liebeskind (1996) similarly believes in a knowledge-based theory of the firm, suggesting that firms exist because they can better protect knowledge from expropriation and imitation than can markets.

Interestingly, knowledge-centered strategy research inevitably confronts a number of HR issues. Knowledge management requires that firms define knowledge, identify existing knowledge bases, and provide mechanisms to promote the creation, protection and transfer of knowledge (Argote and Ingram, 2000; Henderson and Cockburn, 1994; Leibeskind, 1996). While information systems provide a technological repository of knowledge, increasingly firms recognize that the key to successful knowledge management requires attending to the social and cultural systems of the organization (Conference Board, 2000).

Knowledge has long been a topic within the HR literature, whether the focus was on testing applicants for job-related knowledge (Hattrup and Schmitt, 1990), training employees to build their job-related knowledge (Gephart, Marsick, Van Buren and Spiro, 1996), developing participation and communication systems to transfer knowledge (Cooke, 1994), or providing incentives for individuals to apply their knowledge (Gerhart, Milkovich and Murray, 1992). The major distinctions between the strategy and HR literatures with regard to knowledge has to do with the focus of the knowledge and its level. While the HR literature has focused on job related knowledge, the strategy literature has focused on more market-relevant knowledge, such as knowledge regarding customers, competitors, or knowledge relevant to the creation of new products (Grant, 1996; Leibeskind, 1996).

In addition, while HR literature tends to treat knowledge as an individual phenomenon, the strategy and organizational literatures view it more broadly as organizationally shared, accessible, and transferable (cf. Argyris and Schon, 1978; Brown and Duguid, 1991; Snell, Stueber and Lepak, 2001). Knowledge can be viewed as something that characterizes individuals (i.e., human capital), but it can also be shared within groups or networks (i.e., social capital) or institutionalized within organization processes and databases (organizational capital).

These distinctions represent something of a departure for HR researchers. However, the processes of creation, transfer, and exploitation of knowledge provide common ground across the two fields, again highlighting their potential convergence within the RBV paradigm. Although theorists such as Argyris and Schon (1978) argue that all learning begins at the individual level, it is conditioned by the social context and routines within organizations (Nonaka and Takeuchi, 1995). Coleman (1988), for example, noted that social capital has an important influence on the creation of human capital. What seems clear is that these different 'knowledge repositories' complement and influence one another in defining an organization's capabilities (Youndt and Snell, 2001).

But there are substantial differences between HR systems that support individual learning and those that support organizational learning. Leonard-Barton (1992), for example, noted that organizational learning and innovation were built on four inter-related processes and their related values: (1) owning/ solving problems (egalitarianism), (2) integrating internal knowledge (shared knowledge), (3) continuous experimentation (positive risk), and (4) integrating external knowledge (openness to outside). Each of these processes and values works systemically with the others to inculcate organizational learning and innovation. Each process/value combination is in turn supported by different administrative (HR) systems that incorporate elements of staffing, job design, training, career management, rewards, and appraisal. Again, the concept of knowledge brings together the fields of strategy and HR. But a good deal more work needs to be done to integrate these research streams. Strategy theory and research provides the basis for understanding the value of knowledge to the firm and highlights the need to manage it. The HR field has lacked such a perspective, but has provided more theory and research regarding how knowledge is generated, retained, and transferred among individuals comprising the firm.

Integrating strategy and SHRM within the RBV

We have discussed the concepts of core competencies, dynamic capabilities, and knowledge as bridge constructs connecting the fields of strategy and SHRM. We proposed that both fields could benefit greatly from sharing respective areas of expertise. In fact, at the risk of oversimplification, the strategy literature has generated significant amounts of knowledge regarding who (i.e., employees/ executives or groups of employees/executives) provides sources of competitive advantage and why. However, absent from that literature are specific techniques for attracting, developing, motivating, maintaining, or retaining these people. SHRM, on the other hand has generated knowledge regarding the attraction, development, motivation, maintenance, and retention of people. However, it has not been particularly successful yet at identifying who the focus of these systems should be on and why.

The strategy literature has also highlighted the importance of the stock and flow of knowledge for competitive advantage. However, it has not explored in great detail the role that individuals as well as their interactions with others contribute to this. Conversely SHRM has missed much of the organizational view of knowledge, but can provide significant guidance regarding the role that individuals play.

This state of affairs calls for greater integration between these two fields. Figure 1.2 illustrates this potential integration. Overall, the figure depicts people management systems at the left, core competencies at the right, intellectual capital and knowledge management as the bridge concepts between the two, and dynamic capability as a renewal component that ties all four concepts over time.

Note that the basic constructs laid out in Figure 1.1 still appear in this expanded model, yet with a much more detailed set of variables. At the left hand side of the model we place the people management systems construct. This placement does not imply that all competitive advantage begins with people management systems, but rather, that this represents the focus of the HR field. We suggest that these people management systems create value to the extent that they impact the stock, flow, and change of intellectual capital/ knowledge that form the basis of core competencies.

Rather than simply focusing on the concepts of 'skills' and 'behavior' we propose a more detailed analysis with regard to the stock and flow of knowledge. To this end we suggest that the 'skill' concept might be expanded to consider the stock of intellectual capital in the firm, embedded in both people and systems. This stock of human capital consists of human (the knowledge skills, and abilities of people), social (the valuable relationships among people), and organizational (the processes and routines within the firm). It broadens the traditional HR focus beyond simply the people to explore the larger processes and systems that exist within the firm.

The 'behavior' concept within the SHRM literature can similarly be reconceptualized as the flow of knowledge within the firm through its creation, transfer, and integration. This 'knowledge management' behavior becomes increasingly important as information and knowledge play a greater role in firm competitive advantage. It is through the flow of knowledge that firms increase or maintain the stock of intellectual capital.

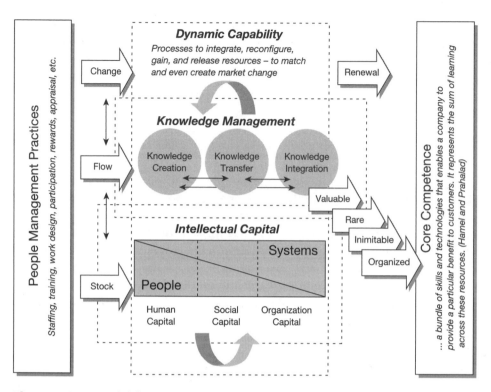

Figure 1.2 *A model for integrating strategy and strategic HRM*

At the right hand side of the model we place the core competence, one of the major foci of the strategy literature. We propose that this core competence arises from the combination of the firms stock of knowledge (human, social, and organizational capital embedded in both people and systems) and the flow of this knowledge though creation, transfer, and integration in a way that is valuable, rare, inimitable, and organized. This provides a framework for more specifically exploring the human component to core competencies, and provides a basis for exploring the linkage between people management systems and core competencies through the management of a firm's stock and flow of knowledge.

Finally, the dynamic capability construct illustrates the interdependent interplay between the workforce and the core competence as it changes over time. It represents the renewal process that organizations must undergo to remain competitive. Dynamic capability requires changing competencies on the part of both the organization and the people who comprise it. It is facilitated by people management systems that promote the change of both the stock and flow of knowledge within the firm that enable a firm to constantly renew its core competencies.

This model by no means serves as a well-developed theoretical framework, but rather simply seeks to point to the areas for collaboration between strategy and SHRM researchers. These two fields share common interests in issues and yet bring complementary skills, knowledge, and perspectives to these issues. The RBV highlights these common interests and provides a framework for developing collaborative effort.

Conclusion

The RBV has significantly and independently influenced the fields of strategy and SHRM. More importantly, however, it has provided a theoretical bridge between these two fields. By turning attention toward the internal resources, capabilities and competencies of the firm such as knowledge, learning, and dynamic capabilities (Hoskisson et al., 1999), it has brought strategy researchers to inescapably face a number of issues with regard to the management of people (Barney, 1996). We would guess that few strategy researchers are well versed in the existing research base regarding the effectiveness of various specific HR tools and techniques for managing people, and thus addressing these issues with necessary specificity.

This internal focus also has provided the traditionally atheoretical field of SHRM with a theoretical foundation from which it can begin exploring the strategic role that people and HR functions can play in organizations (Wright and McMahan, 1992). In addition to the lack of theory, this literature has also displayed little, or at least overly simplistic views of strategy, thus limiting its ability to contribute to the strategy literature (Chadwick and Cappelli, 1998). The RBV provides the framework from which HR researchers and practitioners can better understand the challenges of strategy, and thus be better able to play a positive role in the strategic management of firms.

We propose that both fields will benefit from greater levels of interaction in the future. This interaction should be deeper than simply reading each other's literature, but rather organizing conferences aimed at promoting face-to-face discussions of the common issues and challenges. In fact, we believe that future interdisciplinary research studies conducted jointly by strategy and SHRM researchers would exploit the unique knowledge and expertise of both fields, and synergistically contribute to the generation of new knowledge regarding the roles that people play in organizational competitive advantage.

References

Argote, L. and Ingram, P. (2000) Knowledge transfer: A basis for competitive advantage in firms. *Organizational Behavior and Human Decision Processes*, 82(1): 150–169.

Argyris, C. and Schon, D.A. (1978) *Organizational learning: A theory of action perspective*. Reading, MA: Addison-Wesley.

Arthur, J.B. (1994) Effects of human resource systems on manufacturing performance and turnover. *Academy of Management Journal*, 37(3): 670–687.

Baron, J.N., Davis-Blake, A. and Bielby, W.T. (1986) The structure of opportunity: How promotion ladders vary within and among organizations. *Administrative Science Quarterly*, 31: 248–273.

Barney, J. (1991) Firm resources and sustained competitive advantage. *Journal of Management*, 17(1): 99–120.

Barney, J. (1996) The resource-based theory of the firm. *Organizational Science*, 7, 469.

Barney, J. (2001) Is the resource-based view a useful perspective for strategic management research? Yes. *Academy of Management Review*, 26: 41–56.

Becker, B.E. and Huselid, M.A. (1998) High performance work systems and firm performance: A synthesis of research and managerial applications. *Research in Personnel and Human Resources Management*, 16: 53–101.

Brown, J.S. and Duguid, P. (1991) Organizational learning and communities-of-practice: Toward a unified view of working, learning, and innovation. *Organizational Science*, 2: 40–57.

Boxall, P.F. (1996) The Strategic HRM debate and the resource-based view of the firm. *Human Resource Management Journal*, 6(3): 59–75.

Boxall, P.F. (1998) Human resource strategy and industry-based competition: A conceptual framework and agenda for theoretical development. In P.M. Wright, L.D. Dyer, J.W. Boudreau and G.T. Milkovich (eds), Research in personnel and human resources management (Suppl. 4, pp. 1–29). Madison, WI: IRRA.

Boxall, P.F. and Steeneveld, M. (1999) Human resource strategy and competitive advantage: A longitudinal study of engineering consultancies. *Journal of Management Studies*, 36(4): 443–463.

Cappelli, P. and Singh, H. (1992) Integrating strategic human resources and strategic management. In D. Lewin, O.S. Mitchell and P.D. Sherer (eds), *Research frontiers in industrial relations and human resources* (pp. 165–192). Madison, WI: IRRA.

Chadwick, C. and Cappelli, P. (1998) Alternatives to generic strategy typologies in strategic human resource management. In P.M. Wright, L.D. Dyer, J.W. Boudreau and G.T. Milkovich (eds), *Research in personnel and human resources management* (Suppl. 4, pp. 1–29). Greenwich, CT: JAI Press, Inc.

Coleman, J.S. (1988) Social capital in the creation of human capital. *American Journal of Sociology*, 94: s95–s120.

Conference Board. (2000) *Beyond knowledge management: New ways to work.* Research Report 1262–00RR.

Cooke, W. (1994) Employee participation programs, group-based incentives, and Company performance: A union-nonunion comparison. *Industrial and Labor Relations Review*, 47: 594–609.

Conner, K.R. and Prahalad, C.K. (1996) A resource-based theory of the firm: Knowledge versus opportunism. *Organization Science*, 7: 477–501.

Devanna, M.A., Fombrun, C.J. and Tichy, N.M. (1984) A Framework for Strategic Human Resource Management, *Strategic Human Resource Management* (Chapt. 3, pp. 33–51). New York: Wiley.

Dierickx, I. and Cool, K. (1989) Asset stock accumulation and sustainability of competitive advantage. *Management Science*, 35, 1504–1511.

Drucker, P. (1954) *The practice of management.* New York: Harper.

Edvinsson, L. and Malone, M. (1997) *Intellectual capital.* Cambridge, MA: Harvard Business School Press.

Eisenhardt, K.M. and Martin, J.A. (2000) Dynamic capabilities: What are they? *Strategic Management Journal*, 21: 1105–1121.

Fiol, C.M. and Lyles, M.A. (1985) Organizational learning. *Academy of Management Review*, 10: 803–813.

Finkelstein, S. and Hambrick, D. (1996) *Strategic leadership: Top executives and their effects on organizations.* Minneapolis/St. Paul: West Pub. Co.

Fisher, S.R. and White, M.A. (2000) Downsizing in a learning organization: Are there hidden costs? *Academy of Management Review*, 25(1): 244–251.

Gardner, T.M., Wright, P.M. and Gerhart, B. (2000) The HR-Firm performance relationship: Can it be in the mind of the beholder? Working Paper, Center for Advanced Human Resource Studies, Cornell University.

Gephart, M. Marsick, V., Van Buren, M. and Spiro, M. (1996) Learning Organizations come alive. *Training and Development*, 50: 34–35.

Gerhart, B., Milkovich, G. and Murray, B. (1992) Pay, performance and participation. In D. Lewin, O. Mitchell, and P. Sherer (eds), *Research frontiers in industrial relations and human resources*. Madison, WI: IRRA.

Gerhart, B., Wright, P.M., McMahan, G.C. and Snell, S.A. (2000) Measurement error in research on human resources and firm performance: How much error is there and how does it influence effect size estimates? *Personnel Psychology*, 53: 803–834.

Godfrey, P.C. and Hill, C.W.L. (1995) The problem of unobservables in strategic management research. *Strategic Management Journal*, 16: 519–533.

Grant, R.M. (1996) Toward a knowledge-based theory of the firm. *Strategic Management Journal*, 17 (Winter Special Issue): 108–122.

Hamel, G. and Prahalad, C.K. (1994) Competing for the future. *Harvard Business Review*, 72(4): 122-129.

Hansen, M.T. (1999) The search-transfer problem: The role of weak ties in sharing knowledge across organization sub units. *Administrative Science Quarterly*, 44 (March): 82–111.

Hedlund, G. (1994) A model of knowledge management and the N-form corporation. *Strategic Management Journal*, 15: 73–90.

Hattrup, K. and Schmitt, N. (1990) Prediction of trades apprentices' performance on job sample criteria. *Personnel Psychology*, 43: 453–467.

Henderson, R. and Cockburn, I. (1994) Measuring competence? Exploring firm effects in pharmaceutical research. *Strategic Management Research*, 15: 63–84.

Hitt, M.A., Bierman, L., Shimizu, K. and Kochhar, R. (2001) Direct and moderating effects of human capital on the strategy and performance in professional service firms: A resource-based perspective. *Academy of Management Journal*, 44: 13–28.

Hoskisson, R.E., Hitt, M.A., Wan, W.P., Yiu, D. (1999) Theory and research in strategic management: Swings of a pendulum. *Strategic Management Journal*, 25(3): 417–456.

Huselid, M.A. (1995) The impact of human resource management practices on turnover, productivity, and corporate financial performance. *Academy of Management Journal*, 38(3): 635–672.

Jackson, S.E., Schuler, R.S. and Rivero, J.C. (1989) Organizational characteristics as predictors of personnel practices. *Personnel Psychology*, 42: 727–786.

King, A.W. and Zeithaml, C.P. (2001) Competencies and firm performance: Examining the causal ambiguity paradox. *Strategic Management Journal*, 22: 75–99.

Koch, M.J. and McGrath, R.G. (1996) Improving labor productivity: Human resource management policies do matter. *Strategic Management Journal*, 17: 335–354.

Lado, A.A. and Wilson, M.C. (1994) Human resource systems and sustained competitive advantage: A competency-based perspective. *Academy of Management Review*, 19(4): 699–727.

Leonard-Barton, D. (1992) The factory as a learning laboratory. *Sloan Management Review*, 34(1): 23–38.

Leonard-Barton, D. (1995) *Wellsprings of Knowledge*. Boston: Harvard Business School Press.

Lepak, D.P. and Snell, S.A. (1999) The human resource architecture: Toward a theory of human capital allocation and development. *Academy of Management Review*, 24: 31–48.

Lepak, D.P. and Snell, S.A. (in press) Examining the human resource architecture: The relationships among human capital, employment, and human resource configurations. *Journal of Management*.

Lepak, D.P. Takeuchi, R. and Snell, S.A. (2001) An empirical examination of employment mode use and firm performance. Working paper, University of Maryland.

Liebeskind, J.P. (1996) Knowledge, strategy, and the theory of the firm. *Strategic Management Journal, 17* (Winter Special Issue): 93–107.

MacDuffie, J.P. (1995) Human resource bundles and manufacturing performance: Organizational logic and flexible production systems in the world auto industry. *Industrial & Labor Relations Review*, 48(2): 197–221.

March, J. and Simon, H. (1958) *Organizations*, New York: Wiley.

Matusik, S.F. and Hill, C.W.L. (1998) The utilization of contingent work, knowledge creation, and competitive advantage. *Academy of Management Review*, 23: 680–697.

McMahan, G.C., Virick, M. and Wright, P.M. (1999) Alternative theoretical perspective for strategic human resource management revisited: progress, problems, and prospects. In P.M. Wright, L.D. Dyer, J.W. Boudreau and G.T. Milkovich (eds), *Research in personnel and human resources management* (Suppl. 4, pp. 99–122). Greenwich, CT: JAI Press, Inc.

Miles, R.E. and Snow, C.C. (1978) Organizational strategy, structure and process. New York: McGraw-Hill.

Miles, R.E. and Snow, C.C. (1984) Designing strategic human resources systems. *Organizational Dynamics*, Summer, 36–52.

Nonaka, I. (1991) The knowledge creating company. *Harvard Business Review*, 69(6): 96–104.

Nonaka, I. and Takeuchi, H. (1995) *The knowledge-creating company: How Japanese companies create the dynamics of innovation*. New York: Oxford Press.

Norburn, D. and Birley, S. (1988) The top management team and corporate performance. *Strategic Management Journal*, 9: 225–237.

Nordhaug, O. (1993) *Human capital in organizations: Competence, training and learning*. Oslo/London: Scandanavian University Press/Oxford University Press.

Nordhaug, O. and Gronhaug, K. (1994) Competences as resources in firms. *The International Journal of Human Resource Management*, 5(1): 89–106.

Osterman, P. (1987) Choice of employment systems in internal labor markets. *Industrial Relations*, 26(1): 48–63.

Peteraf, M.A. (1993) The cornerstones of competitive advantage: A resource based view. *Strategic Management Journal*, 14: 179–191.

Penrose, E.T. (1959) *The theory of the growth of the firm*. New York: Wiley.

Porter, M.E. (1980) *Competitive strategy*. New York: Free Press, 34–46.

Prahalad, C.K. and Hamel, G. (1990) The core competence of the corporation. *Harvard Business Review*, May/June 79–91.

Priem, R.L. and Butler, J.E. (2001a) Is the resource based 'view' a useful perspective for strategic management research? *Academy of Management Review*, 26(1): 22–40.

Priem, R.L and Butler, J.E. (2001b) Tautology in the resource based view and the implications of externally determined resource value: Further comments. *Academy of Management Review*, 26(1): 57–66.

Richard, O.C. (2001) Racial diversity, business strategy, and firm performance: A resource-based view. *Academy of Management Journal*, 43(2): 164–177.

Rumelt, R. (1984) Toward a strategic theory of the firm. In R. Lamb (ed.), *Competitive strategic management* (556–570). Englewood Cliffs, NJ: Prentice-Hall.

Snell, S.A., Shadur, M.A. and Wright, P.M. (2001) The era of our ways. In M.A. Hitt, R.E. Freeman and J.S. Harrison (eds), *Handbook of strategic management* (pp. 627–629). Oxford: Blackwell Publishing.

Snell, S.A., Stueber, D. and Lepak, D.P. (2001) Virtual HR departments: Getting out of the middle. In: Robert L. Heneman and David B. Greenberger, *Human resource management in virtual organizations* (Information Age Publishing).

Snell, S.A., Youndt, M.A. and Wright, P.M. (1996) Establishing a framework for research in strategic human resource management: Merging resource theory and organizational learning. In G. Ferris (ed.), *Research in personnel and human resources management* (Vol. 14, pp. 61–90).

Stalk, G., Evans, P. and Schulman, L. (1992) Competing on capabilities: The new rules of corporate strategy. *Harvard Business Review*, 70: 57–69.

Stewart, T.A. (1996) Human resources bites back. *Fortune*, May, 175.

Svieby, K.E. (1997) *The new organizational wealth: Managing and measuring knowledge based assets.* San Francisco: Berrett-Koehler.

Szulanski, G. (1996) Exploring internal stickiness: impediments to the transfer of best practice within the firm. *Strategic Management Journal, 17* (Winter Special Issue): 27–43.

Teece, D.J., Pisano, G. and Shuen, A (1997) Dynamic capabilities and strategic management. *Strategic Management Journal*, 18(7): 509–533.

Thomas, A.B. (1988) Does leadership make a difference in organizational performance? *Administrative Science Quarterly*, 33: 388–400.

Truss, C. and Gratton, L. (1994) Strategic human resource management: A conceptual approach. *International Journal of Human Resource Management*, 5: 663–686.

Tsui, A.S., Pearce, J.L., Porter, L.W. and Tripoli, A.M. (1997) Alternative approaches to the employee-organization relationship: Does investment in employees pay off? *Academy of Management Journal*, 40: 1089–1121.

Walker, J. (1978) Linking human resource planning and strategic planning. *Human Resource Planning*, 1: 1–18.

Wernerfelt, B. (1984) A resource-based view of the firm. *Strategic Management Journal*, 5: 171–180.

Wernerfelt, B. (1995) The resource based view of the firm: Ten years after. *Strategic Management Journal*, 16: 171–174.

Wright, P.M. and Boswell, W. (in press) Desegregating HRM: A Review and Synthesis of Micro and Macro Human Resource Management Research. *Journal of Management.*

Wright, P.M. and Gardner, T.M. (in press) Theoretical and empirical challenges in studying the HR practice-firm performance relationship. In D. Holman, T.D. Wall, C. Clegg, P. Sparrow and A. Howard (eds), *The new workplace: People technology, and organisation.* New York: John Wiley and Sons.

Wright, P.M., Gardner, T.M., Moynihan, L.M., Park, H., Gerhart, B. and Delery, J. (in press) Measurement error in research on human resources and firm performance. Additional data and suggestions for future research. *Personnel Psychology.*

Wright, P.M., McCormick, B., Sherman, W.S., McMahan, G.C. (1999) The role of human resources practices in petro-chemical refinery performance. *The International Journal of Human Resource Management*, 10: 551–571.

Wright, P.M. and McMahan, G.C. (1992) Theoretical perspectives for strategic human resource management. *Journal of Management*, 18(2): 295–320.

Wright, P.M., McMahan, G.C. and McWilliams, A. (1994) Human resources and sustained competitive advantage: A resource-based perspective. *International Journal of Human Resource Management*, 5(2): 301–326.

Wright, P.M., Smart, D.L. and McMahan, G.C. (1995) Matches between human resources and strategy among NCAA basketball teams. *Academy of Management Journal*, 38(4): 1052–1074.

Wright, P.M. and Snell, S.A. (1991) Toward an integrative view of strategic human resource management. *Human Resource Management Review*, 1(3): 203–225.

Wright, P.M. and Snell, S.A. (1998) Toward a unifying framework for exploring fit and flexibility in strategic human resource management. *Academy of Management Review*, 23(4): 756–772.

Youndt, M.A. and Snell, S.A. (2001) Human resource management, intellectual capital, and organizational performance. Working Paper, Skidmore College.

2

The Conduct of Management and the Management of Conduct: Contemporary Managerial Discourse and the Constitution of the 'Competent' Manager

Paul du Gay, Graeme Salaman and Bronwen Rees

Introduction

This paper aims to open up discussion about the reconceptualization of a particular category of person – the manager. It represents an initial attempt to think through certain issues surrounding the contemporary 'making up' of the manager as an active agent in his or her own government (particularly as this process is developing in the United Kingdom and United States).

While contemporary discourses of organizational reform, such as total quality management (TQM), excellence, and so forth, all allocate a crucial role to managers and management the analysis of the so-called 'new managerial work' by social scientists in general and sociologists in particular has tended to be cursory and unilluminating. [...] Our concern in this paper is to focus upon one dimension of the contemporary re-conceptualization of managerial work – the turn to competency. We consider the ways in which the competence approach inherently offers a simultaneous reconstructing of the manager, and defines this reconstruction in terms of qualities that centre on the managers' own self-government and enterprise. Our analysis of the competence approach regards it as a crucial element in contemporary discourses

Source: Paul du Gay, Graeme Salaman and Bronwen Rees (1996) 'The conduct of management and the management of conduct: contemporary managerial discourse and the constitution of the "competent" manager', *Journal of Management Studies*, 33(3): 263–82. Edited version.

of organizational change which essentially locates and defines such change in terms of the required individual attributes (attitudes, behaviours) of the new manager. Within contemporary programmes of organizational change the competence approach plays a key role as a central relay mechanism mediating between structure and individual, and defining the new relationship between these – in terms of qualities managers need to operate competently within organizations that have been transformed into quasi-markets – i.e. enterprisingly. More specifically, we attempt to indicate the ways in which the images and ideals of 'management competency' are made practicable in the workplace.

'Making up' managers

Our first task is to indicate what we mean by the term 'making up' managers. What might this phrase signify? Well, on the one hand, making something up suggests the construction of a fiction. But in what sense can the 'manager' be represented as a fictional character? On the other hand, the idea of being 'made up' suggests a material-cultural process of formation or transformation ('fashioning') whereby the adoption of certain habits and dispositions allows an individual to become – and to become recognized as – a particular sort of person.

What both versions of 'making up' share is a concern with 'invention'. They serve as a corrective to the tendency – associated with both radical sociological critiques of management and prescriptive managerial discourse – to regard a given activity or characteristic as in some sense 'natural'. It is perfectly possible and legitimate to conceive of the 'manager' as a fiction, for example, because that category of person has not always existed. As Pollard (1965), among many others, has indicated, the 'manager' only came into being at a particular historical juncture. Similarly, it is important to note that the dispositions, actions and attributes that constitute 'management' have no natural form, and for this reason must be approached as a series of historically specific assemblages. To be 'made up' – in the second sense of the term – as a manager is therefore to acquire that particular assemblage of attributes and dispositions which defines the activity of management at any given period.

The term 'making up' serves to highlight the way in which conceptions of persons and conceptions of activities are inextricably linked. [...] In other words, particular categories of person and the criteria for their identity are defined by reference to a range of activities that are regarded as 'centrally and normatively important to a culture, a historical period or an investigative context' (Rorty, 1988, p. 6).
[...]
In this paper, we are concerned with investigating the contemporary emergence of the so-called 'competent' manager. In order to chart the 'making up' of this creation we begin by delineating and analysing contemporary conceptions

of organizational reform and the role they allocate to the character of the manager. Having done this we move on to examine the mechanisms – or technologies – through which these dreams and schemes are operationalized and the 'competent' manager is constituted.

Re-imagining organizational life: contemporary managerial discourse and the conduct of management

Throughout the twentieth century the 'character' of the manager has been a regular source of public concern, debate and calls for action (Child, 1969). Indeed, the government of economic life across the present century has entailed a range of attempts to shape and regulate the conduct of management. From 'scientific management' through 'human relations' up to and including contemporary programmes of organizational reform such as total quality management and human resource management, the activities of individuals as managers have become an object of knowledge and the target of expertise. A complex series of links has been established through which the economic priorities of politicians and business persons have been articulated in terms of the required personal characteristics of managers (du Gay, 1991; Miller and Rose, 1990). [...] The relationship between these two seemingly discrete elements – representations and material practices – can be understood by reference to the concept of 'discourse'. For our purposes, a discourse refers to a group of statements that provides a language for talking about a topic and a way of producing a particular kind of knowledge about the topic. Thus, 'discourse' serves to undermine conventional distinctions between 'thought' and 'action', 'language' and 'practice'. The term refers both to the production of knowledge through language and representation and the way that knowledge is institutionalized, shaping social practices and cultural technologies and setting new practices and technologies into play. Therefore, it is possible to say that management discourses 'make up' particular ways for the activity of management to be conceptualized and performed.

In recent years the character of the manager has once again become a focus of considerable (national) concern. A number of reports [...] stressed that British companies were in danger of losing out to foreign competitors in many markets because their 'stock' of managers were not adequately trained and developed in the appropriate skills and techniques necessary to meet the challenges posed by a rapidly changing organizational landscape (Barham et al., 1988; Constable and McCormick, 1987; Handy, 1987; Mangham and Silver, 1986). In order to guarantee its position and to ensure future economic growth and success it was deemed crucial that 'Britain ... do more to develop her managers and do it more systematically' (Handy, 1987, p. 15).

[...]

The representations of organization and management deployed within these reports share a common language and mode of problematization with the dominant discourses of organizational reform [...]. The discourses of human resource management, total quality management, and excellence, to name but some of the most well known, all placed emphasis upon the development of more 'organic', 'flexible' organizational forms and practices which would overcome the perceived stasis, rigidity and inefficiency of more 'bureaucratic' structures and practices (Hill, 1991; Peters, 1987, 1992; Peters and Waterman, 1982; Storey, 1989). In particular, they indicated that organizational transformation would necessitate the production of new norms of organizational and personal conduct and the creation of a 'common corporate culture'.

The norms and values characterizing the conduct of 'excellent' organizations, for example, were articulated in explicit opposition to those deemed to constitute the identity of bureaucratic enterprises. Whereas, it was argued, bureaucratic organization encouraged the development of particular capacities and predispositions among its subjects – strict adherence to procedure, the abnegation of personal moral enthusiasms and so forth – the discourse of 'excellence' stressed the importance of individuals acquiring and exhibiting more 'market oriented', 'proactive', 'empowered' and 'entrepreneurial' attitudes and capacities. 'Bureaucratic culture', it was argued, had to give way to 'new approaches that require people to exercise discretion, take initiative, and assume a much greater responsibility for their own organization and management' (Morgan, 1988, p. 56).

[...]

Within these discourses, it is individual managers who are charged with the task of ensuring that these novel work-based subjects emerge. Managers were represented as having a pivotal role in securing successful organizational change through fostering certain 'entrepreneurial' virtues, first within themselves and then among their subordinates. Thus, in opposition to the 'personally detached and strictly objective expert' deemed to characterize bureaucratic management the 'excellent' manager was represented as a 'charismatic' facilitator, teaching others to learn how to take responsibility for themselves and fostering an 'enterprising' sense of identification, commitment and involvement between employees and the organization for which they worked.

[...]

Entrepreneurial governance and personal conduct

Enterprise and entrepreneurialism occupy an absolutely crucial role in contemporary discourses of organizational reform where the major principle of organizational restructuring is the attempt to introduce market mechanisms, market relationships and market attitudes within the organization. Furthermore, enterprise is, naturally, a necessary and valued quality in a market-dominated system. Thus, 'enterprise' is deployed both as a critique of 'bureaucratic' organizational governance and as a solution to the problems posed by 'globalization' through delineating the principles of a novel method of governing organizational and personal conduct.

But what exactly are the basic principles of 'enterprise' as a rationality of government and how do 'entrepreneurial principles' re-define the conduct of organizational life? Quite obviously, an important feature of entrepreneurial government is the role it accords to the 'enterprise form' as the preferred model for any form of institutional organization and provision of goods and services (Keat, 1990, p. 3; see also Gospel, 1992). However, of equal importance is the way in which the term 'enterprise' also refers to those activities that express and display enterprising qualities. Here 'enterprise' refers to a bundle of characteristics such as initiative, self-reliance and the ability to accept responsibility for oneself and one's actions.

Thus, as Graham Burchell (1993) notes, the defining characteristic of entrepreneurial governance is the 'generalization of an "enterprise form" to all forms of conduct – to the conduct of organizations hitherto seen as being neo-economic, to the conduct of government, and to the conduct of individuals themselves'. [...]

As Burchell (1993, p. 276) has argued, a characteristic feature of this style of government is the crucial role it accords to 'contract' in re-defining social relations. The changes affecting schools, hospitals, government departments and so forth often involve the re-constituting of institutional roles in terms of *contracts strictly defined*, and even more frequently involve a *contract-like way* of representing relationships between institutions and between individuals and institutions. [...]

Thus, 'contractualization' typically consists in assigning the performance of a function or an activity to a distinct unit of management – individual or collective – which is regarded as being accountable for the efficient performance of that function or conduct of that activity. By assuming active responsibility for these activities and functions – both for carrying them out and for their outcomes – these units of management are in effect affirming a certain kind of identity or personality. This identity or personality is essentially entrepreneurial in character.

[...]

As Colin Gordon (1991, pp. 42–5), for example, has argued, entrepreneurial forms of governance such as contractualization involve the re-imagination of the social as a form of the economic. 'This operation works', he argues, 'by the progressive enlargement of the territory of economic theory by a series of redefinitions of its object.'

Economics thus becomes an 'approach' capable in principle of addressing the totality of human behaviour, and, consequently, of envisaging a coherent economic method of programming the totality of governmental action. (Gordon, 1991, p. 43) [...]

[...]

[...] The subject of 'enterprise' is both a 'reactivation and a radical inversion' of traditional 'economic man'. The reactivation consists 'in positing a fundamental human faculty of *choice*, a principle which empowers economic calculation effectively to sweep aside the anthropological categories and frameworks of the human and social sciences'. The great innovation occurs, however, in the conceptualization of the economic agent as an inherently manipulable creation. Whereas, *homo economicus* was originally conceived of as a subject the well-springs of whose activity were ultimately 'untouchable by government', the subject of enterprise is imagined as an agent 'who is perpetually responsive to modifications in its environment'. As Gordon (1991, p. 43) points out, 'economic government here joins hands with behaviourism'. The resultant subject is in a novel sense not just an 'enterprise' but 'the entrepreneur of himself or herself'. In other words, entrepreneurial government 'makes up' the individual as a particular sort of person – as an 'entrepreneur of the self' (Gordon, 1987, p. 300).

This idea of an individual human life as 'an enterprise of the self' suggests that no matter what hand circumstance may have dealt a person, he or she remains always continuously engaged (even if technically 'unemployed') in that one enterprise, and that it is 'part of the continuous business of living to make adequate provision for the preservation, reproduction and reconstruction of one's own human capital' (Gordon, 1991, p. 44).

Because a human being is considered to be continuously engaged in a project to shape his or her life as an autonomous, choosing individual driven by the desire to optimize the worth of its own existence, life for that person is represented as a single, basically undifferentiated arena for the pursuit of that endeavour. [...]

This conception of the individual as an 'entrepreneur of the self' is firmly established at the heart of contemporary programmes of organizational reform (consider for example recent emphasis on managers 'managing their own careers'). In keeping with the entrepreneurial imbrication of economics and behaviourism contemporary programmes of organizational reform characterize employment not as a painful obligation imposed upon individuals, nor as an activity undertaken to meet purely instrumental needs, but rather as a means to self-development. Organizational success is therefore premised upon an engagement by the organization of the self-optimizing impulses of all its members, no matter what their formal role. This ambition is to be made practicable in the workplace through a variety of organizational restructuring techniques such as flattening hierarchies and performance-related pay. The latter, for example, whose deployment throughout the public sector has grown dramatically in the last decade, often involves the development of an on-going 'contract' between an individual employee and their line manager whereby an employee's pay is made more dependent upon whether s/he has met or exceeded certain performance objectives (Millward et al., 1992, pp. 268 and 361; Marsden and Richardson, 1994).

The redefinition of management consists of major shift in the 'contract' between employer and manager: the traditional exchange – of security, long-term tenure in return for compliance and loyalty – has been replaced by a market-centred relationship where the contract is defined by the employer, in terms of a constant, regular and continuous assessment, and therefore possible renewal/termination, of the employment relationship, based on measures of performance. The relationship is now based on the value of the discrete transactions, and its permanence and security are functions of the employee's demonstrated 'added value'.

This redefinition necessarily emphasizes new managerial skills/competencies – competencies necessitated by the newly empowered roles of managers and their staff where they are required to 'own' and to be accountable for their own performance and that of others.

[...]

The redefinition of management not only emphasizes and articulates the skills/competencies managers will need in order to act effectively in their newly empowered and accountable roles, but also reflects the delegation of responsibility to ensure achievement/possession of these competencies, to the managers themselves. The price of this involvement is that individuals themselves must assume responsibility for carrying out these activities and for their outcomes. In keeping with the constitutive principles of enterprise as a rationality of government, performance management and related techniques function as forms of 'responsibilization', which are held to be both economically desirable and personally 'empowering'.

Entrepreneurial organizational governance therefore involves the reconstruction of a wide range of institutions, activities, relationships and staff along the lines of the market. At the same time, guaranteeing that the optimum benefits accrue from the re-structuring of organizations along market lines necessitates the production of particular forms of conduct by all members of an organization. In this sense, governing organizational life in an enterprising manner involves 'making up' new ways for people to be; it refers to the importance of individuals acquiring and exhibiting specific 'enterprising' capacities and dispositions.

Contemporary organizational success is therefore premised upon an engagement by the organization of the 'enterprising capacities' of individuals as subjects. In other words, individuals are to be brought to identify themselves with the goals and objectives of their employing organization to the extent that they interpret them as both dependent upon and enhancing their own skills of self-development, self-direction and self-management. In this way, 'enterprise' plays the role of relay between objectives that are economically desirable and those that are personally seductive, 'teaching the arts of self-realization that will enhance employees as individuals' as well as managers or workers (Rose, 1989, p. 16). This responsibilization of the self, the instilling of a reflexive self-monitoring which will afford self-understanding and self-control, makes paid employment an essential element in the path to self-fulfilment and provides the a priori that links work and non-work together, blurring the boundaries between what is properly inside and what is properly outside the orbit of the organization (Sabel, 1991).

Although both managers and workers are represented as equally amenable to 'entrepreneurial' reconstitution, the former are held to have a particularly important role in securing organizational change through fostering 'enterprise' among the latter (Hill, 1991). [...] Managers are charged with 'leading' their subordinates to 'self-realization' by encouraging them to make a project of themselves, to work on their relations with employment and on all other aspects of their lives in order to develop a style of life and relationship to self that will maximize the worth of their existence to themselves.

> No more close supervision of workers, no more focus on data irrelevant to running the business, no more energy spent on defending turf. The role of managers becomes one of empowerment – providing workers with the information, training, authority and accountability to excel … As workers take on more management tasks, managers must take on more leadership tasks – holding a vision of the business, articulating it to workers and customers, and creating an environment that truly empowers workers. (Champy, 1994)

In other words, managers are charged with reconstructing the conduct and self-image of employees: with encouraging them to acquire the capacities and dispositions that will enable them to become 'enterprising' persons. The current interest in identifying and allocating key management 'competences' is seen as fundamental to this process.

Constructing the competent manager

As we have indicated, proponents of contemporary organizational discourse are adamant that the re-imagined corporation depends for its success upon the pre-dispositions and capacities of its managers. This assumption is also a constitutive feature of the reports into the 'state' of British management mentioned earlier. As Mangham and Silver (1986, p. 2), for example, argue, 'to a large extent … it is the competency of managers that will influence the return that an organization will secure from its investment in both human and material capital'. There are two elements to this focus upon the character of the 'competent' manager.

First, the *role* of management is greatly enhanced – even if the *number* of managers is reduced – in the 'flexible' corporation. As the marker of formal hierarchy and the clear distinctions of task, title and function is problematized managers are allocated *the* major responsibility for ensuring that their 'empowered' subordinates adopt the appropriate 'entrepreneurial' habits of action deemed necessary for organizational success.

Secondly, this enhanced role for the manager also necessitates the adoption of *new managerial attributes, skills and capacities*. Managers […] are 'imagined' very differently from their predecessors because the conception of what their job entails is itself re-classified.

If contemporary discourses of organizational reform construct a particular way of representing and acting upon the character of the manager – one that differs very substantially from previous constructions – through what mechanisms does this new manager emerge? […]

According to Michel Foucault (1986, pp. 225–6) attempts to instrumentalize and operationalize particular rationalities of government take a *technological* form. To investigate the 'making up' of the manager as an active agent in her or his own government therefore necessitates an examination of the seemingly banal mechanisms which make this form of government a practical possibility – 'techniques of notation, computation and calculation; procedures of examination and assessment … the standardization of systems for training and the inculcation of habits' (Miller and Rose, 1990, p. 8).

One of the key mechanisms through which authorities of various sorts have sought to shape, normalize and instrumentalize the conduct of management – to 'make up' the new manager – has been the development of management *competences* (Boam and Sparrow, 1992a; Boyatzis, 1982; MCI, 1991).

▌ The turn to competency

The term 'competence' has proliferated in management theory and practice over the past decade. There are three distinct approaches of which the behavioural focus that we discuss here is just one. A second is the strategic concept of core competences, which focuses more on a specific articulation between product, processes and human resource capability and was first identified by Prahalad and Hamel (1989). The third is that developed by the Management Charter Initiative (MCI), which focuses on minimum standards of functional performance.

The behavioural model of competence has its origins in the research of the McBer Consultancy in the late 1970s in the USA as part of the initiative by the American Management Association to identify the characteristics that distinguish superior from average managerial performance (Iles, 1992). The work was encapsulated in the seminal book *The Competent Manager* (Boyatzis, 1982). At its heart, the initiative turns around the processes by which a relevant 'fit' is achieved between the individual and the role holder. Attempting to identify relevant qualities in existing managerial staff and in potential management recruits between 'person' and 'job' is a staple element of personnel practice.

[...]

[...] The 'competence principle' can be used simply as a means of identifying training and development needs, or at the other end of the scale, it can be used as a tool for the wholesale change of an organizational structure and the individuals within it. Further, there is still considerable debate around the actual meaning of the team 'competence'. At various times it has been defined as knowledge, skill, ability, or behaviour.

Despite these multiple and often conflicting accounts of what the word 'competency' means it is generally agreed that all competency systems are based upon explicit behavioural or outcome-based statements. In other words, they focus on *actual performance*. At the same time, they are also all based upon research with *role-holders*. That is, specific competencies are identified through research with the people who are actually involved in doing specific sorts of work.

According to Woodruffe (1992, p. 17), for example,

> a competency is a dimension of overt, manifest behaviour that allows a person
> to perform competently. Behind it must be both the ability and desire to
> behave in that competent way. For example, the person competent at selling
> will need a competency that includes listening. In turn that includes knowing
> how to listen and choosing to listen. Put more generally, people will only
> produce competent action in a situation if they know how to and if they value
> the consequences of the expected outcomes of the action.

The lists of competences produced by academics, practitioners or consultants, whether they be generically or organizationally derived, focus on 'how' to carry out the job – and generally tend to express the capacities, dispositions and attributes of the managers outlined by Peters, Kanter et al., as being crucial to the emergence of the enterprising manager. For example, the eleven competences elicited by Schroder (1989) for high performers carry many of Peters' requirements: information search; concept formation; conceptual flexibility; interpersonal search; managing interaction; development orientation; self-confidence; presentation impact; proactive orientation; achievement orientation.

In other words, 'competency' refers to certain characteristics that a person exhibits which results in effective job performance (Woodruff, 1992). These characteristics are regarded as generic, though they do receive different emphasis depending, for example, on management level or on the sector within which the organization in question is located – i.e. public or private (Boyatzis, 1982). Even if there is variation and debate in the actual competences used, one clear commonality emerges: and that is the agreement that 'competence' can and should be measured. This we see as the technological form of attempts to instrumentalize and operationalize particular rationalities of government. The notion of the competence is seen as the future way of capturing the most elusive of resources – the human one.

The competency approach

The aim of the competency approach is to provide an integrated system whereby those generic characteristics (whether they be generic to the organization or management in general) that distinguish competent managerial performance are identified, then existing and required levels of competency are assessed through appraisal and, finally, any resultant gaps are addressed through on-going assessment and training and development programmes.

There are two distinct stages in the competency approach: in the first stage competencies are identified; and the second focuses on the extent, and way in which the competence framework is implemented in the organization. For each stage there is a raft of mechanisms by which the individual within an organization can develop him or herself in order to realize their own human potential.

The first element of this competency system – the identification of competencies – involves the deployment of a range of job analysis methods derived from person-oriented approaches such as critical incident technique, repertory grid analysis and behavioural event interviews (Kandola and Pearn, 1992).

Once the competencies have been identified, implementation can be designed. The range of mechanisms and technologies used to engender this implementation will vary depending on the extent to which competences are being used as organization-wide development or purely as a tool for management development.

The size of such a task is not to be underestimated. As Lawler points out:

> In existing organizations, the entire human resource management
> infrastructure needs to be altered or replaced. This is clearly a large task and
> may be resisted by the many employees who are comfortable with traditional
> job descriptions, job-based pay and the bureaucratic approach to management.
> Indeed, many of them may not have the capability of functioning effectively
> in organization that emphasizes the skill-based approach. (Lawler, 1994)

Pivotal to this architecture is the notion of assessment. As the need to make the organization 'competent' is acknowledged, so ever more technologies are introduced to measure this competence. At the outset, when competencies are first identified a 'competency audit' may be held to delineate and assess current managerial competency levels. Assessment centre technologies may well form the backbone of such an audit. Here competences are assessed at one large event instead of sporadically over a longer period of time.

As an on-going feature of competence, appraisal is a key mechanism for ensuring that individuals behave in a way that is appropriate to the overall business plan and culture of the organization. Many organizations will have workshops built into their competency programmes so that managers are trained in appraising both themselves and their subordinates. There has also been growing use of 360 degree feedback, or upward appraisal (Fletcher, 1993; Moravec et al., 1993; Novack, 1993). In this process, feedback is collected 'all around' an employee, from his or her supervisors, subordinates, peers, and even the customer. It provides a comprehensive summary of an employee's skills, abilities, styles and job-related competencies. Indeed the individual actually 'becomes' the manager of his/her own performance.

Enterprising up the competency approach

The attractions of the competency approach to various economic authorities are obvious. In indicating that it is possible to define exactly what is needed in managerial jobs in an organization and precisely what people need to bring to those jobs in order to perform them effectively the expertise of competency offers the promise of improved managerial performance and, as a result, continuous business success.

However, the expertise of competency doesn't simply promise to improve organizational performance, it also offers individual managers the prospect of self-improvement. Indeed, becoming a competent manager is equated with becoming a better, more autonomous, accountable self. And with owning the qualities necessary to take responsibility not only for empowered managerial roles, but for empowered staff, and for their development and improvement: 'adding value' to the corporation, oneself and one's staff. As we indicated earlier, within the new discourses of organizational reform the values of self-management, self-presentation and self-realization are represented as both personally seductive and economically desirable. The competency approach, it is argued, can instrumentalize these values by enabling managers to see 'how' exactly they demonstrate competency in their jobs and by offering them the chance to help themselves become more competent as managers and as individuals in the future (Boam and Sparrow, 1992b, p. xxi).

Thus the competency approach promises to make practicable the dreams and schemes of contemporary discourses of organizational reform. That this promise is taken seriously is evidenced by the growing number of major UK companies – including Cadbury Schweppes, W.H. Smith, British Petroleum, National & Provincial Building Society, Rank Xerox, National Power, and the

Body Shop – which have deployed the competency approach to redefine the role and practice of management in their organizations.

However, as more organizations have taken the competency route, so the approach itself has come in for considerable criticism as hoped-for outcomes have proved elusive or actual changes are adjudged to have been only partially successful (Cockerill, 1989; Sparrow and Boam, 1992).

[...]

The 'failures' associated with the operationalization of competency technologies have not led to their abandonment, but rather to their elaboration and 'refinement'. In other words, while competency technologies have rarely been ajudged to have delivered their promise, this has not signalled the downfall of the approach as a whole. Failures have simply been represented as challenges which the 'development of the methodology' *in line with the values of contemporary organizational discourse* will meet.

Proponents of contemporary organizational discourse continually point to the dramatically altered substance of managerial practice. According to Kanter (1989, p. 85), for example, 'managerial work is undergoing such enormous rapid change that many managers are re-inventing their profession as they go: with little precedent to guide them, they are watching hierarchy fade away and the clear distinctions of title, task, department, even corporation blur'. In the flexible meta-corporation (Sabel, 1991), managers are therefore more dependent upon their own resources. This in turn entails 'more risk and uncertainty ... No longer counting on the corporation requires people to build resources in themselves' (Kanter, 1989, pp. 357–8). The assumption is that 'managers are more personally exposed' as 'reliance on organizations to give shape to a career is being replaced by a reliance on self' (Kanter, 1991, p. 76).

Thus, the substance of the managerial job is altered with 'soft' personal and interpersonal management skills coming to the fore while the more mechanical and administrative elements of (bureaucratic) managerial tasks begin to take a back seat or disappear completely. The success of the organization is therefore increasingly premised upon managers' abilities to foster 'proactive mindsets', 'entrepreneurship', 'self-development' and other 'virtues', first within themselves and then among their subordinates (Morgan, 1988).

This concern with individual 'inner' resources and personal and interpersonal management capacities is another area in which existing competency approaches have come in for criticism. According to Iles and Salaman (1994), for example, many competency models have been criticized for paying insufficient attention to the skills of creativity, sensitivity, imagination and so forth which are increasingly seen to be crucial to the successful conduct of the 'new managerial work'. These so-called 'soft competences' are assumed to be 'difficult to measure under any circumstances and virtually impossible to measure under simulated conditions' (Jacobs, 1989). The inability to technologize these capacities and dispositions, it is argued, undermines the efficacy of the competency approach.

Once again, however, criticism has not led to the abandonment of the competency approach; rather, it has acted as a spur to the production of competency mechanisms that can identify and validate behaviourally observable 'soft' skills. [...]

Concluding remarks – mobilizing managers

In this paper we have sought to open up discussion about the reconceptualization of the character of the manager. More specifically we have attempted to indicate the ways in which new images and ideals of management are made practicable in the workplace.

As Hill (1991, p. 398), for example, has indicated, while contemporary discourses of organizational reform allocate a crucial role to managers, the analysis of the 'new managerial work' by social scientists in general and sociologists in particular has tended to be cursory and unilluminating. [...]

Our concern here has been to take the matter of managerial organization seriously by delineating and examining one component of the contemporary making up of the manager as an active agent in his or her own government: the turn to competency.

It is possible to detect a general consistency in the style of government advocated by contemporary discourses of organizational reform. The essential characteristic of this style of government is the generalization of an 'enterprise form' to all forms of conduct – personal as well as organizational: the promotion of an enterprise culture. This does not mean simply that all desired forms of organizational behaviour will be overtly enterprising; although many will be. It also means that new desired forms of behaviour will reflect the reconstruction of the employee and particularly the manager, in terms of those behaviours/competencies that are required by roles where incumbents are answerable, as it were, for themselves, answerable and accountable for their own demonstrable added value, required to demonstrate their competence within an organization and an employment relationship that being imbued with market principles requires market characteristics. Furthermore, the competent employee and the competent manager must take personal responsibility for demonstrating these required behaviours – for self-marketing. Within these discourses continuous business improvement is premised upon an engagement by the organization of the 'enterprising capacities' of individuals as subjects. In other words, contemporary forms of organizational government encourage their subjects to adopt an entrepreneurial form of practical relationship to themselves as a condition of their effectiveness and of the effectiveness of this form of government. This involves offering individuals – most especially managers, but also workers – involvement in activities previously held to be the responsibility of other, clearly demarcated functions and groups – human resource, finance or contract managers, for example. However, the price of this involvement is that they must assume active responsibility for these activities, both for carrying them out and for their outcomes 'and in so doing they are required to conduct themselves in accordance with the appropriate (or approved) model of action' (Burchell, 1993, p. 276).

A crucial component of contemporary organizational governance is therefore the way in which it relies for its effectivity upon individuals assuming the status of being the subjects of their own existence, upon the ways in which they fashion themselves as certain sorts of person. In other words, contemporary forms of organizational government are premised upon the mobilization of the subjectivity of managers.

This mobilization is effected or instrumentalized technologically. It is made practicable within an organizational context through a range of banal mechanisms which can include, *inter alia*, performance appraisal techniques (Townley, 1989, 1993) novel calculative technologies such as activity-based accounting (Miller and O'Leary, 1993, 1994) and emotion and interpersonal management techniques such as transaction analysis (du Gay, 1996).

Competency systems are but one component, albeit an important one, in the ensemble of activities that 'make up' the manager as an enterprising subject. Furthermore, this process of 'making up' is always contingent and provisional. As we have shown, the institution of novel enterprising technologies is never the cut and dried affair that some management gurus would suggest. Rather than being inscribed upon a *tabula rasa*, enterprising technologies of government emerge within organizations where the structuring of work relations, for example, already involves the fracturing of collections of managers and workers around which 'friend-enemy' groupings have developed (Salaman, 1985).

As such the enterprising self is unlikely to be or to become the sole or exclusive model for forms of work-based identification. The degree to which technologies of enterprise meet with resistance and the forms and effects this resistance takes are, of course, matters for empirical investigation. However, while it may be the case that when the enterprising self is brought into an organization it comes into contact with continuing forms of solidarity and exclusion, this does not erase the significance of its emergence. In other words, the possibility of subverting entrepreneurial norms does not automatically erase their significance as regulatory mechanisms in the lives of individuals.

That individual managers are able to use a range of governmental technologies for their own ends to further their own objectives is not an indication of the failure of such mechanisms. Entrepreneurial norms and techniques of conduct are not necessarily displaced by such activity. As Miller (1992, p. 75) has suggested, they still remain as something to which appeals can be made; they continue to provide the terms in which individuals are judged and judge themselves and as something in the name of which business opportunities can be compared and decisions made. Our discussion of the difficulties of operationalizing competences supports just such a reading. Putting competency systems to work in organizations is never a trouble-free process. None the less, while 'live' competency systems are subject to considerable criticism this does not mean they have 'failed' in some absolute, zero sum sense. As we have indicated, governmental technologies are typically surrounded by systematic attempts to evaluate their strengths and weaknesses. 'Failure' in this sense is an integral component of the working of these technologies. It represents a challenge which the 'development of the methodology' in line with particular values and ideals – in this case the norms of enterprise – is expected to meet.

Note

The financial support of the ESRC (grant no. R000234869) is gratefully acknowledged.

References

Barham, K. et al. (1988) *Management for the Future*. Berkhamstead and London: Ashridge Management College and Foundation for Management Education.

Boam, R. and Sparrow, P. (1992a) 'The rise and rationale of competency-based approaches'. In Boam, R. and Sparrow, P. (eds), *Designing and Achieving Competency*. London: McGraw-Hill, 3–15.

Boam, R. and Sparrow, P. (eds) (1992b) *Designing and Achieving Competency*. London: McGraw-Hill.

Boyatzis, R. (1982) *The Competent Manager*. New York: Wiley.

Burchell, G. (1993) 'Liberal government and techniques of the self'. *Economy and Society*, 22: 267–82.

Champy, J. (1994) 'Time to re-engineer the manager'. *Financial Times*, 14 January, 17.

Child, J. (1969) *British Management Thought*. London: Allen & Unwin.

Cockerill, T. (1989) 'The kind of competence for rapid change'. *Personnel Management*, 21, 9: 52–6.

Constable, J. and McCormick, R. (1987) *The Making of British Managers*. London: BIM/CBI.

Fletcher, C. (1993) 'Appraisal: an idea whose time has come?'. *Personnel Management*, September.

Fletcher, S. (1992) *Competence-Based Assessment Techniques*. London: Kogan Page.

Foucault, M. (1972) *The Archaeology of Knowledge*. London: Tavistock.

Foucault, M. (1986) 'Space, knowledge and power'. In Rabinow, P. (ed.), *The Foucault Reader*. Harmondsworth: Penguin.

du Gay, P. (1991) 'Enterprise culture and the ideology of excellence'. *New Formations*, 13.

du Gay, P. (1996) *Consumption and Identity at Work*. London: Sage.

Gordon, C. (1987) 'The soul of the citizen: Max Weber and Michel Foucault on rationality and government'. In Whimster, S. and Lash, S. (eds), *Max Weber: Rationality and Modernity*. London: Allen & Unwin.

Gordon, C. (1991) 'Governmental rationality: an introduction'. In Burchell, G. et al. (eds), *The Foucault Effect*. Brighton: Harvester Wheatsheaf.

Gospel, H. (1992) *Markets, Firms, and the Management of Labour in Modern Britain*. Cambridge: Cambridge University Press.

Handy, C. (1987) *The Making of Managers*. London: MSC.

Hill, S. (1991) 'How do you manage a flexible firm? The total quality model'. *Work, Employment and Society*, 5, 3: 397–416.

Iles, P. (1992) 'Managing assessment and selection processes'. Block 4, B884 *Human Resource Strategies*. Milton Keynes: Open University.

Iles, P. and Salaman, G. (1994) 'Recruitment and selection'. In Storey, J. (ed.), *Human Resource Management: A Critical Text*. London: Routledge.

Jacobs, R. (1989) 'Getting the measure of management competence'. *Personnel Management*, June, 32–7.

Kandola, R. and Pearn, M. (1992) 'Identifying competencies'. In Boam, R. and Sparrow, P. (eds), *Designing and Achieving Competency*. London: McGraw-Hill, 31–50.

Kanter, R. (1989) *When Giants Learn to Dance*. London: Unwin Hyman.

Kanter, R. (1991) 'The future of bureaucracy and hierarchy in organizational theory: a report from the field'. In Bourdieu, P. and Coleman, J. (eds), *Social Theory for a Changing Society*. Boulder: Westview Press.

Keat, R. (1990) 'Introduction'. In Keat, R. and Abercrombie, N. (eds), *Enterprise Culture*. London: Routledge.

Lawler, E. (1994) 'From job-based to competency-based organizations'. *Journal of Organizational Behaviour*, 15: 3–15.

Lyotard, J.-F. (1984) *The Postmodern Condition*. Translated by G. Bennington and G. Massumi. Minneapolis, MN: University of Minnesota Press.

MCI (Management Charter Initiative) (1991) *Management Standards Implementation Pack*. London: MCI.

Mangham, I. and Silver, M. (1986) *Management Training: Context and Practice*. ESRC Pilot Survey on Management Training.

Marsden, D. and Richardson, R. (1994) 'Performing for pay? The effects of "merit pay" on motivation in a public service'. *British Journal of Industrial Relations*, 32, 2: 243–61.

Miller, P. (1992) 'Accounting and objectivity: the invention of calculating selves and calculable spaces'. *Annals of Scholarship*, 9: 61–86.

Miller, P. and O'Leary, T. (1993) 'Accounting expertise and the politics of the product: economic citizenship and modes of corporate governance'. *Accounting, Organizations and Society*, 18: 187–206.

Miller, P. and O'Leary, T. (1994) 'Accounting, "economic citizenship" and the spatial re-ordering of manufacturing'. *Accounting, Organizations and Society*, 19, 1: 15–43.

Miller, P. and Rose, N. (1990) 'Governing economic life'. *Economy and Society*, 19: 1–31.

Millward, N. et al. (1992) *Workplace Industrial Relations in Transition*. Aldershot: Dartmouth.

Moravec, M. et al. (1993) 'Upward feedback. A 21st century communication tool'. *HR Magazine*, July, 77–81.

Morgan, G. (1988) *Riding the Waves of Change*. San Francisco: Jossey-Bass.

Novack, K. (1993) '360-degree feedback: the whole story'. *Training and Development*, January, 69–72.

Peters, T. (1987) *Thriving On Chaos*. Basingstoke: Macmillan.

Peters, T. (1992) *Liberation Management*. Basingstoke: Macmillan.

Peters, T. and Waterman, R. (1982) *In Search of Excellence*. New York: Harper & Row.

Pollard, S. (1965) *The Genesis of Modern Management*. Harmondsworth: Penguin.

Prahalad, C.K. and Hamel, G. (1989) 'The core competence of the corporation'. *Harvard Business Review*, 68, May/June: 79–91.

Rorty, A. (1988) *Mind In Action*. Boston, MA: Beacon Press.

Rose, N. (1989) 'Governing the enterprising self'. Paper presented to a conference on the Values of the Enterprise Culture, Lancaster University.

Rose, N. (1990) *Governing the Soul*. London: Routledge.

Sabel, C. (1991) 'Moebius strip organizations and open labour markets: some consequences of the re-integration of conception and execution in a volatile economy'. In Bourdieu, P. and Coleman, J. (eds), *Social Theory for a Changing Society*. Boulder: West-view Press.

Salaman, G. (1985) *Working*. London: Tavistock.

Schroder, H.M. (1989) *Managerial Competence: The Key to Excellence*. Dubuque, IA: Kendall-Hunt.

Sparrow, P. and Boam, R. (1992) 'Where do we go from here?'. In Boam, R. and Sparrow, P. (eds), *Designing and Achieving Competency*. London: McGraw-Hill, 175–96.

Storey, J. (ed.) (1989) *New Perspectives on Human Resource Management*. London: Routledge.

Townley, B. (1989) 'Selection and appraisal: reconstituting "social relations"?'. In Storey, J. (ed.), *New Perspectives on Human Resource Management*. London: Routledge, 92–108.

Townley, B. (1993) 'Performance appraisal and the emergence of management'. *Journal of Management Studies*, 30: 221–38.

Woodruffe, C. (1992) 'What is meant by a competency'. In Boam, R. and Sparrow, P. (eds), *Designing and Achieving Competency*. London: McGraw-Hill, 16–30.

3

Foucault, Power/Knowledge, and its Relevance for Human Resource Management

Barbara Townley

A glimpse at human resource management (HRM) texts would seem to give light to a comment by Beer, Spector, Lawrence, Mills, and Walton (1984) that HRM is a series of seemingly disjointed activities. [...] What the heterogeneity of HRM highlights, is the importance of an organizing principle, or analytical focus, as opposed to common sense description, which gives HRM practices a theoretical coherence. HRM's heterogeneity stresses the importance of an order 'that turns a set of bits, which have limited significance on their own, into an intelligible whole' (Turner, 1983: 191).

[...] Underlying most studies of HRM, although often remaining implicit, is what may be identified as a systems maintenance or functionalist perspective. Reflecting concerns with improvement in efficiency that derive from classical management theory, HRM is an organizational mechanism through which goal achievement and survival may be promoted. Its aim is to make the organization more orderly and integrated. In HRM, connotations of goal-directed activity, inputs and outputs, stability, adaptability, and systems maintenance predominate. From this perspective HRM is the black box of production, where organizational inputs – employees – are selected, appraised, trained, developed, and remunerated to deliver the required output of labor. Within this framework HRM practices are all too frequently technique oriented, presented as the tools or instruments that enable the effective attainment of goals – an approach that behaviorist psychology has a tendency

Source: Barbara Townley (1993) 'Foucault, power/knowledge, and its relevance for human resource management', *The Academy of Management Review*, 18(3): 518–45. Edited version.

to reinforce. Research concerns are usually to make HRM practices more efficient, and they reflect the belief that knowledge of them, through the services of its handmaiden, science, will progressively be made more accurate. As such, the study of HRM stands well within a modernist, and largely positivist, tradition.

As a series of categories, selection, appraisal, training, and so forth, have become so familiar that they are not seen as a 'way of ordering,' but as 'an order which is in the phenomena' (Turner, 1983: 192). Here, I wish to set aside these traditional methods of ordering and examine an alternative and, it is argued, more productive line of analysis. I do so by drawing upon the work of Michel Foucault, Professor in the History of Systems of Thought at the College de France, Paris, until his death in 1984. One of the central concerns of Foucault's work is to dispel self-evidencies, that is, to indicate that although elements are part of a familiar landscape, they are not 'natural,' or part of a naturally existing order. Through a number of different examples, Foucault has shown how what counts as truth depends on, or is determined by, the conceptual system in operation. [...] As Philp (1985: 70) noted, 'When we classify objects we operate within a system of possibility – and this system both enables us to do certain things, and limits us to this system and these things.' Foucault's work provides an avenue to illustrate how established ways of ordering limit our analysis, and it also introduces different ways of seeing.

Power, knowledge, and the subject

Ostensibly, Foucault's work covers a wide range of subjects – nominally, psychiatry (1967), the human sciences (1970), medicine (1973), the penal system (1977), and sexuality (1981, 1985, 1986). Dates cited are the first English translations of Foucault, except for essays printed in edited collections. There are, however, a number of underlying themes that those who are familiar with his work might identify as central concerns. Three of these concerns are perhaps most apparent: power, knowledge, and subjectivity. A necessarily brief explication of Foucault's understanding of these concepts is important to illustrate the relevance of his work for HRM.

Dreyfus and Rabinow (1983) stated that part of the difficulty with, and the genius of, Foucault is that he did not accept the usual sociological categories, both in the questions he posed and the concepts he introduced. [...] The reasons for this refusal lie in Foucault's desire to understand more fully *power relations*, that is, how mechanisms of power affect everyday lives. His work is critical of views of power that depict it as a commodity (something held or possessed; something embodied in a person, institution, or structure; something to be used for organizational or individual purposes). He wrote, 'Power is not something that is acquired, seized or shared, something one holds on to or allows to slip away' (Foucault, 1981: 94). Rather, power is relational; it becomes apparent when it is exercised. Because of this relational aspect, power is not associated with a particular institution, but with practices, techniques, and procedures. Power is employed at all levels, and through many dimensions. Denying the concept of power as a commodity has implications for the way it is studied. Thus, questions such as 'who has power?' or 'where, or in what, does power reside?' are changed to what Foucault termed the 'how' of power: those practices, techniques, and procedures that give it effect. He also offered a different understanding of power as, for example, in the political dimensions of visibility (rendering something or someone visible) 'power is exercised by virtue of things being known and people being seen' (Foucault, 1980: 154).

This view of power informs the concept power-knowledge, 'an anchoring device for the unity Foucault gave to his work' (Eribon, 1991: 127). Such a view is perhaps most apparent in Foucault's essay on governmentality, in which he examined techniques used in the management of populations (Burchell, Gordon and Miller, 1991; Foucault, 1991c). Governmentality is a neologism derived from a combination of government and rationality. Government is understood to be not simply political institutions but in a broader sense 'the conduct of conduct: a form of activity aiming to shape, guide or affect the conduct of some person or persons' (Gordon, 1991: 2). Rationality is the idea that before something can be governed or managed, it must first be known. It is the acknowledgement that government is intrinsically dependent upon particular ways of knowing. Programs of government, for example, require vocabularies, ways of representing that which is to be governed, ways of ordering populations (i.e., mechanisms for the supervision and administration of individuals and groups). Rationality is dependent upon specific knowledges and techniques of rendering something knowable and, as a result, governable. Governmentality, therefore, is a reference to those processes through which objects are rendered amenable to intervention and regulation by being formulated in a particular conceptual way. Governmentality places an emphasis on regulatory systems, processes, and methods of thinking about or perceiving a domain, especially those which may be translated into written inscriptions that claim to authentically depict it. These methods, and so forth, include mechanisms for inscription, recording, and calculation: ways of observing; and ways of coding, (e.g., in balance sheets, audits, population tables, censuses). Once an arena is captured or inscribed, knowledge about it may then be translated to other decision-making bodies.

Foucault does not, therefore, acknowledge a neutral concept of knowledge formation, as his play on the word discipline – at once a branch of knowledge and a system of correction and control – exemplifies:

> The exercise of power itself creates and causes to emerge new objects of
> knowledge and accumulates new bodies of information ... the exercise of
> power perpetually creates knowledge and, conversely, knowledge constantly

induces effects of power. … It is not possible for power to be exercised without knowledge, it is impossible for knowledge not to engender power. (Foucault, 1980: 52)

Knowledge is not detached and independent; as a source of illumination, it is integral to the operation of power. From this perspective, procedures for the formation and accumulation of knowledge, including the scientific method, are not, therefore, neutral instruments for the presentation of the real (Steffy and Grimes, 1992). Indeed, scientific discourse and the institutions that produce it are part of the taken-for-granted assumptions of knowledge that should be questioned (Knights, 1992). Procedures for investigation and research (e.g., the use of a classificatory table), although operating as a procedure of knowledge, can operate equally as a technique of power. Knowledge is the operation of discipline. It delineates an analytical space and in constituting an arena of knowledge, provides the basis for action and intervention – the operation of power.

The concept power-knowledge has two implications. First, by showing how mechanisms of disciplinary power are simultaneously instruments for the formation and accumulation of knowledge, Foucault challenged positivism's portrayal of them as independent (Knights, 1992). He dissolved the traditional distinction between power and knowledge, whereby knowledge may lead to power, or power may be enhanced by the acquisition of knowledge. The two are not depicted as having an independent existence. They are coterminous. Second, according to Foucault, rather than being external, or something which operates on something or someone, power is integral or productive in the sense that it *creates* objects. Power is the desire to know. Power is not negative; on the contrary, it is creative. As Foucault (1977: 194) wrote:

> We must cease once and for all to describe the effects of power in negative terms: it 'excludes,' it 'represses,' it 'censors,' it 'abstracts,' it 'masks,' it 'conceals.' In fact, power produces; it produces reality; it produces domains of objects and rituals of truth. The individual and the knowledge that may be gained of him belong to this production.

This creative element of power introduces a third important aspect of Foucault's work: the concept of the individual. Traditional approaches in the social sciences have taken the individual as a self-evident unit with which to begin analysis – an observable reality, a unit continuous in time, possessing an essential personal identity. The individual is the basic unit of analysis underpinning many HRM practices, that is, an essential human subject whose nature is to be discovered or uncovered, and who is to be motivated through the exercise of correct procedures of recruitment, selection, appraisal, training, development, and compensation. Thus, research into HRM practices has been designed to build on previous efforts, in order to make such practices more accurate and less subjective, thereby aiding rational decision making.

Rather than perceive the individual as reducible to an internal core of meaning, from a Foucauldian perspective, the human subject is not 'given' but produced historically, that is, constituted through correlative elements of power and knowledge. 'Certain bodies, certain gestures, certain discourses, certain desires come to be constituted as individuals. The individual ... is I believe one of [power's] prime effects' (Foucault, 1980: 98). When the individual loses his or her privileged epistemological status, it becomes possible to see the individual as a product of the social techniques of power, a perspective that highlights the importance of both identity and identity-securing strategies in the reproduction of power relations (Knights and Willmott, 1985). The focus of analysis becomes the 'knowability' of the individual – the process by which the individual is rendered knowable, or the process by which the individual is constructed or produced. Such an approach to an understanding of identity is explicitly adopted in poststructuralism and feminism, where individuality is not seen as being fixed in its expression (Alvesson and Willmott, 1992; Henriques, Hollway, Urwin, Venn and Walkerdine, 1984). Identity is contingent, provisional, achieved, always in process; not a given or an essential component of the subject. 'Identities are not absolute but always relational; one can only ever be seen to be something in relation to something else' (Clegg, 1989: 159). [...]

Described as analyses of regimes du savoir, Foucault's work traces the formation of knowledge and the power structures that result. By analyzing the processes involved in the construction of knowledge – processes of classification, codification, categorization, precise calibration, providing tables and taxonomies, in short providing nomenclatures or the process of naming – he has shown how discourses on sanity, health, knowledge, and punishment have been developed and the implications that this has had for the individual (the criminal, the madman) who becomes an object of knowledge. [...]

The question that is prompted by a body of knowledge from a Foucauldian perspective, therefore, does not concern the truth or falsity of such processes, or whether the knowledge that is generated is objective or subjective. Issues are not posed in such terms. Rather, the emphasis is on what is involved in rendering an arena or an individual knowable: What are the processes by which they become known? How do these processes become established and used? What are their effects? The emphasis is on the techniques through which human beings understand themselves and others. It emphasizes the importance of studying, in detail, the actual practices that introduce domains and individuals to enunciation and visibility – the mechanisms of inscription, recording, and calculation that constitute the discursive practices that make knowledge of both arenas and the individual possible. The focus, therefore, is how disciplinary practices operate to create order, knowledge, and ultimately, power effects. [...] This idea provides the basis for a rereading of HRM.

Foucault's implications for HRM

To illustrate the relevance of Foucault's work for HRM, we must return to the basic building block on which HRM practices are premised – the employment relationship. [...]

The employment relationship is a paradigm case of a transaction, as Williamson (1975: 59) noted, 'Supplying a satisfying exchange relation is part of the economic problem, broadly construed, [which] has special relevance where the employment relation is involved.' The employment relationship describes only in general terms services to be provided, allowing details to be elaborated later. Baldamus portrayed it in the following way:

> Though it [the employment contract] stipulates precise wage payments for the employer, nothing definite is ever said about effort or efficiency; nor anything about the components of effort, the acceptable intensity of impairment, the intolerable degree of tedium or weariness. Instead it merely mentions hours of work, type of job, occupational status and similar external conditions. At the most there are vague and concealed references to an implied level of effort. ... Thus the formal contract between employer and employee is incomplete in a very fundamental sense. (Baldamus, 1961: 2)

[...]
The dominance of an economic paradigm and reifications that have gained the status of institutions (the market and administration) have blurred the basic unit of analysis that Williamson's framework highlights, namely, the gap, or space, that inevitably exists in a transaction between the parties, in terms of what is promised and what is realized, the indeterminacy of a contract. In the employment relationship this gap is the contrast between promise and performance or the capacity to labor and its realization. In this article I wish to refocus attention on the information gap that arises from the indeterminacy of a contract and, in particular, the requirement to articulate the space that exists between expectation and deliverance of performance.
[...]
Adopting a Foucauldian perspective introduces an alternative analysis of the employment exchange. Following Foucault's eschewal of self-evident categories, the focus is neither institutions (the market, administration) nor individuals (agents, principals). Again, following Foucault, the analysis is not driven by considerations of what (the market, administration) or why (efficiency, shirking, problems of trust, etc.), but how. [...]
The indeterminacy of a contract provides the analytical space that needs to be rendered governable. The employment relationship is an analytical, conceptual space, which has geographic (at work) and temporal (time at work) dimensions. It also involves a subject – the worker. All these dimensions or

spaces must be rendered known and articulated before they can be managed. From the employer's point of view, there are two principal unknowns in the employment relationship: (a) the detail of activity required and (b) the nature of labor, in embodied form, which is required to carry out the activity. Thus, there is the need for knowledge of two dimensions: the nature of work and the nature of its operator.

HRM is presented here as the *construction and production of knowledge*. It attempts to reduce the space resulting from the unspecified nature of a contract. It constitutes a discipline and a discourse, which organizes analytical space – the indeterminacy between promise and performance. HRM serves to render organizations and their participants calculable arenas, offering, through a variety of technologies, the means by which activities and individuals become knowable and governable. HRM disciplines the interior of the organization, organizing time, space, and movement within it. Through various techniques, tasks, behavior, and interactions are categorized and measured. HRM provides measurement of both physical and subjective dimensions of labor offering a technology that renders individuals and their behavior predictable and calculable. In so doing, HRM helps to bridge the gap between promise and performance, between labor power and labor, and it organizes labor into a productive force.

Dividing practices

The administration of personnel is one of the major requirements of an employing organization. The coordination of large numbers of people, and the ability to differentiate between them – the rational and efficient deployment of a population – requires the development of techniques that enable people to be managed en masse. Managing employees requires a vocabulary, that is, a means of knowing and ways of representing and ordering populations. [...] Foucault (1977: 143) wrote:

> One must eliminate the effects of imprecise distributions, the uncontrolled disappearance of individuals, their diffuse circulation. ... [The discipline's] aim was to establish presences and absences, to know where and how to locate individuals, ... to be able at each moment to supervise the conduct of each individual, to assess it, to judge it, to calculate its qualities or merits. It was a procedure, therefore, aimed at knowing, mastering and using.

Disciplines begin with the distribution of individuals in space, locating or fixing them conceptually. The art of distribution may use a series of techniques. Foucault (1977) identified three primary methods through which this is effected: (a) *enclosure* (the creation of a space closed in upon itself), (b) *partitioning* (each individual has his or her own place and each place an individual), and (c) *ranking* (the hierarchical ordering of individuals). Essentially, what

Foucault identified was the process involved in knowing the population and the individual. Discipline organizes techniques of classification and tabulation and introduces individuals into the latter.

Enclosure involves the geographical or spatial separation of a place, and it is reflected in Foucault's studies of the asylum (1967), the hospital (1973), and the prison (1977). In production also, early work organizations tended to be physically enclosed spaces, often surrounded by high walls and fences; they frequently operated under a policy of physically locking the doors once work had commenced (to omit latecomers). Although the physical enclosure of work is now highly modified, some of its conceptual effects remain. The disciplines continue to police the boundaries between work and nonwork. The effects of the discourse of enclosure can be seen most dramatically in the separation between paid and unpaid labor, that is, the public and private divisions that feminist discourse is eager to counter. Work, for example, is conceived of as 'employment in the production of goods and services for remuneration' (Rubin, cited in Pahl, 1988: 13). People are classified according to their location on either side of the enclosure: at home, retired, unemployed, working part-time, and so on. The enclosure of work has had particular implications for definitions of skill and is reflected in gendered divisions of labor. Certain types of labor, particularly emotional labor, nurturing, supporting, and caring are omitted from job descriptions and job analyses, and they receive low levels of remuneration (Hochschild, 1983; Pringle, 1988). [...]

Within the enclosed sphere of work, individuals are further subject to the art of distribution through partitioning. Partitioning operates on space in a much more flexible and detailed way, and it refers to the divisions that are created internal to the work organization. Partitioning produces both horizontal and vertical divisions between individuals. It may occur geographically or spatially, for example, in the division between headquarters and other sites; it also can occur through technology, but, essentially, partitioning imposes an order by constructing a rational classification of living beings. This classification (e.g., manual/nonmanual, blue collar/white collar, productive/nonproductive, core/periphery) involves not only the spatial and the analytic, but also the political ordering of people, and it may be enforced through the operation of internal labor markets, the provisions of closed or union shops, and the enforcement of union jurisdictions.

Further partitioning involves ranking, a process of creating a serial, or hierarchical, ordering among employees. This essentially evaluative procedure raises the problem of how relations between beings or things will be conceived: How will an established and ordered succession between units be brought about? Such an order requires a basis for comparison, that is, a common denominator must be established. Generally, there are two systems of comparing (a) the development of an order through a taxonomy (taxinomia) or (b) the establishment of an order through measurement (mathesis). Both procedures define a relation, stating what is to be associated with what. They allow things to be placed in relation to one another, establishing relations of equality and difference. Both also imply a continuum between things. They facilitate the ordering of a multiple, but also allow for the ordering of individuals. These procedures constitute systems of recording, classifying, and measuring – the operation of governmentality.

Several HRM techniques operate to ensure that individuals become classified and hierarchically ordered along a scale. Job classifications and job ladders are examples of ranking systems creating a hierarchy nominally based on skill, responsibility, or experience. Seniority systems and 'bumping' rights are other mechanisms through which ranking is materialized. So too are salary administration and job evaluation schemes. The latter determine the relative value of a job in terms of education, skill, experience, and responsibility, and such schemes explicitly include ranking systems. Nonanalytical job evaluation schemes, or the ranking method, compare whole jobs against other jobs on some assessment of value or job content, to provide a hierarchy. Analytic evaluation schemes are used to subdivide, or further partition, jobs. In this case, jobs are ranked based on independent, measurable job components, or compensable factors, through factor comparison and the points method. In the pursuit of more objective ranking, same job evaluation schemes are based on a matrix of ranking within compensable factors, for example, know-how becomes classified in terms of managerial skills, human resource skills, and practical procedures, each with further gradations (Hollway, 1984). The ranking of jobs essentially ensures the ordering of a population. There is the presumption that different work roles have a certain minimum similarity that enables them to be represented on a hierarchical continuum. Through the reduction of activities to a taxonomy of job factors, and their subsequent translation into numerical representation or mathesis, the population of jobs becomes ordered to be filled by suitable personnel.

Other familiar tool of personnel management – skills inventories, performance appraisal systems, assessments and evaluation methods, attitude measurements – are all arrangements for ranking, which facilitate a serial ordering of individuals. For example, selection testing, as a systematic procedure for observing an individual's behavior and describing it with the aid of a numerical scale of category system, provides an example of partitioning. Most testing takes place through the means of a taxinomia or grid which allows similarities and differences between people to be recognized. Such similarities and differences render individuals observable, measurable, and quantifiable. The very act of enumerating attributes in a programmatic or codified manner allows for the amount of a particular attribute or quality to be measured and thereafter compared with others. Selection tests provide 'a grid of codability of personal attributes' (Rose, 1988: 181), and they enhance the calculability of individuals by placing them on a comparative scalar measure. Likert scales, for example, render attitudes inscribable and quantifiable, and in doing so enable a population and the individual's place within that population to be known.

Classification schemes are often presented as techniques to analyze labor, reflective of naturally occurring divisions or ordering of ability, skill, aptitude, and so forth. These schemes are, however, very much disciplinary techniques. They proceed by operating primarily through enhancing the 'calculability' of individuals, as each classificatory or ranking system designates each individual to his or her own space, and in doing so makes it possible to establish his or her presence and absence. Such classification schemes locate individuals in reference to the whole, and in doing so they operate to reduce individual singularities. Performance appraisal systems, for example, generally attempt to anchor the individual to some type of behaviorally or numerically anchored measuring system. Thus, for example, a performance dimension might be 'leadership' ability, which might be graded on a five-point scale, ranging from 'well above' to 'well below average.' Verbal anchors may attempt to make this more explicit; for example, 'job knowledge' may range from 'extremely well informed about all aspects of the job' to 'misinformed or lacks knowledge on important job dimensions.' The act of scaling, however, produces gradations, a disciplinary mathesis that determines who is to be seen in relation to whom. It facilitates the hierarchical seriation of a population because overall performance, based on generic dimensions of global rating or the culmination of various individual dimensions, aids comparisons with others. Indeed, the distribution of the individual within the population may be explicitly achieved through ranking, if it takes the form of paired comparisons or forced distributions.

The questions raised from a Foucauldian perspective relate to how and why, and with what effects, boundaries become imposed, maintained, and breached, not whether they are accurate or efficient, or whether they reflect reality. For example, judging individuals according to comparative, scalar models not only acts as a disciplinary process, but also as a *normalizing* one. Ranking, for example, organizes individuals around two poles – one negative, the other positive. 'The distribution according to ranks or grades has a double role; it marks the gaps, hierarchizes qualities, skills and aptitudes but it also punishes and rewards' (Foucault, 1977: 181). This can be seen, for example, in pass rates and cut-off scores. By referring individual actions to a whole in a field of comparison, ranking enables individuals to be known through being differentiated from one another. It measures and hierarchizes according to the value, the abilities, the level, and the nature of individuals. [...]

Articulating the contract

The above are examples of how disciplinary practices may be applied to distribute individuals in space. A continuation of these is the division and articulation of the temporal and physical dimensions of the labor process.

'The labor process was articulated, on the one hand, according to its stages and elementary operations, and on the other hand, according to the individuals, the particular bodies, that carried it out' (Foucault, 1977: 145). From classification and tabulation of a population, the disciplines become more focused, acting on the body, time, and everyday gestures and activities. Disciplines attempt to codify and enumerate as closely as possible time, space, and movement, and they attempt to articulate the analytical space of work.

The timetable provides a general framework for activity. An invention of religious orders, 'specialists in time' (Foucault, 1977: 151), disciplines refine temporal regulation. With the onset of industrialization, time becomes measured and paid. It is divided into quarter hours and minutes. The working day itself is segmented and work assigned within discrete time periods – day shift, night shift, split shifts, overtime, and so on – and regulated through the time card and the time clock. There is bankable time in flexi-hour programs and billable time in the accounting and legal professions, where the hour, divided into quarter hours, or tenths, becomes a mechanism of control.

The actions of the body also must be adjusted to these temporal imperatives, in order to produce an efficiency of movement. This is the temporal elaboration of the act: 'The act is broken down into its elements; the position of the body, limbs, articulations is defined; to each movement are assigned a direction, an aptitude, a duration; their succession is prescribed' (Foucault, 1977: 152). This temporal elaboration involves the prescription of how bodies should act, the nature of gestures and coordination that should be used, and a detailed specification as to how the body should engage with physical objects. [...] Through minute and detailed regulation, disciplines make possible the meticulous control of the body. The individual becomes subject to habits, rules, and orders; he or she operates as 'one wishes, and with the techniques, speed and efficiency one determines' (Foucault, 1977: 138).

In this respect, the disciplines function in a manner prescribed by Taylor's scientific management, and, indeed, a lot of scientific management's recommendations represent the extension to production of disciplines already in operation in other organizations, for example, in schools, in hospitals, and in prisons (Clegg, 1989). To equate disciplines solely with scientific management, however, would be to mistake the ubiquity of their operation and to ignore their continuation in an era in which, we are told, the principles of scientific management no longer apply. They may, for example, be identified in the routine activities of the personnel specialist.

The articulation of activity can be seen, for example, in job analyses and job descriptions, task and skill specifications, appraisal systems using behavioral observation scales, and some training specifications. In all, the nature of performance is detailed with greater precision. For example, job analysis, the nonindividualized impersonal definition of the nature of work, articulates activity. It begins through the creation of a taxonomy. According to functional job analysis, for example, all jobs involve a relationship with data, people, and things, and these relationships can be arranged according to degrees of complexity. Thus, activities become defined and hierarchically arranged on a scale. For example, activities involving relations with people include (from higher to lower skills) mentoring; negotiating; supervising (consulting, instructing, and treating); coaching and persuading; exchanging information; and taking instructions (helping and serving). The relationship with data is codified and ranked in terms of synthesizing, coordinating, innovating, analyzing, computing, compiling, copying, and comparing. These techniques elaborate the construct 'job' through the concept of job skills. Activities are created and serially ordered. Other systems, for example, the Position Analysis Questionnaire, are more elaborate and include measures of time spent on each activity, relative importance of each duty, and learning time in its divisions and hierarchies. The concern with managerial competencies provides the extension of job analysis to managerial jobs – the attempt to articulate and make known managerial activity under the guise of introducing more scientific methods to its study. There is, in all this, the view that detailing managerial competencies is an act of revealing the natural, rather than the product of decisions of an 'already encoded eye' (Foucault, 1970: xx).

The codification and enumeration of activity and movement may be identified in training and performance appraisal systems. For example, interpersonal skills training offers recommendations as to how the individual should engage with the human 'object.' The following, for example, is taken from a skills training document in handling customer complaints. The trainee is recommended to 'smile to make initial welcome contact … smile warmly with direct eye contact … watch customer reactions … note customer's embarrassment by lack of eye contact … keep eye contact with customer, nod when customer makes valid point … give customer full attention … smile … [and after the complaint has been attended to] avoid too much eye contact to allow customer to relax' (Kenney et al., 1981: 82). This articulation of activity may be further reinforced in performance appraisal systems that include behavioral observation scales or behaviorally anchored appraisal scales. Performance assessment with its construction of a system of job factors, evaluation standards, and performance descriptors most obviously involves the production of knowledge. Aspects of activity become more specifically articulated. For example, behavior dimensions of waiter or waitress 'service' may be expanded to include whether the individual 'knows the menu and can inform customers about each item, how it is served, and how it is prepared' or 'asks customers how they would like their meat and eggs done and brings rolls to the table promptly.'

To ensure that both time and activity are rendered productive there is the organization of activity into a series or in a temporal sequence, with each stage successfully graded from the other and leading to a seemingly logical progression. Foucault referred to this as the *capitalization of time*. An example of this may be seen in management by objectives (MBO) systems. The emphasis of the MBO system is that the action plan specifying what is to be achieved should include time limits for particular activities. A person's success with these particular activities is evaluated at the end of each period. In some cases, a person may be reviewed in the middle of the period to see what progress he or she is making. There is a correlation of activity with time, especially if the system is supplemented by regular progress reports. Modifications of the MBO system include a productivity rating index, which combines a time-based index based on the achievement of time-related goals and a quality index that is used to assess how well goals are achieved (Bordman and Melnick, 1990). Again, the MBO system is a process that operates to inscribe activities of workers, thereby creating a visibility, which ultimately becomes the basis for constructing norms and trends. This capitalization of time perhaps reached its zenith in human asset accounting, which as Flamholtz (1985: 244) noted, 'represents a type of balance sheet of the potential services that can be rendered by people at a specified time.' Thus, measuring positional replacement costs, for example, involves not only costs relating to expenses, but also detailed analyses of the time taken and the salaries of those involved in all stages of the activity: requesting a position, choosing a selection method, setting up a place to interview, reviewing applicants, deciding to offer a position (or not offer a position) to an applicant, and so on. Therefore, capitalization of time is the detail of activity through time, related to cost – the partitioning of time, space, and movement allied to a financial equivalent.

Creating the industrial subject

Individuals at work must also be rendered visible. In work organizations there must be systems to inspect workers, to observe workers' presence and application, to inspect the quality of the work, to compare workers to one another, and to classify workers according to skill and speed. As Foucault (1980: 125) recognized, in order to obtain productive service from individuals 'power had to be able to gain access to the bodies of individuals, to their acts, attitudes and modes of every day behavior.'

First it must be recognized that making aspects of the labor process more visible has a direct implication for constituting the individual. The precisely adopted codification of action or activities engenders almost automatically the codification of the individual – the one functions to produce knowledge of the other. Undertaking a complete job analysis lays down the dimensions of the individual in terms of intelligence or aptitudes necessary to do the job. Making activities more visible necessarily renders the individual 'known' in a particular manner. As Foucault (1977: 138) noted, 'Disciplines create force, they turn into an aptitude or capacity that which they seek to increase,' with the result that behavior gradually replaces the 'simple physics of movement.' Equally, systems of classification, partitioning, and ranking contribute to the detailed enumeration of the capabilities of organizational members.

Although the parameters of individuality are constituted in this way, there is still the requirement that the individual be 'known'. As Garland (1987: 853) identified, 'The successful control of an object … requires a degree of understanding of its forces, its reactions, its strengths and weaknesses. The more it is known the more controllable it becomes.' The components of the individual, whatever they may be, personality, attitudes, skill, and so on, must be calculated, assessed, and judged. Therefore, how is an individual rendered an object of knowledge? For Foucault this may be effected in two ways: (a) individuals may become objects of enquiry through being made the subjects of scientific study or (b) individuals, through practices labeled technologies of the self, may situate and define themselves by becoming tied to an identity by a conscience or self-knowledge both coming to see themselves and being seen in a particular way (Foucault, 1983). He distinguished two principal practices or technologies that provide knowledge of the individual: the examination, which constitutes the individual as an object of knowledge, and the confession, which ties the individual to self-knowledge and establishes concepts of subjectivity. Through both activities the individual is rendered more amenable to intervention or management.

The examination, a familiar practice in schools and hospitals, is essentially a method of observing. It is a disciplinary process in which several distinct operations are put into play: It is used to measure in quantitative terms, and to hierarchize in terms of value the abilities, the level, and the nature of individuals. It is a technique that makes individual differences and capacities visible, and it allows for these differences to be inscribed or notated. 'It [the examination] establishes over individuals a visibility through which one differentiates them and judges them' (Foucault, 1977: 184). Through such processes the individual is rendered more easily calculable and manageable. It is the process whereby individuals become compartmentalized, measured, and reported, for the purpose of administrative decision making. As such, the examination operates as a technology of governance acting simultaneously to individualize and standardize. In doing so, its use has become so widespread that it may be found in 'psychiatry, pedagogy, for the diagnosis of diseases to the hiring of labor' (Foucault, 1977: 185).

Where the work force was largely undifferentiated in early factory organization, there was little knowledge of, or interest in, the individual. As classification systems were put into place, greater differentiation arose generally based on observable factors such as skill, age, performance, behavior, and so forth. Later, the mind, or psyche, became identified as the key to gaining knowledge of performance. 'Individuals were moved by attitudes or sentiments … internal states that shaped the ways in which an individual apprehended and evaluated events' (Rose, 1990: 27). New dimensions of subjectivity were introduced that helped bridge the external world of conduct and the internal world of the individual (Hollway, 1991; Rose, 1990). These new dimensions of subjectivity became incorporated into selection procedures in which aspects of the individual are identified, measured, and acted upon. Personality testing (e.g., Cattell's 16PF text, the Minnesota Multiphasic Personality Inventory, and the Eysenck Personality Inventory) introduced a standardization to personality, and the techniques of scaling further introduced the subjective dimensions of individuals to the sphere of knowledge and regulation. This effect is extended in trait and function psychometric testing (Rust and Golombok, 1989). As Rose (1990: 85) noted, 'The internal world of the factory was becoming mapped in psychological terms, and the inner feelings of workers were being transmitted into measurements about which calculations could be made.' The self directions of individuals – the need to achieve, the need for power, the need to self actualize – were incorporated into the production process. Thus, the individual was elaborated on in further classificatory systems and more compartmentalization. Human nature is increasingly objectified, and action is reified. Human types are created. Actions are performed because an actor is an X type person, or X type persons perform such actions. Certain work arrangements suit individuals with a high 'need to achieve' and 'type A' individuals. Personnel discourse, allied with specializations and subdisciplines of behavioral science, occupational psychology, and industrial psychology, further introduces the individual to more progressive objectification and ever more subtle partitioning of human behavior, even to the extent of individuals being located on scales of 'morningness' (Smith, Reilly and Midkiff, 1989). These labels may become incorporated into an individual's self-assessment, the means through which individuals identify their feelings and behavior to themselves and others. It is perhaps in this way that Foucault's (1977: 170) statement that 'disciplines "make" individuals' makes most sense.

The assumptions of the examination are legion: that there is an essential personality that neither changes according to situation nor is definable only in a relational context reflective of interaction; that attributes are distinguishable, isolable, and directly related to a job; that jobs exist rather than being organizational and individual constructs. Essentially, these tests function as a means of measuring and evaluating individuals, rendering them calculable and manageable through 'representing in standard forms human mental capacities and behavioral characteristics which previously had to be described in complex and idiosyncratic language' (Rose, 1988: 195). As Taylor (1986: 76) commented, 'To try to bring it (the individual) under the control of reason is to divide what should be a living unity.'

The examination has two effects: individualization and individuation. The first effect denotes the process of making the individual more identifiable vis-à-vis other individuals or workers, that is, the process of identifying or differentiating individuals. The second effect refers to dividing practices that are internal to the individual, that is, those processes that attempt to identify components of individuality. Through the examination, the individual is rendered more and more an object, which is exemplified by the employee's reduction to a final score as, for example, in graphic rating scales, or overall scores at an assessment center (Bray, Campbell and Grant, 1974). The translation of individuals into numerical equivalents is perhaps the inevitable extension of commodity production. [...]

As presented here, the rationale of HRM is to create the individual 'as an analyzable, describable subject' (Burrell, 1988: 202), to be assessed, judged, measured, and compared with others. There is, however, a difficulty for management when faced with this problem, as McGregor (1972: 136) has noted:

> The individual knows ... more than anyone else about his own capabilities, needs, strengths and weaknesses, and goals. ... No available methods can provide the superior with the knowledge he needs to make such decisions ... ratings, aptitude and personality tests, and the superior's necessarily limited knowledge of the man's performance yield at best an imperfect picture.

The principal technology that Foucault identified for accessing the self-knowledge of the subject is the confession (Foucault, 1981, 1985, 1986, 1988a, 1988b). Although the confession is most readily associated with religious practices, Foucault recognized that the basis of its functioning – avowal, the individual's acknowledgment of his or her actions or thoughts – operates in a range of activities, in education, in medicine, also at work. It may be identified, for example, in application blanks that request individuals to acknowledge their main weaknesses or strengths, their ways of coping with success or disappointment, and their pleasures or regrets over past decisions. Other selection devices, for example, prescreening inventories, ask individuals to be as open and as accurate as possible in acknowledging what words or phrases characterize them 'most of the time,' 'quite often,' or are 'essentially unlike you.' Individuals are asked to admit their responses to, for example, being proud, self-sufficient, considerate, encouraging to others, concerned with status, honest and direct in feelings, concerned with what others think, and so on. Selection interviews also operate on the process of avowal, as for example, behavior-descriptive interview questions designed to tap demonstrated leadership, which ask individuals to recount times when they influenced or countered people on certain issues and how they handled these obstacles. Team players may be required to give examples of how they resolved differences with others when working on a group project. In all this, however, there is a view of the individual as harboring a secret truth; hence, the techniques recommended to interviewers to get the candidate to talk openly.

It is, perhaps, in developmental appraisals that the confessional may be most readily identifiable; in these, individuals may be required to comment on, for example, job satisfaction. (Is this area of your work satisfying? Are your skills overstretched or underused? Have any recent changes affected your job satisfaction?) Part of the value of the confession is that it produces information that becomes part of the individual's self-understanding. It is also important to notice that these practices shade into other practices based not merely on accessing individuals, but allowing or training individuals to access themselves. Training enables individuals to identify what is happening within themselves in order to become more effective. As Rose (1990: 240) noted, 'In compelling, persuading and inciting subjects to disclose themselves, finer and more intimate regions of personal and interpersonal life come under surveillance and are opened up for expert judgement, normative evaluation, classification and correction.'

Confessional procedures operate in two ways. Not only do they require the individual to break the bounds of discretion or forgetfulness, but they also act as processes that confirm identity. These procedures are examples of how 'knowing' individuals operate to tie these people to self-knowledge, constituting them as individuals. Other HRM practices function to constitute the individual in a particular manner through tying him or her to a changed sense of self or identity. This may be seen, for example, in mentoring, as the following recommendation illustrates: 'managers can use mentoring *to help cultivate desired norms* and values in their organization ... through serving as mentors, senior managers guarantee that *role models embody core values* that best promote desired organizational culture' (White, 1990: 46, emphasis added). The process of constituting the subject may be identified in orientation, socialization, and induction programs. Training and development in interpersonal and social skills, communication, and listening skills also constitute individuals in particular ways, tying them to 'appropriate' identities. Appraisal systems may operate so as to inculcate the correct behavioral norms (Townley, 1989). [...]

Equally, the individual may be constituted through *proscribing* certain aspects of identity. Disciplinary procedures most obviously define the parameters of acceptable and nonacceptable behavior, and as such, they contribute to the process of individuals' being able to identify the valid from the invalid. Other mechanisms are more subtle. Hochschild (1983), for example, in her analysis of training programs for flight attendants illustrated the emphasis on managing negative emotions and summoning the ubiquitous smile. The role of these individuals is to become managers of emotion. They, themselves, must suppress anger, any sense of effrontery, that is, their own sense of self, no matter how justified.

All of the above are examples of procedures that constitute the subject with varying degrees of individual engagement and participation. There is the inculcation of required habits, rules, and behavior and socially constructed definitions of the norm. However, the status of the individual, that is, the

individual's right to be different and everything that makes the individual truly individual tends to get lost in these processes.
[...]

Conclusion

To recap the argument, the basic unit of analysis in understanding HRM was identified as the nature of exchange embodied in the employment relationship. Given the essentially indeterminate nature of this relationship, the problematic then becomes how this relational, exchange activity is organized. Foucault's concept of power-knowledge was introduced to illustrate how HRM acts to impose order on the inherently undecidable. Attempting to clarify the indeterminacy of contract requires 'effective instruments for the formation and accumulation of knowledge – methods of observation, techniques of registration, procedures for investigation and research, apparatuses of control' (Foucault, 1980: 102). The construction of knowledge in HRM operates through rules of classification, ordering, and distribution; definitions of activities; fixing of scales; and rules of procedure, which lead to the gradual emergence of a distinct HRM discourse. Associated with these practices are concepts of rationality, scientificity, measurement, grading – the language and the knowledge of the HRM specialist. Through mechanisms of registration, assessment, and classification – areas of study often neglected or dismissed as technical or administrative procedures – it becomes possible to illustrate how a body of knowledge operates to objectify those on whom it is applied. It is also in this discourse that the individual becomes located as an object of knowledge. Classification schemes, offered as techniques of simplification and clarification for the analysis of labor, both as effort and object, become inextricably tied to its disciplinary operation.

A Foucauldian perspective presents an alternative way for perceiving and ordering material. Rather than thinking in functional terms of recruitment, appraisal, remuneration, and so on, in this perspective an emphasis is placed on how HRM employs disciplinary practices to create knowledge and power. These practices fix individuals in conceptual and geographical space, and they order or articulate the labor process. Processes of individualization and individuation create an industrial subject who is analyzable and describable. As an approach, it allows HRM to be analyzed as the 'will to knowledge,' that is, as a system of knowledge and modality of power. It is sufficiently detailed an approach to allow for the 'micropolitics' of power to be addressed and, by providing examples of how the concern with 'knowing' labor as a 'population' can percolate down to its effects on the individual, allows for highly individualized practices to be related to an intelligible whole. In doing so, it also provides the basis for reorienting contemporary, historical, and comparative analyses of HRM.

References

Alvesson, M. and Willmott, H. (1992) On the idea of emancipation in management and organization studies. *Academy of Management Review*, 17: 432–465.

Baldamus, W. (1961) *Efficiency and Effort*. London: Tavistock.

Baron, J., Dobbin, F. and Devereaux Jennings, P. (1986) War and peace: The evolution of modern personnel administration in U.S. industry. *American Journal of Sociology*, 92: 350–383.

Beer, M., Spector, B., Lawrence, P.R., Mills, D.Q. and Walton, R.E. (1984) *Managing Human Assets*. New York: Free Press.

Bordman, S. and Melnick, G. (1990) Keep productivity ratings timely. *Personnel Journal*, 69: 50–51.

Bray, D.W., Campbell, R.J. and Grant, D.L. (1974) *Formative Years in Business: A Long-term AT&T Study of Managerial Lives*. New York: Wiley.

Burchell, G., Gordon, C. and Miller, P. (1991) *The Foucault Effect: Studies in Governmentality*. London: Harvester Wheatsheaf.

Burrell, G. (1988) Modernism, Post-modernism and organizational analysis 2: The contribution of Michel Foucault. *Organization Studies*, 9: 221–235.

Clegg, S. (1989) *Frameworks of Power*. London: Sage.

Commons, J.R. (1934) *Institutional Economics: Its Place in Political Economy*. New York: Macmillan.

Dreyfus, H. and Rabinow, P. (1983) *Michel Foucault, Beyond Structuralism and Hermeneutics*. Brighton, England: Harvester Press.

Eribon, D. (1991) *Michel Foucault*. (B. Wing, Trans.). Cambridge, MA: Harvard University Press.

Flamholtz, E. (1985) *Human Resource Accounting* (2nd edn). San Francisco: Jossey Bass.

Foucault, M. (1967) *Madness and Civilization: A History of Insanity in the Age of Reason*. London: Tavistock.

Foucault, M. (1970) *The Order of Things: An Archeology of the Human Sciences*. London: Tavistock.

Foucault, M. (1972) *The Archaeology of Knowledge*. London: Routledge.

Foucault, M. (1973) *The Birth of the Clinic*. London: Tavistock.

Foucault, M. (1977) *Discipline and Punish: The Birth of the Prison*. London: Penguin.

Foucault, M. (1980) *Power/Knowledge: Selected Interviews and Other Writings by Michel Foucault, 1972–77*. (C. Gordon, ed.). Brighton, England: Harvester.

Foucault, M. (1981) *The History of Sexuality: Vol. 1. The Will to Knowledge*. London: Penguin.

Foucault, M. (1983) The subject and power. In H.L. Dreyfus and P. Rabinow (eds), *Michel Foucault: Beyond Structuralism and Hermeneutics*: 208–226. Chicago: University of Chicago Press.

Foucault, M. (1985) *The History of Sexuality: Vol. 2. The Use of Pleasure*. New York: Pantheon.

Foucault, M. (1986) *The History of Sexuality: Vol. 3. The Care of the Self*. New York: Pantheon.

Foucault, M. (1988a) Technologies of the self. In L. Martin, H. Gutman and P.H. Hutton (eds), *Technologies of the Self*, 16–49. London: Tavistock.

Foucault, M. (1988b) The political technology of individuals. In L. Martin, H. Gutman and P.H. Hutton (eds), *Technologies of the Self*, 145–162. London: Tavistock.

Foucault, M. (1991a) Politics and the study of discourse. In G. Burchell, C. Gordon and P. Miller (eds), *The Foucault Effect: Studies in Governmentality*, 53–72. London: Harvester Wheatsheaf.

Foucault, M. (1991b) Questions of method. In G. Burchell, C. Gordon and P. Miller (eds), *The Foucault Effect: Studies in Governmentality*, 73–86. London: Harvester Wheatsheaf.

Foucault, M. (1991c) Governmentality. In G. Burchell, C. Gordon and P. Miller (eds), *The Foucault Effect: Studies in Governmentality*, 87–104. London: Harvester Wheatsheaf.

Garland, D. (1987) Foucault's discipline and punish, an exposition and critique. *American Bar Foundation Research Journal*, 4: 847–880.

Gordon, C. (1991) Governmental rationality: An introduction. In G. Burchell, C. Gordon and P. Miller (eds), *The Foucault Effect: Studies in Governmentality*, 1–52. London: Harvester Wheatsheaf.

Henriques, J., Hollway, W., Urwin, C., Venn, C. and Walkerdine, V. (eds) (1984) *Changing the Subject*. London: Methuen.

Hochschild, A. (1983) *The Managed Heart: Commercialization of Human Feeling*. Berkeley: University of California Press.

Hollway, W. (1984) Fitting work: Psychological assessment in organizations. In J. Henriques, W. Hollway, C. Urwin, C. Venn and V. Walkerdine (eds) *Changing the Subject*, 26–59. London: Methuen.

Hollway, W. (1991) *Work Psychology and Organizational Behaviour*. London: Sage.

Kenney, J., Donnelly, E. and Reid, M. (1981) *Manpower Training and Development* (2nd edn). London: Institute of Personnel Management.

Knights, D. (1992) Changing spaces: The disruptive impact of a new epistemological location for the study of management. *Academy of Management Review*, 17: 514–536.

Knights, D. and Willmott, H. (1985) Power and identity in theory and practice. *Sociological Review*, 33: 22–46.

Lupton, T. (1974) *Industrial Behaviour and Personnel Management*. London: IPM.

Marsden, R. (1993) The politics of organizational analysis. *Organization Studies*, 14: 93–124.

McGregor, D. (1972) An uneasy look at performance appraisal. *Harvard Business Review*, 50(5): 133–138.

Morgan, G. (1980) Paradigms, metaphors and puzzle solving in organization theory. *Administrative Science Quarterly*, 605–622.

Pahl, R.E. (1988) Editor's introduction: Historical aspects of work, employment, unemployment and the sexual division of labour. In R.E. Pahl (ed.), *On Work: Historical, Comparative and Theoretical Approaches*, 11–15. Oxford: Basil Blackwell.

Philp, M. (1985) Michel Foucault. In Q. Skinner (ed.), *The Return of Grand Theory in the Human Sciences*, 65–82. Cambridge, England: Cambridge University Press.

Pringlo, R. (1988) *Secretaries' talk. Sexuality, power and work*. London: Verso.

Rose, N. (1988) Calculable minds and manageable individuals. *History of the Human Sciences*, 1(2): 179–200.

Rose, N. (1990) *Governing the Soul: The Shaping of the Private Self*. London: Routledge.

Rust, J. and Colombok, S. (1989) *Modern Psychometrics: The Science of Psychological Assessment*. London: Routledge.

Simitis, S. (1986) The juridification of labour relations. *Comparative Labour Law*, 7: 93–142.

Smith, C., Reilly, C. and Midkiff, K. (1989) Evaluation of three circadian rhythm questionnaires with suggestions for an improved measure of morningness. *Journal of Applied Psychology*, 74: 728–738.

Steffy, B. and Grimes, A. (1992) Personnel/organizational psychology: A critique of the discipline. In M. Alvesson and H. Willmott (eds), *Critical Management Studies*, 181–201. London: Sage.

Taylor, C. (1986) Foucault on freedom and truth. In D.C. Hoy (ed.), *Foucault: A Critical Reader*, 69–102. Oxford: Basil Blackwell.

Townley, B. (1989) Selection and appraisal: Reconstituting 'social relations'? In J. Storey (ed.), *New Perspectives on Human Resource Management*, 92–108. London: Routledge.

Townley, B. (1993) Performance appraisal and the emergence of management. *Journal of Management Studies*, 30(2): 27–44.

Turner, S. (1983) Studying organization through Levi Strauss's structuralism. In G. Morgan (ed.), *Beyond Method*, 189–201. Beverly Hills, CA: Sage.

White, H. (1990) The self method of mentoring. *Bureaucrat*, 19(1): 45–48.

Williamson, O. (1975) *Markets and Hierarchies*. New York: Free Press.

4

The Cognitive Perspective on Strategic Decision-making

Charles R. Schwenk

[...]

The cognitions of key decision-makers are receiving increased research attention in strategic management. This is due to the increased recognition of the importance of key decision-makers' perceptions in studying the links between the environment, strategy, and structure as well as a greater awareness of the role of cognitions in strategic issue diagnosis and problem formulation.

Several studies illustrate this recognition [...]. In a longitudinal study of strategic change in a retail chain, Mintzberg and Waters (1982) suggest that in the entrepreneurial mode of strategy-making the development of a new strategy is typically carried out 'in a single informed brain'. They conclude that that is why the entrepreneurial mode is at the centre of the most glorious corporate successes (Mintzberg and Waters, 1982: 496). The study of strategists' cognitions provides information about the workings of these informed brains, and therefore the factors which contribute to some glorious corporate successes (as well as some dismal strategic failures).

Hambrick and Mason (1984) note that strategic decision-making is influenced by the cognitive frames and decision processes of members of organizational 'upper echelons'. Anecdotal evidence in the business press supports this view. Business ventures (particularly if they fail) are often described as being the result of the predispositions and thought processes of key upper-level decision-makers.

Source: Charles R. Schwenk (2002) 'The cognitive perspective on strategic decision-making', in G. Salaman (ed.), *Decision Making for Business: A Reader.* London: SAGE/The Open University. Edited version.

Finally, [...] Dutton et al. suggest that the concepts, beliefs, assumptions, and cause-and-effect understandings of strategists determine how strategic issues will be framed (1983: 310). Lyles notes that subjectivity is involved in the process of problem definition and suggests that strategists' problem definitions will be guided by their past experiences (1981: 62).

Recognizing the importance of cognitions, strategic management researchers have begun to explore their role in strategic management. This research focuses not on individuals and individual differences in cognition but on *cognitive structures and processes* which may in some cases be shared by multiple strategists.

In this article, recent research on four specific topics in strategic cognition will be summarized. These topics include: cognitive heuristics and biases, cognitive frames, strategic assumptions, and analogy and metaphor. [...] In the author's judgement they represent those topics which are the most potentially useful in understanding the ways decision-makers understand and solve strategic problems. [...]

Research on strategic cognition

A useful starting point in a discussion of cognitive processes is the concept of cognitive simplification. Simon (1957, 1976) laid the groundwork for the treatment of cognitive simplification in his discussion of 'bounded rationality' which suggests that decision-makers must construct simplified mental models when dealing with complex problems (1976: 79–96). Further, they can only approximate rationality in their attempts to solve these problems (Simon, 1976; Taylor, 1975). They may be subject to selective perception since they are unable to evaluate comprehensively all variables relevant to a decision (Hogarth, 1980; Mason and Mitroff, 1981). Further, when *groups* are making strategic decisions, they may be subject to perceptual biases associated with groupthink (Janis and Mann, 1977: 129–33).

Mason and Mitroff (1981) and others have observed that strategic problems are, almost by definition, extremely complex. How do strategists with limited information processing capacities deal with this complexity in order to make sense of strategic problems? The material in the next section deals with this question.

Attempts by strategists to understand complex problems may introduce *biases* into their *strategic assumptions*. Strategic assumptions then form the basis for the frames of reference or *schemata* through which decision-makers represent complex strategic problems. Finally, *analogy and metaphor* may be the means by which cognitive maps and schemata from other problem domains are applied to new strategic problems. If new strategic problems cannot be dealt with through analogy, then a complex diagnosis may have to be done. Heuristics and biases may then come into play in developing new strategic assumptions. These points will be elaborated in the research reviews which follow.

Cognitive heuristics and biases

The behavioural decision theory literature provides material for the study of cognitive heuristics and biases in strategic management. Researchers have recently begun to suggest that the decisional biases identified in laboratory contexts may affect strategic decision-making as well [...].

Extensive lists of heuristics and biases have already been developed [...]. Researchers have identified a number of heuristics or 'rules of thumb' which decision-makers use to simplify complex problems and a number of decisional biases which may have an impact on strategic decisions. Tversky and Kahneman (1974), and other behavioural decision theorists have pointed out that the heuristics may provide efficient short cuts in processing information. As Tversky and Kahneman (1974: 1125) state, 'in general, these heuristics are quite useful, but sometimes they lead to severe and systematic error'. [...] Those which seem most likely to affect strategic decisions are listed in Table 4.1.

To illustrate the nature of heuristics and biases, one example of each will be discussed here. Strategic decisions are often influenced by judgements about the probability of certain types of changes in the environment. One

Table 4.1 *Selected heuristics and biases*

Bias	Effects
Availability	Judgements of probability of easily recalled events distorted.
Selective perception	Expectations may bias observations of variables relevant to strategy.
Illusory correlation	Encourages belief that unrelated variables are correlated.
Conversatism	Failure sufficiently to revise forecasts based on new information.
Law of *small* numbers	Overestimation of the degree to which small samples are representative of populations.
Regression bias	Failure to allow for regression to the mean.
Wishful thinking	Probability of desired outcomes judged to be inappropriately high.
Illusion of control	Overestimation of personal control over outcomes.
Logical reconstruction	'Logical' reconstruction of events which cannot be accurately recalled.
Hindsight bias	Overestimation of predictability of past events.

heuristic which may affect such probability judgements is the availability heuristic (Barnes, 1984; Tversky and Kahneman, 1974). Using this heuristic, decision-makers judge a future event to be likely if it is easy to recall past occurrences of the event. In other words, judgements of the likelihood of an event are based on the availability of past occurrences in memory. Generally, frequently occurring events are easier to recall than infrequently occurring events so availability is a good way of judging probability.

However, other things besides frequency can increase the availability of certain types of events in memory. Dramatic vivid events may be easy to recall even if they occur infrequently. Also, recent events may be easier to recall. For this reason, the availability heuristic may distort judgements of probabilities.

One bias which may affect strategic decisions is the illusion of control (Duhaime and Schwenk, 1985; Langer, 1983; Schwenk, 1984, 1986). This bias may affect people's assessments of their chance of success at a venture. Langer reports on six studies which show that subjects making a variety of decisions expressed an expectancy of personal success higher than the objective probability would warrant. They tend to overestimate their skill or the impact it will have on the outcome (Langer, 1983: 59–90).

Langer suggests that we are subject to this illusion of personal control because of the way we collect information. She notes that as people constantly seek ways to control outcomes in the environment, they form hypotheses about the effects of their actions on these outcomes. In her words, they then 'tend to seek out information that supports their hypotheses while innocently ignoring disconfirming evidence' (1983: 24). This type of information search tends to reinforce the illusion of personal control.

Most of the heuristics and biases have been identified in laboratory experiments using relatively structured tasks. Therefore, strategic management researchers have attempted to identify examples of the operation of the biases in actual strategic decisions. The focus on simplification processes for which laboratory and field support exists should increase the chance of identifying cognitive processes which really do affect organizational decisions rather than processes produced only by the artificiality of the laboratory context or the political processes in organizations.

In summary, there is some evidence from the laboratory and the field that availability, the illusion of control, and other biases identified in this research may affect strategic decisions by restricting the range of strategic alternatives considered and the information used to evaluate these alternatives.

It is likely that multiple biases affect strategic decisions. Schwenk (1986) has shown how some of the biases may interact and reinforce each other. For example the availability bias might increase the illusion of control in successful executives. These executives' past experiences of success might be salient to them and therefore more easily recalled when they are assessing their chances of success with a new strategy. Researchers are now attempting to describe the ways individual biases interact to affect such decisions.

Strategic assumptions, cognitive maps, and schemata

The effects of cognitive heuristics and biases may be seen in decision-makers' assumptions about strategic problems. Mason and Mitroff (1981) suggest that assumptions are the basic elements of a strategist's frame of reference or worldview. According to Mason and Mitroff, strategic problems involve organized complexity; in other words, problem variables are interdependent in such a way that solutions to some problems create others (1981: 3–21). Assumptions about such problems are necessary because policy-makers must often take action in the absence of certainty (Mason and Mitroff, 1981). In strategic decisions, many of the most important assumptions deal with the behaviour of groups or individuals who are important to the success of the strategy and who have a *stake* in the outcome of the strategy. Freeman (1984) calls such individuals and groups *stakeholders.*

Since assumptions form the basis of strategies, it is important that they are consistent with the information available to strategists. This requires careful examination of assumptions. However, this is difficult because most policy-makers are unaware of the particular set of assumptions they hold and of methods that can help them in examining and assessing the strength of their assumptions (Mason and Mitroff, 1981: 18). The accuracy of these assumptions may be affected by the cognitive biases previously discussed.

Strategic assumptions form the basis of top managers' frames of reference. Shrivastava (1983), and Shrivastava and Mitroff (1983) suggest that analysis of these frames of reference is helpful in understanding how strategic problems are formulated. Two concepts from the cognitive psychology literature, cognitive maps and schemata have been discussed in connection with strategic problem frames.

The term 'cognitive map' was first used by Tolman (1948) in discussions of learning in laboratory animals and human beings. These cognitive maps consist of concepts about aspects of the decision environment and beliefs about cause-and-effect relationships between them. Such maps serve as interpretive lenses which help decision-makers select certain aspects of an issue as important for diagnosis.

Axelrod (1976) has developed methods for representing cognitive maps diagrammatically. Though they are often used to represent individual worldviews, they may be used to represent shared assumptions among a group of strategic decision-makers which makes them useful in the study of strategic problem formulation. Axelrod notes that the purpose of cognitive mapping is not to represent a person's entire belief system. Rather, it represents the causal assertions of a person with respect to a particular policy domain (Axelrod, 1976: 58). [...]

Bougon et al. (1977) and Weick (1979) suggest that cognitive maps may direct information search in organizations and that cognitive maps may exist at the organizational level. They are discovered or inferred by organization members and used as a basis for action (1979: 52). [...]

Strategic choices are determined by the way strategists conceptualize their environment and industry. [...] Cognitive mapping may help researchers to describe more effectively the ways executives understand relations among industry factors and to determine which factors are taken most seriously by executives in formulating their strategies. Research using cognitive mapping may also help clarify the processes by which industry factors affect strategies. Therefore, this type of analysis might supplement research based on 'objective' assessment of industry factors as determinants of strategy. [...]

The term *schemata* is sometimes used in connection with cognitive maps. From the definitions of the two terms in the literature, the distinction between cognitive maps and schemata is not completely clear. In general, however, 'schemata' is a broader term. A cognitive map may be defined as a particular type of schema or a part of a broader schema (Weick, 1979: 48–53). Schemata have been defined as cognitive representations of attributes and the relationships between them which constitute commonsense social theories (Rumelhart and Ortony, 1977), and as active cognitive structures which frame problems (Neisser, 1976: Ch. 6).

Taylor (1982: 72–3) and Taylor and Crocker (1983), suggest that schemata are abstract conceptions people hold about the social world, and that previously developed schemata may be applied to new problems. Chittipeddi and Gioia (1983: 6) state that schemata are evoked by cues in a problem-solving setting and they provide frames for problems which makes it unnecessary for decision-makers to expend the mental effort necessary to diagnose completely each element of a new strategic problem.

In conclusion, human cognitive limitations introduce biases into the development of strategic assumptions and may lead to simplification in strategic schemata. These biases and simplifications affect strategic decisions when decision-makers' existing schemata are used in diagnosing and framing new strategic problems. Analysis of executives' strategic schemata helps explain strategic choices in response to environmental and industry forces. The use of existing schemata in diagnosing new problems can be better understood through the discussion of analogy which follows.

Analogy in diagnosis

In some ways, each strategic problem is unique. However, when diagnosing or framing a new strategic problem, decision-makers may draw on their experience of situations which seem to be similar. These 'similar situations' may come from relatively straightforward sources like previous strategic decisions, or from relatively imaginative sources like athletic contests. Research on analogy and metaphor in strategic decision-making deals with the transfer of schemata from one domain to another.

Isenberg (1983: 17) has given some interesting examples of the use of metaphor and analogy in defining organizational missions and framing strategic problems. He found that managers created new meanings by comparing a current strategic issue with an issue that a prototypical organization dealt with in a particular manner. For example, a bank CEO frequently used MacDonald's hamburgers as a way of understanding how standardization of branches could be a very powerful marketing tool. When discussing the bank's ability to compete with other banks and its ability to rally its employees around a common goal, he would frequently draw an analogy to the army. The CEO of the same company would sometimes compare and contrast his control systems with those of ITT.

Isenberg also found that in order to make sense of dramatic events, managers in a pharmaceutical company likened these events to experience that they had already had, such as rushing at a fraternity. The process of drawing analogies seems to be very common when organizational actors are trying to understand an ambiguous or novel situation (Louis, 1980).

Analogies are more likely to shape strategic problem formulation when they are *shared* by organizational members. Sapienza (1983) has discussed the development of shared analogies which help frame strategic decisions. The process involves the creation of a shared vocabulary among the decision-makers through discussion of problems and the emergence of shared images among the group to define the problems.

Researchers who study governmental decision-making have insights into the uses of analogy which may be helpful to strategic management researchers. Steinbruner (1974) has discussed reasoning by analogy in foreign policy-making. This involves the application of simple analogies and images to guide complex problem definition. This process helps to reduce the uncertainty perceived in the environment. Since both foreign policy and business strategy decisions are complex, ill-structured, top-level decisions, analogy may affect business strategy as well. The use of analogy affects decision-makers' problem diagnosis and generation of potential solutions in ways which may increase or decrease the quality of strategies.

Reasoning by analogy has been shown to be effective in generating creative solutions to a variety of problems (Gordon, 1961). However in strategic decisions which involve a great deal of uncertainty and complexity, the use of simple analogies may mislead the decision-makers into an over-simplistic view of the situation (Steinbruner, 1974: 115). When decision-makers use analogies to define problems, they may not recognize that there are critical differences between their analogies and the decision situations they face.

The past often provides a ready source of analogies. Present decisions may be viewed as similar to past decisions (Huff, 1982: 123). May (1973) [...] notes that foreign policy decision-makers frame present problems by using analogies to the past. They sometimes select the first analogy which comes to mind rather than searching more widely, or pausing to analyse the analogy and ask in what ways it might be misleading (May, 1973: xi). Gilovich (1981) demonstrated that analogies to the past influenced decision-makers' recommendations about how to resolve a hypothetical international relations crisis in a laboratory experiment. Subjects developed different recommendations depending on whether the scenario they received had information suggesting similarities to the Second World War or to Vietnam.

Huff (1982) notes that a firm may also draw on the analogous experiences of other firms in the industry. She suggests that this may account for the similarities in strategic concepts and frames among firms in a single industry.

In summary, diagnosis of a strategic problem sometimes involves the application of a relevant schema from another domain. Essentially, the decision-maker draws an analogy between the causes and solutions for the current problem and those of past problems. Analogies then specify the ways the problem should be solved, particularly if they are shared by organizational members. Individuals' past experiences of other companies in the industry provide the most common sources of analogy.

Integration and questions for future research

The previous sections summarize four major streams of research on strategic cognitions. These have yet to be integrated into an overall theory of cognition in strategic choice. In this final section, an integrative model is proposed and a number of hypotheses for future research are developed from this model.

Though the relationships between the research streams within the cognitive perspective have not yet been articulated, they can be integrated around two basic concepts; the development of schemata and the application of schemata to the diagnosis of particular strategic problems. Figure 4.1 describes the relationships between the four types of strategic cognitions and the two processes of schemata development and application.

This model is based on the assumption that there are two ways in which understanding of strategic problems is achieved. First, in order to comprehend some types of strategic problems, data may be carefully analysed and a new schema may be developed. For other types of problems, understanding may be achieved by *applying* a previously developed schema to the current strategic problem. This involves less diagnosis and information search.

Mintzberg et al. (1976) have discussed similar ideas in connection with the development of *solutions* to strategic problems. They suggest that in some cases solutions are designed to deal with very new strategic problems. In other cases, pre-existing solutions which were developed for other problems are sought out and applied to the problem. Mintzberg et al. suggest that two fundamentally different thought processes underlie the activities of design and search (1976: 255–6).

In the model in Figure 4.1, heuristics and biases affect the development of strategic assumptions and cognitive maps, which in turn affect the development

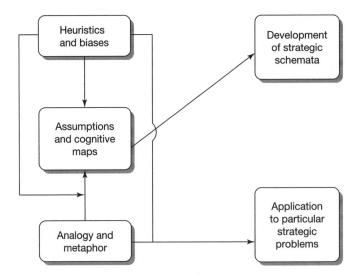

Figure 4.1 *Strategic problem comprehension*

of strategic schemata. The term schemata, being a broader term than cognitive maps, is used to describe the basic cognitive structures through which strategic problems are understood. Schemata may contain cognitive maps as well as assumptions about the strength of the relationship between variables, assessments about decision-makers' degree of confidence, and so forth. Cognitive heuristics and biases may affect the development of cognitive maps. Analogy is the means by which previously developed schemata are applied to new strategic problems. These processes are described in more detail in the following discussions of the development and application of schemata.

The development of schemata

Simon's work (1957, 1976) suggests that schemata are *simplified* models of the relationships between variables relevant to a strategic problem. Given the complexity of strategic problems and the cognitive limitations of strategists, some types of simplification are needed. Heuristics and biases may enter into this simplification process.

Researchers have not yet dealt explicitly with the *types* of biases which might affect the development of strategic assumptions and cognitive maps. However, work on the availability heuristic suggests that strategists' judgements about the causal relationships between variables in their cognitive maps would be distorted by their recollections of vivid events. Research on the illusion of control suggests that the causal role of key individuals would be exaggerated in strategists' assumptions and cognitive maps. The role of environmental variables which are difficult to control would be underestimated.

The previous speculations on the effects of cognitive heuristics and biases on strategic assumptions and cognitive maps provide the basis for several hypotheses to guide future research:

1 Decision-makers subject to the illusion of control will overestimate the causal role of their own actions in constructing their cognitive maps. Since this bias causes decision-makers to overestimate their level of personal control, it should be reflected in their assessments of the number of variables within their cognitive maps which can be influenced or determined by their own actions.

2 Cognitive heuristics and biases will reduce the number of variables included in decision-makers' cognitive maps. Since heuristics and biases serve to simplify strategic problems, they should reduce the number of variables in cognitive maps related to strategic problems.

3 Heuristics and biases will lead to a smaller number of conflicting strategic assumptions in cognitive maps. Conflicting assumptions are possible when dealing with complex problems. Under the influence of heuristics and biases decision-makers may abandon plausible assumptions which conflict with more deeply held assumptions in order to simplify their cognitive maps for dealing with these problems.

4 Decision-makers who report greater numbers of recent successful business decisions will assign a larger causal role to their own actions in their cognitive maps. Langer's (1983) work suggests that recollections of recent successes may increase the illusion of control which should lead decision-makers to overestimate the causal role of their own actions.

Analogy and metaphor may affect the development of cognitive maps dealing with strategic issues. Cognitive maps deal with variables and the causal relationships between them. Analogy and metaphor may suggest causal relationships to decision-makers developing new cognitive maps. For example, referring to Figure 4.1, strategists attempting to determine the effect of new product introduction on competitors' behaviour may draw on analogies to other industries with which they are familiar (Huff, 1982). Or, they may draw on analogies to the past (May, 1973) or to competitive games and sports or other personal experiences (Isenberg, 1983).

These considerations form a hypothesis for future research on the effects of analogy and metaphor on cognitive maps.

5 Differences in strategists' personal experiences and industry experience will affect their choice of analogies in constructing cognitive maps. Strategists with different personal or industry experience will have different analogies to draw upon. This should influence the type of analogies chosen in constructing cognitive maps.

The application of schemata

If a broad definition of the term 'analogy' is adopted, it could be said that *any* application of a previously developed schema to a new strategic problem involves analogy. Analogy and metaphor may be the basic processes by which schemata are transferred from one domain to another.

Those writing on analogy and metaphor have not clearly specified the cognitive processes by which they affect strategic problem comprehension. However, it appears that cognitive heuristics and biases may be involved in this process. For example, the *availability* heuristic might cause decision-makers to use dramatic and vivid events as the basis for their problem-defining analogies, even though these events may bear little resemblance to the problems they are attempting to understand. The *illusion of control* bias may lead decision-makers to use analogies to situations in which they had a great deal of control over outcomes, even though this may not be true of the present situation. Further, this bias may draw decision-makers' attention to aspects of the strategic problem over which they have control. These aspects of the problem then provide the *cues* which are used in selecting an analogy.

These points lead to two final hypotheses:

6 Decision-makers who report greater numbers of recent successful
   business decisions will be more likely to define new strategic problems
   using analogies to situations in which they had a high level of
   personal control. As suggested in the comments on hypothesis 4,
   the illusion of control is more likely in decision-makers who have
   experienced success. This should lead them to define new problems
   in terms of past situations in which they had personal control.
7 Differences in strategists' personal experiences and industry experience
   will determine which cues are used in selecting analogies to define
   new strategic problems. Strategists with different backgrounds are
   likely to attend to different features of new problems when attempting
   to define them. Therefore, it is likely they will focus on different cues
   when selecting a problem-relevant schema as a framework for defining
   the new strategic problems.
   [...]

Conclusion

In general, researchers in strategic management have not paid sufficient attention to strategists' cognitions in the past. As was pointed out earlier in the paper, the study of cognition may improve our understanding of industry and competitive strategy and the ways environmental factors affect strategic decisions. In this chapter, I have surveyed recent research on four specific topics related to strategic cognitions. I have also developed a model which shows the interrelationships between these topics and I have provided an example to illustrate the features of this model.

As was stated at the beginning of the chapter, interest in strategic cognitions is growing because of increased awareness of their role in strategic issue diagnosis and problem formulation. Research on cognitive structures, processes, and biases gives insights into the ways decision-makers with limited cognitive capacities comprehend and solve very complex strategic problems. It may also give insights into the types of errors they make in strategic decision-making. However, no one has yet shown how these separate streams of research relate to each other. Such integration is necessary in order for future research to provide a complete understanding of strategic problem-solving.

A better understanding of strategists' cognitive structures and processes will also provide a basis for better recommendations for improving strategic decision-making. Strategic decision aids can be developed which are more consistent with the ways decision-makers represent strategic problems. Also, once the most important biases are identified, decision aids can be designed to reduce these. Decision aids may also be developed to help decision-makers to examine more carefully the analogies they use to define new problems.

References

Axelrod, R. (1976) *The Structure of Decision: Cognitive Maps of Political Elites*, Princeton, NJ: Princeton University Press.

Barnes, J. (1984) 'Cognitive biases and their impact on strategic planning', *Strategic Management Journal*, 5: 129–38.

Bougon, M., Weick, K. and Binkhorst, B. (1977) 'Cognitions in organizations: an analysis of the Utrecht jazz orchestra', *Administrative Science Quarterly*, 22: 606–39.

Chittipeddi, K. and Gioia, D. (1983) 'A cognitive psychological perspective and the strategic management process'. Paper presented at the National Academy of Management Meetings.

Duhaime, I.D. and Schwenk, C. (1985) 'Conjectures on cognitive simplification in acquisition and divestment decision-making', *Academy of Management Review*, 10: 287–95.

Dutton, J., Fahey, L. and Narayanan, V. (1983) 'Toward understanding strategic issue diagnosis', *Strategic Management Journal*, 4: 307–23.

Freeman, R. (1984) *Strategic Management: A Stakeholder Approach*. Boston: Pitman.

Gilovich, T. (1981) 'Seeing the past in the present: the effect of associations to familiar events on judgements and decisions', *Journal of Personality and Social Psychology*, 40: 797–808.

Gordon, W. (1961) *Synectics*. New York: Harper & Row.

Hambrick, D. and Mason, P. (1984) 'Upper echelons: the organization as a reflection of its top managers', *Academy of Management Review*, 9: 193–206.

Hogarth, R.M. (1980) *Judgement and Choice: The Psychology of Decision*. Chichester: Wiley.

Huff, A. (1982) 'Industry influences on strategy reformulation', *Strategic Management Journal*, 3: 119–31.

Isenberg, D. (1983) 'How senior managers think (and what about)'. Unpublished manuscript, Harvard University.

Janis, I. and Mann, L. (1977) *Decision-Making*. New York: Free Press.

Langer, E.J. (1983) *The Psychology of Control*. Beverly Hills, CA: Sage.

Louis, M.R. (1980) 'A cultural perspective on organizations'. Paper presented at the National Academy of Management Meetings.

Lyles, M. (1981) 'Formulating strategic problems: empirical analysis and model development', *Strategic Management Journal*, 2: 61–75.

Mason, R.O. and Mitroff, I.I. (1981) *Challenging Strategic Planning Assumptions*. New York: Wiley.

May, E. (1973) *'Lessons' of the Past*. New York: Oxford University Press.

Mintzberg, H. and Waters, J. (1982) 'Tracking strategy in the entrepreneurial firm', *Academy of Management Journal*, 25: 465–99.

Mintzberg, H., Raisinghani, P. and Theoret, A. (1976) 'The structure of "unstructured" decision processes', *Administrative Science Quarterly*, 2: 246–75.

Neisser, U. (1976) *Cognition and Reality*. San Francisco, CA: Freeman.

Rumelhart, D. and Ortony, A. (1977) 'The representation of knowledge in memory', in R. Anderson, R. Spiro and W. Montague (eds), *Schooling and the Acquisition of Knowledge*. Hillsdale, NJ: Lawrence Erlbaum.

Sapienza, A.M. (1983) 'A cognitive perspective on strategy formulation'. Paper presented at the Academy of Management National Meetings, Dallas, August.

Schwenk, C. (1984) 'Cognitive simplification processes in strategic decision-making', *Strategic Management Journal*, 5: 111–28.

Schwenk, C. (1986) 'Information, cognitive bias, and commitment to a course of action', *Academy of Management Review*, 11: 298–310.

Shrivastava, P. (1983) 'A typology of organizational learning systems', *Journal of Management Studies*, 20: 7–28.

Shrivastava, P. and Mitroff, I.I. (1983) 'Frames of references managers use: a study in applied sociology of knowledge', in R. Lamb (ed.), *Advances in Strategic Management*, V: 1, Greenwich, CT: JAI Press.

Simon, H.A. (1957) *Models of Man*. New York: Wiley.

Simon, H.A. (1976) *Administrative Behavior* (4th edn). New York: Free Press.

Steinbruner, J.D. (1974) *The Cybernetic Theory of Decision*. Princeton, NJ: Princeton University Press.

Taylor, R.N. (1975) 'Psychological determinants of bounded rationality: implications for decision-making', *Decision Sciences*, 6: 409–29.

Taylor, S. (1982) 'The interface of cognitive and social psychology', in J. Harvey (ed.), *Cognition, Social Behavior and the Environment*. Hillsdale, NJ: Lawrence Erlbaum.

Taylor, S. and Crocker, J. (1983) 'Schematic bases of social information processing', in E. Higgens, C. Herman and J. Zauna, *Social Cognition: The Ontario Symposium*. Hillsdale, NJ: Lawrence Erlbaum.

Tolman, E. (1948) 'Cognitive maps in rats and men', *Psychological Review*, 1(55): 189–208.

Tversky, A. and Kahneman, D. (1974) 'Judgement under uncertainty: heuristics and biases', *Sciences*, 185: 1124–31.

Weick, K. (1979) 'Cognitive processes in organizations', in B. Staw (ed.), *Research in Organizational Behavior*. Greenwich, CT: JAI Press.

Achieving 'Fit': Managers' Theories of How to Manage Innovation

Graeme Salaman and John Storey

The importance of innovation

Innovation is increasingly identified as *the* critical factor in economic competitiveness. Rapid technological change, globalization, the liberalization of trade, intense competition from low-wage economies, the reduction in communication and transport costs, shorter product life cycles and consumers switching between products and providers at an accelerated rate, require firms in advanced high wage economies to achieve competitive advantage through innovation. A range of governments throughout the world have emphasized this point – in Austria, Australia, Canada, France, Germany, The Netherlands, Sweden and the UK – advocating innovation-driven economies (see, for example, OECD 2004).

Furthermore – and this is central to the concerns of this chapter – Government analyses recognize the fundamental role of managers' attitudes, interpretations and knowledge to the encouragement of innovation in organizations. The UK government's recent *Competing in the Global Economy: The Innovation Challenge* (DTI, 2003) contends that 'ultimately innovation depends on the knowledge, skills and creativity of those working in business' (2003: 26).

Academic research supports the strategic value of innovation, stressing the role of internal, organizational determinants: 'Winners in the global market place have been firms that can demonstrate timely responsiveness and rapid and flexible product innovation, coupled with management capability to effectively co-ordinate and re-deploy internal and external competences' (Teece et al., 2002: 183). This ability is the capacity to renew the organization and its competences to be consistent with changing environmental demands (Teece et al., 2002: 183).

Yet while the benefits of innovation as a source of competitive advantage are well rehearsed; the incidence of innovation remains low. The impact of innovation research and policy prescription on managerial behaviour is limited. Hence the frequency and urgency of Governmental exhortation: 'what the literature prescribes and what most firms do are miles apart' (Cooper and Kleinschmidt, 1986: 73).

If there is a gap between theory and practice how can it be explained? Managers are presumably aware of the competitive advantages of innovation (this is something we investigated) but if they establish it as a priority, then why do they not ensure their organizations achieve it? Is the 'problem' one of intention or of capacity? And if they do value innovation how do they go about trying to achieve it?

Another discrepancy explored in this study is between senior managers' claims about the strategic importance of innovation to their organization and the actual achievement of innovation – their actions (or lack of action) to encourage innovation within their organization. Some explain this gap by invoking the charge of hypocrisy; others more charitably, attribute it to managers' rhetoric. But such charges of bad faith are too easy, and are untested. Is the gap deliberate: an attempt to claim the PR advantages of a focus on innovation without a willingness to invest and take the risks necessary to achieve it? Or is it possible that in their own ways managers are actually being consistent – that senior managers who espouse innovation but allow their organizations not to achieve it actually have designed organizations to achieve the levels and types of innovation they really want?

Our approach

This chapter explores practising managers' and organizational researchers' views of the nature and role of innovation and how it is supported or obstructed by their organizations. Innovation is something managers and executives in some organizations want to achieve (although how they define innovation and how they value it vary importantly). It is a priority, a strategic and explicit purpose. If they are committed to innovation they will hold views about how well or badly it is achieved within their organization and why, and what needs to be done for innovation to be encouraged so that their organizations are better at achieving it. If they are committed to innovation they will try to design their organizations to achieve the type of innovation they see as necessary; if they are for various reasons not able to do this, they will be frustrated by the existence and persistence of organizational features which in their view (their theory) block innovation.

The conventional approach to the exploration of innovation in organizations involves the identification and attribution of the grounds for its existence (or non-existence) or persistence (or disappearance). Conventional explanations identify the causal relationships between objective variables – organizational size, the amount of R&D spend, characteristics of the workforce, aspects of the societal or regional culture, the degree of concentration of firms within an industrial cluster, and so on – and factors which are taken as indicators of innovation (for example, patents registered).

Within this tradition, the insights, interpretations and opinions of the managers concerned are not of central interest except in that they contribute information which assists the researcher to develop an 'objective assessment' of the levels of the key variables.

This is not the approach used in this study. We are not interested in gathering and cross-relating objective, quantified data on key determinants and output variables. Our research involved an analysis of how *managers and innovators themselves* explain variations in levels of innovation and specifically their explanations for their organizations' levels of innovation. It is about how people who wish to innovate (or not) and who want their organizations to innovate (or not) set about trying to encourage or argue against innovation. It is not about *our* theories; it is about *their* theories. What could be more sensible and necessary, when seeking to understand innovation within organizations than to know and understand the intentions, plans, experiences, theories, fears and frustrations of those who are, in varying ways, engaged in trying to achieve innovation? Levels of innovation are a result of intention, of deliberate (but clearly not always successful) attempts by organizations and individuals to pursue their ends.

Debates relevant to this study

Two debates within the extensive and wide-ranging innovation literature are relevant to this study. Both address issues critical to our approach to understanding managers' theories of innovation.

The first turns on and addresses issues around the meanings and definition of innovation. The way respondents define and value innovation is a central starting point for our analysis and indeed for our respondents' approach to the management and organization of innovation. Since people act in terms of their definitions we expect, a priori that how managers define and value innovation will be closely and causally related to how their organizations are designed to achieve it.

The second debate analyses factors which encourage or obstruct innovation within organizations. This focuses on the role of innovation in business strategy and new product development, the use of alliances and networks; and the role of cognitive aspects of organizations – mindsets, recipes, routines, mind maps and so on – in encouraging or discouraging innovation and the analysis of the relationships between these cognitive elements and other structural aspects of organization. We briefly review each of these literatures in turn.

Meanings and definitions

The meaning of the term 'innovation' has been and remains contentious and problematical partly because it is constituted in various and different debates, and partly because commentators have identified different types of innovation. The distinctions between product and process innovation and between radical and incremental innovation are fundamental to definitions of innovation and to explorations of the meaning of innovation in organizations (although possibly difficult to apply in practice).

The distinction between achieving improvements to an existing product or process and achieving a radical departure from historic products and practices is one of the most fundamental distinctions in the innovation literature (Moch and Morse, 1977; Freeman and Soete, 1997). Incremental innovation involves relatively minor changes to existing elements; it exploits further the existing design. Radical innovation is based on new principles and so can open up completely new markets, and represents a complete break from the past.

Radical innovation can create difficulties for established firms by challenging their products and technologies and so can be difficult for these firms to achieve. Incremental innovation also presents firms with problems because it tends to lock established firms into pathways which dis-equip them from competing with new entrants who may introduce products and services which entirely subvert their technologies (Christensen, 1997). Incremental innovation reinforces the nature and dominance of existing organizational arrangements and competences, but radical innovation potentially challenges these – 'it forces them [organizations] to ask a new set of questions, to draw on new technical and commercial skills, and to employ new problem solving approaches' (Henderson and Clark, 2002).

The management of innovation: enablers and barriers

This literature is of direct interest to our study. It addresses the issues our respondents were most eager to address: how important innovation is strategically and how organizations can encourage or discourage the incidence of innovation. The literature in this category includes work on business strategy and new product development, and the organizational factors (of varying types) which facilitate or obstruct innovation.

One answer to the basic question – what factors facilitate or obstruct innovation? – is that size and maturity of the organization are fundamental. Entrepreneurship and innovation are often closely linked and both have been associated with size. (Mintzberg and Waters, 1982; Schwenk, 2002) Small firms have been seen as more innovative then large firms. (Tushman and Anderson, 1986; Henderson and Clarke, 2002; Meyer, Brooks and Goes, 1990; Leonard Barton, 1992) Various factors have been seen as significant: 'structural and cultural inertia, internal politics, complacency, fear of cannibalising existing products, fear of destroying existing competences, satisfaction with the status quo, and a general lack of incentive to abandon a certain present (which is profitable) for an uncertain future' (Markides, 2002: 246). One solution is seen as employing alliances and inter-organizational networks (Powell, 1990; Child and Faulkner, 1998; Yoshino and Rangan, 1995).

Large firms have been urged to emulate the characteristics of small entrepreneurial firms (Kanter, 1983), or to combine the characteristics of large and small, mature and new, organic and mechanistic firms – 'ambidexterity' (Tushman and O'Reilly, 1996; Amit and Schoemaker, 1993; Teece, Pisano and Shuen, 1997; Ghemawat et al., 2001).

Others have noted the advantages of large size for innovation (Schumpeter, 1934, 1942; Pavitt, 1991.) Others (for example, Rothwell, 1986) argue that large and small firms interact in a symbiotic way. Lefebvre et al. (1997) report that it is the *perceptions of the chief executives* rather than objective variables which explain technology policy and innovation strategy, because managerial perceptions and orientations tend to correlate with size and age of the organization (Tushman and O'Reilly, 1996: 18). Institutions construct taken-for-granted routines and establish systems and competences which introduce rigidity and become rooted in conformity. Researchers have argued that the organizational qualities necessary for successful and effective operations are dysfunctional for innovation: 'Established firms have difficulty developing and marketing commercially viable new products' (Dougherty, 1992: 77).

Researchers have identified the features of the mature successful firm which can obstruct innovation, noting the role of established skills and routines surrounding their development, deployment and institutionalization. Leonard Barton identifies the role of competences, 'core capabilities' can also become 'core rigidities', an example of what Argyris has called trained incapacity. Klein and Sorra (1996) contend that the main problem which has not received sufficient attention is that of 'implementation failure' arising from organizational climate and user values.

A number of researchers have focused on the nature and role of processes of cognition within organizations, pointing to their possible implications for the nature and extent of innovation. Innovation is an intellectual, cognitive process. If aspects of organization encourage or discourage innovation they do this by influencing how managers and researchers think, and what they think about. The cognitive approach to innovation stresses the importance of the ways in which established forms of thinking, search techniques, modes of analysis and so on, develop over time in response to established technologies, products and associated processes and routines and become constraining in the face of new circumstances.

Valentin et al. (2002), argue the significance of history and complacency born from past certainties and successes: 'past successes and ideological rigidities can foster dysfunctional inertia and mindsets' (p. 58). Tushman and O'Reilly (1996) stress a cultural dimension built up over time with established norms obstructing change. Support for this comes from Lant and Milliken (1992), and Senge (1990). Cyert and March (2002) note how successful organizational search sets the pattern for future search. Managers may also become personally committed to established routines (Lant et al. 2002). Coombs and Hull (1998) show how the knowledge base of a firm reinforces path dependency and thus limits the scope for opportunistic or strategic acquisition of external knowledge. Von Hippel's (1994) concept of 'sticky information' draws attention to the ways in which existing information limits finding or accessing new information.

Moreover, at the management of organizations level of analysis there are some examples of work designed to further the idea of an integrated approach. Currently popular is the 'dynamic capabilities framework' as found (for instance) in the work of Teece and Pisano (1994, 1997). They trace the competitive advantage of firms to a number of *linked* internal capabilities (skills, ways of coordinating and organizational processes) in relation to technological paths and market positions). The management of innovation occurs within this space. Firm activities and associated capabilities are shaped by the firm's asset positions such as the firm's portfolio of knowledge assets along with other complementary assets and the evolutionary path it has followed. It is important to remember why we have rehearsed some elements in recent debates on the management of innovation. This study will not directly test any of these views. Our purpose is not to test them but to explore and understand how, if at all, they are relevant to *respondents' theories* of how innovation is encouraged or discouraged within their organizations. We will now turn to our respondents and see how *they* try to explain the incidence or encourage innovation. The literature discussed indirectly surfaces a number of issues which constitute the heart of this research: How do managers define, value, and comprehend innovation? And do these definitions differ with level, function of other organizational locations? How do managers explain the ways in which their organizations encourage or discourage innovation?

Research method

Our research objectives required that we accessed the perceptions and cognitions of a selection of managers and located these in their organizational contexts. These dual requirements required detailed case study research. We aimed for 20 interviews per case organization and these were to range across senior and middle managers. However, in the small and medium sized organizations we reduced the number of interviews to approximately 10 per organization. In total, 351 interviews were conducted and they lasted on average one and a half hours. Interviews were tape recorded and transcribed and then analysed by multiple members of the research team.

We conducted research in six sectors: pharmaceuticals; banking and finance; manufacturing; telecommunications; media and the voluntary sector. Within each of these sector groups we selected and researched a minimum of two case organizations. Key cases included: NatWest Bank, Zeneca, GPT/Marconi Communications, Nortel, Oxfam and the BBC. The logic in selecting a range of diverse sectors, and indeed these sectors in particular, was that, from a reading of the literature, it could be expected that there might be some sector-specific influences on the way managers would report the way in which innovation was treated in their context.

As the research progressed, managers in the large organizations often suggested that small and medium sized companies would enjoy some distinct advantages in innovation. In order to explore this claim we selected six SMEs. This sample was selected in collaboration with a Chamber of Commerce and Business Link. Their innovation counsellors identified what they judged to be the top innovative companies in the locality and these were then added to our list of organizations to be researched.

Our interest in practitioners' own insights and theories is of course reflective of the wider growth of interest in what Gibbons et al. (1994) refer to as 'mode 2 knowledge production'. This marks a departure from an attachment to a supposedly theoretically pure form of knowledge to a form of knowledge production where findings are closely related to context. Moreover, the latter form also emphasizes knowledge deriving from direct engagement with practical problems. We make no claim that our approach is 'better' in any absolute sense but we do judge that it has a relevant part to play. It is none the less worth noting that some observers have suggested that the inherent nature of the subject of management and business research makes the mode 2 approach especially appropriate (see for example, Tranfield and Starkey, 1998).

Our intention is to describe, analyse and interpret managers' theories of innovation. We move beyond managers' explicit theories to an analysis of underlying themes which were not always explicitly stated or acknowledged by the managers themselves.

Findings

In this section, the findings are presented in three parts: first, managers' interpretations and attitudes towards innovation; second, their interpretations of the role played by organizational structures; and third their interpretations of organizational cultures.

Managers' interpretations of and attitudes towards innovation

Definitions of innovation (and the value placed on these definitions) are crucial elements in managers' analyses of their organizations' innovation performance and potential. Managers insisted that the way their organization defined innovation (in effect they normally meant a combination of the top management message and the way organizational life actually proceeded) and the significance they attached to innovation were central to the way the organization was geared up (or not) to achieve innovation. We found important differences in the way innovation was understood, defined and valued by managers – especially senior managers – in different organizations. In some cases managers – particularly senior managers – defined innovation in relatively traditional terms – as incremental improvement or radical transformation of product or process. In other organizations managers defined anything and everything as a potential object of innovation – for example: 'For us, innovation is absolutely vital to everything we do' (manager, Zeneca).

In some organizations managers defined innovation as an exotic extra ingredient, as something that could with benefit (but often also with risk) be added to the organization – something the organization might *have* – in others innovation was defined as co-terminus with the organization itself: not a desirable but optional extra to be added when possible to everyday, real business, but absolutely essential: something the organization *was*.

Some definitions of innovation were circumscribed and conventional; others were wide-ranging and unconventional. Limited definitions focused on products – and processes – more comprehensive, radical definitions encompassed any and every aspect of organizational structure process and functioning. In the organizations seen as poor innovators, incremental innovation was judged to be the favoured mode and the assumed 'sensible' way to proceed. Conversely, in the organizations which were judged as more positive towards innovation, managers defined it in much wider terms and were far more alert to opportunities for radical innovation.

Our managers believed that the first object of innovation is innovation itself. Traditional, conventional definitions of innovation were seen as major obstacles. In organizations where managers were more positive about their organization's attitude towards innovation, their thinking about innovation was more far-reaching and unconstrained. They went beyond the conventional radical/incremental product distinction and insisted that innovation should apply to the organization itself and to every aspect of the organization's functioning and network of relationships. 'It's about the capacity of the organization to reinvent itself … innovation is constant.'

These differences in definition (and value) were seen by our respondents as closely related to their organizations' performance with respect to innovation. In organizations where respondents were convinced their organization was obstructive towards innovation, they also insisted that this was to a degree because of the way senior managers valued and defined innovation.

In organizations where managers rated their organizations as poor innovators, they argued that senior management was only interested in conventional, un-ambitious, limited and incremental forms of innovation. This suggests that if organizations display an apparent gap between an espoused commitment to innovation and the achievements of the organization this may not be a result of incompetence or error but a logical and deliberate outcome. The apparent gap may be not an error but a success. In these cases senior managers didn't want to achieve innovation beyond the sort of innovation they did achieve – or they only wanted to achieve innovation when it complied with various standards and disciplines.

There is a second way in which definitions of and values placed on innovation may be important: when there are marked differences in definitions and values *within* an organization. The research organizations differed in the degree to which the respondents from an organization shared a definition of innovation and the value they placed on it. In some cases there were marked differences in the ways in which innovation was defined and valued. Successful and less successful innovators – as assessed by the managers – differed sharply in this respect. In successful innovating organizations senior technical staff, executives, and managers agreed on the factors that encouraged and discouraged innovation. In the less successful innovating organizations, while managers and staff agreed on what obstructed and facilitated innovation within their organization, their senior managers articulated a markedly different analysis.

These differences on how to encourage innovation were seen by the technical specialists and managers (but not by senior managers) as a major source of frustration and dissatisfaction (and failure to innovate). Within these organizations the perceived failure to innovate was ascribed not to incompetence, error or confusion but to the deliberate policies of senior management who designed and encouraged organizational structures and systems which were explicitly designed to reduce the risks they associated with innovation or to reduce the incidence of types of innovation they found less desirable. Our informants' insights and narratives helped to reveal that if an organization was obstructive to innovation (regardless of the espoused commitments of senior managers) it was not by accident.

Among the organizations seen as poor innovators, conflict, confusion and ambiguity over organizational direction and purpose were frequently seen as major obstacles to the realization of innovation. And clarity and consensus about the direction and strategy of the organization were seen in successful innovating organizations as one of the most important factors in encouraging innovation. On its own it was not enough; but it was a crucial contextual condition. Our managers were convinced that the starting point for a successful innovating organization was for it to adopt a wide-ranging, ambitious, definition of innovation and to be genuinely committed to achieving it. The stumbling block, they suggested, was not simply or even primarily problems of the appropriate means, but of genuine and serious commitment to the ends.

We found another, more subtle aspect of the value attached to innovation in organizations – a moral and highly judgemental dimension of meaning. For some managers innovation was defined as dangerous, almost inherently irresponsible, childish, creative, unsettling, threatening to the organization and its established controls and disciplines, desirable possibly (as long as it was controlled) but not essential. For other managers these aspects of innovation – its creativeness, its quirkiness, its capacity to break through barriers and constraints, its inherent riskiness, and so on, were seen far more positively – as highly valuable, as strategically essential, creative, exciting, exhilarating, the source of advantage and competitive success.

This crucial difference underpinned radically different organizational approaches to the management of innovation. When senior management saw innovation as a threat, a danger that must be controlled, they were more likely to seek to manage and control it. When innovation was seen as a desirable and exhilarating source of competitive advantage, the stress was less on controlling innovation and more on encouraging it. In both types of organization, managers recognized what the innovation literatures also stress – that the achievement of radical forms of innovation definitionally requires a willingness and commitment at senior levels of the organization to question and critique the existing organizational order. But senior managers differed in their reaction to this. Some welcomed it and stressed how the search for innovation meant that they had to continue to 'smash' the organization to ensure that vested interests and ways of thinking didn't become established. As a senior Nortel manager observed, 'It's a self-critical culture, hence, it's always changing. We like to shake up every three to five years to seek out complacency and shake them out. We seek a balance between order and chaos.'

But, in other organizations, senior managers' attachment to the established order meant that they considered forms of innovation which would threaten this order (and they were right in thinking that it would) and sought to ensure its survival by carefully controlling innovative ideas and projects which threatened it. As a manager in NatWest argued: 'Organizations that are innovative have a knack of being able to create an imperative for change that others may not see. Banks in general have had it too good. So much so that many insiders inevitably say: "why change?" We ourselves tend to leave change until the platform is burning.' We found that senior management commitment to the existing order is causally related to a focus on incremental innovation. Commitment to radical forms of innovation requires a commitment to challenge existing organizational arrangements.

In organizations that were seen by middle managers to be obstructive towards innovation, innovation was defined by the senior managers as something potentially dangerous, as something that must be controlled and tightly regulated. A manager in NatWest observed: 'The bank has managed its business by worrying about not letting in goals ... but we have to score some too.' In GPT, senior managers described innovation as 'an indulgence' that overexcited researchers could pursue for its own sake. In this atmosphere, managers who encouraged innovation spoke of it as an illicit activity that had to be protected and hidden – and given 'air-cover'.

Innovation raises issues of legitimacy. In some organizations innovators required senior sponsorship and protection: innovation was a source of tension and conflict about the allocation of resources (including the deployment of key staff), the appropriate product and service offerings, and operating procedures and infrastructure of the organization which would be needed to support the new activities.

In organizations where a radical and ambitious view of innovation prevailed the underlying view of innovation was far more positive (not in terms of its risks but in terms of its benefits) and a radically different organizational response was accorded it. When innovation was seen as a risk it had to be controlled; when it was a virtue and a benefit it was seen as something to be encouraged and to be welcomed. In organizations where innovation was seen as a risky indulgence, it was carefully and rigorously managed by structural and systematic controls; in organizations where it was defined positively it was encouraged by the pervasive organizational culture and formal controls were minimized.

Whereas in the first sort of organization, innovation was defined as a specialist activity (at best) in the second innovation was expected of everyone. And whereas in the first sort of organization innovation was defined as necessarily subservient to the existing operationally-focused structure and culture of the organization (innovation had to adapt to the 'real' world of the product businesses, the potential self-indulgence of innovation had to be disciplined) in the second sort of organization, the search and need for innovation was regarded as just as important and legitimate a priority around which the organization should be structured as any other.

Managers believe that there is a tension between existing organizational strengths and structures and the ability to innovate. But they differed fundamentally in their response to this view of the inherent limitations to innovation that develop in established organizations. In some cases senior managers accepted it and even welcomed it. They made a virtue out of the ways in which established structures limited innovation and argued that such control was necessary and desirable. If innovation was to be encouraged, tolerated, permitted, it could only do so if it fitted in with existing structures and systems. In other cases – where managers argued that their organizations were good innovators – senior managers insisted that the solution to the paradox was not to adapt innovation to organization but organization to innovation. They saw their role as trying to combat and neutralize the inevitable forces of conservatism that would obstruct innovation and which could emerge only too easily within large organizations.

In some of our organizations (those where managers were unimpressed by their organization's innovation performance) senior managers did indeed seem to be trapped by their commitments to existing organizational arrangements. But this is not how they saw it. They saw themselves as guardians of the integrity and traditions of the organizations, concerned to curtail the risks of innovation, to ensure that valuable resources were not squandered on self-indulgent innovations regardless of market demands, as defenders of the status quo. In contrast, in organizations which were seen as far better innovators, senior managers saw that existing structures could curtail innovation and sought rigorously and radically to overcome these limitations, as reconfiguring organizational skills, resources, and functional competences to match the requirements of a changing environment (Teece et al., 2002: 183).

The nature and role of structures

Although managers' assessment of their organizations' innovation achievements differed starkly, their views of what organizations needed to do to encourage (or discourage) innovation were remarkably similar. Regardless of how the organizations were assessed, the analyses used the same axes and factors: negative factors were simply the opposite or absence of positive factors. The managers used the same basic theory of innovation; what differed fundamentally was the organizational context. Managers who were dissatisfied argued that according to their theory of how innovation should be defined, valued and achieved, their organization employed an inappropriate (restricted) definition of innovation, valued it insufficiently, and allowed organizations features which blocked it. The main differences were less in what managers thought should be done and much more in what organizations actually did.

In successful innovators, managers argued that the organization was supportive of innovation; several factors were identified: a clear and genuine strategic emphasis and value on innovation; clarity of strategic direction; senior managers' positive attitudes towards innovation and risk-taking; the quality of staff and how they were managed and rewarded; supportive structures and processes, and crucially, cultural values which genuinely encouraged innovation; the availability (through various means, formal or informal) of sources of funding. In organizations seen as successful as innovators, managers stressed a combination of elements all mutually supporting each other: strong and genuine empowerment (which means failure must be accepted); a clear sense of strategic direction; what a senior manager in Nortel called 'good visibility' so that senior managers can see what people are doing and ensure it fits.

A key differentiator of successful and unsuccessful innovators was the way the organization tried to 'manage' innovation. Organizations often have some sort of innovation management system, varying from highly formalized to less formalized, centralized to decentralized, business-based to autonomous. Organizations that defined innovation in un-ambitious terms as a potentially dangerous activity requiring discipline and regulation tended to lay particular stress on these formal processes. These poor innovators had the most formal-ized innovation management systems – of which managers were critical claiming that they applied inappropriate criteria and methodology to the assessment of innovation; being more concerned with eliminating risk than encouraging innovation, and focused on securing reassurances of guaranteed levels of financial return which could not possibly be sensibly predicted. These innovation management systems applied disciplines and values from other aspects of the organization, for example applying engineering logics to innovation. Innovation was defined in terms of its potential dangers not its potential benefits; as only acceptable if it was subservient to existing structures and values. One manager commented the innovation management system 'is a filter not a catalyst'.

In the effective innovators there were few complaints of this sort; managers did not complain about the formal system because there was no obvious formal innovation system. Furthermore these managers did not see the need for one. They believed that people with good ideas existed and were encouraged, and that the nature of the organization and its clear purposes, allied to available funding, and associated with a pervasive skill at network-ing encourages innovation. Supportive and inspirational senior management are important not only for practical support, guidance and implementation but also for supplying a supportive moral or cultural dimension. These managers also stressed a culture which encouraged managers and researchers to be empowered, proactive and energized. A senior manager in Nortel observed, 'Innovation occurs across the board in a fairly unmanaged and chaotic way.'

The underlying source of difficulty – displayed in a number of manifesta-tions and variants – was the same: since radical innovation is potentially destructive of – or challenging of – existing arrangements, products, compe-tences, processes, assumptions, structures, the more such factors were main-tained and defended by powerful senior managers, the more innovation was required to comply with constraints and limitations, the less likely it was to occur. Senior managers in organizations which were regarded as successful innovators recognized the need to overcome organizational inertia when they talked of the need to 'balance' operational values with the encouragement of innovation. As a top manager in Nortel Europe argued:

There has to be a balance between the ability to be free to move versus the ability of the organization to be seen to work effectively. I see it as part of my responsibility to periodically 'smash' the organization. Nortel is an almost anarchic company. It is so loose that it is non-hierarchical, it is pretty non-structured. We accept that there is a very thin dividing line between anarchy and empowerment.

Managers in organizations which were defined as less successful innovators were quick to identify aspects of their organizations which in their view blocked innovation. One such feature – a common one – was the structuring of an organization into separate product businesses, with innovation being accountable to these businesses. In this organization senior managers were worried that innovation would become self-indulgent, detached from market applications, irresponsible, unaccountable. Having a strong conviction in the healing powers of market forces, the solution to these worries was to allocate responsibility for innovation to the product businesses, thus ensuring that any innovation that occurred would be closely tied to existing products and closely market-focused. Since the product businesses were managed by annual business plans with demanding levels of targeted performance they were unlikely to squander this years' profits on extravagant innovation projects, especially when these were uncertain of delivery, require long-term develop-ment, or were not tied to existing products and markets. The result was that little innovation was encouraged and what was encouraged was incremental improvement, not radical innovation.

Furthermore, when organizational structures allowed the emergence of dominant product 'barons', managers noted that these barons might resist innovations which would not easily fit into existing organizational demarca-tions or which threatened the power of existing businesses. Radical innova-tion frequently challenges existing product boundaries.

Also, a strong hierarchical approach was also seen to encourage conser-vatism, and discourage innovation. One manager insisted that the low level of innovation was not the result of lack of brains or commitment or enthusiasm but because new radical ideas 'get murdered when you go to the high altar of executive decision-making'.

Managers identified a tension between the sort of organizational and management systems necessary to run a large complex organization in an accountable and efficient manner and the sort of structure that allows, even encourages, variation, experiment, non-standard responses and innovation. However, managers differed in their views of this tension. In organizations seen as effective innovators, the tension was defined in a complex and often subtle manner. Managers recognized it, and accepted that the tension was inevitable while accepting that the relative strength of the two sides of the distinction needed constant attention. ('You want to get to this creative edge of chaos'; manager, Zeneca.) Senior managers in these organizations used different words to describe what they were trying to do ('chaos theory', 'dividing line', 'balance') but in essence they were seeking the same goal: to achieve or discover a viable balance or dividing line between empowerment and established systems, and secondly (and arguable even more importantly) to ensure that this process of discovery was never completed but was a source of on-going debate and review: 'One of the ways in which innovation thrives here is that there's an organizational culture of never being satisfied' (senior manager, Oxfam).

Effective innovators attempted to escape from the obstructive consequences of organizational centralization, control and standardization. But achieving a balance or solution to the simplicities of the loose/tight polarity in itself defined another possible type of inertia: any 'solution' to the loose/tight polarity must itself sooner or later become fixed and inflexible and therefore part of the very polarity from which escape is sought. The solution to this is to ensure a constant process of review and debate about the adequacy of the 'balance' the organization has achieved. In the poor innovators, managers defined this tension in moralized and polarized ways: each pole was seen as good and as negative. In successful innovators the need for control, regulation and predictability is not seen as a heavy cost that must be borne, but on the contrary, as a core value which must be stressed and which should be applied to innovation in order to reduce the dangers of self-indulgent projects. In other words, in poor innovators, the impact of control and standardization on innovation was recognized and valued and seen as an effective way of managing innovation.

In the proficiently innovating companies there was a greater recognition of the complexity of the relationship between organization and innovation. Both organization and innovation were seen as necessary, both as useful, both as potentially costly. Effective innovators seem to have a way out of this unhelpful polarity: for example they recognized that innovation is not an absolute good. There can be too much innovation. If a system is working well, changing it for change's sake is unwise. If people are innovating because they are encouraged to do so, it can introduce excessive amounts of unnecessary variability in procedures.

Second, in these organizations, if innovation is not always or necessarily a positive benefit, neither are tight organizational processes and systems necessarily negative. Sensible systems are necessary to ensure effective, across the board implementation of innovation, and can supply the overall framework (of accountability, direction, necessary professional standards and processes) within which innovation must occur. While an excessively loose organizational structure can result in a fragmentation, or excessive focus on the local task and an insufficient focus on the corporate whole.

Organizational cultures

Culture was seen to play a pivotal role in the encouragement or discouragement of innovation in organizations. Its most powerful positive role is when organizations make available shared ways of thinking that encourage and value innovation: that assume managers and researchers will innovate, and be proactive, that discourage passivity, that castigate those who claim they are unable to find organizational support. Cultures are most important negatively when the prevailing norms do not accord sufficient value to innovation, when compliance and conformity are emphasized; when innovation is seen as illicit, dangerous, threatening; when the organization is presented as an obstacle from which there is no escape and when discussion of all of these is seen as illicit.

In poor innovators, managers identified a number of shared ways of thinking which limited innovation. One possibility was that technical values associated with the nature of the organization's business became applied more generally to the way innovation was managed. For example, engineering values are not surprising in a telecoms business with a real and important reputation for engineering excellence. But, managers claimed, these were less appropriate and indeed was a serious obstruction when applied to the management of innovation. The attitude towards risk inherent in an engineering culture, with its understandable concern with reliability, resulted in an inappropriate cautious approach to the management of innovation.

The dominance of an engineering mindset also resulted in excessive concern for technological innovation at the expense of market-driven innovations, and placed excessive emphasis on product innovation at the expense of channel or process innovations. It also meant that value was placed on attention to detail rather than on an intuitive, far-sighted, approach. In unsuccessful innovators, innovation was limited by the dominance of historically-derived mindsets and values which permeated senior management thinking and culture. In NatWest, for example, there was a lack of urgency and, most of all, a culture which stressed the elimination of risk: 'People are comfortable with the way things were ... They find it hard to change, hard to see the need for change.'

Among the effective innovators, organizational cultures positively encouraged innovation, in three ways.

First, the organization supplies a clear and consensual sense of the direction of the organization so that people are able to see how they could contribute to the achievement of shared purpose. One manager in a good innovator noted: '... I think the role of senior managers is to create a shared vision in the organization. I think that would really channel this innovation and encourage innovation in a productive way ... It gets everybody aligned.'

Second, the cultures encouraged debate and discussion about the ways in which the organization manages innovation. It makes the organization's innovation performance discussible, which ensures that any blockages (and there are bound to be blockages) can be identified, discussed, confronted and resolved. In poor innovators although the development of innovation was, according to managers discouraged by features of the organization, managers were not prepared to identify and confront these obstacles in the organization – although they were prepared to complain about them to our researchers.

Third, a degree of discontent was encouraged; it was acceptable to be critical as part of a search for improvement.

In successful innovators, managers believed that people with good ideas would be able to find sponsorship and support. In unsuccessful innovators on the other hand, managers saw themselves as powerless in the face of organizational obstacles. These organizations also varied in the strength and extent of the structural obstacles, so managers in more innovative organizations had fewer barriers to overcome, but the difference is a moral one: in successful innovators managers stressed that anyone with a good idea *should* be able to overcome organizational difficulties. A senior manager in Nortel for example commented that anyone with a good idea who wasn't able to find funding and sponsorship for their idea should not be in Nortel in the first place. In GPT on the other hand, managers saw themselves as powerless in the face of overwhelming senior resistance and obstruction.

The two types of culture defined and constituted the individual innovator in startlingly different ways. In poor innovators the individual innovator was seen as a solitary, heroic, individual who through personal qualities of energy, genius, and bravery battled *against* and overcame organizational obstacles. In successful innovators the individual innovator was seen as a *product* of the organization: everyone was expected to be able to gain support and sponsorship for innovative ideas, or to be unworthy of the organization.

Discussion: two approaches to innovation – a danger to be controlled or an energy to be tapped?

Managers in organizations ostensibly committed to innovation as a strategic priority used a series of propositions to explain the level of incidence of innovation within their organizations. Regardless of the level of success of their organizations at innovation respondents showed agreement about the key organizational factors which determined the level of innovation.

When respondents used their theory of innovation to understand differences in the production of innovation they differentiated two polarized organizational approaches, one positive, the other negative. They think they know why organizations succeed or fail at innovation and they offered detailed analyses of the ways in which different organizational responses to innovation encourage or obstruct it.

They differentiated two categories of organization. One comprises organizations where the way innovation is defined and valued in the organization and the way the organization tries to manage innovation are unhelpful to the achievement of the sort of innovation the organization actually needs. In the other sort of organization, where managers judged the organization was more successful, the respondents argued that certain structures, processes and values were unhelpful and others helpful, and that on the whole their organization was more disposed to be supportive than obstructive.

In the less successful organizations innovation was seen as dangerous, risky, almost illicit, and somewhat self-indulgent. While recognizing – at least publicly – that innovation was important and strategically significant, senior executives by their actions sought to limit, to control, to corral and constrain it. If innovation was to be allowed or even encouraged, then it could only be permitted so long as it complied with the existing rules, discipline and procedures of the organization. Innovation must fit in with the organization, not the other way around. Innovation was so constrained and regulated that it was permitted little chance of realization or impact. This approach is entirely consistent in its own terms. If innovation is risky it must be regulated. If the risk of innovation is that it takes on its own momentum with little recognition of the needs of the business then the way to control this risk is to make innovation in every way possible regulated and controlled by the business and not the other way around.

Many managers were aware that operational aspects of organizations were intrinsically potentially obstructive to innovation. In the less successful innovators, the inherently controlling and limiting effects of structures and processes were held to be necessary and virtuous. In the more innovative organizations, innovation was defined as inherently exciting, challenging, playful and precious. If organization was potentially at odds with innovation then the organization would have to be changed; here innovation was seen as precious and mobilizing rather than as dangerous and illicit. All else followed from this basic difference. If the organization would have to be changed then the role of senior managers was not to preserve tradition but to help to deconstruct it.

These managers argued that the form of organization most conducive to innovation was one that minimized the factors that were inherently anti-innovation (hierarchy, bureaucracy, regulation and centralization).

This is not the first time that organizational approaches to innovation have been mapped onto a polarized dichotomy: the seminal polarity being that of Burns and Stalker (1961). An interesting question is how that model relates to ours. First, although there is certainly overlap (hierarchy/flexibility; centralization/decentralization), there are also differences: our categories refer more to 'soft' cognitive and cultural variables covering attitudes (explicit and implicit) towards innovation and organization, attitudes towards history and the nature and contribution of leaders. But the greatest difference is that at least in successful innovators this tension between loose/tight forms of organization was itself questioned and seen in a subtle and sophisticated manner. Control was seen as necessary. Too much looseness was seen as wasteful. The solution was not necessarily to replace one form of organization with another but to recognize the contribution of both types of organization and to switch between them as circumstances required.

In arguing this position managers moved beyond Burns and Stalker and echoed the debate about 'ambidexterity' – how to *combine* control and flexibility. In Nortel, senior managers explicitly stressed the need to ensure that the organization was minimally constraining and controlling and maximally empowering and liberating. In Oxfam, senior managers stressed the importance of a balance between the two forces of centralized control and autonomy and empowerment, as one manager said, 'one of the critical things is how you actually try to bring these two things together'. In Zeneca too, as a result of the chief executive's enthusiasm for 'chaos theory' managers accepted that if the organization was to be able to encourage innovation it had to find ways of overcoming some of the core aspects of organization itself: 'Zeneca needs to be much more like an amoebic sort of object than like a solid object.'

In both types, the role of the leadership was seen as crucial. As the CEO of Zeneca remarked, 'So where does innovation take place? How do you get creativity? How do you get to the edge? My job here is more to keep pushing in that direction. And that's a very atypical role for a senior manager.' As we have noted, this distinction between leaders who protected the organizational status quo and leaders who were prepared to radically reform the organization regularly in order to avoid the build-up of conservatism was one of the most important differentiators of all.

This analysis goes beyond the assembly, organization and classification of respondents' views. We also identify underlying patterns and themes. Our analysis of respondents' comments reveals two types of data. One consists of explicit explanations managers offered of the problem or successes of innovation within their organizations. The other consists of our interpretations of what was said or partially said or hinted at or assumed – the meanings and interpretations we derived and developed from managers' comments.

Below we summarize respondents' views in terms of these two levels of analysis. We have polarized the information to point out the contrasts. In reality, most organizations would be positioned along a continuum between these polarities.

The underlying factors are as important as the more obvious factors in that they support and legitimize these explicit factors, and supply a logic which makes them sensible.

The managers agreed on the elements of a theory of innovation – the dimensions they employed in analysing their organizations' attitudes towards and management of innovation – and on the qualities of these dimensions that would produce or obstruct innovation. These dimensions are listed in the left-hand column of Table 5.1. The qualities of each dimension that were seen to encourage or discourage innovation are listed in the central and right hand columns.

In the managers' view, organizations adopted one of two possible positions in terms of the key variables: broadly supportive or obstructive. Table 5.1 summarizes how managers applied their theory of innovation.

Table 5.1 *Managers' explicit theories of innovation applied to their organizations identifies two polarized organizational approaches to innovation*

Core elements of managers' theory of innovation	'Poor' innovators	'Good' innovators
Definition of innovation	Conventional, limited	Radical, all-encompassing
Value placed on innovation	Guarded, qualified, marginal, limited not strategically central	Very high, seen as strategically critical
Structures	Constraining, rigid, long established and strong divisions, centralized, hierarchical, stable	Changeable, flat, fluid, decentralized
Attitude towards structures	Defensive, justifying	Questioning, critical, destructive
Innovation management system	Elaborate, structural formalized, many-layered, thorough, cautious, reduce risk, focus on control	Informal, if present at all, to encourage innovation attempts, culturally transmitted
Specialist/generalist	Innovation a specialist activity and function	Innovation expected of everyone
Role of leadership	To protect against risks of innovation, to defend status quo, to pursue historic strengths, and market applications, to ensure that innovation is controlled and contained. Present	To ensure innovation occurs ubiquitously and continuously across all aspects of the organization. Future
Culture	Deference, compliance, fatalism, cautious	Autonomy, enterprise, assertive, positive
Operational versus innovation emphasis	Operational	Innovation

In the negative approach the organization (or its dominant coalition) adopted a limited and conventional definition of innovation, and was relatively limited in the value it placed on innovation. This was fundamentally different from how innovation was defined by more successful innovators.

The managers saw this as a causal relationship: organizations tended to design their ways of encouraging or controlling innovation in terms that were consistent with their view of its value.

The two types of organization differed in how they were structured, and these differences were seen by all respondents as supporting or blocking innovation. In poor innovators, senior managers viewed their organizations' repressive structures and systems as necessary to control the risky excesses of uncontrolled innovation; they stressed the historic and current value of existing structures and systems. In good innovators senior managers saw their role as mounting critiques and attacks on existing structures in the name of innovation. This suggests that critical to an organization's stance on and approach to innovation is its attitude towards radical change. Radical innovation requires at least the possibility of fundamental change. So senior managers' perceptions of *the need for change*, attitudes towards possible change and beliefs about the current status of the organization are significant for innovation since they determine the perceived 'legitimacy'/'illegitimacy' of innovation.

Poor innovators had elaborate formalized, structured innovation management systems the purpose of which was to reduce the riskiness of innovation; good innovators placed reliance on encouraging innovation (while making sure it remained 'visible') through a culture which encouraged experimentation and innovation. In poor innovators innovation was seen as a specialist activity and there was greater stress laid on the mythic individual innovative hero necessary to overcome organizational limitations.

The managers laid emphasis on the nature, role and contribution of the leader(s) of the organization. In one case the leader defends the organization against the dangers of innovation and protects the status quo against change: innovation if permitted, must accommodate to existing organizational structures and authorities. In the other approach the leader leads the charge on behalf of innovation *against* the organizational status quo. The role of the leader is to find the 'dividing line' between chaos and order.

Organizational cultures vary with the two very different types and missions of leadership: in the poor innovators, these cultures are conservative, stressing the values of the present and the past, wary of innovation and change, stressing danger over opportunity, seeing the organization as the ultimate authority and the individual as passive and powerless. In the good innovators, cultures stress change, emphasize the significance of the individual against the organization, stress enterprise and energy rather than compliance and obedience.

Underlying these explicit elements of managers' views of how their organizations encourage or discourage innovation we discerned a number of less obvious but crucially important themes. These are summarized in Table 5.2. The central column shows how these issues are defined and addressed in poor innovators; the right hand column shows how they were managed in good innovators.

Table 5.2 *Managers' implicit theories of innovation applied to their organizations identifies two polarized organizational approaches to innovation*

Core elements of managers' implicit theory of innovation	'Poor' innovators	'Good' innovators
Underlying attitude towards innovation	Dangerous, potentially improper, irresponsible, childish, conservative	Positive, celebratory, encouraging, radical
Consensus/differentiated definitions	Differentiated	Consensual
Recognition of role of balance, 'ambidexterity'	Conviction that one set of values should dominate	Search for balance, recognition that any 'solution' will fail
Innovating innovation	Traditional view and approach	Open, radical approach
Debate and discussion	Discouraged, not necessary	Encouraged, seen as central
Priority of organization or innovation	Organization, stability	Innovation, change

The underlying attitude towards innovation is crucial. How an organization views, defines and values innovation is the starting point for how it manages innovation. Managers argued that when innovation is obstructed this is rarely accidental or born of ignorance. It arises because senior members of the organization are not persuaded of the importance of innovation, are wary of it, anxious about it, define it too narrowly or negatively, are not prepared to risk the existing structures and values through innovative projects which may endanger them or render them irrelevant. It is not surprising that some firms fail to innovate when their senior managers regard innovation with suspicion and anxiety.

Senior managers in this study recognized the conflict between exploitation and exploration, but while some were convinced the benefits of innovation far outweighed the potential costs, others took the opposite view. In good innovators, managers stressed the need for balance. They eschewed the simplicities of the loose/tight, mechanistic/organic polarity and argued that both were necessary; that good systems and efficient organizational structures were critically important, but that staff empowerment and mobilization under clear strategic direction informed by strong shared values (which stressed individual responsibility) were also critical.

Finally, our material offers a contribution to current attempts at theory building in the areas of innovation, strategy and knowledge which stresses 'the key role of strategic management in appropriately adapting, integrating, and reconfiguring internal and external organisational skills, resources, and functional competences to match the requirements of a changing environment' (Teece et al., 2002: 183). Our study supports the crucial importance of these qualities; and suggests that the key factors underlying the development and deployment of such dynamic capabilities which underpin the development of innovation, are not only a range of organizational features, but an approach and attitude on the part of organizational leaders who, in successful innovators reject a polarized loose/tight dichotomy but stress the need to *balance* exploration and exploitation and to remain unsatisfied by the way this balance is achieved at any one time and to have the issue of innovative capacity a subject of constant open and critical discussion. And underlying this approach is the recognition of the value of innovation and a willingness to prioritize innovation above the status quo and to accept that it cannot be achieved by half measures. A serious and genuine commitment to innovation cannot regard it as an optional extra, a marginal value, a 'bolt on' extra. The ability to innovate is not something an organization *has*; it is something an organization *is*.

Acknowledgement

The research reported here was funded by a grant from the Economic and Social Research Council (ESRC) of the UK (grant number: L125251053).

References

Amit, R. and Schoemaker, P.J.H. (1993) 'Strategic assets and organisational rent.' *Strategic Management Journal*, 14(1): 33–46.

Burns, T. and Stalker, G.M. (1961) *The Management of Innovation*. Oxford: Oxford University Press.

Child, J. and Faulkner, D. (1998) *Strategies of Cooperation*. Oxford: Oxford University Press.

Christensen, C.M. (1997) *The Innovator's Dilemma: When New Technologies Cause Great Firms to Fail*. Boston: Harvard Business School.

Coombs, R. and Hull, R. (1998) '"Knowledge management practices" and path-dependency in innovation.' *Research Policy*, 27(3): 237–254.

Cooper, R. and Kleinschmidt, E. (1986) 'An investigation into the new product process: steps, deficiences and impact.' *Journal of Product Innovation Management*, 3: 71–85.

Cyert, R.M. and March, J.G. (1963) *A Behavioural Theory of the Firm*. Englewood Cliffs, NJ: Prentice-Hall.

Doughtery, D. (1992) 'A practice-centred model of organisational renewal through product innovation.' *Strategic Management Journal*, 13: 77–92.

DTI (2003) *Competing in the Global Economy: The Innovation Challenge*. London: DTI.

Freeman, C. and Soete, L. (1997) *The Economics of Industrial Innovation (Third Edition)*. London: Pinter.

Ghemawat, P., Collins, D.J., Pisano, G. and Rivkin, J.W. (2001) *Strategy and the Business Landscape: Core Concepts*. Englewood Cliffs, NJ: Prentice-Hall.

Gibbons, M., Limoges, C., Nowotny, H. and Trow, M. (1994) *The New Production of Knowledge: The Dynamics of Science and Research in Contemporary Societies*. London: Sage.

Henderson, R.M. and Clark, K.B. (2002) 'Architectural innovation: The reconfiguration of existing product technologies and the failure of established firms'. In M. Mazzucato (ed.), *Strategy for Business*. London: Sage.

Kanter, R.M. (1983) *The Changemasters: Corporate Entrepreneurs at Work*. New York: Routledge.

Klein, K. and Sorra, J. (1996) 'The challenge of innovation implementation.' *Academy of Management Review*, 21(4): 1055–1080.

Lant, T.K. and Milliken, F.J. (1992) 'The role of managerial learning and interpretation in strategic persistence and reorientation: An empirical exploration.' *Strategic Management Journal,* 13(8): 585–608.

Lant, T.K., Milliken, F.J. and Batra, B. (2002) 'The role of managerial learning and interpretation in strategic persistence and reorientation: an empirical exploration.' In G. Salaman (ed.), *Decision Making for Business*. London: Sage, pp. 155–78.

Lefebvre, L., Mason, R. and Lefebvre, E. (1997) 'The influence prism in SMEs: the power of CEOs' perceptions of technology policy and its organisational impacts.' *Management Science*, 43: 856–78.

Leonard-Barton, D. (1992) 'Core capabilities and core rigidities: a paradox in managing new product development.' *Strategic Management Journal*, 13: 111–26.

Markides, C. (2002) 'Strategic innovation in established companies.' In M. Mazzucato (ed.), *Strategy Business*. London: Sage.

Meyer, A.D., Brooks, G. and Goes, J.B. (1990) 'Environmental jots and industry revolutions: organisational responses to discontinuous change.' *Strategic Management Journal*, 11(4): 93–111.

Mintzberg, H. and Waters, J.A. (1982) 'Strategy in an entrepreneurial firm.' *Academy of Management Journal*, 25 (3): 465–500.

Moch, M.K. and Morse, E.V. (1977) 'Size, centralization and organizational adoption of innovation.' *American Sociological Review*, 42(10): 716–725.

OECD (2004) *Science and Innovation Policy: Key Challenges and Opportunities*. Paris: OECD.

Pavitt, K. (1991) 'Key characteristics of the large innovating firm.' *British Journal of Management*, 2(1): 41–50.

Powell, W.W. (1990) 'Neither market nor hierarchy: network forms of organisation.' *Research in Organisational Behaviour*, 12: 295–336.

Rothwell, R. (1986) 'The role of small firms in the emergence of new technologies.' In C. Freeman (ed.), *Design, Innovation and Long Cycles in Economic Development*. London: Frances Pinter, pp. 231–48.

Schumpter, J. (1934) *The Theory of Economic Development*. Cambridge, MA: Harvard University Press.

Schumpeter, J. (1942) *Capitalism, Socialism and Democracy*. New York: Harper and Row.

Schwenk, C.R. (2002) 'The cognitive perspective on strategy decision-making.' In G. Salaman (ed.), *Decision Making for Business*. London: Sage, pp. 179–91.

Senge, P. (1990) *The Fifth Discipline*. New York: Doubleday.

Teece, D.J. and Pisano, G. (1994) 'The dynamic capabilities of firms: an introduction.' *Industrial Change*, 3: 537–56.

Teece, D.J., Pisano, G. and Shuen, A. (1997) 'Dynamic capabilities and strategic management.' *Strategic Management Journal*, 18(7): 509–33.

Teece, D.J., Pisano, G. and Shuen, A. (2002) 'Dynamics capabilities and strategic management'. In M. Mazzucato (ed.), *Strategy in Business*. London: Sage. pp. 177–208.

Tranfield, D. and Starkey, K. (1998) 'The nature, social organisation and promotion of management research: towards policy.' *British Journal of Management*, 9: 341–53.

Tushman, M.L. and Anderson, P. (1986) 'Technological discontinuities and organisational environments.' *Administrative Science Quarterly*, 31: 439–65.

Tushman, M.L. and O'Reilly, C.A. (1996) *Winning Through Innovation: A Practical Guide to Leading Organizational Change and Renewal*. Boston: Harvard Business School Press.

Valetin, E.K. (2002) 'Anatomy of a fatal business strategy.' In G. Salaman (ed.), *Decision Making for Business*. London: Sage, pp. 40–61.

von Hippel, E. (1994) 'Sticky information and the locus of problem solving: implications for innovation.' *Management Science*, 40: 429–439.

Yoshino, M.Y. and Rangan, U.S. (1995) *Strategic Alliances: An Entrepreneurial Approach to Globalization*. Boston: Harvard Business School Press.

Part 2

Strategic Human Resource Management and Business Performance

The chapters in this second part of the book examine the links between human resource management and performance. In other words, these chapters tackle some fundamental and often-asked questions. Most notably: does practising SHRM actually make any difference? What impact does it have? Can the investment of time and money in SHRM be shown to be justified? What kinds of outcomes and impacts does SHRM have? The chapters in this part of the book address these kinds of questions in different ways and at different levels of analysis. They also come to some different conclusions.

The attempt to investigate the association between SHRM and business performance has been one of the most central themes – if not indeed *the* most central theme – underlying HR research during the past few years. Numerous research studies, conferences and articles have focused on this question. The search for the 'HR bundle' (that is, the critical mix of mutually-supportive policies) has been an especially enticing and attractive mission for sponsors of research.

Huselid's chapter is significant because it remains one of the best examples of a systematic, large-scale, survey-based attempt to test the impact of SHRM. Various practices associated with, or rather seen as constituting, SHRM are treated as the independent variable. These include employee involvement, the use of attitude surveys, training, systematic hiring practices, the use of performance appraisal and so on. The dependent variables are both intermediate behavioural impacts (such as labour turnover and productivity) and corporate financial performance. The analysis is also sensitive to issues of potential reverse causality and to internal and external fit. The results of the study suggest evidence of a positive link between SHRM practices and lower employee turnover, higher productivity and superior financial performance.

The study prompted many other attempts to test the association between SHRM and performance. Critics have suggested that there are methodological problems with the use of cross-sectional data and with single-respondent bias. Similarly, it could be argued that much of interest is lost by concentrating on the existence of a practice (such as appraisal) rather than the manner in which it is undertaken. None the less, the search for large-scale statistical evidence of the impact of SHRM will undoubtedly continue and this study is one of the classic examples of the studies in this genre.

Godard's chapter assesses research on the effects of high performance practices (HPPs). In effect, these are the collection of sophisticated HR interventions which Huselid and others have been seeking to evaluate. Godard's chapter adopts a much more sceptical approach to the claims of the SHRM/high performance advocates. Hence, the chapter offers an interesting antidote and riposte to the approach taken in the previous chapter. Godard begins with a careful delineation of the subcategories of high performance systems. He notes that one set of interventions emphasizes the inducement of high commitment among employees as the path to favourable outcomes, while other elements may simply involve various lean and work-intensification measures. To help untangle these elements, he focuses on the high-commitment/team involvement system – the type of approach often also known as mutual gains or partnership. The chapter then systematically examines the array of available data on the outcomes as measured in terms of economic performance, the implications for employees, and implications for unions. On each of these, Godard finds the overall evidence to be unconvincing.

The chapter is useful for two main reasons. First, because of its clear portrayal of the methodological problems that can interfere with conventional studies. Second, because of its analysis of the possible explanations as to why the HPP paradigm has so far not had the kind of widespread take-up and positive set of out-turns that might have been expected. On the latter, a range of possible explanations are considered and ultimately Godard comes to the conclusion that widespread adoption of SHRM and high performance practices cannot be realistically expected unless employers' initiatives are underpinned by a supportive policy and institutional context at national level.

Beyond the grand-scheme approaches which seek to assess the difference made by SHRM as a whole, there are other analyses which seek to examine the HRM and performance outcome link at a more individual practice level. One useful example of this middle-level approach is Chapter 8 by Storey and Sisson which investigates the evidence relating to the impact of performance-related pay. The chapter systematically assesses the assumptions on which performance-related pay interventions are built and then compares these with the research evidence about actual practices. In addition, the chapter also presents findings about the impact of performance-related pay schemes and notes their frequent failures to deliver. In search of the reasons for this mismatch between deeply-held beliefs and assumptions and actual out-turns, the chapter highlights a number of factors which are at play. These include internal contradictions and confusions of motive surrounding the introduction of these schemes. The chapter also describes the range of alternative pay structures.

The three chapters constituting this part of the book take a number of different stances in relation to the investigation of the HR–performance link. Together they reveal that the exploration of this linkage can be and has been attempted at the large-scale survey level in search of a test of the 'best practice' hypothesis; at the sub-stem level where different configurations or modes of employment can be tested in comparison with each other; and at the individual practice level where specific HR techniques can be subject to close scrutiny. It seems likely that research in the future will continue the search for evidence of the difference made by SHRM and that these searches will continue to be pursued at each of these levels.

6

The Impact of Human Resource Management Practices on Turnover, Productivity, and Corporate Financial Performance

Mark A. Huselid

The impact of human resource management (HRM) policies and practices on firm performance is an important topic in the fields of human resource management, industrial relations, and industrial and organizational psychology (Boudreau, 1991; Jones and Wright, 1992; Kleiner, 1990). An increasing body of work contains the argument that the use of *High Performance Work Practices*, including comprehensive employee recruitment and selection procedures, incentive compensation and performance management systems, and extensive employee involvement and training, can improve the knowledge, skills, and abilities of a firm's current and potential employees, increase their motivation, reduce shirking, and enhance retention of quality employees while encouraging nonperformers to leave the firm (Jones and Wright, 1992; US Department of Labor, 1993).

Arguments made in related research are that a firm's current and potential human resources are important considerations in the development and execution of its strategic business plan. This literature, although largely conceptual, concludes that human resource management practices can help to create a source of sustained competitive advantage, especially when they are aligned with a firm's competitive strategy (Begin, 1991; Butler et al., 1991; Cappelli and Singh, 1992; Jackson and Schuler, 1995; Porter, 1985; Schuler, 1992; Wright and McMahan, 1992).

Source: Mark A. Huselid (1995) 'The impact of human resource management practices on turnover, productivity, and corporate financial performance', *Academy of Management Journal*, 38(3): 635–72. Edited version.

In both this largely theoretical literature and the emerging conventional wisdom among human resource professionals there is a growing consensus that organizational human resource policies can, if properly configured, provide a direct and economically significant contribution to firm performance. The presumption is that more effective *systems* of HRM practices, which simultaneously exploit the potential for complementarities or synergies among such practices and help to implement a firm's competitive strategy, are sources of sustained competitive advantage. Unfortunately, very little empirical evidence supports such a belief. What empirical work does exist has largely focused on individual HRM practices to the exclusion of overall HRM systems.

This study departs from the previous human resources literature in three ways. First, the level of analysis used to estimate the firm-level impact of HRM practices is the system, and the perspective is strategic rather than functional. This approach is supported by the development and validation of an instrument that reflects the system of High Performance Work Practices adopted by each firm studied. Secondly, the analytical focus is comprehensive. The dependent variables include both intermediate employment outcomes and firm-level measures of financial performance, and the results are based on a national sample of firms drawn from a wide range of industries. Moreover, the analyses explicitly address two methodological problems confronting survey-based research on this topic: the potential for simultaneity, or reverse causality, between High Performance Work Practices and firm performance and survey response bias. Thirdly, this study also provides one of the first tests of the prediction that the impact of High Performance Work Practices on firm performance is contingent on both the degree of complementarity, or internal fit, among these practices and the degree of alignment, or external fit, between a firm's system of such practices and its competitive strategy.

Theoretical background

Limitations of the prior empirical work

Prior empirical work has consistently found that use of effective human resource management practices enhances firm performance. Specifically, extensive recruitment, selection, and training procedures; formal information sharing, attitude assessment, job design, grievance procedures, and labor-management participation programs; and performance appraisal, promotion, and incentive compensation systems that recognize and reward employee merit have all been widely linked with valued firm-level outcomes. These policies and procedures have been labeled High Performance

Work Practices (US Department of Labor, 1993), a designation I adopt here.

However, if this line of research is to be advanced, several serious limitations in the prior empirical work have to be addressed. Two are methodological, and one involves both conceptual and measurement issues. The first issue concerns the potential simultaneity between High Performance Work Practices and corporate financial performance, a problem exacerbated by the prevalence of cross-sectional data in this line of research. For example, if higher-performing firms are systematically more likely to adopt High Performance Work Practices, then contemporaneous estimates of the impact of these practices on firm performance will be overstated.

A second methodological problem is related to the widespread collection of data via questionnaire. Because survey respondents generally self-select into samples, selectivity or response bias may also affect results.

Systems of HRM practices and the concept of fit

The third significant limitation of prior work is its widespread conceptual focus on single High Performance Work Practices, and the measurement problems inherent in broadening the focus to a system of such practices. A focus on individual practices presents both theoretical and methodological dilemmas, as both recent research (Arthur, 1992; MacDuffie, 1995; Osterman, 1987, 1994) and conventional wisdom would predict that firms adopting High Performance Work Practices in one area are more likely to use them in other areas as well. Therefore, to the extent that any single example reflects a firm's wider propensity to invest in High Performance Work Practices, any estimates of the firm-level impact of the particular practice will be upwardly biased. This likely bias presents a significant limitation for a line of research that attempts to estimate the firm-level impact of a firm's entire human resources function, as the sum of these individual estimates may dramatically overstate their contribution to firm performance.

[...]

In short, although a growing empirical literature focuses generally on the impact of High Performance Work Practices, prior work has been limited in terms of the range of practices evaluated, the dependent variables, and the industry context. For example, a finding that systems of work practices affect turnover or productivity does not necessarily mean that these practices have any effect on firm profits, and the discovery that systems of High Performance Work Practices affect profitability begs the important issue of the processes through which they influence firm financial performance. Therefore, unlike prior work, this study included the full range of organizational human resource practices, examined those practices in terms of their impact on both immediate employment outcomes and corporate financial performance, and did so within the context of a broad range of industries and firm sizes. My initial summary hypotheses can be stated as follows:

> Hypothesis 1a: Systems of High Performance Work Practices will diminish employee turnover and increase productivity and corporate financial performance.

> Hypothesis 1b: Employee turnover and productivity will mediate the relationship between systems of High Performance Work Practices and corporate financial performance.

The second hypothesis will allow for one of the first empirical tests of a diverse theoretical literature positing the importance to firm performance of synergies and fit among human resource practices as well as between those practices and competitive strategy (Milgrom and Roberts, 1993). Baird and Meshoulam (1988) described the first of these complementarities as internal fit. Their primary proposition was that firm performance will be enhanced to the degree that firms adopt human resource management practices that complement and support each another. Thus,

> Hypothesis 2: Complementarities or synergies among High Performance Work Practices will diminish employee turnover and increase productivity and corporate financial performance.

A second form of complementarity, Baird and Meshoulam's (1988) external fit, occurs at the intersection of a firm's system of HRM practices and its competitive strategy. The notion that firm performance will be enhanced by alignment of HRM practices with competitive strategy has gained considerable currency in recent years and in fact underlies much of the recent scholarship in the field (Begin, 1991; Butler et al., 1991; Cappelli and Singh, 1992; Jackson and Schuler, 1995; Schuler, 1992; Wright and McMahan, 1992). Although no empirical work has suggested that firms with better external fit exhibit higher performance, the expectation that they should provides my final hypothesis:

> Hypothesis 3: Alignment of a firm's system of High Performance Work Practices with its competitive strategy will diminish employee turnover and increase productivity and corporate financial performance.

Fit versus 'best practices'

The internal fit perspective suggests that the adoption of an internally consistent system of High Performance Work Practices will be reflected in better firm performance, *ceteris paribus*: it should be possible to identify the best HRM practices, those whose adoption generally leads to valued firm-level outcomes. The external fit perspective raises the conceptual issue of whether any particular human resources policy can be described as a best practice, or whether, instead, the efficacy of any practices can only be determined in the context of a particular firm's strategic and environmental contingencies. Although prior work has yet to provide a direct test of these competing hypotheses, recent research finding strong main effects for the adoption of High Performance Work Practices lends credence to the best practices viewpoint.

The argument that firm performance will be enhanced to the degree a firm's HRM practices are matched with its competitive strategy is, however, compelling. In fact, the internal and external fit hypotheses may not be altogether inconsistent: all else being equal, the use of High Performance Work Practices and good internal fit should lead to positive outcomes for all types of firms. However, at the margin, firms that tailor their work practices to their particular strategic and environmental contingencies should be able to realize additional performance gains. For example, most firms should benefit from the use of formal selection tests, although the results of such tests could be used to select very different types of people, with those differences perhaps depending on competitive strategy. Likewise, the use of formal performance appraisal and incentive compensation systems has been widely found to enhance firm performance. However, each of these practices can be used to elicit very different types of behaviors from employees. In short, the process of linking environmental contingencies with HRM practices may vary across firms, but the tools firms use to effectively manage such links are likely to be consistent. The issue of whether internal, external, or both types of fit affect firm performance is central, and later in this chapter I provide an explicit test of these hypotheses.

Methods

Sample and data collection

A study of this type presents a number of data collection challenges. It requires as broad a sample as possible and at the same time requires that each data point provide comprehensive information on both organizational human resource practices and strategies and firm-level performance. Thus, my sample was drawn from Compact Disclosure, a database containing comprehensive financial information from 10-K reports[1] on nearly 12,000 publicly held US firms. Firms were included in the sample if they had more than a hundred employees and excluded if they were foreign-owned, holding companies, or publicly held divisions or business units of larger firms. These criteria yielded 3,452 firms representing all major industries.

Firm-level data on High Performance Work Practices were collected with a questionnaire mailed to the senior human resources professional in each firm.

Measurement of High Performance Work Practices

[...] Thirteen items broadly represent the domain of High Performance Work Practices identified in prior work (US Department of Labor, 1993). These items also represent important choice variables on which many firms differ significantly (Delaney et al., 1989). However, the substantial conceptual and empirical overlap among these items and my desire to adopt a systems perspective make determination of the independent contribution of each practice to firm performance impractical. Therefore, to uncover the underlying factor structure associated with these practices, I factor-analyzed each item's standard score, using principal component extraction with varimax rotation. Two factors emerged from these analyses; and I constructed a scale for each by averaging the questions loading unambiguously at .30 or greater on a single factor. Table 6.1 shows these results and the questionnaire items.

Following Bailey (1993), I named the first factor 'employee skills and organizational structures'. This factor includes a broad range of practices intended to enhance employees' knowledge, skills, and abilities and thereafter provide a mechanism through which employees can use those attributes in performing their roles. Specifically, a formal job design program and enhanced selectivity will help ensure employee–job fit, and providing formal training will enhance the knowledge, skills, and abilities of both new and old employees. Quality of work life programs, quality circles, and labor–management teams are all forms of participation that allow employees to have direct input into the production process. Likewise, information-sharing programs, formal grievance procedures, and profit- and gain-sharing plans help to increase the probability that employee participation efforts will be effective because such programs provide a formal mechanism for employer–employee communication on work-related issues. The Cronbach's alpha for this scale was .67.

The second factor, which I named 'employee motivation' (Bailey, 1993), is composed of a more narrowly focused set of High Performance Work Practices designed to recognize and reinforce desired employee behaviors. These practices include using formal performance appraisals, linking those appraisals tightly with employee compensation, and focusing on employee merit in promotion decisions. Conceptually, core competencies among employees are developed through selection, training, and the design of work (factor 1, employee skills and organizational structures) and are subsequently reinforced through the second factor, employee motivation. The Cronbach's alpha for the employee motivation scale was .66.
[...]

Table 6.1 *Factor structure of High Performance Work Practices*

Questionnaire Item	1	2	Alpha
Employee skills and organizational structures			.67
What is the proportion of the workforce who are included in a formal information sharing program (e.g., a newsletter)?	.54	.02	
What is the proportion of the workforce whose job has been subjected to a formal job analysis?	.53	.18	
What proportion of nonentry level jobs have been filled from within in recent years?	.52	−.36	
What is the proportion of the workforce who are administered attitude surveys on a regular basis?	.52	−.07	
What is the proportion of the workforce who participate in Quality of Work Life (QWL) programs, Quality circles (QC), and/or labor–management participation teams?	.50	−.04	
What is the proportion of the workforce who have access to company incentive plans, profit-sharing plans, and/or gain-sharing plans?	.39	.17	
What is the average number of hours of training received by a typical employee over the last 12 months?	.37	−.07	
What is the proportion of the workforce who have access to a formal grievance procedure and/or complaint resolution system?	.36	.13	
What proportion of the workforce is administered an employment test prior to hiring?	.32	−.04	
Employee motivation			.66
What is the proportion of the workforce whose performance appraisals are used to determine their compensation?	.17	.83	
What proportion of the workforce receives formal performance appraisals?	.29	.80	
Which of the following promotion decision rules do you use most often? (a) merit or performance rating alone; (b) seniority only if merit is equal; (c) seniority among employees who meet a minimum merit requirement; (d) seniority.	−.07	.56	
For the five positions that your firm hires most frequently, how many qualified applicants do you have per position (on average)?	−.15	.27	
Eigenvalue	2.19	1.76	
Proportion of variance accounted for	16.80	13.60	

Measurement of internal and external fit

Despite prior work arguing that enhanced internal and external fit will enhance firm performance, the relevant research has not specified the functional form that fit can be expected to take. In the business strategy literature, however, Venkatraman (1989) concluded that fit is most commonly measured in terms of a moderated relationship, or interaction, between two variables. For example, the relationship between a firm's competitive strategy and its performance could co-vary with the type of environment in which it operates. A second category of fit that is relevant in this context is the degree of match between two variables. Fit as matching differs from fit as moderation in that an explicit external performance criterion is lacking (Venkatraman, 1989). For example, one might argue that fit has been achieved if a firm's competitive strategy and its structure have been aligned, based on an a priori theoretical prediction, regardless of the outcome. In the following sections, I develop several alternative indexes to assess degree of internal and external High Performance Work Practices fit, using Venkatraman's categories of fit as moderation and fit as matching. Given the paucity of prior work in the area, however, these measures should be considered highly exploratory and the results interpreted with caution.

Internal fit as moderation

Internal fit among work practices could be expected to take the form of complementarity or synergy both within and between the employee skills and organizational structures and employee motivation factors. Thus, the first measure of internal fit I developed consists of the interaction between the degree of human resources policy consistency and the respective factors. Human resources policy consistency was assessed with this Likert-scale survey item: 'How would you describe the *consistency* of your *human resource policies* across any *divisions* or *business units* your firm may have?' (emphasis in original). Unfortunately, this measure is less than ideal for two reasons. First, it has restricted range, as firms that by definition do not adopt human resource policies consistently, such as holding companies, were excluded from the sample. Secondly, because the two factor scales were based on the proportions of coverage of exempt and nonexempt employees throughout a firm, a firm with a high score on these variables must have widely adopted each practice.

The second measure of internal fit as moderation I adopted consists of the interaction between these two measures. Based on the assumption that the returns from investments in employee skills and organizational structures will be higher to the extent that firms have also devoted significant resources to employee motivation, this measure provides a straightforward test of the magnitude of any such returns. This scale is superior to the first internal fit-as-moderation measure in that it does not exhibit the psychometric problems outlined above.

Internal fit as matching

The second broad category of internal fit consists of the degree of match between the two factor scales (Venkatraman, 1989). In the current context, internal fit as matching would occur if a firm were consistently low, medium, or high on both factors. As a test of the matching model of internal fit, I calculated the absolute value of the difference between a firm's scores on the employee skills and organizational structures and employee motivation scales (Venkatraman, 1989).

External fit as moderation

My first measure of external fit as moderation indicates the degree of correspondence between each firm's competitive strategy and its system of High Performance Work Practices. Porter (1985) provided the dominant typology of competitive strategies in the business policy literature; the types specified are cost leadership, differentiation, and focus. To provide an estimate of a firm's competitive strategy, each respondent indicated the proportion of its annual sales derived from each of those strategies. In view of prior work (Jackson and Schuler, 1995; Jackson et al., 1989), I assumed that a predominantly differentiation or focus strategy would require more intensive investments in High Performance Work Practices than would a cost leadership strategy. Thus, to test the external fit-as-moderation hypothesis, I interacted the proportion of sales derived from either a differentiation or focus strategy with scores on the employee skills and organizational structures and employee motivation scales, respectively.

My second measure of external fit as moderation is based on behavioral indication of the emphasis each firm placed on aligning its human resource management practices and competitive strategy. Specifically, respondents indicated whether or not they attempted to implement each of seven strategic human resource management activities for all employees (the Appendix lists these activities). I then constructed an index by adding the number of affirmative responses to each question ($\alpha = .69$). To test my expectation that the returns from investments in both factors will be greater when firms explicitly attempt to link human resources and business objectives, I interacted each firm's score on the strategic 'HRM index' with each factor score.

External fit as matching

Finally, I calculated the fit-as-matching variable by taking the absolute value of the difference between the Z score of the proportion of sales resulting from a differentiation or focus strategy and the respective factor scores (Venkatraman, 1989). This variable indicates the degree to which firms adopting differentiation or focus strategies also employ high levels of High Performance Work Practices and vice versa.

My expectation was that each fit-as-moderation interaction would be positive and significant for the financial performance dependent variables. Given that a lower score for the fit-as-matching variables indicates greater fit, I expected each of these measures to be negative and significant.

Dependent variables

Turnover

The level of turnover within each firm was assessed with a single questionnaire item, 'What is your *average annual rate* of turnover?' (emphasis in original). This question was asked separately for exempt and nonexempt employees, and the level of turnover for each firm is therefore the weighted average across each of these categories.
[...]

Productivity

The logarithm of sales per employee is a widely used measure of organizational productivity and was adopted here to enhance comparability with prior work (Ichniowski, 1990; Pritchard, 1992).
[...]

Corporate financial performance

Prior work on the measurement of corporate financial performance is extensive. Perhaps the primary distinction to be made among the many alternative measures is between measurements of accounting and economic profits (Becker and Olson, 1987; Hirsch, 1991). Economic profits represent the net cash flows that accrue to shareholders; these are represented by capital (stock) market returns. Accounting profits can differ from economic profits as a result of timing issues, adjustments for depreciation, choice of accounting method, and measurement error. Additionally, economic profits are forward-looking and reflect the market's perception of both potential and current profitability, but accounting data reflect an historical perspective. Although there is widespread agreement in the literature that capital market measures are superior to accounting data, accounting data provide additional relevant information (Hirschey and Wichern, 1984). Moreover, accounting data are often the focus of human resource managers who must allocate scarce resources. Therefore, I used both a market-based measure (Tobin's q) and an accounting measure (gross rate of return on capital, or GRATE) of corporate financial performance.

Each is the best available measure of its type (Hall et al., 1988; Hirsch, 1991; Hirschey and Wichern, 1984).[2]

[...]

Control variables

The estimation models were developed to provide unbiased estimates of the impact of High Performance Work Practices on firm performance. Thus, the selection of the control variables for each dependent variable was based on a careful review of the prior empirical work (cf. Huselid, 1993), focusing on those variables likely to be related to both the dependent variables and the use of High Performance Work Practices. The controls for each dependent variable included firm size (total employment), capital intensity, firm- and industry-levels of union coverage, industry concentration, recent (five-year) growth in sales, research and development intensity, firm-specific risk (beta), industry levels of profitability, net sales, total assets, and 34 dummy variables representing 35 two-digit Standard Industrial Classification (SIC) codes. Unfortunately, there was no straightforward measure of firms' total wage bills available for inclusion in the turnover model. However, selling, general, and administrative expenses is a common income statement item that serves as a proxy for employee compensation.

Financial data were taken primarily from Compact Disclosure. I took considerable care to ensure that all data were matched to the same accounting period (1 July 1991 to 30 June 1992). Missing data were retrieved from *Moody's Industrial Manual* or the *Standard & Poor's Stock Price Guide*, where possible. Otherwise, missing data were eliminated listwise for each dependent variable. Stock price data were gathered from the *Investment Statistics Laboratory Daily Stock Price Record* for 31 December. Stock dividend and stock split data were gathered from *Standard & Poor's Stock Price Guide*. Capital intensity was calculated as the logarithm of the ratio of gross property, plant, and equipment over total employment. The five-year trend in sales growth and R&D intensity (the logarithm of the ratio of R&D expenditures to sales) and compensation levels (proxied by selling, general, and administrative expenses) were calculated directly from the accounting data. Firm-level union coverage and total employment were taken from the questionnaire, and industry-level unionization data were taken from Curme et al. (1990). Concentration ratios were calculated by dividing the sum of the largest four firms' sales within each industry by the total sales for that industry. The systematic component in the variability of a firm's stock price (systematic risk, or beta) was calculated using the Center for Research on Stock Prices (CRSP) database and a 250-day period. Initially, betas were only available for 543 firms. Using an auxiliary regression equation, I inputed data for the missing observations ($R^2 = .40$).

Results

Table 6.2 presents means, standard deviations, and correlations. The employee skills and organizational structures and employee motivation scales reflect an average of standard scores, so their means are very near zero. Turnover averaged 18.36 per cent per year, and the logarithm of the productivity averaged 12.05, or annual sales of $171,099 per employee. The mean q was .46, and the average annual gross rate of return was 5.10 per cent. This value for q ($e^{.46} = 1.58$) implies that the market value of the average firm was 58 per cent greater than the current replacement cost of its assets. This result indicates that managements were generally working in the interest of the shareholders to increase the value of their equity. A GRATE value of 5.10 implies that each dollar invested in capital stock generates five cents in annual cash flow. Each of these values is consistent with the results of prior work (Becker and Olson, 1992; Hirsch, 1991). Average total employment was 4,413 (the logarithm of this variable was used in all subsequent analyses); firm-level unionization averaged 11.34 per cent; and industry-level unionization averaged 13.97 per cent. Total employment and union coverage were lower than in most prior work in this area, primarily because previous research has focused on the manufacturing sector, which is more heavily unionized. Finally, as expected, the employee skills and organizational structures scale was negatively related to turnover, while both scales were positively related to productivity and corporate financial performance.

Tables 6.3 through 6.6 present the regression analysis results for Hypotheses 1a and 1b. The first equation in each table contains the first factor scale, employee skills and organizational structures, the second equation contains the employee motivation scale, and the third equation contains both. These analyses provide some indication of the sensitivity of the findings to my specification and a very rough estimate of the degree of bias associated with a focus on individual facets of High Performance Work Practices. As a test of Hypothesis 1b, in the fourth equation in Tables 6.5 and 6.6 I added turnover and productivity to the models for Tobin's q and GRATE.

Turnover

Table 6.3 shows the regression results for turnover. Each equation reached significance at conventional levels, and the control variables generally had the expected signs and significance levels. Although employee skills and organizational structures were consistently negative and significant, employee motivation was not significant in either model. This result is less surprising when it is recognized that the use of incentive compensation

Table 6.2 *Means, standard deviations, and correlations*[a]

Variables	Means	sd.	1	2	3	4	5	6	7	8	9	10	11	12	13	14	15	16	17
1. Turnover	18.36	21.87																	
2. Productivity	12.05	0.99	−.24																
3. Tobin's q	0.46	1.64	−.10	.07															
4. Gross rate of return on assets	5.10	23.00	−.03	.15	.35														
5. Employee skills & organizational structures	0.02	0.52	−.08	.06	.09	.13													
6. Employee motivation	0.00	0.78	.04	.03	.20	.01	.15												
7. Total employment	4,412.80	18,967.45	.13	−.22	.02	.12	.18	−.15											
8. Capital intensity	3.96	1.32	−.29	.48	−.11	.02	.05	−.23	−.01										
9. Firm union coverage	11.34	24.28	−.14	.05	−.09	.02	−.05	−.51	.21	.29									
10. Industry union coverage	13.97	13.55	−.22	.11	−.11	.00	.04	−.36	.19	.40	.36								
11. Concentration ratio	0.38	0.25	.05	−.15	−.03	−.14	−.08	−.12	.17	.02	.08	.16							
12. Sales growth	0.61	1.08	.06	.06	.13	.01	−.03	.12	−.02	−.04	−.16	−.03	.10						
13. R&D intensity	0.03	0.06	−.09	−.01	.10	−.11	−.01	.18	−.14	.06	−.12	−.12	.03	.04					
14. Systematic risk	1.06	0.32	.09	−.08	.05	−.05	.00	.19	.06	−.23	−.18	−.20	.08	.09	.10				
15. Selling, general & administrative expenses[b]	286.54	1,622.02	−.02	.31	.09	.18	.23	.00	.77	.21	.16	.13	.00	−.11	−.01				
16. HRM policy consistency	4.54	1.10	−.10	−.04	.01	.04	.14	.23	−.12	−.06	−.12	−.07	−.08	.00	.03	−.03	−.08		
17. Differentiation/focus	−0.01	1.02	−.03	−.10	.12	−.02	.05	.18	−.03	−.13	−.15	−.15	.00	.01	.10	.06	.01	.05	
18. Strategic HRM index	3.36	1.98	−.02	.01	.00	.08	.33	.06	.25	−.01	.08	.01	−.04	.01	−.04	.07	.24	.05	.05

[a] $N = 816$. All correlations greater than or equal to .05 are significant at the .05 level; those > .07 are significant at the .01 level, and those > .10 are significant at the .001 level (one-tailed tests). Raw means are reported for total employment and selling, general, and administrative expenses to ease interpretation. The logarithms for these variables are used in all subsequent analyses.
[b] In millions of dollars.

Table 6.3 *Results of regression analysis for turnover*

Variables	Model I		Model 2		Model 3	
	b	**s.e.**	**b**	**s.e.**	**b**	**s.e.**
Constant	44.965***	9.418	46.363***	9.420	44.758***	9.486
Logarithm of total employment	2.656***	0.772	2.507***	0.778	2.637***	0.783
Capital intensity	−2.229***	0.659	−2.279***	0.663	−2.240***	0.663
Firm union coverage	−0.088***	0.029	−0.089***	0.032	−0.090***	0.032
Industry union coverage	0.222***	0.080	−0.225***	0.080	−0.222***	0.080
Concentration ratio	−1.376	3.611	−1.369	3.617	−1.360	3.615
Sales growth	0.329	0.592	0.362	0.592	0.332	0.593
R&D/sales	−3.509	11.298	−3.211	11.409	−3.278	11.403
Systematic risk	1.490	2.158	1.577	2.177	1.532	2.176
Selling, general, & administrative expenses	−2.168***	0.749	−2.175***	0.763	−2.145***	0.763
Employee skills & organizational structures	−1.769*	1.245			−1.743*	1.258
Employee motivation			−0.359	1.036	−0.162	1.045
R^2	0.385***		0.383***		0.385***	
ΔR^2	0.002[a]		0.120[a]		0.002[a]	
F for ΔR^2	2.017		0.730		1.020	
N	855		855		855	

[a] These statistics reflect the incremental variance accounted for when employee skills and organizational structures and employee motivation, respectively, are added to the complete specification for each model. The impact of High Performance Work Practices on the dependent variable is underestimated by this statistic because the assumptions that the independent variables are orthogonal and have been entered on the basis of a clear causal ordering are not appropriate in the current study. This caveat applies to all reported results.

* $p < .10$, one-tailed test
** $p < .05$, one-tailed test
*** $p < .01$, one-tailed test

systems may actually encourage employees who are performing poorly to leave a firm.

I next estimated the practical significance of the impact of High Performance Work Practices on turnover, from the results of the third equation shown in Table 6.3. With all other variables held at their means, firms with employee skills and organizational structures and employee motivation scores three standard deviations below the mean exhibited 21.48 per cent turnover, but firms with scores three standard deviations above the mean had 15.36 per cent turnover. This 40 per cent decrease of course would be the maximum expected effect of High Performance Work Practices, because it implies that a firm has moved from the total absence of any effective human resource programs to complete participation across all dimensions. A more representative estimate can be made by calculating the effect of a one-standard-deviation increase in each practice scale on turnover. Each such increase reduced turnover 1.30 raw percentage points, or 7.05 per cent relative to the mean. Considering that this model controls for firm size, the impact of unions, and employee compensation (selling, general, and administrative expenses), this effect is practically as well as statistically significant. In fact, this specification provides a highly restrictive test of the impact of High Performance Work Practices on turnover, as the inclusion of selling, general, and administrative expenses controls not only for employee wage levels but also for any direct costs associated with the implementation of these practices. Removing this variable and thus allowing the effect of High Performance Work Practices on compensation to be reflected in the direct effect of such practices increased the magnitude of their impact on turnover by more than 20 per cent.

Productivity

Table 6.4 presents the regression results for productivity. As above, each equation reached significance at conventional levels, and the control variables generally had the expected signs and significance levels. When employee skills and organizational structures and employee motivation were entered individually (models 4 and 5), each was positive and significant at conventional levels. In model 6, which includes both employee skills and organizational structures and employee motivation, only the coefficient for the later remained significant. This finding graphically demonstrates the need to adopt a system perspective in evaluating the links between High Performance Work Practices and firm-level outcomes and the way in which focusing on a subset of human resources management practices may overstate their effects. In fact, these analyses are likely to understate the biases associated with a focus on individual High Performance Work Practices, as I focus here on the impact of omitting an entire facet of these practices, rather than a single practice.

To estimate the practical significance of the impact of High Performance Work Practices on productivity, I next calculated the impact of a one-standard-deviation increase in each practices scale on the numerator of productivity (net sales) while holding total employment and all other variables at their means. These analyses were based on model 6 from Table 6.4. The findings indicate that each one-standard-deviation increase raises sales an average of $27,044 per employee. This substantial figure represents nearly 16 per cent of the mean sales per employee ($171,099). However, this is a

Table 6.4 *Results of regression analysis for productivity*

Variables	Model 4 b	Model 4 s.e.	Model 5 b	Model 5 s.e.	Model 6 b	Model 6 s.e.
Constant	10.919***	0.227	10.899***	0.225	10.899***	0.225
Logarithm of total employment	−0.123***	0.018	−0.119***	0.017	−0.123***	0.018
Capital intensity	0.399***	0.025	0.404***	0.025	0.403***	0.024
Firm union coverage	0.000	0.001	0.001	0.001	0.001	0.001
Industry union coverage	0.001	0.003	0.001	0.003	0.000	0.003
Concentration ratio	−0.240*	0.146	−0.251**	0.145	−0.251*	0.145
Sales growth	0.105***	0.024	0.100***	0.024	0.101***	0.024
R&D/sales	−0.771**	0.457	−1.004***	0.457	−1.002**	0.457
Systematic risk	0.083	0.087	0.042	0.087	0.043	0.087
Turnover	−0.003**	0.001	−0.003**	0.001	−0.003**	0.001
Employee skills & organizational structures	0.073*	0.050			0.046	0.051
Employee motivation			0.160***	0.041	0.154***	0.041
R^2	0.490***		0.498***		0.498***	
ΔR^2	0.001[a]		0.010[a]		0.010[a]	
F for ΔR^2	2.100		15.448***		8.136***	
N	855		855		855	

[a] These statistics reflect the incremental variance accounted for when employee skills and organizational structures and employee motivation, respectively, are added to the complete specification for each model. The impact of High Performance Work Practices on the dependent variable is underestimated by this statistic because the assumptions that the independent variables are orthogonal and have been entered on the basis of a clear causal ordering are not appropriate in the current study. This caveat applies to all reported results.

* $p < .10$, one-tailed test
** $p < .05$, one-tailed test
*** $p < .01$, one-tailed test

single-period estimate, and spending on High Performance Work Practices should be thought of as an investment that can reasonably be assumed to produce gains for longer than a single year. If the effects of increasing such practices are arbitrarily assumed to accrue for a five-year period at an 8 per cent discount rate, the present value increase in sales will be $107,979 per employee. It should be noted that the assumption underlying this spec-ification is that High Performance Work Practices increase sales for a fixed number of employees rather than increase efficiency (lower employment) given a constant level of sales. Otherwise identical specifications that modeled sales as a function of total employment produced very similar results.

Corporate financial performance

Table 6.5 presents the results for Tobin's q, and Table 6.6 shows the same specifications for the gross rate of return on assets. Each equation reached significance at conventional levels, and the control variables generally had the expected signs and significance levels. The results for q showed the employee skills and organizational structures and employee motivation scales to be significant in each equation. For GRATE, employee skills and organizational structures were positive and significant in each model but employee motivation was not. Although the diversity in these results reinforces the importance of researchers' considering multiple outcomes when evaluating the impact of human resources department activities (Tsui, 1990), the structure of incentive systems in many firms may help to explain them. Given the numerous problems associated with the use of accounting measures of firm performance in incentive compensation systems (Gerhart and Milkovich, 1992), many firms have begun to explicitly link employee compensation with capital market returns. This shift may help to explain why employee motivation has a much stronger impact on the market-based performance measure than on the accounting returns-based measure.

I next assessed the practical significance of the impact of High Performance Work Practices on firm profits. To do so, I estimated the impact of a one-standard-deviation increase on the numerator of both Tobin's q and GRATE while holding their denominators and all other variables at their means. These analyses were based on models 9 and 13 from Tables 6.5 and 6.6, respectively. In terms of market value, the per employee effect of increasing such practices one standard deviation was $18,641 (relative to q). Such an increase in market value is not likely to occur immediately, however. A more likely scenario is that investments in High Performance Work Practices create an asset that provides an annual return. If one assumes (again, arbitrarily) that these returns accrue over a five-year period at an 8 per cent discount rate, then such an investment would provide an annuity of $4,669 per employee per year.

Estimates of the practical effects of increasing use of these practices can also be made on the basis of annual accounting profits. Relative to GRATE, each one-standard-deviation increase in High Performance Work Practices increased cash flow $3,814. These figures are remarkably close to the five-year annuity values calculated above.

Summary of financial performance results

In short, although there is strong support for the hypotheses predicting that High Performance Work Practices will affect firm performance and important

Table 6.5 *Results of regression analysis results for Tobin's q*

Variables	Model 7 b	Model 7 s.e.	Model 8 b	Model 8 s.e.	Model 9 b	Model 9 s.e.	Model 10 b	Model 10 s.e.
Constant	0.672*	0.505	0.515	0.495	0.642	0.502	-2.166*	0.995
Log of total employment	0.065**	0.040	0.082**	0.039	0.067**	0.040	0.106***	0.041
Capital intensity	-0.125***	0.054	-0.115**	0.054	-0.119**	0.054	-0.251***	0.063
Firm union coverage	0.000	0.002	0.004	0.003	0.004*	0.003	0.003	0.003
Industry union coverage	-0.002	0.007	-0.003	0.007	-0.003	0.007	-0.005	0.007
Concentration ratio	-0.443*	0.326	-0.469*	0.325	-0.471*	0.324	-0.400	0.321
Sales growth	0.205***	0.053	0.195***	0.053	0.198***	0.054	0.172***	0.054
R&D/sales	2.354***	1.009	1.935***	1.013	1.937**	1.013	2.198**	1.005
Systematic risk	-0.039	0.194	-0.115	0.194	-0.112	0.194	-0.099	0.192
Employee skills & organizational structures	0.215*	0.113			0.165*	0.113	0.139	0.112
Employee motivation			0.297***	0.090	0.277***	0.091	0.227***	0.091
Turnover							-0.007***	0.003
Productivity							0.271***	0.078
R^2	0.138***		0.146***		0.148***		0.167***	
ΔR^2	0.004[a]		0.012[a]		0.014[a]		0.033[a]	
F for ΔR^2	3.635*		10.842***		6.483***		7.781***	
N	826		826		826		826	

[a] These statistics reflect the incremental variance accounted for when employee skills and organizational structures, employee motivation, turnover, and productivity, respectively, are added to the complete specification for each model. The impact of High Performance Work Practices on the dependent variable is underestimated by this statistic because the assumptions that the independent variables are orthogonal and have been entered on the basis of a clear causal ordering are not appropriate in the current study.

* $p < .10$, one-tailed test

** $p < .05$, one-tailed test

*** $p < .01$, one-tailed test

Table 6.6 Results of regression analysis for gross rate of return on assets (GRATE)

Variables	Model 11 b	Model 11 s.e.	Model 12 b	Model 12 s.e.	Model 13 b	Model 13 s.e.	Model 14 b	Model 14 s.e.
Constant	-0.126**	0.072	-0.159**	0.072	-0.125***	0.072	-0.588***	0.140
Log of total employment	0.019***	0.006	0.023***	0.006	0.019***	0.006	0.025***	0.006
Capital intensity	0.011*	0.007	0.012*	0.008	0.011*	0.008	-0.009	0.009
Firm union coverage	0.000	0.000	0.000	0.000	0.000	0.000	0.000	0.000
Industry union coverage	0.000	0.001	0.000	0.001	0.000	0.001	0.001	0.000
Concentration ratio	-0.077**	0.046	-0.075**	0.046	-0.076**	0.045	-0.065*	0.046
Sales growth	0.008	0.007	0.008	0.007	0.008	0.007	0.004	0.008
R&D/sales	-0.213*	0.144	-0.202**	0.146	-0.201**	0.145	-0.153**	0.145
Systematic risk	-0.050*	0.027	-0.049*	0.028	-0.048*	0.027	-0.048	0.027
Employee skills & organizational structures	0.041**	0.016			0.043**	0.016	0.040*	0.016
Employee motivation			-0.003	0.013	-0.008	0.013	-0.015	0.013
Turnover							0.000	0.000
Productivity							0.044***	0.011
R^2	0.117***		0.109***		0.117***		0.137***	
ΔR^2	0.008[a]		0.001[a]		0.008[a]		0.027[a]	
F for ΔR^2	6.649***		0.680***		3.356***		6.157***	
N	826		826		826		826	

[a] These statistics reflect the incremental variance accounted for when employee skills and organizational structures, employee motivation, turnover, and productivity, respectively, are added to the complete specification for each model. The impact of High Performance Work Practices on the dependent variable is underestimated by this statistic because the assumptions that the independent variables are orthogonal and have been entered on the basis of a clear causal ordering are not appropriate in the current study.

* $p < .10$, one-tailed test

** $p < .05$, one-tailed test

*** $p < .01$, one-tailed test

employment outcomes, the results are not completely unambiguous. Notably, the significant effects found are also financially meaningful. Moreover, where these effects are meaningful their magnitude is consistent across very different measures of financial performance. For example, a one-standard-deviation increase in High Performance Work Practices yields a $27,044 increase in sales and a $3,814 increase in profits. The ratio of these variables (cash flow to sales) at 14 per cent is very near the sample mean of 10 per cent. And assuming that the market value of a firm reflects the discounted net present value of all future cash flows, the present value of these cash flows ($15,277 at 8 per cent for five years) is remarkably close to the estimated per employee impact on firm market value of $18,614. The point of these analyses is to demonstrate that High Performance Work Practices have impacts of similar magnitude on each dependent variable of interest. In fact, these results show a remarkable level of internal consistency, especially given the fact that they are based on measures of firm performance that are only moderately intercorrelated.

Sources of the gains from High Performance Work Practices

The next series of analyses examined the processes through which High Performance Work Practices affect corporate financial performance. Specifically, Hypothesis lb states that employee turnover and productivity will mediate the relationship between systems of work practices and corporate financial performance. Following Baron and Kenny (1986), I first regressed the mediating variables (turnover and productivity) on the practices scales (see Tables 6.3 and 6.4). The next step was to regress each dependent variable on those scales (see models 7, 8 and 9 in Table 6.5 and models 11, 12, and 13 in Table 6.6). The significant effects shown in each case are necessary but not sufficient conditions to establish that mediation exists. Finally, as an estimate of the magnitude of any mediation effect, I regressed the dependent variables on the work practices scales and the mediating variables. These results are shown in the final models in Tables 6.5 and 6.6. Here, the decrement in the coefficients for the employee skills and organizational structures and employee motivation scales as turnover and productivity are entered into the profitability equations providing an estimate of the degree to which the effects of High Performance Work Practices on firm performance can be attributed to these factors.

As expected, the coefficient on each practices scale becomes smaller once turnover and productivity have been entered into the models. The magnitude of this effect can be shown by calculating the proportionate change in the impact of High Performance Work Practices on corporate financial performance that can be attributed to the inclusion of turnover and productivity.

Although, on the average, the coefficients on the two scales fall by approximately 20 per cent each when turnover and productivity are entered into the models, the joint effect is to reduce the estimated financial impact of High Performance Work Practices on q by 74 per cent and on GRATE by 77 per cent. This effect is sizable and suggests that a significant proportion of the impact of High Performance Work Practices on corporate financial performance is attributable to either lower turnover or higher employee productivity, or to both. The fact that turnover and productivity are temporally antecedent to my measures of firm profits and that the contemporaneous estimates of the profitability effects were highly similar increases my confidence in these results.

Evidence of complementarity

The final phase in the analyses was to evaluate the influence of internal and external fit on the dependent variables. Owing to space constraints, I focus here on firm profits, but the results for turnover and productivity were similar.

Internal fit as moderation

The first measure of fit I developed was the interaction between the degree of human resources policy consistency and each of the scales measuring High Performance Work Practices. These results were uniformly non-significant. Conversely, the second measure of internal fit, the interaction between the employee skills and organizational structures and employee motivation scales, was positive and significant for both Tobin's q and GRATE.

Internal fit as matching

The internal fit-as-matching variable, which assesses the degree to which a firm adopts the same level of High Performance Work Practices throughout its operations, was negative and significant for GRATE but nonsignificant for q.

External fit as moderation

The first external fit-as-moderation variables reflect the interaction between the proportion of sales associated with differentiation and focus strategies and the employee skills and organizational structures and employee motivation scales respectively. These results were uniformly nonsignificant.

The second measures of external fit as moderation reflects the interaction between firms' scores on the strategic HRM index and the practices scales. With the exception of the interaction between this index and employee motivation for GRATE, these analyses were also uniformly nonsignificant.

External fit as matching

Finally, the fit-as-matching variables for external fit show the coefficient for q to be positive – in the unanticipated direction – and significant, but non-significant elsewhere.

In summary, most of the coefficients on the fit measures had the expected signs, and the interaction of employee skills and organizational structures and employee motivation was consistently positive and significant. But despite the strong theoretical expectation that better internal and external fit would be reflected in better financial performance, on the whole the results did not support the contention that either type of fit has any incremental value over the main effects associated with the use of High Performance Work Practices.

[...]

▋ Discussion

Prior work in both the academic and popular press has argued that the use of High Performance Work Practices will be reflected in better firm performance. This study provides broad evidence in support of these assertions. Across a wide range of industries and firm sizes, I found considerable support for the hypothesis that investments in such practices are associated with lower employee turnover and greater productivity and corporate financial performance. That my results were consistent across diverse measures of firm performance and corrections for selectivity and simultaneity biases lends considerable confidence to these conclusions.

The magnitude of the returns for investments in High Performance Work Practices is substantial. A one-standard-deviation increase in such practices is associated with a relative 7.05 per cent decrease in turnover and, on a per employee basis, $27,044 more in sales and $18,641 and $3,814 more in market value and profits, respectively. These internally consistent and economically and statistically significant values suggest that firms can indeed obtain substantial financial benefits from investing in the practices studied here. In addition, these estimates imply a constant level of investment in such practices each year. If an increase requires only a one-time expense (as perhaps could be the case with recruiting or selection costs), these values will be underestimates of the impact of High Performance Work Practices on firm performance. Moreover, these calculations only include a firm's portion of the gains from increasing use of these practices. Presumably, some of the value created by adopting more effective HRM practices will accrue to employees, in the form of higher wages and benefits (Becker and Olson, 1987). Since higher levels of High Performance Work Practices lead to lower turnover, and presumably greater employment security, there appears to be considerable justification for encouraging firms to make such investments from a public policy perspective.

The impact of High Performance Work Practices on corporate financial performance is in part due to their influence on employee turnover and productivity. The identification of some of the processes through which these practices affect firm profits helps to establish the plausibility of a link with corporate financial performance. However, some of their influence on firm profits remains unaccounted for, and the source of these remaining gains is an important topic for future research.

But despite the compelling theoretical argument that better internal and external fit will increase firm performance, I found only modest evidence of such an effect for internal fit and little evidence for external fit. These findings are in fact consistent with recent attempts to model fit in the organizational strategy literature (Venkatraman, 1989), and they are perhaps unsurprising given the preliminary nature of the measures of fit I developed. And given the substantial main effects associated with systems of High Performance Work Practices, one might conclude that the simple adoption of such practices is more important than any efforts to ensure these policies are internally consistent or aligned with firm competitive strategy. However, the theoretical arguments for internal and external fit remain compelling, and research based on refined theoretical and psychometric development of these constructs is clearly required before such a conclusion can be accepted with any confidence. The very large theoretical literature in the fields of human resources management based on the premise that fit makes a difference cries out for more work in this area, and the primary import of the current findings may in fact be to call attention to this important line of research.

Finally, the reader is cautioned to recognize the limitations associated with the use of cross-sectional data when an attempt to draw conclusions about causality is made. Although the use in this work of simultaneous equations, corrections for response bias, measures of current and subsequent years' profits, extensive control variables, and a large and diverse sample mitigate many of the traditional methodological concerns, longitudinal data on both High Performance Work Practices and firm performance are needed to conclusively replicate the findings presented here. But such data are extremely costly to generate and are as yet unavailable.

This caveat is not intended to obviate the central conclusions of this study, however. Although traditional economic theory would suggest that the gains associated with the adoption of High Performance Work Practices cannot survive into perpetuity (because the returns from these investments will be driven toward equilibrium as more and more firms make them), the substantial variance in the HRM practices adopted by domestic firms and the expectation that investments in such practices help to create firm-specific human capital that is difficult to imitate suggest that, at least in the near term, such returns are available for the taking.

Appendix: Components of the Strategic Human Resources Management Index*

1   Match the characteristics of managers to the strategic plan of the firm.
2   Identify managerial characteristics necessary to run the firm in the long term.
3   Modify the compensation system to encourage managers to achieve long-term strategic objectives.
4   Change staffing patterns to help implement business or corporate strategies.
5   Evaluate key personnel based on their potential for carrying out strategic goals.
6   Conduct job analyses based on what the job may entail in the future.
7   Conduct development programs designed to support strategic changes.

*Adapted from Devanna et al. (1982).

Notes

1   10-K reprints are informational documents filed with the Securities and Exchange Commission.
2   A particular focus of this chapter concerns estimation of the financial impact of HRM practices. Huselid uses two measures of financial performance: Tobin's q and GRATE. Tobin's q is the ratio of the market value of a company to the estimated replacement cost of its assets. It can be interpreted as a measure of the strength of competitive advantage held by a firm. GRATE (gross rate of return on capital) is the ratio of cash flow to gross capital stock, and is an accounting-based measure of return on assets.

References

Arthur, J.B. (1992) 'The link between business strategy and industrial relations systems in American steel minimills', *Industrial and Labor Relations Review*, 45: 488–506.
Bailey, T. (1993) 'Discretionary effort and the organization of work: employee participation and work reform since Hawthorne'. Working paper, Columbia University, New York.
Baird, L. and Meshoulam, I. (1988) 'Managing two fits of strategic human resource management', *Academy of Management Review*, 13: 116–28.
Baron, R.M. and Kenny, D.A. (1986) 'The moderator-mediator variable distinction in social psychological research: conceptual, strategic, and statistical considerations', *Journal of Personality and Social Psychology*, 51: 1173–82.

Becker, B.E. and Olson, C.A. (1987) 'Labor relations and firm performance', in M.M. Kleiner, R.N. Block, M. Roomkin and S.W. Salsburg (eds), *Human Resources and the Performance of the Firm.* Washington, DC: BNA Press. pp. 43–85.

Becker, B.E. and Olson, C.A. (1992) 'Unions and firm profits', *Industrial Relations*, 31: 395–415.

Begin, J.P. (1991) *Strategic Employment Policy: An Organizational Systems Perspective.* Englewood Cliffs, NJ: Prentice-Hall.

Boudreau, J.W. (1991) 'Utility analysis in human resource management decisions', in M.D. Dunnette and L.M. Hough (eds), *Handbook of Industrial and Organizational Psychology* (2nd edn), vol. 2. Palo Alto, CA: Consulting Psychologists Press. pp. 621–745.

Butler, J.E., Ferris, G.R. and Napier, N.K. (1991) *Strategy and Human Resources Management.* Cincinnati: South-Western.

Cappelli, P. and Singh, H. (1992) 'Integrating strategic human resources and strategic management', in D. Lewin, O.S. Mitchell and P. Sherer (eds), *Research Frontiers in Industrial Relations and Human Resources.* Madison, WI: Industrial Relations Research Association. pp. 165–92.

Curme, M.A., Hirsch, B.T. and McPherson, D.A. (1990) 'Union membership and contract coverage in the United States', *Industrial and Labor Relations Review*, 44: 5–33.

Delaney, J.T., Lewin, D. and Ichniowski, C. (1989) *Human Resource Policies and Practices in American Firms.* Washington, DC: US Government Printing Office.

Devanna, M.A., Fombrun, C., Tichy, N. and Warren, L. (1982) 'Strategic planning and human resource management', *Human Resource Management*, 22: 11–17.

Gerhart, B. and Milkovich, G.T. (1992) 'Employee compensation: research and practice', in M.D. Dunnette and L.M. Hough (eds), *Handbook of Industrial and Organizational Psychology* (2nd edn), vol. 3. Palo Alto, CA: Consulting Psychologists Press. pp. 481–569.

Hall, B.H., Cummins, C., Laderman, E.S. and Mundy, J. (1988) 'The R&D master file documentation'. Technical working paper no. 72. National Bureau of Economic Research, Cambridge, MA.

Hirsch, B.T. (1991) *Labor Unions and the Economic Performance of Firms.* Kalamazoo, MI: W.E. Upjohn Institute for Employment Research.

Hirschey, M. and Wichern, D.W. (1984) 'Accounting and market-value measures of profitability: consistency, determinants, and uses', *Journal of Business and Economic Statistics*, 2: 375–83.

Huselid, M.A. (1993) 'Essays on human resource management practices, turnover, productivity, and firm performance'. Unpublished doctoral dissertation, State University of New York at Buffalo.

Ichniowski, C. (1990) 'Manufacturing businesses'. NBER working paper series no. 3449. National Bureau of Economic Research. Cambridge, MA.

Jackson, S.E. and Schuler, R.S. (1995) 'Understanding human resource management in the context of organizations and their environments', in J.T. Spence, J.M. Darley and D.J. Foss (eds), *Annual Review of Psychology*, vol. 46. Palo Alto, CA: Annual Reviews Inc. pp. 237–64.

Jackson, S.E., Schuler, R.S. and Rivero, J.C. (1989) 'Organizational characteristics as predictors of personnel practices', *Personnel Psychology*, 42: 727–86.

Jones, G.R. and Wright, P.M. (1992) 'An economic approach to conceptualizing the utility of human resource management practices', in K. Rowland and G. Ferris (eds), *Research in Personnel and Human Resource Management*, vol. 10. Greenwich, CT: JAI Press. pp. 271–99.

Kleiner, M.M. (1990) 'The role of industrial relations in firm performance', in J.A. Fossum and J. Mattson (eds), *Employee and Labor Relations.* Washington, DC: BNA Press. 4.23–4.43.

MacDuffie, J.P. (1995) 'Human resource bundles and manufacturing performance: organizational logic and flexible production systems in the world auto industry', *Industrial and Labor Relations Review*, 48: 197–221.

Milgrom, P. and Roberts, J. (1993) 'Complementarities and fit: strategy, structure, and organizational change'. Working paper, Stanford University, Stanford, CA.

Osterman, P. (1987) 'Choice of employment systems in internal labor markets', *Industrial Relations*, 26: 46–57.

Osterman, P. (1994) 'How common is workplace transformation and how can we explain who adopts it? Results from a national survey', *Industrial and Labor Relations Review*, 47: 173–88.

Porter, M.E. (1985) *Competitive Advantage: Creating and Sustaining Superior Performance*. New York: Free Press.

Pritchard, R.D. (1992) 'Organizational productivity', in M.D. Dunnette and L.M. Hough (eds), *Handbook of Industrial and Organizational Psychology* (2nd edn), vol. 3. Palo Alto, CA: Consulting Psychologists Press. pp. 443–71.

Schuler, R.S. (1992) 'Strategic human resource management: linking people with the needs of the business', *Organizational Dynamics*, 20: 19–32.

Tsui, A.S. (1990) 'A multiple-constituency model of effectiveness: an empirical examination at the human resource subunit level', *Administrative Science Quarterly*, 35: 458–83.

US Department of Labor (1993) *High Performance Work Practices and Firm Performance*. Washington, DC: US Government Printing Office.

Venkatraman, N. (1989) 'The concept of fit in strategy research: toward a verbal and statistical correspondence', *Academy of Management Review*, 14: 423–44.

Wright, P.M. and McMahan, G.C. (1992) 'Theoretical perspectives for strategic human resource management', *Journal of Management*, 18(2): 295–320.

7

A Critical Assessment of the High-performance Paradigm

John Godard

Introduction

The high-performance paradigm has come to be promoted as 'best practice' for employers on the grounds that the practices associated with it yield performance levels above those associated with more traditional workplace and employment relations practices. According to proponents, these practices do so largely by enabling and motivating workers to develop, share and apply their knowledge and skills more fully than do traditional practices, with positive implications for the quality of jobs as well as for performance. In the field of industrial relations, many (e.g. Heckscher, 1988: 114–52; Kochan and Osterman, 1994: 141–68; Marshall, 1992: 307–8; Rubinstein and Kochan, 2001: 133–5) have further argued that their implementation also creates opportunities for union renewal, enabling unions to discard their traditional, adversarial role in favour of a new, partnership one. Thus, the high-performance paradigm is best practice not only for employers, but also for workers and, potentially, for their unions.

Under this view, the high-performance paradigm has seemed an ideal solution to public policy dilemmas that have faced western economies over the past quarter century. It has promised not only improved national competitiveness, but also high-skill, high-pay jobs, progressive treatment for workers and an end to adversarial labour relations. It would seem to have been especially attractive to government officials and policy elites, because it allows greater scope for state involvement than have the neoliberal policies of the past few decades, providing these elites with a renewed and expanded role. Moreover, it has

Source: John Godard (2004) 'A critical assessment of the high-performance paradigm', *British Journal of Industrial Relations*, 42(2): 349–78. Edited version.

in theory yielded a positive-sum solution to workplace problems, enabling proponents to address labour market problems not through stronger rights for workers, but rather through practices that also happen to enhance performance. Not surprisingly, therefore, this paradigm has proved popular in policy circles, often under the guise of a 'mutual gains' (Kochan and Osterman, 1994: 45–77) or partnership approach (see Guest and Peccei, 2001: 213–16).

Despite this paradigm's apparent promise, concerns have been raised as to whether, indeed, the practices associated with it have been shown to have meaningful performance effects and what their effects on workers and unions actually are. As argued in Godard and Delaney (2000: 488–93), there is a need to pay closer scrutiny to these concerns and to the possibility that there are more fundamental limitations to the high-performance paradigm than typically acknowledged by proponents. This paper in effect picks up where the Godard–Delaney paper leaves off, updating and extending the arguments of that paper. However, where the Godard–Delaney paper focused on the implications of the high-performance paradigm for industrial relations as a field, concern in the present paper is about whether this paradigm can really be considered to represent best practice for liberal market economies (the USA, the UK and Canada). I thus adopt more of a public policy orientation, assigning equal weight to worker, union and employer outcomes.

I begin by briefly identifying alternative variants of the high-performance model to be referred to in this paper. I then review and critically assess the relevant research on the implications of high-performance practices (HPPs) for employer performance, for workers and for unions. I find that the performance effects of HPPs may be more limited than has been assumed, and that their implications for both workers and unions are at best uncertain. Next, I explore possible reasons for these findings, first considering arguments suggested by proponents, then proposing an alternative, political economy approach, one that accounts more fully for the underlying structure of the employment relation in liberal market economies. Finally, I discuss the implications of the analysis, arguing that the promise of the high-performance paradigm appears to have been a false one, and hence that it is more a question of having state policies and laws that promote what I refer to as 'good' work and employment practices, ensuring quality jobs, progressive employer practices and meaningful representation and voice, rather than promoting an absolute, optimum model that fails to account for the institutional conditions of the employment relation.

The high-performance paradigm

A wide variety of practices have been associated with the high-performance paradigm (see Becker and Gerhart, 1996: 785). For the present, however, this paradigm can be defined in accordance with two types of practice: alternative work practices, and high-commitment employment practices. Alternative work practices that have been identified include: (1) alternative job design practices, including work teams (autonomous or non-autonomous), job enrichment, job rotation and related reforms; and (2) formal participatory practices, including quality circles or problem-solving groups, town hall meetings, team briefings and joint steering committees. Of these practices, work teams and quality circles can be considered as most central to the high-performance paradigm.

High-commitment employment practices that have been identified include: (1) sophisticated selection and training, emphasizing values and human relations skills as well as knowledge skills; (2) behaviour-based appraisal and advancement criteria; (3) single status policies; (4) contingent pay systems, especially pay-for-knowledge, group bonuses, and profit sharing; (5) job security; (6) above-market pay and benefits; (7) grievance systems; and others. Although the first four of these categories may be largely unique to the high-performance paradigm, the remainder largely represent traditional personnel practices and hence are not. However, proponents of the high-performance paradigm often argue that both sets of practices are critical to the effectiveness of high-performance work systems (e.g. Kochan and Osterman, 1994: 45–58; Pfeffer, 1998: 64–98), and they have been included in studies measuring the extent to which the high-performance paradigm has been adopted.

There is considerable variation in how HPPs have been adopted in practice (Godard, 1998a: 19–21; Geary and Dobbins, 2001: 3–6). But for the analytical purposes it is useful to distinguish between 'lean' and 'team' systems. Both may be implemented in the context of a quality improvement programme, which some view as critical to the effectiveness of HPPs (see Wood, 1999: 370–1). However, the former typically entails conventional supervision and a just-in-time system, while the latter typically entails truly autonomous teams and no just-in-time system (Appelbaum and Batt, 1994: 7; Berggren, 1992: 9; Shaiken et al., 1997: 17–19). It is also useful to distinguish between 'involvement' and 'intensification' approaches. While the former can be thought of as achieving gains through high employee commitment and hence by relying on high-commitment employment practices, the latter can be thought of as achieving gains through cost reduction and work intensification, and hence not by relying extensively on these practices (see Ramsay et al., 2001: 505).

These distinctions will be employed throughout this paper. As revealed in Figure 7.1, in combination they suggest four possible systems, each of which has some precedent in the literature. But what may be referred to as a 'team involvement' system, characterized by a team system and an involvement approach, is most advocated by proponents of the high-performance paradigm, especially those concerned with mutual gains or partnership. The analysis to follow therefore uses the term 'high-performance paradigm' to refer to this approach.

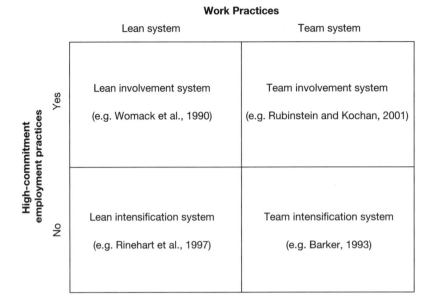

Figure 7.1 *High-performance systems*

HPPs and economic performance

Most proponents of the high-performance paradigm either argue or imply that HPPs are of virtually universal benefit to employers. A general assumption seems to be that this benefit increases with the number of practices adopted. However, it is often argued that HPPs are complementary to, and hence interact with, each other, so that their true potential is not fully realized unless they are adopted in combination or as part of a full-blown high-performance system (the 'complementarities' thesis). It is also sometimes argued that these effects are not fully realized unless integrated with or matched to a particular employer strategy (the 'matching' thesis). Studies addressing these and related arguments are too numerous and complex to assess fully here and have in any case been reviewed elsewhere. (For recent reviews, see Cappelli and Neumark, 2001: 738–43; Godard, 2001b: 25–7; Wood, 1999; Wood and Wall, 2002.) Thus, I provide only a brief overview, to illustrate the character of these studies and some of the issues and limitations that have been identified with them in the literature.

Huselid's initial (1995) cross-sectional analysis of 1992 mail survey data from 968 US firms, matched with Compustat financial data, remains perhaps the most noted study of the performance effects of HPPs. He explored the associations between two additive indices of HPPs and objective measures of firm performance, including labour turnover, sales per employee and an indicator of financial performance. Huselid interpreted his results as finding strong positive effects, even after controlling for a variety of alternative explanations for variation in performance. Other studies have reported similar findings, but typically within specific industries, such as steel finishing (Ichniowski et al., 1997), steel min-imills (Arthur, 1992, 1994), automobile assembly (MacDuffie, 1995) and apparel manufacturing (Berg et al., 1996). In addition to reporting a positive general association for HPPs, a number of these and other studies have also reported support for the complementarities and the matching thesis (Ichniowski et al., 1997; Huselid and Becker, 1997; Becker and Huselid, 1998: 75; Hoque, 1999).

These studies have been interpreted by proponents as providing strong evidence in support of the high-performance paradigm (e.g. Pfeffer, 1998: 31–62; Ichniowski et al., 1996: 312–21). Yet other studies suggest that high-performance systems are fragile (Clarke, 1997: 859) and that they are often scaled back or discontinued altogether after a few years have elapsed (Drago, 1988: 338–9; Eaton, 1994: 378–80), even in those very workplaces that have been held out as success stories by proponents (see Heckscher and Schurman, 1997: 325; Osterman, 2000: 97).

More important, recent studies have found little support for the high-performance paradigm. In an analysis of longitudinal data from the National Employer Surveys in the USA, Cappelli and Neumark (2001: 753–66) found HPPs to be associated with increased labour costs, to have weak productivity effects at best, and to bear no association with labour efficiency in manufacturing establishments. In an analysis of employer survey data matched with publicly available financial data for 260 US firms over a 10-year period, Freeman et al. (2000: 9–12) also found HPPs to have little effect. Guest et al. (2003), in an analysis of telephone interview data matched with published performance data from 366 British corporations, found little or no association between their index of HRM practices (which consisted mostly of HPPs) and objective performance measures once causality issues were addressed, despite positive associations with subjective performance outcomes.

In my own longitudinal study of 78 Canadian firms, I found that employment practices believed to complement alternative work practices had few positive associations with the perceived gains from these work practices, and that in some cases these associations were negative (Godard, 2001b: 39–40). I also found these perceived gains to increase most at low to moderate levels of adoption, and to plateau or even decline at high levels (Godard, 2001b: 42). These latter results are contrary to the complementarities thesis. Other studies, including the recent Cappelli–Neumark study, have been unable to find interactions between HPPs, again contrary to the complementarities thesis (see Cappalli and Neumark, 2001: 744, 760). Finally, a number of studies have been unable to find much support for the matching thesis. (See Wood, 1999: 386–96 for a review.)

More critical assessments of the performance effects literature also suggest that most if not all studies contain one or more potentially serious limitation. Limitations that have been identified across the studies include the reliance on single respondent data (Gerhart et al., 1999; Ichniowski et al., 1996: 309); the use of single items to measure complex work arrangements (e.g. teamwork: see Cully et al., 1999: 43); over-representation of traditional practices not unique to the high-performance paradigm (for example, Huselid included formal job analysis, grievance systems and job ladders – see Godard and Delaney, 2000: 410); under-representation of work practice items in measures of HPP adoption (Godard, 2001b: 46); inconsistencies in the HPPs included and how they are measured (Becker and Gerhart, 1996: 795–6; Godard and Delaney, 2000: 489–90; Wood, 1999: 403); possible cause–effect, selection and omitted variables biases (Becker and Gerhart, 1996: 794–5; Edwards and Wright, 2001: 574–6; Godard and Delaney, 2000: 488–9; Ichniowski et al., 1996: 305–7; Lewin, 2001: 276; Purcell, 1999: 29–31); and replication problems (Addison and Belfield, 2001: 357).[1]

These problems suggest that we should have limited confidence in research on the performance effects of HPPs. They also reflect the very considerable difficulties in attempting to establish the implications of a complex set of social relations and practices for performance outcomes (Purcell, 1999: 37). In particular, owing to the varied nature of HPPs and the difficulties in controlling for alternative explanations of employer performance, serious measurement and specification problems may be endemic to such research, possibly rendering it futile.

More relevant to the present analysis, however, are possible biases in how this research has been conducted and interpreted. As Wood (1999: 391, 403–4) has shown, authors have displayed a tendency to emphasize results that appear to support the high-performance paradigm while skating over those that do not. It is also possible that the expectation of positive effects has led researchers to engage in specification searches until this expectation has been met, and referees to evaluate papers more critically if it is not (see Levine, 2001).

More importantly, most workplaces in these studies have had only limited levels of HPP adoption. Because these studies have also often included a number of traditional personnel practices, it is possible that they only show that workplaces with such practices, coupled perhaps with a few HPPs, perform better than those without them (see Godard and Delaney, 2000: 490). Consistent with this possibility, studies that employ a classification method (e.g. Arthur, 1994; Betcherman et al., 1994; Cutcher-Gershenfeld, 1991; MacDuffie, 1995; Forth and Millward, 2004: 33) typically suggest that workplaces characterized by intermediate levels of HPP adoption perform almost as well as do high-adoption workplaces, although they both enjoy significant gains over their low-adoption counterparts. This may indicate that there tend to be diminishing returns at higher levels of adoption, rather than the increasing returns predicted by the complementarities thesis.

Many of the studies claiming support for the complementarities thesis may also be called into question. For example, Ichniowski et al. (1997: 309–12) report that three bundles representing distinct combinations of HPPs significantly added to the variance already explained by individual practices alone. But they do not report the magnitude of these effects, nor whether the one bundle representing the full adoption of HPPs made a difference independently of the other bundles. Becker and Huselid (1998: 75) report large performance gains at high levels of HPP adoption, but they appear only to have explored bivariate associations, and their measure of HPP adoption did not include any job design practices.

Similar problems may apply to studies claiming support for the strategy-matching thesis. For example, Huselid and Becker (1997: 14–17) report that an index of respondent assessments of HR effectiveness and alignment with strategy bore a significant association with performance even when controlling for an index of HR system practices. They also report that a cluster representing firms that were high on both indices accounted for more variance than did the two indices combined. But in the former case they did not test for interactions between the two clusters; in the latter they compared coefficients across separate regressions, one with their high-performance cluster and one with their two indices. They did not report whether their cluster made a difference after controlling for the two indices.

Finally, although the term 'contingencies' is typically used to refer to the complementarities and strategy-matching thesis, little attention has been paid to whether the performance effects of HPPs may also be contingent on more structural variables such as establishment size, technology (especially the capital–labour ratio) and market context. This may be important, because such a finding would suggest that the high-performance paradigm might not be universally effective even if complementary practices were adopted and firms adopted a matching strategy. In my longitudinal study of 78 Canadian workplaces with HPP programmes, I in fact found structural variables to be associated with managerial perceptions of HPP gains on a variety of performance dimensions (Godard, 2001b: 40–1). There is also evidence that the level of HPP adoption varies in accordance with structural variables (Osterman, 1994: 182; Godard, 1997: 217–25; 1998b: 45–6), which may reflect the implications of these variables for HPP effectiveness.

Overall, these concerns suggest that we should treat broad-brush claims about the performance effects of HPPs, and about research findings claiming to observe them, with a healthy degree of scepticism. There is little reason to doubt that HPPs are highly effective in some workplaces, and the adoption of at least some HPPs can likely contribute to performance in most workplaces. However, as I will argue more fully below, it is also likely that proponents not only overestimate the positive effects of high levels of adoption of these practices, but also underestimate the costs – costs that are often not reflected in the performance measures used by researchers (Cappelli and Neumark, 2001: 743). Even if high levels of HPP adoption can yield significant gains, these may be offset by such costs in a great many workplaces. As a result it may be that, for most employers, the full adoption of the high-performance paradigm often yields little or no overall advantage over traditional personnel practices with a few HPPs grafted on, a possibility that would seem to be consistent with a reading of available research results. Full adoption may even have negative performance effects for some or even many employers.

The implications of HPPs for workers

Under the high-performance paradigm, HPPs should have positive implications for workers. In theory, they give rise to both an improved quality of work life, with positive social and psychological implications, and higher pay and job security. I address each of these possibilities in turn.

Although a number of studies have reported positive social and psychological implications (see Godard, 2001a: 778–80), a number have also found HPPs, particularly alternative work practices, to be associated with high levels of work intensity and stress (see Landsbergis et al., 1999: 122–3; Smith, 1997: 320–22). Perhaps most noteworthy in this respect is Barker's (1993) analysis of autonomous teams in a US manufacturing plant, in which he concluded that workers as individuals felt pressured by strong performance norms, a circumstance he referred to as 'concertive' control. There is also evidence that, even where HPPs are initially received positively by workers, support tends to decay over time, as experience accumulates (Bruno and Jordan, 1999: 178–80; McKinlay and Taylor, 1996: 483–6; Rinehart et al., 1997: 159–79).

Much of the relevant research exploring the implications of HPPs for workers, however, has been limited to one or a few organizations, or has assessed the effects of one or a few specific practices (usually autonomous teams or quality circles) without controlling for other practices that might affect results, or has focused on the effects of an entire programme of HPPs rather than on how these effects vary depending on programme characteristics or the configuration of practices adopted (see Godard, 2001a: 778–9).

Yet there are a number of recent studies that do not suffer from these limitations. One such study has been by Appelbaum et al. (2000), who analysed data from 4400 workers in 44 US plants in the steel, apparel, and medical electronic instruments and imaging industry, reporting separate regressions for each. The practices included in this study appeared to have some positive implications for trust, commitment and satisfaction, and no implications for stress levels. Yet the results varied considerably depending on the industry and the dependent variable. Moreover, the authors included only four practices: autonomy in decision making; communication with others outside of one's work area; membership in a self-directed team; and membership in an off-line team. The first two of these have always varied considerably in workplaces, independently of whether a high-performance programme is in place (e.g. see de Menezes et al., 2002: 19). Thus, the results for these measures cannot be interpreted as reflecting the effects of HPPs per se. The two remaining measures – self-directed teams and off-line teams – made very little difference, and where they did their effects were negative almost as often as they were positive.

Drawing on the 1998 Workplace and Employee Relations Survey (WERS) data set, Delbridge and Whitfield (2001) analysed the associations between selected work practices, measured at the workplace level, for perceptions of influence over how the job is done, the pace of work, and the range of tasks, all measured at the employee level. They found that practices providing for broad employee participation in decision making (e.g. briefing groups, joint consultation councils) tended to have positive effects, and those focused more at what they refer to as the point of production (e.g. work teams, quality circles) to have only limited effects. Of particular note, they also found that workers perceived less influence in workplaces where teams had specific responsibility for products or services, even though such teams tend to be defining features of the high-performance paradigm. Whether workers could select their own leader also had positive effects for perceptions of influence over how the job is done, but not for the other two influence measures.

Harley (2001) and Ramsay et al. (2001) also report findings from the 1998 WERS data. Harley found that employees in workplaces with autonomous team systems reported no more or less favourable work experiences than those in workplaces without any form of teams. He chose not to report results for workplaces that were in between, with semi- or non-autonomous teams (Harley, 2001: 731). Ramsay et al. found that one of three additive HPP scales created from a factor analysis bore a positive association with both commitment and reported strain, a finding that is consistent with Barker's argument about concertive control. However, the former result was not statistically significant once a variable measuring satisfaction with management relations was controlled for (2001: 515). The two other scales also bore no associations, though they were arguably less representative of high-performance systems. Ramsay et al. did not address the implications of individual HPPs.

Freeman et al. (2000: 14–19) report results from a survey of 2408 employees in US private-sector firms with 25 or more employees. This survey asked respondents in what was labelled an 'employee involvement' programme their opinions about these programmes. Three-quarters of the respondents participating in these programmes stated that it would be 'bad' or 'very bad' if the programme were discontinued. These respondents also consistently reported higher levels of influence and job satisfaction than those not subject to such a programme. However, these differences were relatively small. For example, while 74 per cent of the former reported that they 'look forward to going to work', 63 per cent of the latter also did so. The measure of employee involvement used was also a single-item, dichotomous variable measuring whether an employee involvement programme was in place (reported in Freeman and Rogers, 1999: 167), and so did not allow the authors to establish whether the content of employee involvement programmes or the extent to which they had been adopted mattered.

Based on a 1997 telephone survey of 1000 British employees, Guest (1999) reported a positive association between an additive index of HPPs and one labelled the 'psychological contract', comprising items measuring perceived fairness, trust, and management delivery on promises and commitments. However, his HPP index contained a number of evaluative measures (e.g. 'serious attempt to make jobs … interesting'), introducing the likelihood of a percept–percept bias, and only one of his component items directly measured work practices. Moreover, his HPP index was statistically insignificant in regressions on additional outcome variables, including job satisfaction, pressure at work, employment security and motivation. Although he concludes that this is because high-commitment practices operate through the psychological contract, he presents no evidence to this effect.[2]

Using data from a random telephone survey of 508 Canadian labour force participants in 1997, I found an additive scale measuring respondent involvement in eight different alternative work practices to be positively associated with scales measuring belongingness, empowerment, task involvement, role stress, and ultimately job satisfaction, self-esteem, commitment, motivation and organizational citizenship behaviour. Yet these associations held only at low to moderate levels of adoption. At higher levels, they declined in magnitude or even became negative – despite possible selectivity biases. Moreover, consistent with the Ramsay et al. (2001) results, I found positive associations for role stress, commitment and motivation, associations that did not change at higher adoption levels. These results suggest that the positive effects of work practices taper off and even decline at high levels of adoption, but that corresponding increases in concertive control, and hence stress, do not.

I also constructed measures of team organization (autonomous teams, no JIT system), lean organization (supervised teams, a JIT system), 'post-lean' organization (autonomous teams and JIT), and 'traditional' group work (supervised teams, no JIT). Only traditional group work was consistently associated with more positive work attitudes and outcomes after controlling for other work practices. (The reference category was traditional individualized work). When I analysed the implications of specific practices and programmes for worker attitudes and outcomes, I found group work and information sharing (e.g. team briefings) to have positive implications, but team autonomy, team responsibility for a good or service, JIT systems and re-engineering to have negative ones. In particular, team responsibility for a good or service was positively associated with work overload, role stress and after-work fatigue, findings that are broadly consistent with those of Delbridge and Whitfield and of Barker.[3]

These findings tend to be supported by White et al. (2003), who analysed data from national surveys of British employees in 1992 and 2000 to assess the implications of working hours and selected high-performance practices for work–family balance. They found that high-performance practices tended to have a negative job-to-home spillover, although this finding applied primarily to appraisal systems and performance-related pay rather than to job design variables such as teamworking, which were statistically insignificant.

It is likely that the effects of HPPs depend on whether management adopts an intensification or an involvement approach. For example, case studies finding negative effects for workers have often tended to be in what Drago (1996) has termed 'disposable workplaces', in which workers are coerced to co-operate, either because employers are readily able to relocate operations or because of harsh market conditions. This may be especially true of the auto and auto parts industries, which have been the focus of many of these studies, and which the research suggests tends to follow an intensification rather than an involvement approach to work organization (Delbridge, 1998: 178–92; Fucini and Fucini, 1990; Garrahan and Stewart, 1992: 228–46; Graham, 1995: 222–36; Parker and Slaughter, 1995; Rinehart et al., 1997: 78–84). However, there do not appear to have been any studies exploring whether high-commitment employment practices, which likely signal an involvement approach, moderate the effects of alternative work practices on workers.

Although most research addressing the implications of HPPs for workers have focused on social and psychological outcomes, a growing number of studies have also addressed their implications for more objective outcomes such as pay and job security. Again, the evidence is mixed (also see Handel and Gittleman, 2004: 72–4). In an analysis of workplace level data from 2945 US establishments collected in 1994, Cappelli (1996) found TQM and work-teams to be associated with both wages and skill levels. In their study of manufacturing workplaces, Cappelli and Neumark (2001: 760) interpreted a finding of higher labour costs per worker as reflecting higher compensation levels. However, the only practices that were consistently significant were teamwork training and TQM; the holding of regular problem-solving meetings was significant in only one of four specifications, while self-managing teams and cross-training were not significant in any specification. In an analysis of his 1992 and 1997 survey data, Osterman (2000: 190) found the number of HPPs adopted as of 1992 to be associated with a higher likelihood of layoffs in subsequent years and with no real gain in wages. He also found that the HPPs in his study bore no association with wage levels. In an analysis of both workplace-level and individual-level data obtained from the US Bureau of Labor Statistics 1995 Survey of Employer-Provided Training, Handel and Gittleman also found little evidence that HPPs are associated with higher wages (2004: 90–4).

Using individual data from the Appelbaum et al. (2000) data set (discussed above), Bailey et al. (2001) found an additive scale consisting of their four practices to be associated with a 16 per cent premium in apparel and a 10 per cent premium in steel when workers with the highest scores on this scale were compared with those with the lowest scores. But they found no effects for those in the medical electronics and imaging industry. Moreover, as discussed earlier, two of the items in their scale cannot necessarily be viewed as HPPs. In this regard, Bailey et al. explored the effects of the two practices that can be so viewed – self-directed teams and off-line participation – in separate regressions. The former had statistically significant effects only in apparel (a 10 per cent increase), and the latter only in steel (a 2.5 per cent increase). They also found that the results for apparel suffered from an endogeneity problem (Bailey et al., 2001: 539).

Employing data from the 1998 WERS, Forth and Millward (2004) explored the associations between nine HPPs, measured at the workplace level, with pay, measured at the individual level. Of the nine practices, only job security and information disclosure bore positive associations with wages, and a simple additive index bore an association only at high levels of adoption (seven or more practices). When they categorized their sample into 'traditional', 'mixed' and 'high-involvement' workplaces, they observed an 8 per cent premium for high-involvement workplaces (compared with traditional), and no premium for mixed. Yet when they constrained their high-involvement category to include only those workplaces where teams appointed their own leader or could decide how their work was done, they observed no effect. They also found that the wage premium for their original high-involvement category held only in workplaces with a job security guarantee, and those workplaces in this category with a strong union paid wages that were 10 per cent higher than those without a strong union.

The Forth–Millward results seem to be consistent with my results addressing the social and psychological effects of alternative work practices, suggesting that autonomous teams may affect worker wellbeing negatively. They also suggest that practices long considered to reflect good employment, including traditional group work, job security and strong unions, may yield pay outcomes that are better than those yielded by the high-performance paradigm. However, the finding for mixed workplaces tends to contradict such a conclusion. Unfortunately, the Forth–Millward analysis did not include the various personnel practices in the WERS data set and so did not explore whether these mattered.

Overall, it would seem that the implications of HPPs, and especially alternative work practices, for worker pay and security is at best mixed, and that their implications for social-psychological variables is more complex than has been assumed by proponents. It is again possible that practices traditionally considered to yield positive outcomes for workers, such as traditional group work and information-sharing, are as effective as, or even more effective than, the practices most identified with the high-performance paradigm (especially autonomous teamwork). Although group work and information-sharing are associated with the high-performance paradigm, both hearken back to the findings of the Hawthorne researchers and so may not be viewed as in any sense new.

The implications of HPPs for unions

As noted earlier, many proponents have argued that high-performance programmes allow unions to develop a new role, where they effectively become partners with management in the pursuit of mutual gains. Others, however, have argued that they may weaken member support for a union (e.g. Fisher, 1997; Parker and Slaughter, 1988), because they provide workers with alternative, individualized means of exercising voice, and help to ensure fair treatment (see e.g. Taylor, 1994: 131). In addition, their emphasis on co-operation may undermine a union's essentially adversarial role and create a climate that is hostile to those with pro-union sentiments. Finally, a lack of adequate participation rights for unions under the law means that any partnership that is achieved is likely to be on employer terms and hence to prove unequal and unstable (Streeck, 1992: 326; 1995: 329).

Practices associated with the high-performance paradigm have in some (if not many) cases been used as means to avoid unions, especially in the USA. (Kochan, 1980: 153–81; 184–7; Kochan et al., 1986a: 47–80; Jacoby, 1997: 113–23). But the importance of this relative to other objectives is not always clear. In my study of 141 Canadian employers with high-performance programmes, one-quarter of respondents in firms that were less than 80 per cent unionized ($n = 70$) admitted this objective to be of at least moderate importance in the decision to adopt HPPs, and a third assessed it to be an outcome of these practices (Godard, 1998a: 26–7). However, 19 out of 20 respondents rated at least one other objective (e.g. cost reduction, quality improvement) to be more important than union avoidance. If these findings can be taken at face value, it would appear that union avoidance is often both an objective and an outcome of high-performance programmes, but rarely is it the sole or even most important one.

A sizeable number of studies have explored whether there is an a priori association between HPPs and union presence. Of these, only Huselid and Rau's (1996) study of US firms and Roche's (1998) study of Irish firms have found a negative association. The preponderance of multivariate research finds no significant association (de Menezes et al., 2002: 32; Eaton and Voos, 1994: 73–9; Godard, 1997: 219; Gittleman et al., 1998: 109; Osterman, 1994; Wood, 1996; Wood and de Menezes, 1998). However, it may be that non-union employers use these practices for union avoidance purposes only where there is a significant likelihood of unionization. This could be especially important in nations where weak labour law protections for unions make it easier to defeat union organizing drives through more direct means (e.g. threats), as in the USA, or simply to refuse to recognize them, as in the UK prior to the 1999 Employment Relations Act. Under these conditions, non-union employers may have less reason to adopt HPPs for union avoidance purposes. While HPPs may be adopted to avoid unions in firms subject to the threat of unionization, the number of such firms may be relatively small, thus lessening the chances of observing a statistically significant negative association. Any observed negative association may also be offset to the extent that union employers have as great an incentive to adopt HPPs as do their non-union counterparts, whether in order to try to weaken the union (Taylor, 1994: 128), to counter any negative economic effects (e.g. wage premiums), or to achieve more positive employee relations.

More direct evidence is provided by research exploring the implications of HPPs for union organizing and worker propensities to vote for a union. In their study of US firms, Fiorito et al. (1987: 124–5) found that, where these practices were adopted by non-union firms in the USA, the likelihood of a union becoming established was reduced. Another US study, by Kochan et al. (1986b: 498), found this to be especially true when the employer placed a high priority on avoiding unions. The Freeman et al. study (2000: 30) referred to above found that only one in four workers in workplaces with employee involvement schemes would vote for a union, compared with four in ten in workplaces without such a programme. In an analysis of employer–employee linked data from the 1991 US National Organizations Survey (NOS), Fiorito and Young (1998) found a modest association between an index of employer-reported HPPs and individual voting preferences, although their index did not contain any direct measures of work practices. In a subsequent analysis of employee data from the 1994 US Worker Representation and Participation Survey, Fiorito (2001) found the number of HPPs reported by employees to have negative but relatively small effects on voting preferences. Fiorito argued that both of his analyses suffered from important data limitations and might underestimate these effects. But if taken at face value, they point to modest negative effects on voting propensities.

As suggested above, concerns have also been raised about the implications of HPPs for unions where already established. There is some North American case research (see Allen and van Norman, 1996; Frost, 2000; Verma and McKersie, 1986; Verma, 1989) concluding that HPPs appear to harm support for a union if it does not co-operate, but to have neutral or even positive effects where it does. Roche and Geary (2002: 682–3) also found modest support for this position in their study of Irish airports.

Much may, however, depend on whether unions are actually provided with an opportunity to participate in the adoption of HPPs, and have sufficient power and institutional security to ensure that some form of meaningful partnership can be achieved (Roche and Geary, 2002: 662, 682). Otherwise, unions may find themselves undermined, an argument that appears to be supported by Kelly's (1996: 86) analysis of the fortunes of UK unions adopting a partnership strategy. Moreover, in cases where unions do not accept an offer to participate, it may be because of employer unwillingness to provide meaningful assurances or influence. A study of two UK spirits companies

(Marks et al., 1998: 220–3) finds evidence that unions may be marginalized and member support undermined if they decide to co-operate under such circumstances.

Research also suggests that collaboration with the employer can generate problems for local unions over time. For example, in the Saturn experiment in the USA the local union has suffered from internal tensions and conflicts (Rubinstein and Kochan, 2001: 80–99). This is especially noteworthy in view of the high profile given this experiment by proponents of the high-performance paradigm. A Canadian study finds similar problems in other workplaces (Wells, 1993). This study is unique, because it examined the implications over time of high-performance programmes for unions in five companies held out as exemplars in an earlier, federal government report (Mansell, 1987). Contrary to this report, the author found that high-performance programmes resulted in strains between the union's traditional role and the more co-operative one demanded of it. As a result, these practices seemed to survive only where the union was already weak. Otherwise, the union found it necessary to revert to its traditional adversarial role. This study also found that a few of the companies used their experiences with these programmes as models for establishing non-union workplaces.

It would thus appear that the implications of HPPs for established unions are unclear, although they may offer some benefit where unions are offered, and accept, a meaningful partnership role. Where a union is not established, the available research suggests that on balance HPPs have negative implications. These appear on the whole to be weak, and they are by no means unequivocal. However, anti-union employer practices appear to have become predominant over the past few decades. This has been especially apparent in the USA and to a lesser extent Canada, but it has also been reflected in the UK (Kelly, 1996), where employers have been unwilling (especially prior to the Employment Relations Act) to recognize unions where they are not already established (Machin, 2000: 642–3). Thus, even if HPPs were shown to have no negative implications for unions, it may be argued that this is relative to anti-union practices (i.e. practices to discourage unions), which have become the norm among employers. Regardless of the intentions underlying them, HPPs do not appear on balance to engender levels of union acceptance by employers traditionally considered to represent sound industrial relations policy. If they did, we would observe positive associations between HPPs and both union presence and organizing success, as ultimately reflected in increased union density. Yet this has not been the case.

The high-performance paradigm revisited

It would seem that support for the high-performance paradigm is at best limited. Because the available evidence typically addresses the average effects of this paradigm across all workplaces or workers in a given sample, it does not rule out the possibility that the promise of this paradigm has been, or can be, realized in some or even many workplaces. Indeed, proponents have identified such cases (Kochan and Osterman, 1994; Pfeffer, 1994). But it would appear that, on average, the full adoption of this paradigm may not yield outcomes that are appreciably more positive than those yielded by practices that have long been associated with good management, including professional personnel practices (e.g. job ladders, employment security, grievance systems, formal training, above-market pay), group work organization, information-sharing and accommodative union relations policies. Indeed, it is even possible that high levels of adoption yield outcomes that are appreciably less positive than traditional good practice. This is especially so with regards to the implications of HPPs for workers and their unions. Yet, even from an employer perspective, it is not clear that the theoretical benefits of the high-performance paradigm are on average borne out in practice.

Reinforcing this latter possibility is the apparent unwillingness of most employers to fully adopt HPPs. Instead, it would appear that most employers may be settling on partial adoption. For example, although Osterman's 1997 US survey of 462 workplaces with more than 50 employees found that 85 per cent had at least one of the four work practices asked about, and that 71 per cent had at least two, it also found that only 16 per cent of respondents had all four (Osterman, 2000: 186). Results reported by Gittleman et al. (1998: 105) suggest that the observed frequency of these practices may be more than halved when workplaces with fewer than 50 employees are included. Using data from the 1997 US Census Bureau's National Employer Survey of 3167 establishments with over 20 employees, Ellwood et al. (2000: 69–78) found that, although half had adopted at least three of the seven HPPs included in their study, only 8 per cent had adopted more than four, and only 1.4 per cent had autonomous teams, work-related meetings and job rotation for 50 per cent or more of their non managers. These results were largely unchanged from the 1994 National Employer Survey.

In the UK, the 1998 WERS revealed that, although 71 per cent had at least three of the 15 HPPs asked about, only 14 per cent had eight or more (Cully et al., 1999: 110). Moreover, while 35 per cent met the criteria for semi-autonomous teams, only 3 per cent selected their own leader and hence could be considered truly autonomous (Cully et al., 1999: 43). In Canada a 1999 Statistics Canada survey of 3142 establishments with over 10 employees found that, although half reported some form of information-sharing and a quarter reported problem-solving teams, only 10 per cent reported self-directed work groups (Morisette and Rosa, 2003: 25).

Proponents of the high-performance paradigm have generally argued that the research findings do not reflect a problem with the paradigm itself: instead, the problem is essentially a managerial one, reflecting the wrong managerial values and beliefs (e.g. Kochan et al., 1986a: 14; Rubinstein and

Kochan, 2001: 107–12), or a lack of knowledge, expertise or financial resources adequate for the full and effective implementation of HPPs, especially in small firms (e.g. Kochan and Osterman, 1994: 170–1). There has been no research directly addressing the latter possibility, although it would provide one explanation for why small employers are less likely to adopt HPPs (e.g. Osterman, 1994: 182; Gittleman et al., 1998: 109). With regard to the former, Osterman (1994: 182) reported that a single item asking whether employers should accept responsibility for the well-being of employees, intended to measure employer values, was significantly associated with work practice adoption in his 1992 survey of 694 US manufacturing establishments. However, in my study of 293 Canadian employers, I found managerial values and beliefs specific to HPPs to account for only 7 and 6.5 per cent of the variance in the reported intensity of HPP adoption and in worker say in work-related decisions, respectively, while more structural, context variables (e.g. size, technology, market pressures) accounted for 12 and 30 per cent (Godard, 1997: 221).

A further possible managerial explanation is that, owing to the limited adoption of this paradigm, many studies are not adequately testing the effects of the high-performance paradigm when fully adopted. But as discussed earlier, the performance effects research suggests that, if anything, the effects of HPPs may drop off or even decline at high levels of adoption. A similar argument can be made for some of the findings on worker effects, especially my own study of 508 employed Canadians. Such results may reflect failures of implementation (Pfeffer, 1994: 223–54), in which case it could be argued that better implementation processes would yield results more consistent with the high-performance paradigm and might lead to higher sustainability and levels of adoption over time. In my research on Canadian employers, however, I found that implementation processes tend to have only limited implications for reported HPP effectiveness (Godard, 1999: 694–6).

Yet another possibility is that the problem is one of market failures rather than of either management failures or limitations to the high-performance paradigm itself. Two market failures arguments have been advanced by proponents of the high-performance paradigm, each of which could help to explain why both the adoption and the beneficial effects of the high-performance paradigm have been limited. The first is that employers are discouraged from investing in the high levels of training required by team involvement systems because of the risk of poaching by other employers (e.g. Levine, 1995: 107–9; Kochan and Osterman, 1994: 171). The second is that financial markets place pressures on employers to adopt a short-term orientation and hence to use HPPs as a means of cutting costs and maximizing short-term performance rather than building trust and partnership over the long term (Kochan and Osterman, 1994: 111–14; Levine, 1995: 87–91). This latter argument has been especially popular among UK commentators attempting to explain why, in contrast to their German counterparts, UK employers resort to 'opportunistic pragmatism' in the management of human resources (Armstrong, 1989: 155; Sisson and Storey, 1993: 76–7; Legge, 1995: 135–7).

These arguments are somewhat more compelling than their more managerial counterparts, if only because most HPPs have long been widely advocated in some form in the management literature, and hence should have been more fully adopted by now if the problem was simply one of management. Yet, as for their managerial counterparts, support for these explanations is at present limited. Contrary to the poaching explanation, some studies find that HPPs are associated with lower turnover rates (e.g. Huselid, 1995; Arthur, 1994), although even this relationship may not be universal (Morisette and Rosa, 2003). The only direct attempt to assess the implications of the time horizon is found in Osterman's study of US workplaces (1994: 182), where a measure of this construct was statistically insignificant.

There may be additional possible explanations for the limited research support for the high-performance paradigm. But it is necessary at some point to consider the possibility that the promise of this paradigm as a policy alternative is a false one, and that, while the problems associated with it may be attributable in part to both managerial and market failures, these explanations simply do not go far enough. The full adoption of this paradigm may have positive effects in some workplaces. However, these effects may be inherently more limited than assumed and, in a great many workplaces, may not be sufficient to justify full adoption. I now discuss why this may be the case, adopting what I refer to as a political economy approach. This approach focuses on the way in which the employment relation is constituted in liberal market economies, and the implications this has for the politics and economics underlying the exercise of managerial authority.

A political economy approach to understanding the limitations to HPPs

Where more conventional explanations for the apparent limitations of the high-performance paradigm focus on managerial and, to a lesser extent, market failures, the political economy approach attributes them to a more fundamental institutional failure arising out of the nature of the employment relation itself in liberal market economies. Under the political economy approach advanced here, the employment relation is viewed as a relation of subordination under conditions of interest conflict (see Godard, 1998b: 34–46; 2001b: 27–9). When an individual enters into an employment relation, he/she legally subordinates him/herself to the exercise of employer authority. In contemporary liberal market economies, he/she has few if any co-decision rights, and his/her legal status is that of a human resource, but a resource none the less, to be employed as an instrument for the attainment of employer ends. This has a number of important implications for both the politics and the economics of HPPs, each of which can explain one or more of the limitations identified above for the high-performance paradigm.

First, and most important, the structure of the employment relation and the purposes to which authority is exercised mean that employee interests are subordinated to those of owners. This does not mean that it is necessarily in the interests of employers to neglect employee interests or to sacrifice those interests where conflicts arise. It does mean, however, that employees always have a reason not to trust employers, and hence that trust and legitimacy are always potentially problematic. Thus, although some level of consent and co-operation may be readily achieved if employers adopt the appropriate policies, the high levels of commitment that proponents associate with a comprehensive adoption of HPPs may be far more difficult to achieve than is assumed. This could help to explain why the main performance benefits of these practices may accrue at low to moderate levels of adoption, and begin to diminish at high levels.

> Hypothesis 1: HPPs have declining marginal returns owing to underlying sources of distrust and commitment problems arising out of the structure of the employment relation.

Second, although workers and their union representatives may initially decide to co-operate in the adoption of these practices, they may do so only as long as they have little reason to suspect managerial motives. But as soon as management finds it necessary or in its interests to make a decision that is perceived to violate the 'psychological contract' associated with these practices, underlying distrust is likely to surface, and co-operation is likely to be replaced by resistance or, at best, apathy. This would help to explain why, as discussed earlier, high-performance programmes tend to be fragile, often seeming to have a limited life span, and why workers appear to become disillusioned with them over time.

> Hypothesis 2: High-performance programmes tend to be fragile to the extent that management is free to make decisions that are in violation of the psychological contract on which co-operation is based.

Third, not only may the pay-offs from HPPs be smaller in many workplaces than proponents appear to assume, but the costs of achieving these pay-offs may be substantial (Cooke, 1992: 132; Cappelli and Neumark, 2001: 760), especially where an involvement approach is adopted. These costs can reflect higher wages, more training, possible inefficiencies arising from participatory decision processes, and various resource requirements needed to maintain high involvement levels. Because of them, it may make sense for many employers to adopt an intensification approach, implementing alternative work practices in a way that entails little real empowerment and hence does not require high involvement levels. This approach may generate lower pay-offs. But even if it does, this may be more than compensated for by lower costs. This would help to explain the apparent prevalence of intensification approaches.

> Hypothesis 3: Because of the costs associated with an involvement approach, it is in the interests of some or many employers to adopt an intensification approach.

Fourth, the effectiveness of an intensification approach may be expected to vary. In circumstances where employees have little reason to fear that their workplace will be shut down if they do not co-operate, or where they have comparable labour market alternatives, they are likely to resist such an approach. But where these conditions do not hold resistance is likely to be lower, as employees are essentially coerced to co-operate. Under such a circumstance, an intensification approach is likely to be effective for management. This explains why an intensification approach appears to be more prevalent in so-called disposable workplaces.

> Hypothesis 4: Where employees have reason to fear a shutdown, and where job opportunities are limited, the payoffs to an intensification approach, and hence the likelihood that one is adopted, are greater.

Fifth, even in workplaces not suited to an intensification approach, we might expect the costs of high levels of adoption often to outweigh the benefits, especially if there are diminishing returns to HPP adoption, as suggested under hypothesis. This may explain why employers seem typically to adopt only low to moderate levels of these practices, and to do so as add-ons to traditional personnel practices associated with good management. It may also provide a further explanation for the limited life span of many high-performance programmes. Once implemented, employers may find the benefits to be lower than expected and hence to not justify the costs, thus leading them to cut back or eliminate this programmes altogether.

> Hypothesis 5: Owing to cost–benefit trade-offs, it is in the interests of many employers to adopt only low to moderate levels of HPPs, often as add-ons to traditional practices.

Sixth, because the costs of an involvement approach can be high, it is necessary for employers to ensure high benefits if the programme is to be a success. Thus, even where employers do not strictly opt for an intensification approach, it may in many cases be necessary to create a high-pressure environment if the performance gains needed to justify a high level of adoption are to be achieved. Workers may therefore be subjected to considerable pressures to work still harder, even it through norms enforced by peers rather than from direct employer pressures. This would be consistent with Barker's findings, and would explain my finding that high levels of adoption appear to have primarily negative implications for workers. It would also provide a further explanation for why high levels of adoption remain relatively rare and difficult to sustain. That is, because of high levels of pressure, and hence stress, experienced by employees, the gains associated with high levels of adoption are even more difficult to sustain and the potential for conflict even higher than otherwise.

> Hypothesis 6: The costs of adopting a team involvement system mean that workers are subject to increased performance pressures and stress levels and that this approach is difficult to sustain.

Seventh, and following from the above points, the costs and the benefits of high-performance programmes, and hence their net pay-offs, may depend on contextual conditions. It can be argued that, if there are diminishing returns to employer expenditures on employee motivation and control, then it is in the interests of employers to make expenditures to that point where the gains from further expenditures no longer exceed, but instead just equal, the costs. This point, and hence the level of expenditure that is rational for the employer, can vary considerably depending on worker attitudes and expectations, the costs to employers of quits, strikes or workplace recalcitrance, and available cost economies in the implementation of high-performance programmes (see Godard, 1998b: 37–44). These considerations can in turn be expected to vary in accordance with structural variables such as establishment size, capital intensity and market context. Although precise determination of the most rational level of HPP adoption is unlikely, employer attempts to balance costs and benefits in a way that is suitable to these considerations mean that adoption of HPPs can thus be expected to vary in accordance with structural variables. This argument received support in my study of the role of structural relative to ideology variables in 293 Canadian firms (Godard, 1997: 217–25), referred to earlier, and provides a more cogent explanation than offered by others observing structural variation (e.g. Kochan and Osterman, 1994: 81–109).

> Hypothesis 7: The extent to which it is in management's interests to adopt HPPs associated with a team involvement system varies with structural variables such as size, technology and market relations.

These arguments, and the hypotheses that derive from them, can be considered to engender a political economic approach, because they address the essentially political problems of distrust and conflict that arise out of the nature of the employment relation and the associated economic costs of HPP adoption in liberal market economies. They are not incompatible with those advanced by proponents of the high-performance paradigm. Indeed, market failure explanations are compatible with those advanced here: poaching concerns may heighten the perceived costs of a team involvement system, while short-termism may heighten both worker distrust and the pressures on employers to violate promises. But the explanations offered here suggest that the underlying problem is with the design of the employment relation in liberal market economies and is hence institutional. Therefore they go further than the other explanations, helping to establish why many of the obstacles proponents identify appear to be so deeply ingrained.

Implications

Three implications follow. First, the limitations to the high-performance paradigm identified in this paper may be greatest in liberal market economies. In co-ordinated market economies (e.g. Germany), where firms are managed more as stakeholder institutions, where workers have strong co-decision and representation rights, and where there are stronger protections against lay-off, problems of trust (Hypothesis 1) are likely to be substantially reduced; employer freedom to make unilateral decisions that undermine trust (Hypothesis 2) is likely to be limited; HPPs are more likely to be implemented in ways that benefit workers (Hypotheses 3 and 4); the benefits relative to the costs of these practices (Hypothesis 5) are likely to be increased; the performance pressures on workers (Hypothesis 6) are likely to be reduced or at least addressed; and the portion of employers who find it in their interests to adopt a team involvement system (Hypothesis 7) may be increased. Thus, to the extent that liberal market economies undergo institutional changes that mimic social market economies, the limitations to the high-performance model may be reduced.

Second, the very content of the high-performance paradigm may reflect the institutional context of liberal market economies (e.g. see Roth, 1997; Streeck, 1996). Because trust is in the first instance less problematic in co-ordinated market economies, there is less need of many of the high-commitment practices associated with the team involvement system in these economies. Moreover, participatory practices identified with the high-performance paradigm are rendered redundant by the existence of legally institutionalized systems for information-sharing and consultation. Finally, the ways in which new forms of work organization are adopted (e.g. lean production) are likely to be substantially different, owing to differing institutional realities (Streeck, 1996). Thus, if liberal market economies were to develop institutional arrangements more similar to those of co-ordinated market economies, it is likely that the practices and processes currently promoted under the high-performance paradigm would need to be substantially changed.

A third implication is that promotion of the high-performance paradigm as a major policy paradigm for liberal market economies is misguided. If so, there is need to promote an alternative. The analysis in this paper suggests that, on average, the high-performance paradigm may not represent an improvement over, and may even be less effective than, traditional personnel practices, especially if these practices are coupled with group work and information-sharing and with accommodative union relations practices. But any such paradigm would need to entail recognition that such practices may not go far enough, especially with regards to the provision of employee voice. It would also need to entail recognition that it is not always in the interests of employers to adhere to such practices. Thus, it would go beyond attempting to alter employer norms. It would also require the promotion of legal reforms that, in conjunction with complementary public policies, alter the institutional environments within which employers act so as to ensure that some combination of high-quality work, progressive employment practices and meaningful representation and voice are available to most or all workers (see Godard, 2002, 2003a).

The extent to which such reforms could gain sufficient political support is of course open to question. Much would likely depend on the extent to which they were consistent with the institutional and state traditions of the economies in question and with their current economic and political realities (Godard, 2002: 251–2, 273–7). It is thus unlikely that they could entail a substantial change in how the employment relation is constituted or even in elements of the socioeconomic environment identified by proponents of the high-performance paradigm. But it may well be possible to enact reforms that are consistent with established institutions and which do not entail undue efficiency costs. In the UK, for example, the adoption of recent EU works council directives, coupled with the discourse that has developed around the concept of partnership, may provide the foundations for an alternative paradigm, one that could support more substantive reforms than have been attempted to date but are compatible with broader institutions Conditions would appear to be less favourable in the USA and Canada. But the failings of union recognition systems in these countries may have created a void conducive to reforms. This may be especially so in Canada, where tradition is more conducive to direct public policy interventions (see Godard, 2004).

Conclusions

This paper has reviewed the research addressing the implications of the high-performance practices for employers, workers and unions, finding that, when compared with traditional personnel practices (e.g. formal training, grievance systems), group work organization, information-sharing and accommodative union relations policies, the high-performance paradigm may, on average, yield marginal performance gains while tending to have ambiguous if not negative effects for workers and unions. It had also argued that, although there are many possible reasons for these findings, it is likely that the problems run deeper than proponents of the high-performance paradigm assume. These problems can be accounted for under a political economy approach. Under this approach, conflicts embedded in the structure of the employment relation may substantially limit the effectiveness of the high-performance paradigm for employers, render it highly fragile, and explain its variable adoption, depending on workplace context variables. These same conflicts may also explain why high-performance practices are often implemented in ways that tend to have negative effects for workers and unions. In short it may simply be that it is in the interests of only a minority of employers to adopt the high-performance paradigm fully and that, even when it is adopted, it may not have positive implications for workers or their unions.

These findings have implications for public policy-makers. Specifically, there is a need to recognize that there may not be a universal coincidence of interests, in which what is good for employers is also always good for workers and their unions. There is thus need for state policies, laws and institutions that promote good management practices. Doing so would be based on the recognition that, not only is it not always in the interests of employers to adopt such practices, but also that, even where it is, such practices often may not go far enough, and in any case should not be matters for employer volition but should instead entail legal rights.

Although this paper has been written primarily from a public policy perspective, its findings also have implications for employers and unions. For employers, there is need to recognize that the promise of the high-performance paradigm may be a false one. It may make better sense for most to adopt what have always been considered to be good management practices, possibly with some alternative work practices grafted on. These practices may not yield the high levels of commitment promised by the high-performance paradigm, but they can be expected to yield reasonable levels of consent and realistic levels of performance.

For labour leaders, there is need to recognize that high-performance practices and the partnership arrangements sometimes associated with them need not be harmful to workers or unions, but that they can be, and that they do not in any case appear to represent the best way forward. Rather, it is the design of laws and institutions, not managerial perspicacity, on which any meaningful advances for workers and their unions are likely to depend. The future of unions likely depends on their ability to develop and promote a public policy paradigm that engenders such advances.

Notes

1 At least two additional limitations may be identified. The first is a tendency for HPPs to explain low levels of variance. For example, in Huselid's initial study (1995), the introduction of his HPP indices increased the *R*-squared by only 0.01 in his productivity regressions, and by only 0.014 in his financial performance regressions. Second, in panel studies (e.g. Huselid and Becker, 1996) there has been a tendency for observed performance effects to drop substantially once the error term is controlled for, possibly indicating that 'competent' managements introduce HPPs, and that it is management competence, rather than HPPs, that explains higher performance. I thank an anonymous referee for these points.

2 As reported in a personal correspondence with the author, however, there were statistically significant correlations between his HPP measure and a number of these dependent variables, in the 0.15–0.30 range.

3 Notably, subsequent analysis of the same data set (Godard, 2002) also revealed that, at least for workers, new work practices tend to have substitution rather than complementary effects. In particular, teamwork had negative interactions with quality circles and information-sharing. Interactions with selected employment practices also tended to be weak and were often in the wrong direction.

References

Addison, J.T. and Belfield, C. (2001) 'Updating the determinants of firm performance: estimation using the 1998 UK Workplace Employee Relations Survey'. *British Journal of Industrial Relations*, 39: 341–66.

Allen, R. and Van Norman, K. (1996) 'Employee involvement programs: the non-involvement of unions revisited'. *Journal of Labor Research*, 17: 479–98.

Appelbaum, E. and Batt, R. (1994) *The New American Workplace*. Ithaca, NY: ILR Press.

Appelbaum, E., Bailey T., Berg, P. and Kalleberg, A. (2000) *Manufacturing Advantage: Why High-performance Work Systems Pay Off*. Ithaca, NY: Cornell University Press.

Armstrong, P. (1989) 'Limits and possibilities for HRM in an age of management accountancy'. In J. Storey (ed.), *New Perspectives on Human Resource Management*. London: Routledge, pp. 154–66.

Arthur, J. (1992) 'The link between business strategy and industrial relations systems in American steel minimills'. *Industrial and Labor Relations Review*, 45: 488–506.

Arthur, J. (1994) 'Effects of human resource systems on manufacturing performance and turnover'. *Academy of Management Journal*, 37: 670–87.

Bailey, T., Berg, P. and Sandy, C. (2001) 'The effect of high-performance work practices on employee earnings in the steel, apparel, and medical electronic and imaging industries'. *Industrial and Labor Relations Review*, 54 (2A – extra issue): 525–41.

Barker, J.R. (1993) 'Tightening the iron cage: concertive control in self-managing teams'. *Administrative Science Quarterly*, 38: 408–37.

Becker, G. and Gerhart, B. (1996) 'The impact of human resource management on organizational performance'. *Academy of Management Journal*, 39: 779–801.

Becker, G. and Huselid, M. (1998) 'High-performance work practices and firm performance: a synthesis of research and managerial implications'. In G. Ferris (ed.), *Research in Personnel and Human Resources*, vol. 16. Stamford, Conn.: JAI Press.

Berg, P., Appelbaum, E., Bailey, T. and Kalleberg, A. (1996) 'The performance effects of modular production in the apparel industry'. *Industrial Relations*, 35: 356–74.

Berggren, C. (1992) *Alternatives to Lean Production*. Ithaca, NY: ILR Press.

Betcherman, G., McMullen, K., Leckie, N. and Caron, C. (1994) *The Canadian Workplace in Transition* Kingston: Ontario: IRC Press.

Brockner, J. and Hess, T. (1986) 'Self-esteem and task performance in quality circles'. *Academy of Management Journal*, 29: 617–23.

Bruno, R. and Jordan, L. (1999) 'From high hopes to disillusionment: the evolution of worker attitudes at Mitsubishi Motors'. In D. Lewin and B. Kaufman (eds), *Advances in Industrial and Labor Relations*, vol. 7: 153–82.

Cappelli, P. (1996) 'Technology and wage structures: implications for establishment wage structures'. *New England Economic Review*. Special issue (May/June): 139–54.

Cappelli, P. and Neumark, D. (2001) 'Do "high-performance" work practices improve establishment level outcomes?' *Industrial and Labor Relations Review*, 54: 737–76.

Clarke, L. (1997) 'Changing work systems, changing social relations? A Canadian General Motors plant'. *Relations Industrielles*, 52: 839–65.

Cooke, W. (1992) 'Product quality improvement through employee participation'. *Industrial and Labor Relations Review*, 46: 119–34.

Cully, M., Woodland, S., O'Reilly, A. and Dix, G. (1999) *Britain at Work*. London: Routledge.

Cutcher-Gershenfeld, J. (1991) 'The impact on economic performance of a transformation in workplace relations'. *Industrial and Labor Relations Review*, 44: 241–60.

Delaney, J. and Godard, J. (2001) 'An IR perspective on the high-performance paradigm'. *Human Resource Management Review*, 11: 395–429.

Delbridge, R. (1998) *Life on the Line in Contemporary Manufacturing*. Oxford: Oxford University Press.

Delbridge, R. and Whitfield, K. (2001) 'Employee perceptions of job influence and organizational participation'. *Industrial Relations*, 40: 472–89.

de Menezes, L., Wood, S. and Lasaosa, A. (2002). 'The foundations of human resource management in Britain: evidence from the Workplace Employee Relations Survey'. Unpublished paper, Goldsmith's College, University of London.

Drago, R. (1988) 'Quality circle survival: an exploratory analysis'. *Industrial Relations*, 27: 336–51.

Drago, R. (1996) 'Workplace transformation and the disposable workplace: employee involvement in Australia'. *Industrial Relations*, 35: 526–43.

Eaton, A.E. (1994) 'Factors contributing to the survival of employee participation programs in unionized settings'. *Industrial and Labor Relations Review*, 47: 371–89.

Eaton, A.E. and Voos, P. (1994) 'Productivity enhancing innovations in work organization, compensation, and employee participation in the union vs. the non-union sectors'. In D. Lewin and D. Sockell (eds), *Advances in Industrial and Labor Relations*, vol. 6: 63–110.

Edwards, P. and Wright, M. (2001) 'High-involvement work systems and performance outcomes: the strength of variable, contingent, and context-bound relationships'. *International Journal of Human Resource Management*, 12: 568–85.

Ellwood, D., Blank, R., Blasi, J., Kruse, D., Niskanen, W. and Lynn-Dyson, K. (2000) *A Working Nation*. New York: Russell Sage Foundation.

Emory, F.E. and Trist, E. (1981 [1946]) 'Socio-technical systems'. In C.W. Churchman and M. Verhuist (eds), *Management Science Models and Techniques*, vol. 2. Oxford: Pergamon; reprinted in F.E. Emory (ed.), *Systems Thinking*, vol. 1. New York: Viking-Penguin.

Ezzamel, M. and Willmott, H. (1998) 'Accounting for teamwork: a critical study of group-based systems of organizational control'. *Administrative Science Quarterly*. 43: 358–96.

Fiorito, J. (2001) 'Human resource management practices and worker desire for representation'. *Journal of Labour Research*, 12: 334–54.

Fiorito, J. and Young, A. (1998) 'Union voting intentions: HR policies, organizational characteristics, and attitudes'. In K. Bronfrenbrenner, S. Friedman, R.W. Hurd, R.A. Oswald and R. Seeber (eds), *Organizing to Win*. Ithaca, NY: ILR Press.

Fiorito, J., Lowman, C. and Nelson, F. (1987) 'The impact of human resource policies on union organizing'. *Industrial Relations* 26(1): 113–26.

Fisher, J. (1997) 'The challenge of change: the positive agenda of the TGWU'. *International Journal of Human Resource Management*, 8: 797–806.

Forth, J. and Millward, N. (2004) 'High involvement management and pay in Britain'. *Industrial Relations*, 43(1): 98–119.

Foulkes, F. (1980) *Personnel Policies in Large Non-Union Companies*. Englewood Cliffs, NJ: Prentice-Hall.

Freeman, J. and Rogers, J. (1999) *What Workers Want*. Ithaca, NY: Cornell University Press.

Freeman, R., Kleiner, M. and Ostroff, C. (2000) 'The anatomy of employee involvement and its effects on firms and workers'. Working Paper no. 8050, National Bureau of Economic Research, Cambridge, Mass.

Frost, A. (2000) 'Explaining variation in workplace restructuring: the role of local union capabilities'. *Industrial and Labor Relations Review*, 53: 559–78.

Fucini, J. and Fucini, S. (1990) *Working for the Japanese: Inside Mazda's American Auto Plant*. New York: Free Press.

Garrahan, P. and Stewart, P. (1992) *The Nissan Enigma: Flexibility at Work in a Local Economy*. London: Mansell.

Geary, J.F. and Dobbins, A. (2001) 'Teamworking: a new dynamic in pursuit of management control'. *Human Resource Management Journal*, 11(1): 3–27.

Gerhart, B., Wright, P.M. and McMahon, G. (2000) 'Measurement error in research of human resources and firm performance'. *Personnel Psychology*, 52: 803–34.

Gittleman, M., Horrigan, M. and Joyce, M. (1998) 'Flexible workplace practices: evidence from a nationally representative survey'. *Industrial and Labor Relations Review*, 52: 99–115.

Godard, J. (1997) 'Whither strategic choice: do managerial IR ideologies matter?' *Industrial Relations*, 36: 206–28.

Godard, J. (1998a) 'Workplace reforms, managerial objectives, and managerial outcomes'. *International Journal of Human Resource Management*, 9: 18–40.

Godard, J. (1998b) 'An organizational theory of variation in the management of labor'. In D. Lewin and B. Kaufman (eds), *Advances in Industrial and Labor Relations*, vol. 8: 25–66.

Godard, J. (1999) 'Do implementation processes and rationales matter? The case of workplace reforms'. *Journal of Management Studies*, 36: 679–704.

Godard, J. (2001a) 'High-performance *and* the transformation of work? The implications of alternative work practices for the nature and experience of work'. *Industrial and Labor Relations Review*, 54: 776–805.

Godard, J. (2001b) 'Beyond the high-performance paradigm? An analysis of managerial perceptions of reform program effectiveness'. *British Journal of Industrial Relations*, 38: 25–52.

Godard, J. (2002) 'Institutional environments, employer practices, and states in liberal market economies'. *Industrial Relations*, 41: 249–86.

Godard, J. (2003a) 'Labour unions, workplace rights, and Canadian public policy'. *Canadian Public Policy*, 29(4): 449–67.

Godard, J. (2003b) 'Do labor laws matter? The density decline and convergence thesis revisited'. *Industrial Relations*, 42: 458–92.

Godard, J. (2004) 'The US and Canadian labour movements: markets vs. states and societies'. In G. Wood and M. Harcourt (eds), *Trade Unions and the Crisis of Democracy: Strategies and Perspectives*. Manchester: Manchester University Press.

Godard, J. and Delaney, J. (2000) 'Reflections on the high-performance paradigm's implications for IR as a field'. *Industrial and Labor Relations Review*, 53: 482–502.

Graham, L. (1995) *On the Line at Subaru-Izuzu: The Japanese Model and the American Worker*. Ithaca, NY: Cornell University Press.

Guest, D. (1999) 'Human resource management: the workers' verdict'. *Human Resource Management Journal*, 9: 5–25.

Guest, D. and Peccei, R. (2001) 'Partnership at work: mutuality and the balance of advantage'. *British Journal of Industrial Relations*, 39: 207–36.

Guest, D., Michie, J., Conway, N. and Sheehan, M. (2003) 'Human resource management and corporate performance in the UK'. *British Journal of Industrial Relations*, 41: 291–314.

Handel, M. and Gittleman, M. (2004) 'Is there a wage payoff to innovative work practices?' *Industrial Relations*, 43(1): 67–97.

Harley, B. (2001) 'Team membership and the experience of work in Britain: an analysis of WERS98 data'. *Work, Employment, and Society*, 15: 721–42.

Havlovic, S.J. (1991) 'Quality of working life and human resource outcomes'. *Industrial Relations*, 30: 469–79.

Heckscher, C. (1988) *The New Unionism: Employee Involvement in the Changing Corporation*. New York: Basic Books.

Heckscher, C. and Schurman, S. (1997) 'Can labour–management co-operation deliver jobs and justice?' *Industrial Relations Journal*, 28: 323–30.

Hoque, K. (1999) 'Human resource management and performance in the UK hotel industry'. *British Journal of Industrial Relations*, 37: 419–43.

Huselid, M.A. (1995) 'The impact of human resource management practices on turnover, productivity, and corporate financial performance'. *Academy of Management Journal*, 38: 635–72.

Huselid, M.A. and Becker, G. (1996) 'Methodological issues in cross-sectional and panel estimates of the human resource-firm performance link'. *Industrial Relations*, 35: 400–22.

Huselid, M.A. and Becker, G. (1997) 'The impact of high-performance work systems, implementation effectiveness, and alignment on shareholder wealth'. Paper presented at the 1997 Academy of Management Annual Conference, Boston, Mass.

Huselid, M.A. and Rau, B.L. (1996) 'The determinants of high-performance work systems: cross sectional and longitudinal analysis'. Unpublished paper.

Ichniowski, C., Kochan, T., Levine, D., Olson, O. and Strauss, G. (1996) 'What works at work'. *Industrial Relations*, 35: 299–333.

Ichniowski, C., Shaw, K. and Prennushi, G. (1997) 'The effects of human resource management practices on productivity: a study of steel finishing lines'. *American Economic Review*, 87: 291–313.

Jacoby, S.M. (1997) *Modern Manors: Welfare Capitalism Since the New Deal*. Princeton: Princeton University Press.

Kelly, J. (1996) 'Union militancy and social partnership'. In P. Ackers, C. Smith and P. Smith (eds), *The New Workplace and Trade Unionism*. London: Routledge.

Kochan, T. (1980) *Collective Bargaining and Industrial Relations; From Theory to Policy and Practice*. Homewood, Ill.: Irwin.

Kochan, T. (1999) 'Social partnership in Britain: good for profits, bad for jobs and unions'. *Communist Review*, 3(10): 124–37.

Kochan, T. and Osterman, P. (1994) *The Mutual Gains Enterprise*. Boston, Mass: Harvard Business School Press.

Kochan, T., Katz, H. and McKersie, R. (1986a) *The Transformation of Industrial Relations*. New York: Basic Books.

Kochan, T., McKersie, R. and Chalykoff, J. (1986b) 'The effects of corporate strategy and workplace innovations on union representation'. *Industrial and Labor Relations Review*, 39: 487–501.

Landsbergis, P., Cahill, J. and Schnall, P. (1999) 'The impact of lean production and related new systems of work organization on worker health'. *Journal of Occupational Health Psychology*, 4: 108–30.

Legge, K. (1995) *Human Resource Management: Rhetorics and Realities*. London: Macmillan.

Levine, D. (1995) *Reinventing the Workplace*. Washington: Brookings Institution.

Levine, D. (2001) Editor's Introduction to 'The Employment Effects of Minimum Wages'. *Industrial Relations*, 40: 161–2.

Lewin, D. (2001) 'Low involvement work practices and business performance'. *Proceedings of the 53rd Annual Meeting*. Urbana-Champaigne, Ill.: Industrial Relations Research Association.

MacDuffie, J.P. (1995) 'Human resource bundles and manufacturing performance: organizational logic and flexible production systems in the world auto industry'. *Industrial and Labor Relations Review*, 48: 197–221.

Machin, S. (2000) 'Union decline in Britain'. *British Journal of Industrial Relations*, 38: 631–46.

Mansell, J. (1987) *Workplace Innovations in Canada*. Ottawa: Economic Council of Canada.

Marks, A., Findlay, P., Hine, J., McKinlay, A. and Thompson, P. (1998) 'The politics of partnership? Innovation in employment relations in the Scottish spirits industry'. *British Journal of Industrial Relations*, 36: 209–26.

Marshall, R. (1992) 'Work organization, unions, and economic performance'. In L. Mishel and P. Voos (eds), *Unions and Economic Competitiveness*. Armonk, NY: M.E. Sharpe, pp. 247–86.

McKinlay, A. and Taylor, P. (1996) 'Commitment and conflict: worker resistance to HRM in the micro-electronics industry'. In B. Towers (ed.), *The Handbook of Human Resource Management*, 2nd edn. Oxford: Blackwell, pp. 467–87.

Morissette, R. and Rosa, J.M. (2003) 'Alternative work practices and quit rates: methodological issues and empirical evidence for Canada'. Catalogue no. 11F0019MIE, no. 199. Ottawa: Statistics Canada Business and Labour Market Analysis Division.

Osterman, P. (1994) 'How common is workplace transformation and who adopts it?' *Industrial and Labor Relations Review*, 47: 173–87.

Osterman, P. (2000) 'Work reorganization in an era of restructuring'. *Industrial and Labor Relations Review*, 53: 179–96.

Parker, M. and Slaughter, J. (1995) 'Unions and management by stress'. In S. Babson (ed.), *Lean Work: Empowerment and Exploitation in the Global Auto Industry*. Detroit, Mich.: Wayne State University Press.

Parker, M. and Slaughter, J. (1988) *Choosing Sides: Unions and the Team Concept*. Boston, Mass.: South End Press.

Pfeffer, J. (1994) *Competitive Advantage through People*. Boston, Mass.: Harvard Business School Press.

Pfeffer, J. (1998) *The Human Equation*. Boston, Mass: Harvard Business School Press.

Purcell, J. (1999) 'Best practice and best fit: chimera or cul-de-sac?' *Human Resource Management Journal*, 9: 26–41.

Ramsay, H., Scholarios, D. and Harley, B. (2001) 'Employees and high-performance work systems'. *British Journal of Industrial Relations*, 39: 501–32.

Rinehart, J., Huxley, C. and Robertson, D. (1997) *Just Another Car Factory? Lean Production and its Discontents*. Ithaca, NY: ILR Press.

Roche, W. (1998) 'In search of commitment oriented human resource management practices and the conditions that sustain them'. *Journal of Management Studies*, 36: 653–78.

Roche, W. and Geary, J.F. (2002) 'Advocates, critics and union involvement in workplace part-nerships: Irish airports'. *British Journal of Industrial Relations*, 40: 659–88.

Roth, S. (1997) 'Germany: labor's perspective on lean production'. In T. Kochan, R. Lansbury and J.P. MacDuffie (eds), *After Lean Production*. Ithaca, NY: ILR Press.

Rubinstein, S. and Kochan, T. (2001) *Learning from Saturn*. Ithaca, NY: Cornell University Press.

Shaiken, H., Lopez, S. and Mankita, I. (1997) 'Two routes to team production: Saturn and Chrysler compared'. *Industrial Relations*, 36: 17–46.

Sisson, K. and Storey, J. (1993) *Managing Human Resources and Industrial Relations*. Milton Keynes: Open University Press.

Smith, V. (1997) 'New forms of work organization'. *Annual Review of Sociology*, 23: 315–39.

Streeck, W. (1992) 'National diversity, regime competition, and institutional deadlock: problems in forming a European industrial relations system'. *Journal of Public Policy*, 12: 310–30.

Streeck, W. (1995) 'Works councils in Western Europe: from consultation to participation'. In J. Rogers and W. Streeck (eds), *Works Councils: Consultation, Representation, and Co-operation in Industrial Relations*. Chicago: University of Chicago Press.

Streeck, W. (1996) 'Lean production in the German automobile industry: a test case for convergence theory'. In S. Berger and R. Dore (eds), *National Diversity and Global Capitalism*, Ithaca, NY: Cornell University Press.

Taylor, R. (1994) *The Future of Trade Unions*. London: Andre Deutsch.

Trist, E.A. and Bamforth, K.W. (1951) 'Some social and psychological consequences of the Longwall method of coal getting'. *Human Relations*, 4(1): 3–38.

Verma, A. (1989) 'Joint participation programs: self help or suicide for Labor?' *Industrial Relations*, 28: 401–10.

Verma, A. and McKersie, R. (1986) 'Employee involvement: the implications of non-involvement by unions'. *Industrial and Labor Relations Review*, 40: 556–68.

Wells, D. (1993) 'Are strong unions compatible with the new model of human resource management?' *Relations Industrielles*, 48(1): 56–85.

White, M., Hill, S., McGovern, P., Mills, C. and Smeaton, D. (2003) 'High-performance' management practices, working hours and work–life balance'. *British Journal of Industrial Relations*, 41: 175–96.

Womack, J., Jones, D. and Roos, D. (1990) *The Machine that Changed the World*. New York: Rawson.

Wood, S. (1996) 'High-commitment management and unionization in the UK'. *International Journal of Human Resource Management*, 7: 41–58.

Wood, S. (1999) 'Human resource management and performance'. *International Management Review*, 1: 367–413.

Wood, S. and de Menezes. L. (1998) 'High-commitment management in the UK: evidence from the Workplace Industrial Relations Survey and the Employers' Manpower and Skill Practices Survey'. *Human Relations*, 51: 485–515.

Wood, S. and Wall, T. (2002) 'Human resource management and business performance'. In P. Warr (ed.), *The Psychology of Work*. Hammondsworth: Penguin, pp. 351–74.

8

Performance-related Pay

John Storey and Keith Sisson

Two main types of individual PRP (performance-related pay) scheme are to be found: one involves the linking of pay to performance as measured by the achievement of specific individual objectives and the other – sometimes known as merit rating – assesses performance in terms of certain behavioural traits such as problem-solving, reliability, initiative, cooperation, and so on. A number of recent surveys, which are reviewed in Kessler (1993), confirm substantial growth in both types, especially among non-manual employees, many of whom have traditionally been paid salaries with automatic annual increments related to length of service. Unlike some previous trends in pay systems, the public sector as well as the private sector is affected; for example, among the 500,000 non-industrial civil servants, assessed performance is now integral to salary progression for most grades.

However, despite the outpouring of advice and consultancy that is available, the signs are that in many organizations individual PRP is leading to major problems. Not only is the introduction of PRP being badly handled, the near-obsession with individual PRP means that other features essential to performance management are being ignored or not being given the attention they deserve. We suggest that the single-minded determination to install individual PRP (despite the lack of firm evidence concerning its efficacy) is reflective of the wider move towards individualism and away from collectivism.

If one ignores for the moment the substantial body of evidence which casts doubt on the links between pay and performance, the case for individual PRP sounds very plausible. It is difficult to quarrel with the overall objective of performance pay which has been described as 'to improve performance by converting the paybill from an indiscriminate machine to a more finely tuned

Source: John Storey and Keith Sission (1993) 'Performance-related pay', in John Storey and Keith Sission (eds), *Managing Human Resources.* Buckingham: Open University. Edited version.

mechanism, sensitive and responsive to a company's and employees' needs' (Brading and Wright, 1990: 1). Equally, there appears to be nothing exceptional about the kinds of specific objectives which organizations are said to be looking for in introducing PRP (see Table 8.1), especially if the possibility of group as opposed to individual PRP is taken into account.

Table 8.1 *The logic of performance pay*

1 It focuses effort where the organization wants it (specified in performance plans, objectives or targets).
2 It supports a performance-orientated culture (pay for results not effort).
3 It emphasizes individual performance or teamwork as appropriate (group-based schemes foster cooperation, personal schemes focus on individual contribution).
4 It strengthens the performance planning process (the setting of objectives and performance standards will carry more weight).
5 It rewards the right people (high rewards to those whose performance is commensurately high).
6 It can motivate all the people (a well-designed scheme will be motivating to all participants).

Source: Brading and Wright (1990: 1)

However, as Kessler's (1993) review of the research evidence suggests, there is a significant gap between assumptions and reality in those many organizations which have introduced individual PRP. A common feature is a failure to think through the introduction of performance-related pay in a coherent manner. Thus, in many cases the establishment of formal performance criteria leaves a great deal to be desired – 'objectives' and 'behaviours' which bear little relationship to work practice are being engineered purely for the purposes of having an individual PRP scheme. In the performance assessment process, which lies at the heart of individual PRP, there are complaints about subjectivity and inconsistency which are often compounded by lack of attention to the training of managers in carrying out appraisal and to the administrative procedures for monitoring arrangements. The links between performance and the level of pay are not always clear and effective – in many cases, it is argued, the amount of the incentive element is far too small to make any material difference. It has also been noted that excessive emphasis on extrinsic motivation in the form of pay can result in damage to intrinsic motivation (Deci, 1975). Motivation which comes from pride in work may be undermined.

Perhaps the most worrying aspect, however, is that individual PRP would seem to contradict or sit uneasily with a number of other policies and objectives which managers profess to be pursuing. One of these is the emphasis which many organizations are putting on teamwork. In many cases, notably where operations are inter-linked, individual PRP would appear to be totally inappropriate. Focusing on individual performance goals in such situations can undermine team spirit and cooperation. At the very least, employees may focus their attention on individual targets (especially if they are artificially contrived for the pay system) at the expense of the performance of the unit. Even so, there currently appears to be a widespread insistence on having individual PRP – come what may. Arguably, this clamour for the latest flavour of the month is as good an example as any of the kind of *lack* of strategic thinking in HR and industrial relations (IR).

Why? The discussion in Kessler (1993) is extremely helpful here. He identifies two analytical approaches to understanding managers' choices of pay systems which draw attention to the confusion of motives that appear to be present in many organizations. The first approach sees the choice of pay system as part of a relatively ordered and rational process in which managers pick the scheme which is appropriate to its needs. This, the contingency approach, has a long tradition in the writing about pay systems in the UK (Lupton and Gowler's *Selecting a Wage Payment System*, which was published as long ago as 1969, is a well-known example and is still probably the best guide there is). The second approach sees the choice of the payment system as a far less ordered or rational management process. Rather, it is a largely political or ideological process acquiring symbolic value to support particular interests or values. In this case the details of the scheme, and how it is introduced and monitored, are likely to be seen as largely irrelevant by decision makers. It is the message sent by the introduction of the scheme that matters most.

It is difficult to escape the conclusion that it is the second view that it is most appropriate to adopt, namely that individual PRP is being introduced for largely ideological reasons. The messages which senior managers would appear to be wishing to give are also fairly clear. First, there is to be a change in the culture of the organization. It is no accident, for example, that some of the most publicized individual PRP schemes have been in the [...] privatized public utilities. Secondly, managers must manage. A key implication of individual PRP is that managers have to take responsibility for performance management: requiring them to take tough decisions about the payments that are going to be made to individual employees is seen as a critical element in the process. Thirdly, and perhaps most important, there is the focus on the individual; the implication, at the very least, is that trade unions and collective bargaining will play a lesser role in pay determination.

It is also possible to suggest two further and related considerations. One is the inherent belief of top managers – it seems to be almost an article of faith – that pay is the prime motivator in performance. The second is their conviction that not only is managing through the payment system the most effective means of managing HR and IR, but it is also sufficient for doing so. This last point is worth stressing because it has much wider implications. Much is made in the personnel management literature of different types of 'contract'. UK management, it seems, feels much more comfortable – largely because of historical reasons – with the cash nexus or subcontracting relationship than it does with the other forms of contract which carry mutual obligations.

Key issues in reward management

There is no dispute about the overall significance of the reward system in performance management. In the words of Collins (1991: 78), the reward system is important in attracting and retaining employees of the required quality, underpinning the drive to improve performance, and supporting the ability to change.

However, as will be clear from reading any standard textbook (see, for example, Torrington and Hall, 1991), one of the great debates in personnel management is whether the system of rewards, in Herzberg's (1966) terms, is to be seen as a 'motivator' or 'hygiene' factor. Is the system of rewards, in other words, to be seen primarily as a positive incentive to greater performance or, if employees feel that it is unfair, as a source of disincentive? Our view is that it is sensible to start from the second position. This is because, in the head-long rush to individual PRP, there has been a tendency in many UK organizations to neglect other key components of reward systems. Certainly the research evidence suggests that there is considerable scope for improvement in a number of the areas involved.

An appropriate pay structure

Two main aspects are involved. One relates to internal pay relationships or differentials; the other to external pay relationships or relativities. Both these are fundamentally important because they are inextricably tied up with notions of fairness. The problem is that fairness is not an absolute but a relative concept. Pay relationships provide the critical measure of the worth or status which the individual is accorded in the organization and in society more generally; their fairness is judged in comparison to others. If they are felt to be unfair, they can be a major disincentive. In Brown's words:

> The most ingenious of bonus systems and the best of supervision are of little use if the underlying pay structure is felt to be unfair. Consequently, the prudent personnel manager devotes far less time to devising new pay incentives than to tending old notions of fairness. (1989: 252–3)

The recommended method of setting the basis for pay differentials which are felt to be fair is job evaluation. This is simply a procedure for allowing comparisons between jobs in a systematic way. A variety of methods is available, but four main types can be found: ranking; paired comparisons; grading or job classification; and points rating (ACAS, 1988: 7–8; and NBPI, 1968).

Typically, UK companies have operated with a minimum of five or six grades. A number of the Japanese companies who have invested in the UK, notably Nissan, have chosen to work with only two major grades. If a major objective is to improve flexibility, it is argued, too many grades can present major obstacles – job evaluation, by definition, involves the preparation of job descriptions. The tighter these are drawn for the purposes of distinguishing one job from another, the greater the inflexibility.

External pay relationships or relativities, the second aspect of pay structure, have in the past been an issue of considerable controversy. [...] Currently, to return to the point made earlier about the ideological explanation of management behaviour, they are supposed to be a non-issue. The main considerations in pay determination, it is argued, ought to be the specific circumstances of the individual organization – the ability to pay, in other words, is of paramount importance. The problem is that the issue will not go away. Organizations have to have regard to what potential competitors for their employees are paying. Otherwise, they risk losing their best people. In the main they do this through market surveys. In the case of managers, for example, considerable use is made of the Hay system to judge the appropriateness of pay levels. In the case of manual workers the local employers' organization is very often the source of the data. In the public services, groups like the armed forces, senior civil servants, doctors, nurses, and teachers have formal review bodies responsible for making recommendations on the basis of comparisons.

Single status

Most commentators accept that the division between manual and non-manual workers, which is grounded in history, cannot be justified and makes little sense. A key reason is that the very existence of these status differences makes it extremely difficult to win the kind of cooperation and commitment that organizations claim to be seeking. There is no defensible reason, for example, why a 50-year-old skilled craftsman, who has worked 30 years with an organization should have inferior sick pay or pension arrangements to his 18-year-old offspring who only recently joined as a junior. A second reason is that in many organizations it is increasingly difficult to distinguish on any objective basis between manual and non-manual jobs. A third reason is that, as the non-pay items increase in their cost, management want greater return from them. Indeed, in the USA the so-called 'cafeteria principle' is becoming increasingly important: in the attempt to draw attention to the costs and benefits of these elements, employees are encouraged to choose between different combinations of non-pay benefits instead of taking them for granted.

Such concerns have not been translated into practice, however, despite predictions about the decline of the status gap (Price and Price, 1993). Certainly [...] there have been moves to harmonize some of the terms and conditions of manual and non-manual workers. Sick pay is a case in point. Examples of single status arrangements, however, remain the exception rather than the rule. [...]

Admittedly, there are some major problems in moving towards single status arrangements. One is cost. Sizeable increases may be involved and many organizations are in no position to pay the bill. Especially important is the cost of security that would be involved in many organizations as a result of the different notice provisions which would arise. Another is trade union opposition. Much of this has come in particular from non-manual unions who are afraid of losing their particular advantages or who fear that they will be 'held back' while others catch up. In many cases, there is a suspicion that managers simply do not perceive the status divide to be a major cause for real concern. On the contrary, the divide could be seen as bringing positive advantages to management. Rightly or wrongly, managements in some organizations feel that it enables them to enjoy the tactical advantage of playing one group off against another.

Group performance pay

Kessler's (1993) review [...] notes that the incidence of 'collective performance schemes, especially those which cover the unit or the company, is relatively low'. Indeed, the ACAS (1988: 18) survey [...] suggested that just over half of the establishments in the sample had some form of group or collective bonus system. The majority of these affected the immediate work group only, however. A mere 13 per cent of workplaces had schemes which covered the workplace or the enterprise as a whole.

There is a widespread view that the direct incentive in group schemes is low because the performance–reward link is too remote. Even so, the relatively low incidence of such schemes is surprising for several reasons. First, there are a number of important variables which can be the basis of performance schemes such as output, cost reduction, sales and quality. [...] Secondly, much work is team work and many of the problems associated with individual PRP schemes are overcome with appropriately designed group schemes – especially if the low level of the payment in many individual PRP schemes is taken into account. Thirdly, group bonus schemes are one of the most effective forms of communication to employees about such key issues as productivity, costs and quality.

Profit sharing

A further possibility in the private sector is profit sharing. Profit sharing, which has received considerable support from the government in the form of tax incentives through the Financial Acts involves linking pay or some element of pay to profits either in the form of direct cash payments or shares.

The empirical evidence also provides a useful starting point here. There has, it is true, been a significant increase in the coverage of profit sharing since the early 1980s. It is by no means extensive, however. Only 36 per cent of the workplaces in the ACAS (1988: 20) survey [...] reported some form of profit sharing and share ownership. Significantly too, in the light of the discussion above about the status divide, the majority of these schemes affected non-manual workers only, however. Only about one-third of the workplaces with profit-sharing schemes or between 12 per cent and 13 per cent of the total applied them to both manual and non-manual workers.

The nature of the Inland Revenue arrangements may have been a deterrent here. But this applies only to government schemes. Here too then there would appear to be considerable scope for improvement in the performance management stakes.

Conclusion

Any serious consideration of the topic 'managing human resources and industrial relations' inevitably involves a critical review of current practice. We have sought to continue this but, in addition, to switch the emphasis onto a positive, practical plane by showing how a practitioner, [...] might set about the process of reform at the organizational level. The practical steps outlined re-confirm [that] – there are no easy quick-fixes to be found for this realm of management. None the less, [...] there are a great many things that can be done to ensure that the adage that 'people are our most important asset' becomes something more than a shibboleth.

References

Advisory, Conciliation and Arbitration Service (ACAS) (1988) *Developments in Payment Systems.* Occasional Paper No. 45. London: ACAS.

Brading, E. and Wright, V. (1990) 'Performance-related pay', *Personnel Management Factsheets*, No. 30. London: Personnel Publications.

Brown, W.A. (1989) 'Managing remuneration', in K. Sisson (ed.), *Personnel Management in Britain.* Oxford: Blackwell.

Collins, M. (1991) *Human Resource Management Audit.* Birmingham: North Western and West Midlands Regional Health Authorities.

Deci, E.L. (1975) *Intrinsic Motivation.* New York: Plenum Press.

Herzberg, F. (1966) *Work and the Nature of Man.* Cleveland, OH: World Publishing.

Kessler, I. (1993) 'Performance pay', in K. Sisson (ed.), *Personnel Management in Britain* (2nd edn). Oxford: Blackwell.

Lupton, T. and Gowler, D. (1969) *Selecting a Wage Payment System*, Research Paper 111. London: Engineering Employers' Federation.

National Board for Prices and Incomes (NBPI) (1968) *Job Evaluation.* Report No. 83. London: HMSO.

Price, E. and Price, R.J. (1993) 'The decline and fall of the status divide', in K. Sisson (ed.), *Personnel Management in Britain* (2nd edn). Oxford: Blackwell.

Torrington, D. and Hall, L. (1991) *Personnel Management: A New Approach.* London: Prentice-Hall.

Part 3

The Emergence of New Organizational Forms and Relationships

The four chapters in this part of the book examine changing organizational forms and relationships. The interplay between organizational structures, forms and relationships – most especially those developments which involve cross-boundary working – has been one of the fascinating themes during the past few years. Traditional analytical silos such as 'bureaucratic structures' and 'industrial relations' have been dissolved as development in the way work is organized has been seen to carry implications for both organizational forms and relationships. For example, the growth in networking and quasi-market arrangements are equally relevant from an organizational form perspective as from a work-relations perspective.

The chapter by Storey provides a conceptual mapping of the new organizational forms and at the same time seeks to examine the link between these organizational reforms and the policies associated with SHRM. The linkages are found to operate at a number of levels. At the highest level, it is possible to interpret both tendencies as expressions of the rise of 'enterprise'. For example, many of the tenets of SHRM within the standard bureaucratic form urge, and seek to impel, expressions of intrapreneurship, flexibility and customer-orientation. Likewise, the various reforms of bureaucracy – including shifts to devolved, enterprising, sub-units can be interpreted as expressions of the same underlying idea. Further, the initiatives which mark departures from hierarchy and bureaucracy (e.g. supply chain management, alliances, federations, joint ventures, partnerships and networks) all carry implications for the practice of SHRM and these are explored in this chapter.

In Chapter 10, Rubery et al. also assess the linkages between changing organizational forms, the reshaping of work, and the changing nature of work relations. In particular, the chapter focuses on the development of the more complex organizational forms such as cross-organizational networking, partnerships, alliances and the use of external agencies. Under these conditions the notion of the conventional employer–employee relationship is difficult to sustain. They suggest that there are unexplored links between new organizational forms on the one hand and the employment relationship on the other. SHRM has traditionally tended to concentrate, and arguably still does concentrate, on relations within single organizations (i.e. one employer to many employees situations) – rarely considering the implications of cross-organizational working. This chapter fills in some of the gaps in conventional analyses. For example, it identifies aspects of the employment relationship under conditions of outsourcing, joint ventures and networked organizations. The massive scope for ambiguity in the areas of pay, performance management and organizational commitment are a particular focus of this chapter.

In Chapter 11, Guest sets out the variety of options facing managers and others in the design of employment strategies and associated patterns of relationships. What is especially interesting about this chapter is the cross-cutting of human resource management and industrial relations possibilities. This is shown to give rise to four types of relationship patterns: (1) a new realism which combines a significant emphasis both upon SHRM policies and industrial relations (thus allowing for both individualistic and collectivist relations); (2) traditional collectivism where priority is given to industrial relations, but with little if any attention to SHRM policies; (3) individualized SHRM – that is where high priority is given to HR policies with a view to engaging the individual commitment but with little or no attention to industrial relations; and (4) the 'black hole' scenario where an employer neglects both SHRM and industrial relations. Thus in laying bare these four different patterns and by indicating the various strands of evidence in relation to each, Guest makes a valuable contribution to the understanding of the complexities of contemporary conditions.

Bunting's chapter examines evolving forms of work relationships – or rather the evolving attempts to engage workers in deeper forms of relationships. She warns of the dangers inherent in the new forms of emotional and spiritual engagement with employer brands. The shifts from contractual to commitment-based and emotional-based relationships are explored and critiqued. The case examples of Microsoft, Orange and Asda are used in order to illustrate how the attempts to raise the stakes in relationship-management extend across different kinds of work and different skill levels. It has long been noted that one of the key objectives of SHRM, and one of its differentiating features compared with other employment paradigms, has been its focus on winning 'commitment'. Mere rule-conformance or acquiescence was not enough. SHRM was part of the movement which sought hearts and minds. The contribution of this chapter is that, by allowing managers at Microsoft, Orange and Asda to speak for themselves, the nature and extent of their ambitions (and their expectations and demands) for new levels of employee engagement is made graphically apparent. The extent to which employees buy-in to the new values is shown to be more open to question, but none the less the managerial intent to move beyond traditional forms of labour-management contracting is evident.

New Organizational Forms and Their Links with HR

John Storey

Introduction

The purpose of this chapter is to explore the interconnections and linkages between organizational forms and human resource management. In recent years, many organizations have sought to redraw their structures and their forms. For example, the UK National Health Service has experimented with market-based and network-based forms. In the 1990s the BBC launched a series of initiatives designed to introduce 'internal-markets' and to promote producer choice including the choice to outsource production services. Numerous private sector organizations have outsourced call-centre work and manufacturing to India, China and other East Asian countries. Such attempts to redesign organizational forms carry important HR implications; in some senses they themselves constitute alternative ways of people management.

Some analysts suggest that the shift in organization structure and form is fundamental. For example, Gabriel (2005) argues that there has been a shift from the rigid, rational, bureaucratic form which characterized a society of 'massive, concrete buildings and massive concrete organizations' to a society of 'flexible but fragile work arrangements and flexible but fragile organizations' (2005: 10). Similar conclusions about fundamental changes to organizations and organizational forms have also been reached by others (Courpasson and Reed, 2004). Globalization, entrepreneurialism and informationalism are seen to be driving a radical shift to a twenty-first century characterized by the 'age of the network' (Castells, 2001; Sabel, 2003). But the 'post bureaucracy thesis' has triggered much debate (Courpasson and Reed, 2004) and some analysts have wanted to make the case for preserving certain values associated with bureaucracy (du Gay, 2000, 2004).

It is to be expected that the linkages between new organizational forms and HR may be of one, or more, of the following:

1 that new forms, impelled by exogenous forces (such as globalization or deregulation), carry implications for human resource practices;
2 that human resource philosophy and policies carry implications for, and help reshape preferred models of organizational form;
3 that both of the above obtain simultaneously.

The prime purpose of the chapter is not to try to locate the prime mover here. Rather, the aim is to explore the consistencies and inconsistencies in the fit between these aspects of organizing. Developments are evidently occurring in the forms and structuring adopted and displayed by organizations; likewise, developments are occurring in the ways in which people are managed through HR systems and processes. The purpose of the chapter is to assess whether these twin sets of developments are in harmony or whether new tensions are created and challenges presented for HR and/or organizational design. It is also possible that developments in organizational form and developments in HRM are in fact part of the same broader phenomenon – new devices to try to reduce costs, reduce risk and deliver customer-responsive service.

New forms – such as the break-up of large internal labour markets, outsourcing, supply chain management, alliances and partnerships – have been equally if not more instrumental in redrawing and reshaping the nature and the contours of work relations than any of the more detailed alterations to selection methods, training, payment or performance evaluation devices.

To a large extent the aspirations and principles underlying many recent structural changes seem to reflect those which also underpin the ideas of HRM. There are even the same 'hard' and 'soft' logics at play. From an organizational restructuring point of view the 'hard' aspects are to be found in the drastic cuts in 'headcounts', the 'downsizing' and the 'outsourcing'. The 'soft' side of the rationale is to be found in the ideas of 'empowerment', the 'learning' that is required to cope with multiple demanding tasks, and the 'teamworking' that is invoked.

Organizational structuring and restructuring are intimately intertwined with many aspects of human resource management. For example, different structures carry different implications for career opportunities, for job design and job satisfaction, for learning and development opportunities, for power distance, work content and skill levels. But the interconnections between organizational structures and human resource management strategies are complex. Integral to the logic of the large organizations which grew after the end of the Second World War was the method described by Edwards (1979) as the 'bureaucratic control' system. This strategy was based around internal labour markets and the winning of employee commitment through the prospect of long-term career advancement, job security, welfare packages and seniority pay systems. The elaborate job ladders were underpinned by company-provided training and development. Where they existed, trade unions also supported these firms' internal labour markets. Such arrangements were, in some ways, also well suited to the principles of human resource management. The material elements were in place to encourage a psychological contract based on commitment; extensive investment in training and development made sense; the system ought to have encouraged careful recruitment and selection, systematic appraisal and elaborate performance management systems. To this extent the fit between this organizational model and human resource management was rather promising. But there were limitations. The argument was mounted that bureaucratic form tended to foster complacency and the link with customers became tenuous; as competitive conditions changed, these systems found it hard to adapt; bureaucracy was used to command and control; initiative was stifled. Hence, in these ways the *departure* from the bureaucratic control system could be interpreted as rather more in tune with the principles of human resource management than would its preservation.

The premise of the chapter is that changes to organizational structures and forms are occurring in two broad categories. First, there are adjustments being made to 'reform' the classic bureaucratic form. Second, there are some indications of more radical departures from that template. In both instances, the aim of the chapter is to consider what implications these changes carry for HRM.

The 'reform' of bureaucracy and HR

The uncertain place of bureaucracy in an 'age of enterprise' has attracted considerable academic scrutiny (see for example the Special Issue of *Organization*, January 2004). Numerous reform initiatives suggest a desire to amend the bureaucratic form. Various types of restructuring have taken place within conventional organizational boundaries. Firms and other organizations have decentralized, they have reduced their size, and they have devolved responsibility. For example, large centralized corporations have experimented with divisionalized forms, with strategic business units, empowered teams and with changes to operations and processes in the form of 'lean organizations' (Womack and Jones, 1996).

The key attributes of bureaucracy in the descriptive, social science, sense can be summarized as a clear division of work with stipulated boundaries to responsibilities; officials given authority to carry out their assigned functions; referral by role occupants to formal rules and procedures which ensure predictability and routinization of decisions; a well-defined hierarchy of authority; appointment to posts arranged not through patronage or bribery but on the basis of technical competence.

The model in its totality gave rise to impersonality – this was one of its intended characteristics. It had the advantage of overcoming nepotism, favouritism and arbitrary decision-making. The principles seemed well suited to the administrative needs of the new democratic states and the emerging large industrial enterprises. But the 'unanticipated consequences' and 'dysfunctions' of bureaucracy pointed out by various organizational analysts (March and Simon, 1958; Merton, 1957; Selznick, 1966; Gouldner, 1954) helped fuel the dissatisfaction with bureaucracy. The emphasis on control is seen to prompt rigidity of behaviour and defensive routines. The division of task and responsibility can elevate departmental goals above whole system goals – that is, lead to suboptimizing behaviour. Rules and procedures can also become ends in themselves.

Various *amendments* to bureaucracy have been noted. One version is the idea that new forms of 'soft bureaucracy' can be detected (Courpasson, 2000; Reed, 1999). Another movement has been to seek to reduce centralized hierarchy by managing a shift to more decentralized organizations. The consequences of such a change depends upon the 'socially negotiated' sensemaking of middle managers (Balogun and Johnson, 2004). A related 'reform' has been the shift from hierarchy to 'modular' forms in order to increase flexibility (Schilling and Steensma, 2001). These semi-independent units require coordination through a mix of contractual-like deals and the design of mutually-beneficial relations. An adjunct type is the project based organization. These are characterized by decentralization, short-term goals, an emphasis on project performance and distributed work practices (Bresnen et al., 2004).

Another important strand in the drive against bureaucracy has been the ideological shift which urged the primacy of the market. This logic led to extensive deregulation and the consequent pressure on large organizations which had previously enjoyed oligopolistic conditions. It also manifested itself in the pressure to depart drastically from internal transactions and management in favour of actual or near-market 'contracts'. This type of market-based contractual relationship inevitably removed the need, the cause and the opportunity to persist with each of the characteristic elements of bureaucracy described above.

Faced with rapidly changing environments, many employers have responded by downsizing and in the process have also retreated from long-term commitments to employees which the internal labour market model allowed and facilitated. Littler and Innes (2004) have analysed patterns of downsizing across the world. In the United States it is estimated that over one million middle managers lost their jobs as organizations flattened organizational structures.

As a result of these kinds of change, Hamel and Prahalad noted,

> In many companies, one cannot speak meaningfully of a 'corporate strategy' because the corporate strategy is little more than the aggregation of the independent strategies of standalone business units. Where the corporate role has been largely devolved, corporate officers have no particular responsibilities other than investor relations, acquisitions and disposals, and resource allocation across independent business units. (1994: 288)

Naturally, there are drawbacks to this arrangement – synergies and the advantages of the big company are lost. Opportunities remain unexploited, the potential to use core competencies across units is undermined.

So far, we have noted changes to organizational structures and forms which essentially seek to reform the existing bureaucratic paradigm. The next section explores initiatives which suggest a more fundamental break with that paradigm.

Departures from bureaucracy: beyond organizational structure

Increasingly, attention is being paid to the connections made across organizational boundaries. Alliances, federations, joint ventures, partnerships and networks are seen as increasingly important. Information and communication technologies carry the capacity to transcend organizational boundaries and allow work to be done in new ways on a distributed basis. The past identity of an organization, resting as it did on a physical place and associated perhaps with distinct products, is becoming less important and even less valid.

Much of the work on the extra-organizational forms has been undertaken by economists. The human resource dimensions of these developments have been very much under-explored. We will identify the human resource management dimensions of each major structural initiative as we proceed through each section; then, in the final section, we address the implications for the *strategic* potential in HRM presented by these structural developments.

Figure 9.1 locates the diverse initiatives on a conceptual map. Hence, the various forms which are creating so much interest are located in reference to four key dimensions. They indicate a progression towards increasing externalization of relations; to diversified activities, to performance-based control and to an open-market mode of regulation (see the dimensions on all four sides of Figure 9.1). For the past few years it would be fair to say that the general thrust (possibly as much expressed in sentiment and aspiration as in concrete action) has been in the direction away from the conventional bureaucratic mode in the bottom left and more towards the various forms in the upper-right direction.

Supply chain management and process management

A radical innovation in the way in which companies regard their structural arrangements has been the rise in popularity of the idea of dismissing function and products as structural principles in favour of a rigorous focus on supply chains and processes. A supply chain and process analysis can extend through, and beyond, organizational boundaries. The starting point is an analysis of the value-adding activities and an attempt to identify and eliminate the non value-adding components (Storey, 2002).

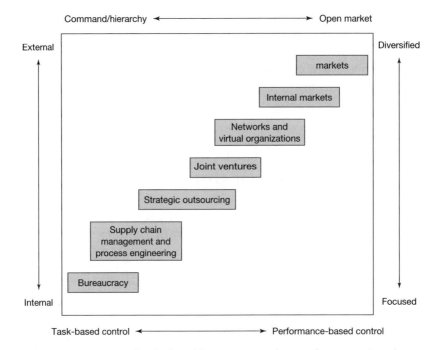

Figure 9.1 *A spectrum of relationship structures beyond conventional organizational boundaries*

Such a zero-based analysis is claimed to be very far-reaching in its implications for organizational structures and human resource management. Thus, 'everything that has been learned in the twentieth century about enterprises applies only to task-oriented organizations, everything must be rethought' (Hammer and Champy, 1992). In this statement the originators of the business process re-engineering concept make clear their radical intent. The central idea of re-engineering is that companies should re-orient themselves around their core processes – the start to finish sequence of activities which create customer value. The human resource management implications are extensive. Re-engineering, it is claimed, means the end of narrow jobs, the end of supervisory management, of traditional career paths and much more.

Process innovation combines the adoption of a process view of the business with the 'application of innovation' to the key processes (Benner and Tushman, 2002). It can apply to services such as healthcare just as much as manufacturing (McNulty and Ferlie, 2002). The objectives are drastic cost reductions, and major improvements in quality, flexibility and service levels.

The key elements of process innovation are said to be:

■ a 'fresh start', 'blank sheet' review;
■ a process rather than functional view of the whole organization;
■ cross functional solutions;

- step change;
- the exploitation of information technology;
- attention to work activities on and off the shopfloor;
- adoption of a customer's view of the organization/producing value for customers;
- processes must have owners.

Hammer (1996) in *Beyond Reengineering* explains how the 'process-centred organization' differs from traditional functional structures. The origins are traced to the late 1980s when a few companies such as Ford, Taco Bell and Texas Instruments began programmes of business improvements which differed in kind from the usual run-of-the-mill variety. They engaged in radical changes and redesigned their processes. The implications for HR according to Hammer are far-reaching:

> For a world of process-centred organizations everything must be rethought: the kinds of work that people do, the jobs they hold, the skills they need, the ways in which their performance is measured and rewarded, the careers they follow, the roles managers play, the principles of strategy that enterprises follow. (1996: xiii)

This scenario is not, he maintains, mere speculation: the concepts and techniques are already in use today. The take-up of re-engineering world-wide has been very extensive. In Britain, for example, it has been reported that 70 per cent of large organizations have embarked on what their own managers say was a BPR programme. In America, Ingersoll Rand, Shell, Levi Strauss, Ford, GTE, Chrysler 'are all concentrating on their processes' (1996: 8). In 2005 one still finds major organizations seeking to adopt a process-based review of their organization and operation.

Human resource management considerations

The first human resource management task is to ensure that everyone in the organization and across its wider reaches is aware of these processes. Shifting from a traditional mode of operating to a process-based one is no easy task. Employees fear that a process re-engineering initiative means job losses and extensive change. They are usually correct on both counts. Even years after the introduction of such a change employees may harbour resentment and blame the consultancy firm that was used. The implications for future commitment-winning measures can be problematical. Second, HR needs to help in the changing of mindsets and behaviours which are required under such a radically different organizational form. One such crucial change is the abandonment of the task specialization discussed above.

In a process organization, workers engaged in operating a machine will need to see themselves, maintains Davenport, as there not merely to run the machine but to contribute to the 'order fulfilment process'. Hence, if production-flow backs-up, these operatives will be expected to investigate and then seek to resolve the problem. Such behaviour will simply be part of the new job. Indeed, language is so important to process re-engineering, say the gurus, that 'worker' should really be replaced by the term 'process performer'.

An additional step from a HRM point of view is that process measurements are important in order to track performance and for planning improvements. This is allied to process management which entails a continual focus on process improvement and process redesign. A process-centred organization entails and requires 'a fundamental reconceptualization of what organizations are all about. It permeates every aspect of the business: how people see themselves and their jobs, how they are assessed and paid, what managers do and the definition and hence strategy and positioning of the business' (Hammer and Champy, 1992).

Further, new roles are required. 'Process performer' roles have already been noted; in addition, there is a need for 'process leaders', 'process owners' and 'process managers' whose jobs are to engage in process design and redesign, coaching, and advocacy. This last means it is the process owner's job to obtain the necessary financial and other resources to meet the process needs; and to occupy a seat on the 'process council' (which is a forum of process owners and heads of remaining support services to discuss the business as a whole). Such a body is seen as necessary to avoid functional silos being replaced by 'process tunnels' or process protectorates.

This kind of process focus implies jobs that are much enlarged: jobs which require understanding, insight, autonomy, responsibility and decision-making. Supervision is not supposed to be required. Hammer (1996) talks bluntly about 'the end of the organization chart'. There are no departments or departmental managers and very little hierarchy. Significant instead are 'centres of excellence'. These are to be thought of as in-house versions of professional associations. They are supposed to enable skill formation and continual development. In addition, they are intended to provide channels of communication which enable the sharing of knowledge and expertise.

Because there are no managers the best performers in a process organization do not become diverted into watching over others; they are freed-up to do what they do best. Corporations, Hammer says, must adjust their reward systems accordingly. The old deal (or psychological contract) was based on obedience, loyalty and diligence in exchange for long-term security. The new deal exchanges initiative for opportunity.

These new entities are not only more co-operative internally they are also inclined to be co-operatively interactive with external organizations too. Internal and external walls are broken down. Partnership here is not driven by goodwill as such but rather by 'enlightened self interest. The goal is not to change the way companies feel about their trading partners but the way they interact with them. Better interaction may well serve to modify feelings as a later consequence of mutual benefit received. But the tangible things, the underlying hard systems of operations must be changed first' (1996: 173). It goes beyond outsourcing; it entails a co-operative endeavour where the partners excel together or sink together. Compartmentalism ultimately is not even possible at the level of the firm.

A more fundamental concern is that the model is based on a unitary view of the firm. In a telling section, Hammer criticizes those corporate heads who so readily nowadays mouth the mantra of the primacy of 'shareholder value'. This is not what business enterprises are about he maintains, rather they are there for 'customer value'. While his main justification for this is couched in terms of the lack of guidance afforded by the former and the comparative clarity of needed behaviours under the latter, the underlying issue is never properly addressed: how does the worker/process performer come to identify so strongly with this enterprise? While it may be the case that a customer focus could be more persuasive than a sole concentration of shareholder value, it hardly seems sufficient.

Strategic outsourcing

'Outsourcing' refers to the situation when a company subcontracts to another supplier work that it was previously performing in-house. Strictly speaking therefore it does not denote all forms of purchasing from suppliers, though the distinction between being a former producer of the service or product and simply being a purchaser is in practice very blurred. Essentially, outsourcing entails the externalizing of production and services. It is a manifestation of the classic 'make or buy' decision. The phenomenon has, as yet, generally found little recognition in the human resource management textbooks. In recent times it has been one of the more popular ways to cut costs and to refocus on core competencies. One graphic sign of the trend was that by the mid-1990s the labour agency Manpower Inc. had displaced General Motors as the largest employer in the United States. While some sporadic signs of insourcing can be found, the general trend has been towards continued outsourcing. For example, in the US, the growth of offshore IT outsourcing in the two-year period 2003–5 was estimated at 55 per cent (www.intergroup.com).

In practice, there are many different types of outsourcing activity and usage. Some of the instances are piecemeal and opportunistic with little strategic character. Office cleaning is an example in most circumstances. The commissioning client has low vulnerability in relation to this kind of service and likewise the contribution to competitive advantage is not likely to be high. But for other services the outsourcing decision might arise from a very close analysis of the value chain and this can permit strategic use of outsourcing. Determining just what is core can, however, be problematical. For example, Nike outsources all of its manufacturing; Apple Computers outsources 70 per cent of its components, while GM has outsourced its car body painting activities.

The reasons for the growth of outsourcing are many. In a complex, fast-moving, market it is a speedy way to gain access to specialist services. Alternatively, it can be a means to reduce costs by sourcing from low-cost producers many of whom are likely to be non-unionized. In this regard, advances in information and communication technologies have played a part in that companies headquartered in high wage cosmopolitan areas can outsource routine billing and so on to remote stations almost anywhere in the world.

Problems of scrap can be drastically reduced or even eliminated as defective components can simply be rejected. Outsourcing also enables flexibility in that supply can be more readily turned on or off – at least in theory. In some instances it is merely a device to respond to pressures of 'headcount control' – that is, a means, on paper at least, to show that the critical measure of direct employee numbers is being kept under control. But, according to the more cutting-edge theories of 'winning' companies, the outsourcing phenomenon is, above all, a manifestation of enterprises clearing-out peripheral, distracting activities, in order to focus on core functions and core competencies. Quinn (1992) argued that companies should concentrate on those 'core competencies' (these, he says are usually intellectual or service activities) in which they can be best in the world. The other activities should be outsourced.

Human resource management considerations

In addition to the commonly outsourced services such as catering, security, IT services and the like, various HR functions can themselves be outsourced. To date, the most popular candidates have been training, retirement planning, outplacement services, relocation, counselling, and various forms of consultancy. American Express, for example, has outsourced its retirement plan and benefits system. In February 2005, BT signed a renewed contract with Accenture for the provision of HR transactional work including recruitment, payroll, employee benefits, health and safety and some HR advisory services. This new long-term (10-year) deal covers 87,000 BT employees in the UK and 180,000 pensioners plus another 10,000 BT employees in 37 countries. BT's Group HR Director said that the agreement would enable BT's own remaining in-house HR staff to concentrate on the strategic aspects of the HR role.

There are many consequences for organizational structures and human resource management deriving from outsourcing though it seems likely that the full consequences have not as yet been fully grasped or even researched. Organizational hierarchies are much flatter, there is reduced scope for inter-functional activity and therefore a lower need for coordination. The priority management task becomes not the handling of physical and capital assets but the management of intellectual processes and the management of staff who are not direct employees of the company. Negotiation of contracts with the providers becomes critical. There are issues of confidentiality, risk sharing, continual improvement and so on. Even where there are clear opt-out clauses for non-compliance the management of the actual occurrences may prove difficult.

A critical strategic human resource management issue is the potential loss of expertise in certain areas which may be difficult to recover. There is a danger of a serious 'hollowing-out' of the organization. The modern tenets of organizational learning, corporate culture and shared visions may all be put in some jeopardy if this occurs. Likewise, the sources of innovation needed in order to keep pace with rapidly changing markets may be put in jeopardy if a company is heavily reliant on strictly delineated services from a host of out-side suppliers. Arranging the wherewithal to forestall this problem is an important HR challenge under conditions of extensive outsourcing.

The HR function could potentially assume a key role when outsourcing occurs. In fact HR departments reportedly already play a role in some 65 per cent of all company outsourcing cases in the United States (up from about 35 per cent in the past 5 years). So, while the search and selection team ideally involves a top executive, the respective department manager and a legal expert, human resources often plays a critical role as facilitators and coordinators of the entire process. It has been suggested that it is a natural role for human resource professionals to play because of their communication and administrative skills.

Part of the human resource management function is to attract and retain people who have the appropriate skill sets required under the new conditions. A series of decisions to buy rather than to make, taken individually, may make economic sense, but collectively they may undermine the ability of a firm to compete.

While not all contracted staff are in the vulnerable, low pay category, there has been some widening of inequalities as the remaining few permanent staff enjoy higher earnings, fringe benefits and better access to skill acquisition. This presents a further challenge to the maintenance of an organization which is low on formal control structures but is supposed to score high on shared values.

Joint ventures, mergers and alliances

Joint ventures and strategic alliances have become a common feature of the business horizon. In the UK, joint ventures and alliances have also been very popular. For example, BT alone has more than 70 joint ventures and overseas distribution arrangements. Some pharmaceutical companies form as many as 20 to 30 new alliances per annum.

Through joint ventures, organizations are able to achieve a number of objectives. Large companies using their marketing expertise and systems can bring new products developed by smaller companies to market rather faster than a small company acting alone. For example, this is common in the area of genetic research enterprises. Additionally, large companies may seek a joint venture in order to gain a foothold in new product areas and to acquire new expertise rapidly. This has been the case with large agrochemical companies which have allied with small and medium sized biotechnology companies. A third reason for joint ventures is to enable the partners to reduce their cost base by pooling resources. Companies have often cut their staffing levels and reduced their distribution costs. A fourth factor is that certain developing countries such as India and China may disallow inward investment which is not tied to some form of joint venture with a domestic concern. Salomon Brothers, the American investment bank, and Dresdner Bank of Germany have both entered into joint ventures with Chinese financial companies as a result. Likewise, Royal Dutch/Shell invested in a power generation plant in India in a joint venture with Essar Group, an Indian industrial company.

Despite these attractions and the frequency of occurrence, failure is high and one of the most frequently-cited causes of such failures has been that the organizational and HRM issues were not adequately addressed.

Human resource management considerations

The human resource management aspects have usually been neglected by companies embarking on new alliances and joint ventures. There are, however, a few exceptions. Merck, for example, in the USA has a high reputation for the way it uses the HR role in managing joint ventures. Numerous joint ventures, both national and international in character, have been entered into by Merck and in each case the HR staff have been involved from the outset. Staffing solutions are devised, procedures and policies drawn up. Communication and education are given an especially high priority in order to ensure that the partners not only understand each other but can learn from each other. The overall HRM challenge involves blending corporate cultures, compensation schemes, and overcoming staffing problems.

A variant on the joint venture is an arrangement whereby companies enter into co-operative arrangements to invest in and share common services – such as a local training facility. In a more formal way this is exemplified by the Shared Service Centre (SSC) established for the BBC by a joint venture company formed by Coopers & Lybrand (now known as Pricewaterhouse-Coopers) and EDS, the US systems group. A 10-year contract has been signed under which staff will eventually work for the joint venture company – but on BBC premises. The shared service centre has allowed the finance function the opportunity to offer career development to two quite different groups of staff. High quality finance staff 'are not going to spend a lifetime pushing debits and credits. We want to build skills in the value-added areas', claimed the Finance Director. In time other companies may use the SSC as it effectively becomes an outsourcing centre. For the present time it is located inside the BBC. Shared service arrangements have also been launched by General Electric, Seagram, Bristol Myers Squib and Whirlpool. Essentially an SSC does all those tasks that do not need to be kept close to the heart of a business. Placing an order with a supplier is a decision that must be taken at the centre – but the payment of the bill and recording of the transaction can be done at the SSC. Meanwhile, the staff working on processing transactions find themselves in a larger, single, organization with greater career opportunities. There has also been a need to put in place management structures to ensure the main customer/contractor is able to keep a measure of strategic control (Jim Kelly, *Financial Times*, July 1997).

Networks and virtual organizations

Network forms have attracted immense attention in recent years as signalled by the Special Issue devoted to the theme in both the *Academy of Management Journal* (December 2004) and the *Academy of Management Executive* (November 2003).

An organization such as Benetton is characterized by its organized network of market relations based on complex forms of contracting. It operates a retail system based entirely on franchising. On the other hand, its sourcing for garments is based on a putting-out system which has a long history. Nowadays, information and communication technology allows the total complex system to operate with rapid feedback enabling it to operate with the absolute minimum of stock. In this system it is the wider network rather than the organization which is the interesting unit of analysis – indeed arguably Benetton, as such, is not an 'organization' at all in the conventional sense (Clegg, 1990). Organizations such as Coca-Cola and Visa, despite their strong worldwide presence are likewise not traditional organizations. It is very hard to pin down the 'ownership' of these forms, some of them have no fixed assets: some commentators maintain that they really are 'virtual organizations'.

A network organization has been defined as an economic entity that operates through a cluster of compact business units, driven by the market, with few levels of decision-making and a willingness to outsource whatever can be better done elsewhere (Snow, 1992). It can be expected that new management functions will be needed – for example, brokers, architects, lead-operators and caretakers.

This free-flow across organizational boundaries can reach a stage when the organization per se becomes indefinable and unrecognizable – what Davidow and Malone (1992) have described as the 'virtual organization'. They ask:

> What will the virtual corporation look like? There is no single answer. To the outside observer it will appear almost edgeless, with permeable and continuously

changing interfaces between company, supplier and customers. From inside the firm the view will be no less amorphous, with traditional offices, departments and operating divisions constantly reforming according to need. Job responsibilities will constantly shift, as will lines of authority – even the very definition of employee will change as some customers and suppliers begin to spend more time in the company than will some of the firm's own workers. (1992: 5–6)

Human resource management considerations

The inherent capability of ICT to allow 'virtual teams' to operate across the globe raises new questions for HR. Typically, these include whether to encourage face-to-face interaction or not, if so how much, and to what extent they should be empowered. A study by Kirkman and Rosen (2004) of 35 virtual sales and service teams revealed that team empowerment was positively associated with both process improvement and customer satisfaction. The degree of face-to-face interaction, however, played a mediating rather than a direct role in that its effects depended upon the amount of empowerment. Other studies too have found that social cohesion and network range affect the efficacy of knowledge transfer within a network (e.g. Reagons and McEvily, 2003). People management choices are thus closely associated with organizational choices.

The management or coordination of network organizations likewise demands attention to HR issues. The underlying logic of network organizations as presented by their advocates and practitioners is that 'know-how' and resource capability are now critical factors and these are increasingly difficult to locate within the boundaries of a single organization. Know-how and capability are increasing distributed across a network of different business and contractors. But if this is so, the human resource management challenge to identify, retain, develop and appropriate such scarce resources are immense.

Part of the know-how resides in the identification of the parties and the capability to bring them together. In the 'the boundaryless organization' there are huge uncertainties about who, if anyone, is managing these processes. External boundaries are barriers between firms and the outside world including customers and suppliers but also government agencies, special interest groups and the community at large. In traditional organizations there are clear demarcation lines separating 'insiders' from 'outsiders'. Role expectations were relatively clear. Management dealt with the former group and had mechanisms and techniques to help them do this. But these traditional methods are of doubtful validity in the network situation.

Under the network arrangement, there are contracts of a more commercial nature. Equally, there are connecting lines based on repeat business, trust and reputation. Mindsets and attitudes have to change considerably. Traditional methods of negotiation, competition, win–lose, information withholding, power plays and the like may cause difficulties.

Increasingly, boundary maintenance behaviour is seen as having dysfunctional consequences. When the boundaries are dissolved or drastically reduced, customers and suppliers may be treated as joint partners. Employees, as such, may be hard to identify. A range of parties may be expected to help the firm solve problems and to innovate. Effective network organizations need to make permeable the external boundaries that divide them from their customers and suppliers. The key concept here is that of the value chain. This is the set of linkages which create services and products of value to the end user. In the traditional view each company is supposed to maximize its own success with disregard for that of others. The over-riding idea is that of competition. Under the new value chain concept the idea is to loosen external boundaries so as to create a win–win across the whole value chain.

Under the network concept co-operative relations between organizations are given high priority. As the cost of innovation increases, as complexity increases and everything changes so much faster, many companies have come to the conclusion that they simply cannot work alone (Storey and Salaman, 2005). Business partners, customers and suppliers are urged to work together to co-produce value. This entails reconfiguring roles and relationships. The use of co-operative arrangements of a network kind has long been well developed in Japan. The *keitsu* consists of cross-locking companies often straddling very different sectors. They have shares in each others' equity but there is no governing holding company.

The successful value chain companies co-operate in both strategic and operational business planning. Network organizations require managers and staff to change their assumptions and behaviours. Instead of developing plans and strategies independently, planning needs to be coordinated and even shared with other participants in the network. Information therefore must not be hoarded and protected but shared to allow joint problem solving. Moreover, measurement and auditing systems need to be coordinated.

Organizational members therefore need to adjust their mindsets so that the well-being of the whole value chain is kept in mind and enhanced. For example GE Appliances collaborated with key suppliers. Together they can plan for and respond more quickly to changes in the production schedules. Production, inventory, sales, specification and scheduling data can be coordinated. A monthly data package is shared with 25 main suppliers. An organization may be considered well linked into its value chain if it scores high on a set of measures of joint development in marketing plans, product development planning, production and inventory planning, distribution planning and information systems planning. And for the management of resources and capabilities the indicators would be shared resources as opposed to separate resources in the areas of technical expertise, financial expertise, management skills, information systems and training and development.

How, and why, does a company become a core organization in a network's value chain? The main identifying feature of a core organization is that it 'manages the network' – a role that is not, however, legally recognized. The actual process of managing such a network is a difficult one and it requires skills for which, as yet, little or no formal training is usually offered. The role of the core may be conceptualized as the provider and/or user of goods and services, and as the link organization. There is the possibility that the role of the core organization may change over time as exemplified by Esso's shift away from being a petrol station franchiser to becoming a link organization by moving into forecourt convenience stores.

According to proponents of networks, the human resource management implications include the involvement of as many employees as possible so that they become familiar with customer and supplier needs. This can be done through inviting customers and suppliers to meetings where outlines of plans, goals and problems can be explained. Also, by sending employees on customer and supplier field trips to encounter the detailed operations of day-to-day work. And by collecting and collating customer and supplier information. An additional stage can involve experiments with collaboration through, for example, organizing cross-value-chain task forces; or sharing technical services. And a more ambitious step involves companies integrating their information systems and reconfiguring roles and responsibilities in the light of the collaboration achieved across the networks.

Implications for strategic human resource management

The host of structural developments reviewed in this chapter such as strategic outsourcing and joint ventures have sometimes been argued as offering a major opportunity for human resource management to raise its strategic profile. This case rests partly on the observation that the many failures in initiatives of this kind have been traced to the shortcomings in human resource management and therefore this presents a strategic opportunity. It also rests in part on the point that many of the challenges thrown up by such initiatives put a premium on strategic thinking about human resource issues.

There is, however, an altogether different case that can be made: this suggests that these structural developments are highly inimical to a strategic approach to human resource management and that they rather express and impel the short-term financial denominator management approach in place of the sustained, numerator approaches extolled, for example, by Hamel and Prahalad.

There are a number of reasons for this impeding of the strategic potential. Outsourcing and other moves to market-based contractual arrangements are likely to reduce the investment by the organization in long-term skill formation activities. This is likely to apply as much to management development as it is to employee development and training more generally. There are still uncertainties about the possible loss of intellectual capital when extensive outsourcing occurs. An organization which contracts for services may, even though it initially gains a cheaper and perhaps more specialized service in the short-term, lose the capability to undertake an activity close to its core.

This set of reservations is of course not an argument for simply retaining large internal labour markets. What seems to be required is a new type of strategic management within the context of the new form of 'boundaryless' or extended 'organization'. But managing these looser boundaries requires new skills (Lynn, 2005) and the full nature of these new skills has as yet to be fully realized.

Classic bureaucracies harbour a *dual potential*. They can emphasize the rigid rules, multiple hierarchical levels and impede horizontal communication along with a command and control approach to worker management. Or, they may emphasize the psychological contract of security for long-term commitment and loyalty along with an infrastructure of training and development and corporate identity. In so far as the classic form has not been entirely abandoned, these dualities remain.

But, as we have seen in this chapter, there have also been very many and very significant departures from this classic form. The alternatives have been numerous. Descriptions and prescriptions of these have proliferated. And, to a large extent, the alternatives are still unfolding. No one has a firm fix on the emergent form. Various key attributes have been championed: prominent front runners have been the process-oriented company, the network, joint ventures and strategic alliances, the boundaryless organization and the virtual organization. We have argued in this chapter that there are some significant overlaps in these conceptualizations. For example, Ashkenas et al.'s (1995) concept of 'boundarylessness' both within and between enterprises shares very many features with Davidow and Malone's (1992) 'virtual organization'. Likewise, Nonaka's (1995) description and proselytizing of the features of 'the knowledge creating company' shares a great deal in common with Senge (1992) on 'the learning organization', Quinn (1992) on 'the intelligent enterprise', and even Hamel and Prahalad (1994) on the vital strategic importance of building core competencies.

Thus, similarities and overlaps abound. Each management consultant and would-be guru is seeking to crystallize a complex set of developments into a central idea which can be made appealing, be packaged and sold. The variations around certain underlying themes should not therefore be too surprising. This is not to say, however, that the whole set can simply be dismissed as manipulated 'fads'. The numerous accounts of the nature of 'the new organization' are capturing, albeit in a selective and partial way, critical features of important trends in organizational (re-)formation.

Approximately forty years ago, the classic organizational scholar J.D. Thompson noted the paradox that for organizations to be efficient they require stability and order, but to be effective they require external adaptability and change (Thompson, 1967). Many of the tensions we have noted in this chapter stem from this fundamental paradox. The various attempts to manage those tensions as shown in this chapter tend to generate new challenges for HRM.

References

Ashkenas, R., Ulrich, D., Tick, J. and Kerr, S. (1995) *The Boundaryless Organization: Breaking the Chains of Organizational Structure*. San Francisco: Jossey-Bass.

Balogun, J. and Johnson, G. (2004) 'Organizational restructuring and middle manager sensemaking.' *Academy of Management Journal*, 47(4): 523–549.

Benner, M.J. and Tushman, M. (2002) 'Process management and technological innovation: a longitudinal study of the photographic and paint industries.' *Administrative Science Quarterly* 47: 676–706.

Bresnen, M., Gousservskaia, A. and Swan, J. (2004) 'Embedding new managerial knowledge in project based organizations.' *Organization Studies*, 25(9): 1535–1556.

Castells, M. (2001) *The Rise of the Network Society*. Oxford: Blackwell.

Clegg, S. (1990) *Modern Organizations: Organization Studies in a Postmodern World*. London: Sage.

Courpasson, D. (2000) 'Managerial strategies of domination: Power in soft bureaucracies.' *Organization Studies*, 21(1): 141–162.

Courpasson, D. and Reed, M. (2004) 'Bureaucracy in the age of enterprise.' *Organization*, 11(1): 5–12.

Davidow, W.H. and Malone, M.S. (1992) *The Virtual Corporation: Structuring and Revitalizing the Corporation for the 21st Century*. New York: Harper Business.

du Gay, P. (2000) *In Praise of Bureaucracy*. London: Sage.

du Gay, P. (2004) 'Against Enterprise (but not against enterprise).' *Organization* 11(1): 37–59.

Edwards, R. (1979) *Contested Terrain: The Transformation of the Workplace in the Twentieth Century*. London: Heinemann.

Gabriel, Y. (2005) 'Glass cages and glass palaces: images of organization in image conscious times.' *Organization*, 12(1): 9–27.

Gouldner, A. (1954) *Patterns of Industrial Bureaucracy*. New York: The Free Press.

Hamel, G. and Prahalad, C.K. (1994) *Competing for the Future*. Boston: Harvard Business School Press.

Hammer, M. (1996) *Beyond Reengineering*. London: HarperCollins.

Hammer, M. and Champy, J. (1992) *Reengineering the Corporation*. London: HarperCollins.

Kirkman, B.L. and Rosen, B. (2004) 'The impact of team empowerment on virtual team performance: The moderating role of face to face interaction.' *Academy of Management Journal*, 47(2): 175–192.

Littler, C.R. and Innes, P. (2004) 'The paradox of managerial downsizing', *Organization Studies*, 25(7): 1159–1184.

Lynn, M.L. (2005) 'Organizational buffering: managing boundaries and cores.' *Organization Studies*, 26(1): 37–61.

March, J.G. and Simon, H.A. (1958) *Organizations*. New York: Wiley.

McNulty, T. and Ferlie, E. (2002) *Re-engineering Healthcare: The Complexities of Organizational Transformation*. Oxford: Oxford University Press.

Merton, R. (1957) *Social Theory and Social Structure*. Chicago: Free Press.

Nonaka, I. and Takeuchi, H. (1995) *The Knowledge-Creating Company: How Japanese Companies Create the Dynamics of Innovation*. Oxford: Oxford University Press.

Quinn, J.B. (1992) *Intelligent Enterprise*. New York: Free Press.

Reagons, R. and McEvily, A. (2003) 'Network structure and knowledge transfer: the effects of cohesion and range.' *Administrative Science Quarterly*, 48: 240–267.

Reed, M. (1999) 'From the iron cage to the gaze? The Dynamics of organizational control in late modernity' in G. Morgan and L. Engwall (eds), *Regulation in Organizations*. London: Routledge.

Sabel, C. (2003) *Cognition, Structure, Governance and Power*. European Group for Organization Studies, Copenhagen.

Schilling, M. and Steensma, H.K. (2001) 'The use of modular organizational forms: an industry level analysis.' *Academy of Management Journal*, 44: 1149–1168.

Selznick, P. (1966) *TVA and the Grass Roots*. Berkeley: University of California Press.

Senge, P. (1992) *The Fifth Discipline: The Art and Practice of the Learning Organization*. London: Century Business.

Snow, C. and Miles, R. (1992) 'Managing 21st century network organizations', *Organizational Dynamics*, 20: 5–20.

Storey, J. (2002) 'What are the general manager issues in supply chain management?' *Journal of General Management*, 27(4): 65–79.

Storey, J. and Salaman, G. (2005) *Managers of Innovation: Insights into Making Innovation Happen*. Oxford: Blackwell.

Thompson, J.D. (1967) *Organizations in Action*. New York: McGraw-Hill.

Womack, J.P. and Jones, D.J. (1996) *Lean Thinking*. New York: Simon & Schuster.

10

Changing Organizational Forms and the Employment Relationship

Jill Rubery, Jill Earnshaw, Mick Marchington,
Fang Lee Cooke and Steven Vincent

Multiple employers: a missing concept in the debate on the changing nature of work and changing structure of organizations

There is a burgeoning literature on both the changing nature of work and employment and on the changing nature of organizations. Both sets of literature, from different starting points and perspectives, have in our view failed to deal adequately with the links between changing organizational forms and changing employment relationships.

Within the employment and work-orientated literature, there has been a widespread debate on the ending of the standard employment contract and associated changes to notions of job security, fuelled by the proliferation of contractual forms and uncertainty over employment status and the destabilization and reshaping of bureaucratic organizations (Burchell et al., 1999b; Cappelli, 1997; Casey et al., 1997; Gallie and White, 1998; Peck and Theodore, 1998; Rodgers and Rodgers, 1988). The focus of employment law has been expanded, in parallel with this development, from a narrow concern with employer–employee relations to a broader concern with employer–worker relations with the term 'workers' used to include a wider range of employment relationships than direct employees. This focus on more flexibility in careers and contracts has coincided with an increasing emphasis, however, on the

Source: Jill Rubery, Jill Earnshaw, Mick Marchington, Fang Lee Cooke and Steven Vincent (2002) 'Changing organizational forms and the employment relationship', *Journal of Management Studies*, 39(5): 645–72. Edited version.

importance of commitment to the organization and on the psychological contract with the employer as critical factors in enhanced competitiveness (Guest, 1998).

Within the human resource literature there has been very limited analysis of the impact of inter-organizational alliances, networks and partnerships. By way of contrast, these new organizational forms have provided a dominant focus in recent literature in the fields of organizational analysis, industrial organization and innovation theory (see Oliver and Ebers, 1998, for a survey of the field). Much of the discussion of flexibility within the work organization and employment literature has been limited to flexibility within single organizations. It has only usually been expanded to include the use of sub-contracting and temporary employment agencies as a substitute for direct employment. With the possible exception of work by Hunter et al. (1996) and Scarbrough (2000), there has been little examination of partnership and network arrangements that organizations develop. More unstable career patterns and the increased passing-on of risk to employees are recognized to be creating problems for organizational commitment and for the trust relation at the heart of the psychological contract. Yet the implications of cross-organizational relationships and partnerships for organizational commitment, as well as for both the psychological and legal contracts underlying the employment relationships, have been largely ignored.

A similar lacuna can be identified within the organizational and innovation literature. Much has been written on the factors driving trends towards more permeable organizational boundaries, including the changing nature of transaction costs (Schendel, 1995; Semlinger, 1991; Williamson, 1985), the search for flexible and low cost ways of expanding the resource base of organizations (Montgomery, 1995; Stinchcombe, 1990) and the increasing need to generate opportunities for learning and sharing of knowledge (Matusik and Hill, 1998). Many of these factors implicitly depend on the nature of employment relations and on the capacities of employees both to respond to learning opportunities and to resist temptations for opportunistic behaviour. Despite the centrality of employment of these developments, detailed and direct consideration of employment issues is rare, except through stylized analyses based on assumptions that it is possible to predict and control the likelihood of opportunistic behaviour through appropriate management tools and incentives (Matusik and Hill, 1998). For the most part, these permeable organizations are still referred to as if they consist of a single entity with single interests. The success of the joint venture, alliance or network is identified as dependent both upon appropriate management tools and the establishment of trust relations. The development of inter-firm trust relations is conceived and discussed as if they are independent of trust relations within employment relationships.

The aim of this paper is to address the missing links in these various literatures. We identify the key areas where the permeable nature of organizations and the development of multi-employer relationships introduce new problems and ambiguities, both into the employment relationship and into the potential gains and 'efficiencies' to be derived from partnerships and networks. The first part of the paper focuses on the lack of consideration of multi-employer relationships in these various debates and literatures and identifies the potential significance of filling such gaps. The second part addresses the issue of managing employment relationships in a multi-employer context. Here we identify the scope for mixed messages and conflicts and contradictions in, for example, reward systems, performance objectives and organizational commitment. Conflicting pressures also apply to the choice of mode of employment organization and management. Multi-employer relationships can be identified as simultaneously creating impulses towards the use of more intense and direct forms of control associated with the notion of contract, and also towards increased reliance on autonomous, empowered and motivated employees.

Employment relations have traditionally and typically been conceived as involving a single employer–employee relationship. The complexities in the relationship are seen to derive from the social, legal and institutional conditions which embed and surround the employment relationship and which derive from considerations both internal and external to the organization. Accordingly, conflicts and contradictions between the objectives of the employer and the broader social and legal context are well known and discussed. The argument made here is that conflicts and contradictions arise also out of inter-organizational relationships which create confusions and ambiguities in the shaping of the employment relationship in both its legal and its social, institutional and psychological form. In the next two sections, we look at this argument from the perspective of employment law issues, and follow it up with a discussion of the implications of the development of permeable organizational boundaries for such key concepts as organizational commitment and organizational learning.

Broadening the legal definition of the employer–employee relationship: from employees to workers and from single employer to multi-employer?

The contract of employment can be regarded as being the cornerstone of the employment relationship (Deakin, 1986). In the UK, by statute (Employment Rights Act 1996) an 'employee' is defined as a person who works under a contract of employment, the tacit assumption being that 'the employer' is the other party to the contract. In the 1970s the importance of being regarded in law as an employee of a single employer was brought sharply into focus by the introduction of employment protection based on a model of permanent, full-time employment for a single employer. On the whole, these new rights were available only to employees and acquired by completion of a continuous period of two years' employment, working at least 16 hours per week for a single employer. Individuals working under a 'contract for services', i.e., the self-employed, were excluded because their relationship with their employer or employers was not seen to be one of dependency.

Over time there has been a move to broaden the application of employment rights for two main reasons. Firstly the application of the single employer–employee definition proved to be more difficult in practice than was anticipated as there was no simple bilateral divide between the two forms of contractual relationship, and the most that courts and tribunals could do was to pin-point whereabouts a given individual fell along the spectrum of dependency. Secondly, during the 1980s, the growth in 'atypical' employment (Felstead and Jewson, 1999; O'Reilly and Fagan, 1998; Rodgers and Rodgers, 1988) and in particular the various forms of 'dependent' self-employment, meant that the distinction between employment and self-employment became increasingly blurred and less easy to distinguish. Moreover an increasing proportion of the workforce fell outside the safety net of employment protection (Leighton and Painter, 1987). In consequence, new pieces of protective legislation since the early 1990s have not been limited to 'employees'. Instead, their benefits have been conferred on 'workers', defined as:

> Those who undertake to do or perform any work or services for another party to the contract whose status is not, by virtue of the contract, that of a client or customer of any profession or business undertaking carried on by the individual. (see e.g. section 230, Employment Rights 1996)

In particular, it has been the use of this term in the UK Working Time Regulations 1998 and the National Minimum Wage Act 1998 which has highlighted the government's recognition of the inadequacy of the term 'employee' as defined in case law, to cover the sort of relationship under which many individuals now work. Research by Burchell et al. (1999a) suggested that up to 5 per cent of all those in employment could be affected by an extension of existing employment protection rights to 'workers', and a provision was subsequently included in the Employment Relations Act 1999 giving power to the Secretary of State to do so at a future date.

However, just as there has been an increasing mismatch between the definition of an 'employee' and the reality of modern-day working patterns, so too the development of more complex organizational forms leads to a questioning of the notion of who is the employer, and a perception that the legal framework of the employment relationship may need to be adjusted to take into account the way in which work may be organized in the future. Table 10.1 provides some illustrative examples of the problems which these types of organizational forms may generate for the maintenance of a concept of a single employer.

Table 10.1 *Types of organizational arrangements which may lead to ambiguities*

Organizational arrangement	Ambiguities in control and performance
Dependent self employment and sub-contractors	Main 'employer' responsible for health and safety for all on site (overlapping with responsibilities of subsidiary employers).
Temporary agency workers	Agency, as the employer, not able to control the work or to verify basis for discipline cases.
Franchise	Franchisor may control work processes through contract and/or issue grievance/discipline framework to franchisees.
Multi-employer site	Third party may be affected by performance of contract between two other parties and may be involved in monitoring performance of companies/employees with which/whom it has no contract.
Partnerships and supply chain relationships	Partners may either request that specific employees are deployed on partnership activities or require information on the qualifications, experience, training etc of the partner's employees.
Outsourcing (whether within or outside TUPE)	Outsourced employees may have work checked/verified by managers in client company if latter retains authority/knowledge.
Outsourcing under TUPE	Terms and conditions of transferred employees may be preserved but frozen; differ from those left behind *and* from other employees in company to which they are transferred.

[...]

Multi-employer sites may lead to monitoring of performance of workforces by organizations where there are no direct contractual relationships; for example, where the 'owner' of the site or facilities is affected by the performance of other companies on site, it may monitor performance of a contract to which it is not directly a party. These performance indicators may be used in the appraisal or discipline of individual employees or teams of employees employed by another organization. In another example of indirect control by a non-employer, organizations involved in a partnership or supply chain relationship may influence the deployment of staff in the partner organization by making explicit requests for certain individuals to be assigned to the tasks. This external control of the employees' work may have subsequent implications for, for example, promotion opportunities or even decisions over compulsory redundancies. However, these requests may be made on only partial information concerning the efficiency of the employees concerned, perhaps based mainly on knowledge of the preferred individual, while the other employees are rejected simply because the partner organization has no direct knowledge of their work. Partner companies may also request detailed information on qualifications, training and experience of the workforce deployed on their contracts. Indeed, this form of control over the quality of work is explicitly encouraged in the relational contracting literature, but again these quality indicators may lead to discrimination against potentially equally productive employees who lack formal qualifications.

Under some forms of outsourcing, there may be even more direct control by the external client organization of work undertaken by the employees of the subcontracting company if the client company retains a role in checking and verifying work. This may apply particularly where there remains a legal or statutory duty on the client firm to ensure the quality and accuracy of the service provided by the subcontractor. Indeed, to an increasing extent, arrangements arising out of transfers of undertakings are producing situations in which there is an artificiality in the notion of a single employer–employee relationship. In its simplest form, a transfer of an undertaking occurs where one employer sells his or her business to another. To protect the transferor's employees in such a situation, the Transfer of Undertakings (Protection of Employment) 'TUPE' Regulations 1981 require that, in effect, the employees are to be treated as part of the business and transferred with it on their current terms and conditions. When this occurs, the transferee becomes the employer of the transferred employees and the transferor then disappears from the picture. However in reality, the TUPE Regulations have featured most prominently in situations in which the transferor maintains a connection with the undertaking transferred, a situation which particularly applies to the transfer of services from the public sector. Even when the main services transferred have been ancillary services, such as cleaning or catering, which in a sense could be divorced from the transferor's main business operation, there is a need for continuing coordination between transferor and transferee. What we are now seeing, for example in the case of PFIs, is a remaining close alliance between the transferor and transferee after the transfer. Although the transferee becomes in law the employer of the staff transferred, they remain on the premises of the transferor and work 'with' staff who have not been transferred. Moreover, although the transferred employees retain their terms and conditions of employment, they are not fully integrated into the new organization and may continue to have quite divergent terms and conditions, both from new direct recruits and from pre-existing employees in the outsourcing company. Nor do they retain the right to have their terms and conditions upgraded along with the employees who remain with the old employer and with whom they may continue to work alongside in the same workplace.

From these illustrative examples of different multi-employer contexts, we can identify the following areas of employment law and practice where the existence of multi-employers or the absence of a single employer can be identified as creating ambiguities. This is summarized in Table 10.2.

Table 10.2 *Main areas of ambiguity in employment*

Employment issue	Ambiguities in the employment relationship
Supervision and control	Employer not present at workplace or more than one 'employer' present. Employee on loan/on secondment to another 'employer'.
Discipline	Differences in rules between 'employers'; who is responsible for monitoring performance, identifying disciplinary issues, initiating actions, verifying information.
Grievance	For example, duties not to harass staff apply to contract staff, not just direct employees; can employees have a grievance against employer if harassed by manager/ employee of another organization?
Terms and conditions – equal pay issues	TUPE and outsourcing may result in different pay for work of same or broadly equivalent value for *either* employees of same organization *or* employees of different organizations but working side by side in same workplace.
Health and safety responsibilities and other legal/statutory obligations	Responsibility for health and safety of workers/ general public lies with main employer/owner of site, but can managers of main employer instruct employees of other employers not to behave in ways which endanger health and safety?
	Main employer may have responsibility for overall delivery of service (e.g. hospital); responsibilities indirectly enforced on non-employees through performance-related contracts with other employers.
Loyalty and confidentiality	Duties of loyalty and confidentiality to employer may be difficult to interpret where conflicts of interest arise between own employer and those of the employer in the workplace where the employee is located.
Trade union recognition	Multi-employer relationships may complicate the definition and constitution of appropriate bargaining units for trade union recognition.

Supervision and control issues arise when the 'employer' is not physically present at the workplace. These problems apply in a range of circumstances, for example with salespeople or employees who provide care in the community, and there are various management devices used for controlling effort levels and quality of work in these circumstances, from performance incentives to random inspections. However, in the context of multi-employers, the issues are more complex as there are potentially other 'employers' present at the workplace who may exercise their own control over the work process. Discipline is another thorny area, for although the employer, for example a temporary agency, may have its own disciplinary procedures, it is hard to see how these can be operated in isolation from those of the particular client firm in which a worker is placed. At the most basic level, questions arise as to whose rules apply as well as how discipline can be initiated and by whom. What would happen in a situation in which the worker commits an act which is regarded as misconduct by the client firm but not (or not to the same extent) by the agency? It may be the case, for example, that a certain type of conduct is regarded by the particular client as gross misconduct warranting summary dismissal, but attracts only a warning in the agency's procedure.

Tricky questions may also arise in relation to grievances, for instance where an agency worker is subjected to harassment by the manager of the client firm. In this case, it is important to note that the Sex Discrimination Act 1975 and the Race Relations Act 1976 specifically cover discrimination against contract workers (see *Harrods Ltd v. Remick* (1997) IRLR 583), thereby establishing duties from managers in multi-employer situations towards those who are working for or associated with but not employees of the organization. Nevertheless, there remain major problems with inconsistent application of procedures which are exacerbated in situations where the rules are laid down by more than one employer.

[...]

The ambiguous nature of the employer–employee relationship in these sorts of complex organizational forms means that not only may employees find it difficult to adapt to the culture of the organization which is legally their 'employer', but that they may experience conflict in relation to duties of loyalty and confidentiality. Since such duties normally arise by virtue of an implied term in every contract of employment, it follows that they are owed to the 'legal' employer. Yet if individuals are working on the premises of another employer or in some sort of joint venture or other alliance with such an employer's staff, it is not difficult to see that issues involving a conflict of interest may arise. The employee of one of the collaborating employers may come across information as a result of their secondment to the other 'employer' which is of direct relevance to his or her legal employer; for example, information concerning the future of the collaboration, or information that was withheld before the collaboration was established but might be of material relevance to the decision to set up the alliance or partnership. It is difficult to see how, in this situation, the 'non-legal' employer could impose any kind of confidentiality clause on the individuals who may gain access to information (which may be of interest to their own employer). Presumably these would be matters which would have to be covered at contractual level in any agreement between the two employers. Awareness of these potential conflicts of interest could lead to contractual arrangements based on low trust and limited disclosure of information which would restrict the efficiency of the partnership or alliance. These issues are recognized in the organizational literature on networks and partnerships, with a focus on actions taken to prevent the limitation or adoption of valuable resources. However, this discussion is not extended to consider the role of employment law in such conflicts of interests, or the more general issues of duty and loyalty which may arise when the employees concerned normally have limited access to knowledge which organizations wish to withhold from competitors.

[...]

Blurring the boundaries of the organization: the neglect of employment relations

In contrast to other literature, the fields of organizational analysis, industrial organization and strategic management have taken up the issue of changing organizational forms and the associated trend towards permeable organizational boundaries as a major area of research focus (see Oliver and Ebers, 1998 for a survey). This focus is clearly linked to concerns over the role of knowledge and learning in competitive strategies, and the implications of new technologies for organizational forms. However, missing from these analyses is an explicit and developed discussion of the employment relationship and how this may both shape the initial decisions to open up organizational boundaries and how the networks and alliances are operated in practice. Moreover, the predicted gains from such arrangements may be critically dependent upon the actual roles that employees of both organizations play in implementing partnerships, joint ventures or outsourcing arrangements. Some authors do make reference to the need for those involved in alliances and networks to be embedded in high trust systems or to be 'empowered' workers, not subject to tight direct control if the expected learning synergies are to materialize (Anand and Khanna, 2000; Kale et al., 2000). However, while trust relationships refer both to relations between companies and to employer–employee relations, the potential for complementary or conflicting interactions between these two dimensions is not fully analyzed.

There are three main arguments that have been developed to explain the growth of these complex or permeable organizational forms. First there is the notion of transaction costs, traditionally used to explain the development of the bureaucratic organization. Changes to the level of transaction costs, associated in particular with information technology, is seen as one factor explaining trends towards less integrated firms (Schendel, 1995; Semlinger, 1991; Williamson, 1985). The opportunity to develop virtual organizations based on complex network and subcontract relations has been considerably enhanced by the development of ICT although complex 'putting out' systems are not dependent on ICT and predated the integrated organization (Marglin, 1976). New technologies do provide new opportunities for control or surveillance by the contracting employer, thereby countering the argument put forward by Marglin and others that integrated workplaces were needed to establish control over the labour process. However, these control systems may also have their own built in rigidities. Inter-organizational relationships and partnerships may require, at least in the initial bedding down period, the exercise of initiative to cope with areas of uncertainty surrounding the interorganizational partnerships.

Second, the resource-based theory of the firm (Montgomery, 1995; Penrose, 1959) suggests that organizations compete through the development of firm-specific assets and knowledge. This may lead both to the outsourcing of stable activities which are not central to the development of the resource base and to the formation of joint ventures or alliances when organizations seek to expand into new or novel areas (Coombs and Battaglia, 1998; Coombs and Ketchen, 1999). This approach complements the resource-based theories of human resource management (Boxall, 1996) but does not address directly the complexities of managing relationships across organizations as a factor which may inhibit the development of dynamic efficiencies, particularly if organizations make ill-judged decisions as to which of their activities should be considered key competencies or which activities are better developed internally or through alliances. A top down view of organizational effectiveness may lead organizations to overlook the significant role played by relatively low paid workers in the maintenance, for example, of customer relations and company image (Fearfull, 1992).

According to the third approach, permeable organizations may provide an effective means of learning and knowledge acquisition in situations where these are significant factors in competitiveness. Some of the literature combines this approach with the resource-based theory of the firm. Distinctions are thus made between conditions under which it is – or is not – in the interests of an organization to open up its boundaries to knowledge acquisition and learning. Organizations with significant firm-specific knowledge on which they base their competitive strengths may tend not to open up their boundaries unless these assets can be protected against imitation by competitors. However, given the growth in these network arrangements and in the apparent importance of firm-specific knowledge in competition, recent work has sought to find explanations as to why these arrangements may still come into play. Organizations with specific-knowledge assets may still be interested, Coombs and Ketchen (1999) argue, in networks and partnerships involving other organizations with similar stakes in company-specific knowledge. If both sides have interests in ring-fencing their resource base of specific assets, it may be possible to enter into partnership arrangements where these assets are protected. Implicitly such arguments identify power relations between organizations as important factors in determining whether or not new organizational forms will emerge.

By and large, however, these analyses focus only on inter-organizational power relations on the assumption that asset specificity takes the form of organizational routines and knowledge which is independent from the specific skills, knowledge and behaviour of individual employees. Exactly how agreements to protect asset specificity are translated into behaviour by employees and exactly how the learning from the partnerships and network arrangements occurs is for the most part left unspecified. Where attempts are made to make these processes more explicit, the effect is to reveal a rather simplistic and stylized approach to employment relations. For example, Matusik and Hill (1998) suggest that it is wrong to argue that firms for which private knowledge is important will not use contingent workers (such as consultants) for fear of leakage of their private knowledge base. In dynamic changing markets these firms need to find cheap and effective ways both to update their public knowledge base – that is, knowledge in the public domain – and to encourage a creative fusion between new public knowledge and the private knowledge base. However, to achieve these twin objectives they are reliant on their employees in two ways: first on their loyalty and commitment to guard against contingent workers gaining access to specific knowledge, and second on their motivation to learn from the contingent workers. The loyalty factor is effectively taken for granted and motivation is believed achievable through the adoption of a formal strategy valuing knowledge acquisition and the development of appropriate structures such as teamworking or advice networks. However, a cursory examination of human resource management in practice reveals that the adoption of formal policies and practices does not necessarily generate desired levels of loyalty or motivation. This may be particularly the case where employees of the organization are expected to develop a heightened commitment to the interests of the organization, in opposition to the interests of contingent workers, yet are still expected to work alongside contingent workers in teams, sharing ideas, insights and knowledge. The reliance on these motivational techniques and structures reveals the uncertainty of actual outcomes and the significance of employment relations to the decisions to open up organizational boundaries. [...]

To take this analysis a little further, we examine some of the key employment aspects which are missing from most of the analyses of different organizational forms. First, the current interest in networked organizations is based on the notion that this is an effective way to gain access to skilled labour. Yet there is little analysis of how skilled labour is provided and reproduced. If the responsibilities for training and learning are passed to individuals, then this may critically affect the ways in which individuals operate within the network

(Cappelli et al., 1997). Their main concern will be to use their skills and learning for developing their own careers, and this factor may inhibit or change the process of sharing knowledge and learning. Where employers take responsibility, their concerns may be to prevent those employers who fail to contribute to the pool gaining access to the skill base.

Within outsourcing decisions there are also concerns relating to the skill base and its reproduction. Short term cost reductions can be achieved either through reducing training costs or by simplifying work procedures to reduce skill input. These strategies may work in a situation of outsourcing in the short term if there is a plentiful supply of trained labour and if the client firm retains managers with wider skills and knowledge, enabling them to supervise and manage the outsourcing relationship. Yet in the longer term, the wider skills base of the client firm management may diminish if there is no longer direct experience of the process in-house and there is a fall in the overall supply of skilled labour in the external market. Even outsourcing of low paid and apparently routinized work may run into problems where either the outsourcer fails to provide a competent service or where the process of outsourcing requires the development of a close relationship between the client company and the outsourcer to maintain a 'seamless' image and good customer relations. These problems are exacerbated where there is no clear focus of responsibility and lengthy disputes arise over which party needs to take action or bear the cost to solve unanticipated problems. A clear example of this is where large organizations decide to focus on their core competencies and outsource responsibility for dealing with customer complaints.

Joint ventures, alliances and partnerships are often entered into with the explicit aim of expanding the dynamic capabilities of the firm based on the acquisition of knowledge and the sharing of learning (Coombs and Battaglia, 1998). However, the embodiment of knowledge and learning within individuals creates problems for dividing the spoils of such ventures. These problems go beyond the simple derivation of formulae for rent sharing which dominates the strategic alliance literature. Knowledge and learning belongs to individuals and has to be incorporated into the behaviour of others in the firm if it is to have more general effects. The likelihood of this taking place will depend inter alia on the employment relationship. Furthermore, individuals cannot divide their own knowledge and this may lead to different rates of return to the collaborating organizations, dependent upon whether it is their employees or those of the other organization who have acquired most knowledge and learning. Heterogeneous employment systems have been identified as conducive to learning among individual employees (Anand and Khanna, 2000), but these systems may not be well orientated towards passing on that learning and knowledge to other individuals or groups, or incorporating it into the normal functioning of organizations. This may be particularly the case where organizations function on the basis of relatively autonomous individuals or teams. Table 10.3 summarizes the major issues in relation to efficiency and employment relations in a number of different organizational forms.

Table 10.3 *Questions of employment relations in the realization of gains from extending organizational boundaries*

Organizational form	Assumed basis for synergy/efficiency	Role of employment relationship
Networked organizations	Drawing upon larger pool of expertise than can be trained/developed/retained in-house	Issue of who takes responsibility for training and development; if individual then knowledge/training will be used in interests of individual's career. Incentive structure for creating/sharing knowledge and expertise depends upon conditions in employment relationship.
Outsourcing	Reduction in costs	Power relations between contractors or between contracting organization and employees influences costs outcome. Short term cost savings may not ensure reproduction of skill base.
	Concentration on core competencies	Outsource areas not apparently related to core competencies but danger of assumption that low wage/apparently routinized work not significant for organizational performance.
Joint ventures/ partnerships/ strategic alliances	To maximize resource base of firm/dynamic capabilities	Human resources central to the resource based theory of firm; but contradictions/conflicts in managing and developing human resources not taken into account. Contracts to share intellectual property rights between joint ventures, but knowledge/expertise located in individuals, employed by one or other organization.
	Learning and knowledge across organizational boundaries	High levels of heterogeneity based on autonomous work relationships found to favour learning but too heterogeneous systems may inhibit absorption of new knowledge and learning within the organization. Learning and imparting of knowledge dependent upon, for example, employee turnover, teamworking, loyalty and commitment to employer, capacity and willingness to impart knowledge to others.

While these potential difficulties are recognized within some parts of the organizational literature, the focus again tends to be on the need to develop particular systems or management styles to overcome these problems. Employee motivation may not be as easily manipulable as this focus on management techniques suggests. Moreover, the very development of permeable boundaries to organizations calls into question issues of organizational commitment on which the effectiveness of many of these management techniques appear to rely. However, while organizational analysis perhaps takes a too simplistic approach to the management of employees, the literature which focuses directly on employee motivation and commitment – the human resource management literature – has perhaps paid too little attention to the development of permeable boundaries to organizations.

Human resource management: bounded by notions of the single employer

In recent years, the human resource management literature has expanded greatly, typically around the distinction between so-called 'soft' and 'hard' versions of HRM (Legge, 1995; Sisson, 1994; Storey, 1995, 2001). The former has also been referred to as high commitment management (Wood, 1999) or 'best practice' HRM, and it has been fuelled by contributions both from the USA (Pfeffer, 1994, 1998; Walton, 1985) and from the UK (Guest et al., 2000). The basic argument is simple: organizations need to invest in a range of human capital-enhancing practices, such as extensive training and learning, teamworking and employee involvement, and high levels of pay in order to capture and mobilize the contributions of employees. The notion of employer and organization is treated as unproblematic within this approach, and the techniques that are adopted for identifying which human resource practices have been adopted by an organization rely typically on a single response from a single respondent. Recent work by Guest (1998) and Guest et al. (2000), which is based on responses from employees to a CIPD survey, typifies this sort of analysis. Employers are categorized and differentiated according to the number of specified HR practices that are present at the workplace. There is no opportunity to examine differences within – as opposed to between – workplaces, even though some surveys ask about the proportion of workers covered by various practices, thereby implicitly making allowance for internal variation (Huselid, 1995). Accordingly, it is not possible to differentiate between different groups of workers at establishments that are home to multiple employers or include employees working for a range of different employers at the same workplace. All are treated as if they receive the same set of benefits.

Those studies that draw upon the 'hard' or contingent approaches to HRM specifically relate the choice of human resource strategies and practices to the peculiar features of the firm and its environment, and they have also featured prominently in recent analyses (Purcell, 1995, 1999; Boxall and Purcell, 2000). Unlike the 'soft' approaches that seek to identify particular sets of HR practice that may be able to enhance performance in all workplaces, these studies argue that different HR practices may be appropriate in different organizations. The choice of which HR practice to adopt depends on factors such as product or labour market circumstances, size or technology employed. However, as with the 'best practice' approaches, the contingent explanations have not been applied to network organizations, alliances or partnerships. In particular, they are bound to be limited in seeking to explain how two different organizations in quite different market situations can agree to adopt a coherent approach to human resource management. In a similar vein, contingent explanations may have difficulty in understanding how workers from different organizations – such as an employment agency and a local authority – who operate alongside each other can be subject to different terms and conditions.

Both approaches have been subject to extensive critical comment, in particular in relation to the universal applicability of the 'best practice' approach (Marchington and Grugulis, 2000) and the methodological base upon which it is built (Purcell, 1999). It has been difficult to assess whether or not the contingency approaches apply in practice, and there are doubts about whether or not grand strategic visions can ever be achieved in reality (Storey, 1995; Marchington and Wilkinson, 1996). In addition to these problems however, neither perspective provides a framework which is adequate to take into account the complexities introduced by the permeable organization when systems of HRM and performance management operate across organizational boundaries. First, both implicitly assume that managers are able to adopt certain sets of HR practices that are likely to be acceptable to what are essentially seen as 'passive' employees. The management of people is treated as if it were a technical function performed on human resources in much the same way that capital and land are treated. Coff (1997) is one of the few to recognize that there are likely to be substantial problems in putting HR practices into effect because employees have 'independent wills'. This is something that is also almost unheard of in the 'best practice' approaches.

Secondly, both are built around notions of employees showing commitment and loyalty to a specific organization, and the emphasis is on organizations developing particular cultures that are likely to appeal to employees. As Guest (1998: 42) notes, 'the concept of organizational commitment is at the heart of any analysis of HRM'. However, it is acknowledged that commitment is notoriously hard to define, and we need to be clear whether or not the reference is to the employing organization (locally or at corporate level), the work group, the trade union or the occupation, or indeed something else. In situations where the notion of the single employer is open to question – such as in the case of multiple employers on a single site, or when call centres are staffed with people from agencies who work alongside those from the 'host' employer, or in the case of a PFI – the problem is further compounded. As no distinction tends to be made between different categories of worker in most surveys, it is inevitable that variations in practice and other complexities in the employment relationship are ignored. Even studies that might be expected to differentiate amongst those working at a particular site, such as when there is likely to be a high utilization of temporary and/or agency labour, seem to assume that one set of HR practices is common to all employees. For example, Hoque's (1999) study of hotels did not specifically mention any differences between permanent and temporary labour despite the fact that this sector is renowned for the high usage of the latter. Hutchinson et al.'s (2000) study of an RAC call centre dealt in terms of common HR practices that made up high commitment management approach despite the fact that this establishment made extensive use of temporaries, mostly students, at certain times of the year. Similarly, Gittell's (2000) study of relational co-ordination during flight departures at an airport only made reference to cross-functional as opposed to cross-organizational links. Airports are characterized by significant inter-employer relations, and many workers may actually have changed employer during recent times.

When attempting to analyse HRM and performance, it seems strange not to consider inter-organizational relations in a study such as this. One potential solution to the problem of organizational commitment in a context of uncertainty and fragmentation is to look to a trade-off between short term organizational commitment (Rajan, 1997) in return for transferable skills offered through experience with the employer. Employees' desire for transferable skills may provide an alternative motivational carrot to long term organizational career structures (Martin, et al., 1998). However, as Cappelli et al. (1997) point out, although, under these kinds of arrangements, compliance with organizational goals may be achieved, workers lack any real identification either with the organization or its strategies. Moreover, the offer of transferable skills does not overcome the problems of potential conflicting organizational commitments in a multi-employer setting.

Thirdly, both approaches operate on the assumption that employers are seeking sustained competitive advantage through the use of a consistent and ubiquitous management style. The likelihood of a sustained and consistent approach diminishes the more that employees come into contact with other organizations and their employees, as strong and consistent policies may in fact hamper rather than assist in the process of managing cross-organizational relationships.

Finally, both approaches refer to employees as opposed to workers, so discounting implicitly those people who work at the organization on a range of temporary contracts, perhaps supplied by an agency. Given recent changes in the law, which now refer to workers rather than employees, it seems time to shift our analysis to take note of this. The management of employment consists of attempts to elicit worker commitment to organizational goals and enhance their contribution, but it also comprises efforts to discipline and control what is felt to be unacceptable behaviour by workers. This becomes particularly pertinent when people employed by different organizations or on different forms of contract face disciplinary action for committing similar offences, especially if different rules and procedures are in place.

Recently, partnership agreements between employers and trade unions have been added to the raft of human capital enhancing HR practices that are used by employers committed to the notion of 'best practice' HRM (see Guest and Peccei, 1998; Marchington, 1998). Since these, like the other HR practices in the mix, rely on employees (or unions) demonstrating their commitment to mutuality, and viewing other organizations as competitors to be beaten, this makes it very difficult to conceive of relations across organizational boundaries. Moreover it is rarely made clear whether or not the partnership agreements cover all the activities of the organization including its subcontracting, joint ventures and alliances. If not, the trade unions may find themselves involved in managing an ever smaller core of activities, or indeed residing over the transfer of perhaps the main parts of the activity to other organizational arrangements.

Mixing the messages: conflicts and contradictions in the employment relationship in a multi-employer environment

In this section our attention turns to considering the potential for multi-employer relationships to introduce yet further tension and indeed conflicts and contradictions into the employment relationship, over and above those that are already present in a straightforward single employer–employee relationship. There are many potential areas where such contradictions and ambiguities may arise, but here we focus on just three: pay, performance management and organizational commitment.

Pay and conditions

Pay systems within organizations are notoriously subject to conflicting pressures and influences and reflect as much past history as current needs and realities. The main sources of influence on pay are the need to recruit and retain workers, to relate pay to accepted skill and supervisory hierarchies, and to provide incentives for, or at least to avoid disincentives for, activities consistent with the overall business strategy or goals of the organization. Each organization will make different compromises between these potentially conflicting objectives (Rubery, 1997). Moreover, organizations have different abilities to pay and have experienced different trajectories and histories relating to pay bargaining and pay determination. By and large, pay systems can only evolve gradually because of resistance to real cuts in money wages; as a result changes normally come about through differential rates of increase, not through complete restructuring of pay relationships. This fine and often delicate balance between different functions of the pay system is clearly open to disruption from the introduction of influences from the pay systems and structures of other organizations.

If the main arena for comparison is the workplace and individuals working alongside other individuals in similar or comparable jobs, then the introduction of multi-employer relationships based on different pay structures has considerable potential to disturb and disrupt. In some cases the introduction of multiple pay levels for the same job is an explicit part of management strategy, for example the use of temporary agencies to supply workers on different terms and conditions from permanent staff. This can be considered a multi-employer disruption which has the approval of the main employer and is designed to cut costs. However, even here the disruption to notions of a fair rate for the job may not be sustainable in the longer term, at least not without some modifications to the policy (Grimshaw et al., 2001). Often organizations feel obliged to offer direct contracts to longstanding temporary staff as wide pay differentials based solely on employment status and not skill levels may become unsustainable over time. Wide wage disparities may also encourage high rates of turnover among temporary workers, thereby reducing the effectiveness of the strategy. Moreover, over time organizations may try to pay lower wage increases to permanent staff and so move their rates closer to temporary workers on the grounds that the existence of differentials suggests they are paying over the market rate. Alternatively, they may move towards using temporary staff mainly as a screening process for entry into long term jobs.

Other pressures may arise at multi-employer sites that are less planned and may cause disruption to relationships in ways not anticipated by employers. For example, those collaborating in joint ventures, project teams or alliances may find themselves working alongside similar or more junior colleagues who are rewarded at higher rates. Staff of franchisees may be sent on training courses covering both direct employees of the franchisor and employees of other franchisees only to find that their terms and conditions differ widely from those doing comparable work under the same brand name. Here the differences emerge out of the decentralization of pay decisions to the franchisee. Further complications arise where an organization which is providing outsourcing facilities to clients is under pressure to offer different terms and conditions to fit the requirements of the client; here we can point to the example cited by

Scarbrough (2000) of a supply chain relationship resulting in internal differentiation. The client company tried to persuade the organization to establish a different set of conditions for employees working on a dedicated line but this led to resentment among other staff who were less favourably treated.

The most clear cut problems arise for staff affected by a TUPE transfer. In these circumstances the employees still retain their terms and conditions set by their previous employer but this may result in disruptions to pay hierarchies and systems for a number of reasons. First of all, although pay rates may be preserved, the transferred employees may find themselves subject to a harsher performance regime, thereby disrupting or reneging on the implicit wage-effort bargain. This may create particular problems if they continue working side by side with non-TUPE transferred staff from the previous employer. The introduction of TUPE transferred staff into an outsourcing organization may also create disruptions within its pay system. The TUPE transferred staff may have different pay rates and holiday and other entitlements from the direct non-transferred employees and this could cause resentment if they work alongside each other doing similar jobs. If the outsourcing organization has a variety of TUPE transferred staff from a range of contracts, it may have an equally wide range of terms and conditions. The legal position with respect to the time period over which harmonization may take place is unclear and the only practical solution may be to maintain staff in different workplaces. This creates further problems if staff need to be redeployed across workplaces due to business fluctuations or for promotion. The outsourcing organization may have to require staff to change contracts as well as workplaces if they transfer on a voluntary basis to other sites. Differentials between workplaces are not in these circumstances in any sense systematically related to skill and job content. Furthermore, the range of pay systems in place may create problems if the outsourcer wishes to establish an effective pay system for supervisory and managerial staff as unless the supervisory staff are also specific to each workplace, the notion of fair differentials between supervised and supervisor might have to be considered with respect to the highest rather than the lowest paid workplace.

These variations in pay levels and systems introduced through multi-employer relationships may also serve to highlight the absence of a link in general between pay and skill. However, equal pay legislation provides under certain circumstances, for this link to be introduced. While currently multi-employer relations are not normally subject to equal pay legislation where the jobs span more than one employer, individual employers may face difficulties in adjusting their pay structures in line with equal pay law if they also wish to adjust pay systems to take into account multi-employer influences. Moreover, the sense of grievance that pay is not related to skill may be enhanced when employees work side by side with other workers doing similar jobs for higher pay even if they are not able currently to translate that grievance into an equal pay case.

Performance management

A major trend in recent years has been the development of performance indicators and performance management, and this to some extent reflects the shift towards permeable organizational boundaries; performance criteria form an important part of the detailed specifications in the contracts between organizations and these in turn may provide the basis for employee performance targets. For example, it has been suggested that there is a direct relationship between the tightness of contract specifications and 'the harshness of the employment regime that may follow' (Kessler et al., 1999: 5). The responsibility for setting performance standards for groups or even individuals may lie not with the direct employer but with the client. Moreover, the client may be involved in actually monitoring performance and passing information back to the direct employer, to provide the basis for either positive or negative appraisals. In the case of the latter, the employer may in some cases rely entirely on third party provided information as the basis of discipline and even dismissal. This is almost always effectively the case where the worker concerned is not under the direct control of the employer but of the client, as with temporary workers, but it could apply more widely. Franchisors may effectively specify and monitor not only the performance of franchisees but also of their employees where the specifications which bind the franchisee also relate to aspects of the work process of those employed by them. One organization may collect information on the performance of other organizations at the same site even though it does not have any direct contractual link with them because their performance may have an impact on demand for its services. At an airport, for example, there may be concern about the activity of baggage handling companies because performance in these key services affects the overall demand for airport services. Such information may well be used as the basis for inquiring into performance of particular shifts or even individual groups and employees. Where disciplinary issues arise there is sometimes a need for joint action by, effectively, two employers. For example, this could apply at an outsourcer using temporary workers supplied by an agency with whom they had entered into a partnership arrangement and where managers from the agency were always present on-site. If a disciplinary matter arises, action would need to be taken jointly and/or in parallel by the managers of the site and the temporary agency managers. In other cases, this neat solution to the division of responsibilities and rights as employers and clients would not be possible because of physical distance and separation.

While the involvement of third parties and multi-employers, directly or indirectly, in monitoring, appraising and disciplining employees certainly adds a layer of complexity and ambiguity into the standard employment relationship, other problems arise when the performance of an employee or group of employees is critically dependent on the action and behaviour of an organization, or employees from an organization which is not their employer. Many outsourcing relationships rely for successful operation on cooperation and exchange of information between organizations but this cooperation and information sharing may be limited and even deliberately withheld, leading to problems of how to assess the actual performance of the employees affected by the breakdown of relationships. In the context of the NHS, Deakin and Walsh (1996: 37) comment that 'the purchaser is often dependent on the provider for knowledge of what has to be done, or even what should be done, so that information becomes a key battleground in service management'. In an outsourcing company, problems can arise due to unforeseen difficulties in dealing with customer enquiries in a context, for example, where customers are annoyed after having been sold unsuitable contracts. The contract setting up a call centre operation may provide tight specifications for number of calls to be dealt with per hour but these may not be achievable in unanticipated hostile environments. In this case, the call centre company had to resort to a renegotiation of the contract to ensure appropriate staffing levels and try to appease temporary staff who feel they have been placed under undue pressure to sort out problems which were not of their making and which were not taken into account in their job specification.

Organizational commitment

As stated above, notions of organizational commitment lie at the heart of human resource management literature and in the rhetoric of practitioners. This focus on organizational commitment, however, sits uncomfortably with the shift to new forms of organization and partnerships, and with the increasing use of outsourcing. This paradox can be resolved to some extent in the public sector where there is a more explicit policy of using partnerships and networks to change organizational culture. In this context, the rhetoric of commitment is still used, but this is commitment to public service *provision* and not commitment or loyalty to a public service *organization*. However, the impact of policies which are destabilizing workplaces and employment relationships on commitment to service delivery is often not called directly into question. Many of the organizations which are engaged in multi-employer relationships are using a variety of techniques to attempt to overcome the confusion between the identity of the employer and the identity of the organization with which the employee is supposed to show some form of commitment. For example, organizations which are outsourcing their customer focused operations are spending time and energy in training call centre and temporary agency staff in aspects of their brand or organizational image. Here the client is taking on a major part of the training role as it is arguably only the client who can impart the information on the company image and brand. Limits to company loyalty soon emerge, however, when problems are encountered in maintaining good customer relations due to factors outside and beyond the control of staff; we have already mentioned above the case of high labour turnover rates when staff are faced with hostile customers over events which were not the responsibility of the temporary agency staff or even of the organization in whose premises they were working.

Organizations are sometimes very aware of the contradictions between using a fragmented employment system and attempting to develop a strong brand name or to present a seamless image to customers. In one case, this awareness led to a requirement that freelance staff operating as trainers on behalf of the organization should give the impression to clients that they were full-time permanent employees of that organization, an impression bolstered by the issue of personal business cards in the organization's name. Further problems arise over mismatches between the apparent goals of organizations working in partnership and the performance goals assigned to individual managers. For example, if an organization splits its training arm from its main operations but explicitly intends the training organization to provide the in-house training needs of the main organization, this arrangement is unlikely to work unless individual managers within the main organization are provided with incentives to use this preferred supplier rather than using cheaper sources of training cheaper elsewhere. Thus, organizations have not only to agree on joint goals and aims but also have to develop incentive structures down the hierarchy which reinforce these organizational goals. Similar problems can arise within integrated organizations, of course, but where these are fragmented and operate as separate businesses, the incentive structures for successful partnerships may need to be more explicitly developed.

Towards contract or status: conflicting pressures from managing multi-employer relationships

So far we have considered the conflicting signals that arise in multi-employer situations and the problems these can create for human resource policies and practices. In this section, we address the issue of how these multi-employer relationships are likely to impact upon the form of the employment relationship and on management's approach to employment relations and control. Even within unambiguous single employer organizations there are recognized to be fundamental problems in managing the employment relationship. These problems arise out of the tensions between controlling and monitoring the employment relationship on the one hand, and seeking to use the employment relationship to confer comparative advantage on the organization by capturing the capacities of the employees to contribute to effective performance. These conflicting tendencies lead to alternative modes of managing employment, referred to by Streeck (1987) as contract and status. In short, contractual approaches to management provide opportunities to specify the quantity of employment and the minimum services to be provided in return for the wage in a context of essentially low trust. In contrast, management through status focuses on encouraging workers to provide 'extra-functional' contributions as a consequence of voluntary commitment engendered through high trust relationships. Status relationships, according to Streeck (1987: 293), involve 'the replacement of specific contractual obligations as the main mechanisms of controlling the exchange between workers and employing organizations, by general, unspecific and long term commitments on both sides to cooperation'.

The paradox, according to Streeck, is that the development of new ways of managing employment in the 1980s and 1990s led to both an expansion of contractual relations and an expansion of status. Both provide different ways of managing uncertainty. The same paradox appears to apply to situations of multi-employers; on the one hand, the very fact that there is no single unambiguous employer tends to lead to a proliferation of monitoring and control systems and a tightening of contractual conditions. On the other hand, the entry into multi-employer partnerships and networks is critically dependent upon the development of successful collaborative relationships, often based on personal capacities and on the provision of extra-functional contributions by the workers concerned. Research into inter-organizational contracting has indeed revealed that, contrary to perhaps a priori expectations, business partnerships tend to be underspecified in contractual terms, for a variety of reasons (Deakin and Michie, 1997). In particular it is found that contractual relationships based on trust are more likely to provide a basis for realizing synergies and sharing information and knowledge while protecting against opportunistic behaviour, than arrangements based on tightly specified contractual obligations which cannot anticipate all the potential areas of conflict or all the areas where unanticipated solutions will be required. Moreover, by concentrating on actions needed in the event of failure, such contractual approaches may undermine the relationship before it has even been established (Deakin and Michie, 1997). This focus on trust has by and large been considered with respect to trust between *organizations*, although trust relationships are recognized to be forged in practice by individuals, most of whom may be in an employment relationship. Trust in an inter-organizational relationship is thus also dependent upon trust within the employment relationship itself, and it may be extremely

Table 10.4 *Towards contract or status?*

Issue	Return to contract	Extension of status
Performance	Strict contractual requirements between partners related to task performance	Reliance on employees' initiative and tact to manage relations between partners, to share knowledge; to 'chart unknown territories'
Autonomy	Strict regulation of responsibilities/allocation of authorization duties	Use of new forms to grow the business, develop spin-offs/synergies – reliance on self-motivated workers
Job content	Emphasis on codified knowledge/processes as a means of control of labour process/brand image	Need to update knowledge/retain exclusive access to knowledge as basis for partnerships/efficiencies
Recruitment and selection	Use tight contractual control rather than personal selection and development of trust relations	Use professional status/qualification/ experience as basis for selection for temporary/short term assignments
Training	Narrow task specific training; company branding	Training from multi-employers; broadening of range of tasks/experience; use of training and qualification as quality indicator; reliance on self-trained/self-motivated workers
Time	Strict time accounting used to control relationship between employers/allocate costs/implement costs savings	Task and performance related contracts implemented through extended work time of employees/managers

difficult, for example, for an organization to rely on its employees to forge a trust-based partnership while moving towards a more contract-based management of the employment relationship with its own employees. Such paradoxical tendencies cannot always be avoided, however, and the use of outsourcing may lead to 'new problems such as transaction costs, erosion of trust between principals and agents, and rent seeking' (Boyne, 1998: 695).

The breakdown of trust may lead agents to 'work to contract', a sure sign of inefficiency and failure within contracts in general and within the employment relationship in particular (Boyne, 1998).

[...]

Conclusions

Filling in the missing links between the literature on new organizational forms on the one hand and the employment relationship on the other should serve a dual purpose. First, it makes more explicit how the causes of uncertainty and ambiguity are related to the performance and efficiency gains to be derived from new organizational forms. The organizational literature has recognized the dependency of the new forms on, for example, the realization of the potential gains from learning; according to Huber (1991, cited in Matusik and Hill, 1998) organizational learning cannot be assumed to be an automatic outcome of networks and partnerships. While there is recognition of this ambiguity, the resolution is seen to lie first in establishing such networks and partnerships only where the objective conditions are right for them to yield net gains and secondly in adopting appropriate management styles and techniques. However, as we have argued above, there also needs to be considerably more attention paid to the predictability of these potential gains if they are primarily dependent upon human agents than if these processes were integrated into in-house operations. 'Unobserved heterogeneity' in the outcomes of partnerships needs to be tied much more closely into the analysis of how these systems are put into place and operationalized as part of a labour process and employment relationship, and not treated simply as a relationship at an abstract level between organizations. Much of the current interest and activity in networking and partnerships may be based as much on acts of faith as on fully considered analyses of how these arrangements will actually benefit the participating organizations. Greater awareness of the risks involved and of the preconditions for success, such as highly developed trust within the employment relationship, might act not as barriers to growth and modernization but as cautionary reminders of the possibilities of failure as well as success.

Introducing notions of multi-employer relationships into the literature on the employment relationship also calls into question the single employer assumptions underpinning both the approach to employment law and employment rights and to the management of the employment relationship. The questioning of the appropriateness of the assumption of a single employer in employment law adds a further dimension to the debate about how to provide effective protection for employees in a period of diversifying employment statuses. That diversity can be seen to include complex multi-employer relationships and not simply issues of atypical employment contracts. The recognition of multi-employers and multiple organizations also adds a further complexity to the notion of organizational commitment, a concept already under pressure due to increased job insecurity and the growing liklihood of boundaryless rather than bureaucratic careers as the dominant employment form of the future (Arthur and Rousseau, 1996). Here the problem is not just one of short time commitment to an organization but of the presence of multiple employers leading to potentially contradictory pressures for organizational commitment. In these circumstances, it would be sensible not to place too much faith in the power and pervasiveness of notions of commitment, as evidenced in the doctrines of human resource management. The introduction of multi-employer relationships calls into question any notion of a single best way or best approach to employment management. Employment law in the future may have to take into account these multi-employer relationships, thereby creating problems for individual employers establishing 'best practice' routines or systems designed to ensure against any need for direct recourse to the law for individual employees. Where employment relationships span more than one employer, such systems may be more difficult to design and implement. Similarly, in the field of human resource management, it may be impossible for managers to avoid making more use of direct contractual systems of control while at the same time increasing the autonomy of employees to take charge of and manage complex relationships. Information technology can only provide at best a partial solution to these control problems. It is possible that inter-organizational relationships will continue to depend upon a dual approach, based both on contract and on status.

References

Anand, B.N. and Khanna, T. (2000) 'Do firms learn to create volume? The case of alliances'. *Strategic Management Journal*, 21: 295–315.

Arthur, M.B. and Rousseau, D.M. (eds) (1996) *The Boundaryless Career: A New Employment Principle for a New Organizational Era*. Oxford: Oxford University Press.

Boxall, P. (1996) 'The strategic HRM debate and the resource-based view of the firm'. *Human Resource Management Journal*, 6, 3: 59–75.

Boxall, P. and Purcell, J. (2000) 'Strategic human resource management: where have we come from and where should we be going?'. *International Journal of Management Reviews*, 2, 2: 183–203.

Boyne, G.A. (1998) 'Competitive tendering in local government: a review of theory and evidence'. *Public Administration*, 76, Winter, 695–712.

Burchell, B., Deakin, S. and Honey, S. (1999a) *The Employment Status of Individuals in Non-standard Employment*. Department of Trade and Industry EMAR Research Series, Number 6.

Burchell, B., Day, D., Hudson, M., Ladipo, D., Mankelow, R., Nolan, J., Reed, H., Wichert, I. and Wilkinson, F. (1999b) *Job Insecurity and Work Intensification: Flexibility and the Changing Boundaries of Work*. York: Joseph Rowntree Foundation, York Publishing Services Ltd.

Cappelli P., Bassi, L., Katz, H., Knoke, D., Osterman, P. and Useem, M. (eds) (1997) *Change at Work*. Oxford: Oxford University Press.

Casey, B., Metcalf, H. and Millward, N. (1997) *Employers' Use of Flexible Labour*. London: Policy Studies Institute.

Coff, R. (1997) 'Human assets and management dilemmas: coping with hazards on the road to resource-based theory'. *Academy of Management Review*, 22, 2: 374–402.

Coombs, R. and Battaglia, P. (1998) 'Outsourcing of Business Services and the Boundaries of the Firm', CRIC Working Paper No 5, June, The University of Manchester.

Coombs, J.G. and Ketchen, D.J. (1999) 'Explaining interfirm cooperation and performance: toward a reconciliation of predictions from the resource-based view and organizational economics'. *Strategic Management Journal*, 20: 867–88.

Deakin, S. (1986) 'Labour law and the developing employment relationship in the UK'. *Cambridge Journal of Economics*, 10: 225–46.

Deakin, S. and Michie, J. (1997) 'Contracts and competition: an introduction'. *Cambridge Journal of Economics*, 21, 2: 121–5.

Deakin, S. and Walsh, K. (1996) 'The enabling state: the role of markets and contracts'. *Public Administration*, 74, Spring, 33–48.

Fearfull, A. (1992) 'The introduction of information and office technologies: the great divide?'. *Work, Employment and Society*, 6, 3: 423–42.

Felstead, A. and Jewson, N. (eds) (1999) *Global Trends in Flexible Labour*. Basingstoke: London.

Gallie, D. and White, M. (1998) *Restructuring the Employment Relationship*. Oxford: Clarendon Press.

Gittell, J.H. (2000) 'Organizing work to support relational co-ordination'. *International Journal of Human Resource Management*, 11, 3: 517–39.

Grimshaw, D., Ward, K., Rubery, J. and Beynon, H. (2001) 'Organizations and the transformation of the internal labour market'. *Work, Employment and Society*, 15, 1: 25–54.

Guest, D. (1998) 'Beyond human resource management: commitment and the contract culture'. In Sparrow, P. and Marchington, M. (eds), *Human Resource Management: The New Agenda*. London: Pitman, 37–51.

Guest, D. and Conway, N. (1998) *Fairness at Work and the Psychological Contract: Issues in People Management*. London: Institute of Personnel and Development.

Guest, D. and Peccei, R. (1998) *The Partnership Company*. London: Involvement and Participation Association.

Guest, D., Michie, J., Sheehan, M., Conway, N. and Metochi, M. (2000) *Effective People Management*. Chartered Institute of Personnel and Development Research Report, London.

Hoque, K. (1999) 'Human resource management and performance in the UK hotel industry'. *British Journal of Industrial Relations*, 37, 3: 419–43.

Huber, G.P. (1991) 'Organizational learning: the contributing processes and the literatures'. *Organization Science*, 2, 88–115.

Hunter, L., Beaumont, P. and Sinclair, D. (1996) 'A "partnership" approach to human resource management'. *Journal of Management Studies*, 33, 2: 235–57.

Huselid, M.A. (1995) 'The impact of human resource management practices on turnover, productivity and corporate financial performance'. *Academy of Management Journal*, 38, 3: 635–72.

Hutchinson, S., Purcell, J. and Kinnie, N. (2000) 'Evolving high commitment management and the experience of the RAC call centre'. *Human Resource Management Journal*, 10, 1: 63–78.

Kale, P., Singh, H. and Perlmutter, H. (2000) 'Learning and protection of proprietary assets in strategic alliances: building relational capital'. *Strategic Management Journal*, 21: 217–37.

Kessler, I., Coyle-Shapiro, J. and Purcell, J. (1999) 'Outsourcing and the employee perspective'. *Human Resource Management Journal*, 9, 2: 5–19.

Legge, K. (1995) *Human Resource Management: Rhetorics and Realities*. London: Macmillan.

Leighton, P. and Painter, R.W. (1987) 'Who are vulnerable workers?'. In Leighton, P. and Painter, R.W. (eds), 'Vulnerable Workers in the UK Labour Market: Some Challenges for Labour Law', *Employee Relations*, 9, 5: 3–8.

Marchington, M. (1998) 'Partnership in context: towards a European model?'. In Sparrow, P. and Marchington, M. *Human Resource Management: The New Agenda*, Financial Times, Pitman Publishing, 208–28.

Marchington, M. and Grugulis, I. (2000) '"Best Practice" human resource management: perfect opportunity or dangerous illusion?'. *International Journal of Human Resource Management*, 11, 4: 905–25.

Marchington, M. and Wilkinson, A. (1996) *Core Personnel and Development*. London: Institute of Personnel and Development.

Marglin, S. (1976) 'What do bosses do?'. In Gorz, A. (ed.), *The Division of Labour*. Brighton: Harvester.

Martin, G., Staines, M. and Pate, J. (1998) 'Linking job insecurity and career development in a new psychological contract'. *Human Resource Management Journal*, 8, 3: 20–40.

Matusik, S.F. and Hill, C.W.L. (1998) 'The utilization of contingent work, knowledge creation and competitive advantage'. *Academy of Management Review*, 23, 4: 680–98.

Montgomery, C.A. (1995) *Resource-based and Evolutionary Theories of the Firm. Towards a Synthesis*. Boston, MA: Kluwer.

Oliver, A.L. and Ebers, M. (1998) 'Networking network studies: an analysis of conceptual configurations in the study of inter-organizational relationships'. *Organization Studies*, 19, 4: 549–83.

O'Reilly, J. and Fagan, C. (1998) *Part-time Prospects; Part-time Employment in Europe, North America and the Pacific Rim*. London: Routledge.

Peck, J. and Theodore, N. (1998) 'The business of contingent work: growth and restructuring in Chicago's temporary employment industry'. *Work, Employment and Society*, 12, 4: 655–74.

Penrose, E. (1959) *The Theory of the Growth of the Firm*. Oxford: Blackwell.

Pfeffer, J. (1994) *Competitive Advantage Through People*. Boston, MA: Harvard Business School Press.

Pfeffer, J. (1998) *The Human Equation: Building Profits by Putting People First*. Boston: Harvard Business School Press.

Purcell, J. (1995) 'Corporate strategy and its link with human resource management'. In Storey, J. (ed.), *Human Resource Management: A Critical Text*. London: Routledge.

Purcell, J. (1999) 'The search for best practice and best fit in human resource management: chimera or cul-de-sac?'. *Human Resource Management Journal*, 9, 3: 26–41.

Rajan, A. (1997) 'Employability in the finance sector: rhetoric vs. reality'. *Human Resource Management Journal*, 7, 1: 67–78.

Rodgers, G. and Rodgers, J. (eds) (1988) *Precarious Jobs in Labour Market Regulation: The Growth of Atypical Employment in Western Europe*. Geneva: International Institute for Labour Studies.

Rubery, J. (1997) 'Wages and the labour market'. *British Journal of Industrial Relations*, 35, 337–66.

Scarbrough, H. (2000) 'The HR implications of supply chain relationships'. *Human Resource Management Journal*, 10, 1: 5–17.

Schendel, D. (1995) 'Introduction to "technological transformation and the new competitive landscape"'. *Strategic Management Journal*, 16, 1–6.

Semlinger, K. (1991) 'New developments in subcontracting: mixed market and hierarchy'. In Amin, A. and Dietrich, M. (eds), *Towards a New Europe? Structural Changes in the European Economy*. Edward Elgar.

Sisson, K. (ed.) (1994) *Personnel Management in Britain*. London: Blackwell.

Stinchcombe, A.L. (1990) *Information and Technologies*. Berkeley, CA: University of California Press.

Storey, J. (ed.) (1995) *Human Resource Management: A Critical Text*. London: Routledge.

Storey, J. (ed.) (2001) *Human Resource Management: A Critical Text*, 2nd edition. London: Routledge.

Streeck, W. (1987) 'The uncertainties of management in the management of uncertainty: employers, labour relations and industrial adjustments in the 1980s'. *Work, Employment and Society*, 1, 3: 281–308.

Walton, R. (1985) 'From control to commitment in the workplace'. *Harvard Business Review*, March–April, 77–84.

Williamson, O.E. (1985) *The Economic Institutions of Capitalism*. New York: Free Press.

Wood, S. (1999) 'Human resource management and performance'. *International Journal of Management Reviews*, 1, 4: 367–413.

11

Human Resource Management, Trade Unions and Industrial Relations

David E. Guest

The rising interest in human resource management (HRM) throughout the 1980s coincided with a steady decline in the significance of industrial relations as a central feature of economic performance and policy. It also coincided with a decline in the membership and influence of trade unions – during the 1980s, trade union membership declined from 53 per cent to 33 per cent. Industrial conflict displayed a similar decline, so that in the early 1990s, strikes were at their lowest level for many decades.

It was tempting in the 1980s to seek an association between the apparent rise of HRM and the decline of trade unions and industrial relations. Part of the temptation lay in the knowledge that the early models of HRM were drawn mainly from successful American non-union firms. In the [late] 1990s the emerging evidence paints a much more complex picture. To begin to understand it, we need to set both HRM and industrial relations within the wider economic and political system.

The central thrust of economic, industrial and legislative policy in the UK for well over a decade has been to create a market-driven economy. From an industrial relations perspective, the most telling feature of this policy has been the successive pieces of legislation designed to limit the role and rights of trade unions. This legislative programme has moved the unions in particular, and industrial relations in general, from the centre to the periphery of corporate concern. For many firms, industrial relations are no longer a contingent variable, helping to shape their business policy in the way they might have done ten or fifteen years earlier.

Organizations now have more choice about industrial relations. Do they also have a choice about HRM? If we follow the new market philosophy, then

---

Source: David E. Guest (1995) 'Human Resource Management, Trade Unions and Industrial Relations, in J. Storey (ed.), *HRM: A Critical Text*. London: Thomson. Edited version.

HRM should be driven by market factors. The point to emphasize here is that innovation, and more particularly, quality-based strategies, require for their success a workforce that is committed to the organization. To take a well-known example, an airline competing through quality must, at the point of customer contact, have staff with the autonomy and motivation to provide the kind of high-quality service that will 'delight' the customer. This will require enthusiasm and initiative on the part of the staff, and trust to permit autonomy on the part of the organization. This 'psychological contract' is a core element of the concept of organizational commitment. But if commitment is a central concept in an HR strategy for managing the workforce, where does this leave industrial relations? Commitment is an essentially unitarist concept. Is it possible to be committed to both a company and a trade union, or is such dual commitment impossible? To understand the possible relationships between HRM and industrial relations and the role of trade unions in this market-driven economy, we must explore in more detail the concept of commitment and the feasibility of dual commitment.

The third strategy for competitive advantage, based on cost leadership, fits well with the political drive to present the UK as a cheap manufacturing base. The underlying assumptions are more pluralist in nature, to the extent that management will seek to minimize labour costs, while workers may well seek to maximize them. The context is therefore ripe for traditional industrial relations and apparently less suitable for the kind of HRM which has as its core the concept of organizational commitment. This certainly tends to be the conclusion of those writing from a strategic perspective. However, the legislation that has freed up the market has also extended the choice for employers. They may believe they can reduce costs more effectively without a trade union. The choice is therefore no longer HRM versus industrial relations; the new alternative is to have neither, and to get rid of all the expensive baggage with which each is associated. It follows that we need to incorporate this wider range of options in any review of trends in HRM and industrial relations.

Many of the strategic options available to management appear to challenge the role of trade unions and offer a potentially bleak view of their future. In some workplaces they may survive because they have always been there. Since they are built into the system, they can be accommodated as long as they are not a drain on resources. But whenever a major strategic review occurs – for example, in the context of a takeover, or a rationalization programme – their role is likely to be challenged. The logic of a market-driven HRM strategy is that where high organizational commitment is sought, unions are irrelevant. Where cost advantage is the goal, unions and industrial relations systems appear to carry higher costs. If possible, it will be preferable to do without them. This scenario is one of continuing gradual decline in membership and influence, unless the unions can respond with new strategies of their own. Paradoxically, HRM, far from threatening the union role, may present one basis for a new union strategy.

Following the themes raised in this introduction, the chapter is divided into two main parts. The first examines organizational commitment and dual commitment as a basis for considering the interaction between HRM and trade unionism. The second examines the evidence on the choices being made by employers in the UK about the type of HRM and industrial relations they wish to pursue.

Commitment and the theory of human resource management and industrial relations

Models of HRM (see, for example, Beer et al., 1985; Guest, 1987) place organizational commitment at their core. Indeed it is the central feature that distinguishes HRM from traditional personnel management/industrial relations systems. Furthermore, it has been suggested (Guest, 1989) that if the four key HRM policy goals are strategic integration, quality, flexibility and commitment, then only commitment to the organization need present a direct challenge to trade unionism. It provides the basis for the contrasting values and assumptions underpinning normative views of HRM and industrial relations which have been presented by Walton (1985), Guest (1987) and Storey (1992). The key contrasting dimensions are presented in Table 11.1.

Table 11.1 *HRM's key dimensions*

Dimension	Industrial relations	Human resource management
Psychological contract	Compliance	Commitment
Behaviour referent	Norms, custom and practice	Values/mission
Relations	Low trust, pluralist, collective	High-trust, unitarist, individual
Organization and design	Formal roles, hierarchy, division of labour, managerial controls	Flexible roles, flat structure, teamwork/autonomy, self-control

Organizational commitment is central to [the HRM] approach for several reasons. First, by holding out the prospect that committed workers will be highly motivated and will go 'beyond contract', it promises higher performance. Secondly, committed workers can be expected to exercise responsible autonomy or self-monitoring and self-control, removing the need for supervisory and inspection staff and producing efficiency gains. Thirdly, committed workers are more likely to stay with the organization, thereby ensuring a return on the investment in careful selection, training and development. Finally, but central to the discussion of HRM and industrial relations, it is assumed that a worker who is committed to the organization is unlikely to become involved in 'industrial relations' or any type of collective activity which might reduce the quality and quantity of their contribution to the organization. This is aided by moving away from the traditional psychological contract of 'a fair day's work for a fair day's pay', thereby reducing the potential for the effort bargain to operate as a potential focus for conflict and grievance. The commitment contract implies that, instead, the staff will go that extra mile for the company.

Placing organizational commitment at the core of the definition of HRM acknowledges the deliberate attempt to win the hearts and minds of the workforce. The traditional definition of organizational commitment (Mowday et al., 1982), and the one most relevant to this analysis, defines it as consisting of three components: an identification with the goals and values of the organization, a desire to belong to the organization, and a willingness to display effort on behalf of the organization. Union commitment can be defined in precisely the same way (Gordon et al., 1980). The key issue then becomes the compatibility of the goals and values of the company and the union. If they are compatible, then it is possible to display high commitment to both company and union. At the same time, it raises fundamental questions about the role of the union and the nature of the values for which it stands. Alternatively, we need to consider how far workers can live with the inherent conflict and ambiguity of identification with two potentially opposing sets of values. Research by Reichers (1985, 1986), for example, has suggested that workers can express commitment to potentially conflicting targets such as work group, career and company. These issues have stimulated research on dual commitment to company and union.

The choices about commitment to company and union can be presented in a simple matrix:

		Commitment to company	
		High	Low
Commitment to	High	1	2
union	Low	3	4

A matrix of this sort is a useful starting point for analysis of commitment to company and union. It is important to bear in mind that it is an over-simplification in two important respects. The first is that there may be intermediate levels of commitment to both company and union, reflecting, perhaps, a kind of conditional approval of both. The second, building on the work of Reichers and others, is that there are other potential focuses of commitment. These include a career, a profession and the family. Commitment to any of these may also conflict with commitment to either company and/or union.

One important strand of research has examined the antecedents of commitment to company and union. If the factors that shape commitment to each are different, then it should be possible for them to coexist, since a change on a factor affecting company commitment need not influence union commitment. On the other hand, if they are caused by the same factor, either they operate from the same end of a continuum and become indistinguishable, which may be the case with some Japanese 'in-house' unions, or they operate from competing ends of the same continuum and therefore are incompatible. The first case might include the quality of working conditions, the second might be the right to hold union mass meetings in working time. The underlying theories are concerned with cognitive dissonance and role conflict. From the limited number of studies of the antecedents, the view seems to be emerging that union and company commitment, although psychologically similar constructs with similar classes of antecedent and outcome, are caused by different specific factors.

In one interesting study, Barling, Wade and Fullager (1990) had the opportunity to examine dual commitment in the aftermath of a strike. They found marked differences between those who viewed the industrial relations climate positively and negatively. In the former group, there was a correlation of 0.06 between commitment to a union and to the company but among those who perceived a poor industrial relations climate, the correlation was –0.52. This takes us one step further in suggesting that it is not just the existence of conflict but the way it is perceived and interpreted that influences the feasibility of dual commitment.

There has only been a limited amount of research on this topic in the UK. Guest and Dewe (1991), in a study of workers in three organizations in the electronics industry, found little evidence of dual commitment, where commitment was defined in terms of identification with company and union. Indeed, the predominant mode was commitment to neither company nor trade union. On the other hand, use of the same questions in other countries elicited evidence of higher levels of dual commitment in Sweden and West Germany, though, perhaps surprisingly, not in Japan (Guest and Dewe, 1991). The European evidence does provide further indirect support for the importance of the industrial relations climate.

If we accept the tenor of this research, and with it the implication that dual commitment is possible within a positive industrial relations climate, we then need to know something about the characteristics of this climate. As a minimum, if it is an industrial relations climate (Dastmalchian et al., 1991), this implies the legitimacy of a pluralist perspective, in which both company and union have distinctive roles. There is choice about how far these are grounded in legislation, as is the case in most of Europe, and how far they rest on the voluntaristic assumptions of those in key positions on both sides. Whatever the context, the role of the unions can vary considerably.

At least three models for the union role in the context of dual commitment can be identified. In the first, typified by some Japanese organizations, the role of the union at the local level is very much that of another arm of the company. One important manifestation of this is that the head of the union may move into a senior management position. A second approach, typified by Germany and Sweden, integrates industrial relations with the political system, and is therefore enshrined in legislation. One important element in this is the distinction between the issues dealt with at plant and company level and those handled at national level. In these countries, the more contentious issues, particularly those concerning pay and working hours, have mostly been handled at the national level. At the local level the works council has dealt with more operational issues, often issues of mutual concern.

The third model is the voluntaristic UK approach, now reshaped by the new legislative framework. The tradition of bargaining at company or even plant level has reinforced a pluralist perspective. At the same time, it is important to recognize that relations in most workplaces are relatively harmonious and that the propensity for industrial action has always been low. However, the absence of legislative or cultural forces encouraging dual commitment makes its presence more fragile and more susceptible to the choices and actions of the key stakeholders. The important point about this system is that it is inherently less stable and provides a less predictable basis for dual commitment.

[...]

The evidence of limited dual commitment presents challenges for the unions. It would be unwise for unions to rely on one of the traditional bases of commitment to the union, namely a presumed belief in trade unionism (Guest and Dewe, 1988). Unions must find a new basis for commitment. The apparent failure of many companies to generate enthusiastic commitment among their workforce suggests that opportunities for unions still exist. If management is tempted to pursue a 'hard' version of HRM, this might backfire, providing further scope for unions. These and other policy options for unions will be considered later in the chapter. First we analyse recent developments at the interface of HRM and industrial relations as a basis for understanding company policy and practice.

Developments in industrial relations and human resource management

If we extrapolate from the discussion of dual commitment, which is essentially concerned with the response at the individual level, to the analysis of policy options facing organizations, we can present the broad alternatives in a similar way:

		HRM priority	
		High	Low
Industrial	High	1	2
relations priority	Low	3	4

Option 1 gives priority to both industrial relations and HRM, implies that dual commitment is feasible and assumes a positive industrial relations climate. It might be termed 'the new realism' and is reflected, for example, in recent publications from the IPA (1992). Option 2 represents the stereotype of the traditional UK approach. It assumes that trade unions are well established and that HRM has not figured significantly on the management agenda. This approach, a traditional collectivism, is probably most likely to be found in parts of the public sector. Option 3 represents the stereotype of individual-ized HRM, popularly associated with American electronics firms, where an individualistic philosophy assumes no need for trade unions or for any other type of collective activity. Option 4 reflects a view that cost advantage can best be achieved by avoiding both industrial relations and HRM. For those with a vested interest in industrial relations and HRM, and possibly for the workers affected by it, it represents a kind of 'black hole'. It is a neglected area of study which is just beginning to receive more attention. It is impor-tant because it helps to refocus a debate which can slip too easily into an analysis of the choice of either unions or HRM by suggesting the possibility of neither.

Within this framework we can analyse evidence on recent trends in industrial relations and HRM to determine developments in and between these options. Ideally, such evidence looks at industrial relations and HR trends together. This requires either sophisticated analysis of complex data sets or case studies. There are a number of both, although a lot of the evidence is more limited in scope. In this chapter we will emphasize developments in industrial relations, rather than in specific areas of HRM policy and practice.

In any analysis of trends in industrial relations related directly or indirectly to HRM, we might wish to look at evidence such as:

■ union recognition and derecognition
■ developments in the 'new' industrial relations, such as single table bargaining and no-strike deals
■ the role of unions in any changes affecting industrial relations
■ the importance of industrial relations as an issue
■ the outcomes of industrial relations, including levels of conduct activity, any union mark-up and productivity.

We will analyse developments as they apply to each of the four options/quadrants in the model.

1 The New Realism – a high emphasis on HRM and industrial relations

Kochan, Katz and McKersie (1986), proclaiming the transformation of American industrial relations, cited a limited number of cases illustrative of a collaborative joint endeavour to shape a new relationship between management and union. It would be dangerous to over-emphasize the importance of any new emergent pattern of industrial relations in the USA. However, it is this type of pattern that we might expect in those organizations in the UK where attempts are made by managers to pursue an approach that integrates HRM and industrial relations.

Evidence about a joint approach can best be gleaned from case studies. There are a number of cases which appear to fit this pattern. One of the best known is Nissan (Wickens, 1987, 1993). He argues that the analysis developed initially by Walton (1985), which contrasts control/compliance and commitment philosophies, presents a false dichotomy. In the car industry, he suggests, you need both. He further argues that, by and large, leading Japanese organizations in Japan, and Nissan in the UK, have achieved this. He accepts the need for a representative system for workers and the need to promote workers' interests, and in particular to ensure job security. But he further emphasizes that this must be based on cooperation rather than confrontation. Wickens deserves attention as one of the small band of senior managers who have tackled these issues at both the intellectual and operational levels.

Many of the other examples of serious attempts at a joint approach – Rover being a case in point – come from the car industry, where the unions are very well entrenched but where market forces demand improvements in productivity and quality. Indeed the circumstances are similar to those in the cases cited by Kochan et al. (1986).

In new plants, one point at which high priority is given to both HRM and industrial relations is at the time of the so-called 'beauty contest', where unions have competed for recognition rights. From the union side, this constitutes a form of concession bargaining based on who promises an agreement closest to the management ideal. In some cases, such as the well-publicized ones of Toshiba (Trevor, 1988) and Nissan (Wickens, 1987) and the similar but less well-known case of the Japanese/American joint venture IBC Vehicles, the positive initial relationship has continued. However, negotiations and all important representative meetings take place between management and a works council. The council represents all the workforce and union shop stewards have to stand for election alongside non-union workers. There is, therefore, a pluralist system, based on a management agenda and the principle of mutuality, but one where the role of the union is somewhat ambiguous.

Another source of evidence about new collaborative arrangements comes from analysis of single-union and single-table bargaining. The third workplace industrial relations survey (WIRS 3) (Millward et al., 1992) found no evidence of major growth in these areas. Nevertheless such arrangements are almost always the result of employer initiatives, and both employers and unions seem satisfied with them. They have facilitated greater flexibility, more multi-skilling, the removal of union demarcations and improvements in quality. From a union perspective they have produced extensions in consultation and moves towards single status.

The cases described by Storey (1992) provide some of the best information on recent trends, although again we must note that many of the cases are drawn from large companies which are household names, or at least indus-trial relations names. Storey concludes that there is little evidence of any frontal attack on unions, but equally little attempt to involve the unions in the planning and implementation of change. In most cases where unions have been well established in the past, the two systems of industrial relations and HRM operate side by side but with a tendency for management to give increasing weight to systems of employee involvement, and in particular communication, which tend to by-pass the union.

Storey's (1992) finding that the two systems can coexist and remain rela-tively compartmentalized is not in doubt; but it does raise interesting ques-tions about the impact of the systems and more particularly the HRM system. If industrial relations remain healthy in the context of HRM, there are at least five possible explanations. First, the HRM may be so ineffective that it is having a minimal impact on values and commitment. Secondly, the 'hard' version is being used, and this leaves a level of anxiety such that workers continue to support the traditional industrial relations system and the trade union as a safeguard and safety net. Thirdly, management, while supporting HRM, rec-ognize the value of retaining collective arrangements because of their conve-nience, particularly in those establishments where large numbers are employed. Fourthly, it is possible that the system of mutuality is viable and a mutually beneficial collaboration between management and unions can operate, resulting in the maintenance of both systems. Fifthly, the industrial relations system may continue as a largely symbolic 'empty shell', insufficiently important for management to confront and eliminate, but retaining the outward appearance of health to the casual observer.

There are very few well-documented cases of a robust trade unionism in the context of enthusiastic HRM policies. As Storey notes of Rover, the unions were invited to the party, but some declined the invitation. At Ford, the party was of a rather different sort – an attempt to form a new partnership, but with less HRM and more concern for quality of working life, including a range of health and education programmes. This fits the American model described by Kochan et al. (1986) and which included Ford in America as one of its cases. The policy choice for the unions is whether they should decline the invitation, sulk at home and be ignored, or have their own party.

The implication of Storey's analysis and of other available data is that there has been little attempt by management and unions to forge a new partnership which gives high priority to both HRM and industrial relations through some process of integration. Instead, managers have taken a lot of piecemeal HRM initiatives, and in so doing have ignored or by-passed the industrial relations system. It continues to exist, accepted by management as having a legitimate, sometimes useful, but limited role. On the surface, it may appear that HRM and industrial relations both receive a high priority. Often, in the case of both, it will be an illusion.

2 Traditional Collectivism – priority to industrial relations without HRM

The second main policy choice is to retain the traditional pluralist industrial relations arrangements within an essentially unchanged industrial relations system. The evidence from WIRS 3 (Millward et al., 1992) suggests that in many places where trade unions have been well established, the industrial relations system appears to continue to operate much as before. However, the empty-shell argument may apply with or without more vigorous HRM policies. Management may continue to use the industrial relations system, but accord it much less priority. Indeed it has been suggested (Smith and Morton, 1993) that from a management perspective it is safer to marginalize the unions than formally to derecognize them and risk provoking a confrontation; better to let them wither on the vine than receive a reviving fertilizer.

An alternative management view may be that it is easier to continue to operate with a union, since it provides a useful, well-established channel for communication and for the handling of grievance, discipline and safety issues. In its absence, management would need to develop its own alternative, which could be both costly and difficult to operate effectively. The trade union and the shop stewards remain a useful lubricant.

The anecdotal case evidence suggests that it is mainly in the public sector and some industries that have been removed from it, that traditional industrial relations continue to operate largely in the absence of HRM. In the privatized docks, the Transport and General Workers' Union has negotiated new working arrangements including, in some cases, worker cooperatives (Turnbull and Weston, 1993). However in some ports, derecognition has occurred and at Felixstowe the union members have conceded wage-cuts as part of a package to avoid derecognition. Large parts of the public sector, including the health service, the police service, local government and education, retain well-established industrial relations systems and, with a few exceptions, no real attempt to introduce HRM. The unions may play a less central role, but they are still significant players, as the response to a number of government initiatives in education and the police service has shown.

WIRS 3 contains mixed news about the traditional institutional industrial relations. Brown (1993) estimates that on the basis of the WIRS 3 data, only 47 per cent of the working population were covered by collective agreements in 1990, compared with 64 per cent in 1984 and 72 per cent in 1973. WIRS 3 also shows some decline in the number of shop stewards, more especially in those plants with modest or low union density, increasing the risk that they are drifting towards derecognition. Furthermore, it reveals a decline in the use of the union channel of communication and consultation and a marked decline in both the pre- and post-entry closed shop. Metcalf (1993) has reviewed the evidence on the union mark-up. Although it is hard to unravel, it does appear that the union mark-up – the extent to which a union presence results in higher wages, and therefore a major rationale for unions' existence – has declined.

The good news from WIRS 3 for the trade unions is that in most workplaces where trade unions have in the past been well established, trade union membership and organization has stood up well. Furthermore, any union presence was associated with positive benefits for the workforce. There was less wage inequality and less use of reward systems likely to engender greater inequality. There were more channels of communication, and more types of information were communicated. Workers in non-union plants were two and a half times as likely to be dismissed as those in unionized plants. Such evidence seriously challenges the empty-shell argument. Unions have been able to protect and promote workers' interests. Overall, WIRS 3 reveals that at 32 per cent of establishments, managers reported constraints on their ability to organize work as they wished, but this rose to 46 per cent in unionized workplaces.

3 Individualized HRM – high priority to HRM with no industrial relations

One of the issues to address in considering the growth of HRM is whether companies are taking HRM seriously and, to the extent that they are, whether this includes operating without unions and an industrial relations system. We could debate what is meant by 'taking HRM seriously', but for many observers one criterion would be an attempt at strategic integration. However, a weaker test is to look at the way in which specific policy initiatives are implemented. A review of recent UK trends in selection, training and reward systems (Guest, 1993) and reports on developments in employee involvement (Marchington et al., 1992) suggest that the approach is essentially piecemeal and opportunistic.

It is interesting to note that in the UK, our models of companies successfully practising HRM are all becoming somewhat dated. Few new names have emerged to add to those of the mid-1980s. Analysis of new establishments in the WIRS 3 sample indicates that it is predominantly the North American-owned firms that appear to promote a high HRM non-union approach. In other new establishments there is a low likelihood of union recognition, but also no particular emphasis on HRM (Guest and Hoque, 1993).

Several companies in the oil industry – a sector which has always had a high reputation for innovation in industrial relations and personnel management – have recently taken steps to derecognize trade unions. The reasoning behind this appears to be that unions are a constraint on the kind of flexibility that market conditions demand, namely functional flexibility to increase productivity, and numerical flexibility, reflected in the use of more contract labour and fixed-term contracts. Despite the market focus on cost advantage, this strategy contains elements of an integrated HRM approach which the companies apparently believe is easier to achieve with a significantly reduced union presence.

4 The Black Hole – no HRM and no industrial relations

If HRM loses its attractions as a policy priority, or at best becomes no more than a set of piecemeal techniques, and there is no compelling reason to operate within a traditional industrial relations system, the alternative is to emphasize neither. In market terms this may imply a strategy based on cost advantage. Labour is viewed as a variable cost, perhaps resulting in increasing emphasis on short-term contracts.

There are several types of evidence which suggest that this option is becoming more prevalent. The first is the well-documented decline in trade union membership and trade union density. This decline continues to be partly structural, but is reinforced by two new factors. The first is a growth in partial or complete derecognition. The most convincing evidence for this comes from the recent company-level survey of industrial relations (Marginson et al., 1993), which shows that 19 per cent of the companies in the sample had partially or wholly derecognized unions at least at one site; this compares with 7 per cent where recognition had been extended.

The second type of evidence is the changing pattern of union recognition at new establishments. Disney et al. (1993), in their analysis of the workplace industrial relations surveys, have shown that the pattern of recognition at new plants has changed. They argue that the industrial relations climate at the time of the start-up is a crucial factor and that it was different in the 1980s compared with the previous decade. As a result, it was 28 per cent less likely, other things being equal, that a union would be recognized at a new establishment set up in the 1980s compared with one started in the 1970s. More specifically, WIRS 3 reveals that in 1990, only 24 per cent of establishments less than ten years old recognized a union. This compares with 45 per cent of establishments less than ten years old in 1980. It appears (Disney et al., 1993) that the trend away from recognition began prior to 1980, and apart from a minor hiccup in the late 1980s, has continued to gather strength.

All the evidence suggests that when confronted with a decision about whether or not to recognize a trade union, companies are increasingly deciding not to do so. It is possible to conclude that this is now the dominant pattern in new establishments; indeed, it raises the question of why unions are recognized at all. The available evidence indicates that a union presence elsewhere in the company is a key positive influence on trade union recognition at new establishments. One interpretation of this is that management accepts, on the basis of experience, that unions have some value.

If a union is not recognized, there is little evidence that management replaces it with an HRM strategy to obtain full utilization of the workforce, by gaining its commitment to company goals and values. Millward (1993) has begun to paint a picture of policy and practice in non-union firms, based on the WIRS 3 survey data. There are fewer procedures and fewer health and safety representatives. There are also fewer channels of information and consultation, less information from management and fewer personnel specialists. Although the workplace climate is described as better than in unionized establishments, there are more dismissals, more compulsory redundancies, more notices to quit and more low pay, alongside a greater dispersion of pay. Pay also appears to be both more often performance-related and more market-determined. For the workforce, this emerging non-union environment is bleak and insecure.

Despite the WIRS 3 evidence which reports a continuing growth in the influence of personnel departments, from which a case might be made for the effective promotion of either industrial relations or HRM, it seems more likely, as Marginson et al. (1993) emphasize, that a financial controller model is dominating board thinking about how to manage the workforce. This does not fit comfortably with an HRM strategy in which labour is a relatively fixed cost, or with an industrial relations perspective which sees labour as a countervailing force, with the power to negotiate additional wage costs. Returning to the four options presented at the start of this section, the trend is away from the traditional collectivism of a representative industrial relations system, but the drift is towards the black hole of no industrial relations and no HRM, rather than towards individualized HRM or the new realism.

References

Barling, J., Wade, B. and Fullager, C. (1990) 'Predicting employee commitment to company and union: divergent models', *Journal of Occupational Psychology*, 63(1): 49–61.

Beer, M., Spector, B., Lawrence, P., Quinn Mills, D. and Walton, R. (1985) *Human Resource Management: A General Manager's Perspective*. Glencoe, IL: The Free Press.

Brown, W. (1993) 'The contraction of collective bargaining in Britain', *British Journal of Industrial Relations*, 31(2): 189–200.

Dastmalchian, A., Blyton, P. and Adamson, R. (1991) *The Climate of Workplace Relations*. London: Routledge.

Disney, R., Gosling, A. and Machin, S. (1993) 'What has happened to trade union recognition in Britain'. CEP Discussion Paper No. 130. London: LSE.

Gordon, M., Philpot, J., Burt, R., Thompson, C. and Spiller, W. (1980) 'Commitment to the union: development of a measure and an examination of its correlates', *Journal of Applied Psychology*, 65: 479–99.

Guest, D. (1987) 'Human resource management and industrial relations', *Journal of Management Studies*, 24(5): 503–21.

Guest, D. (1989) 'Human resource management: its implications for industrial relations and trade unions', in J. Storey (ed.), *New Perspectives on Human Resource Management*. London: Routledge.

Guest, D. (1993) 'Current perspectives on human resource management in the United Kingdom', in C. Brewster (ed.), *Current Trends in Human Resource Management in Europe*. London: Kogan Page.

Guest, D. and Dewe, P. (1988) 'Why do workers belong to trade unions? A social-psychological study in the UK electronics industry', *British Journal of Industrial Relations*, 29(1): 75–96.

Guest, D. and Dewe, P. (1991) 'Company or trade union; which wins workers' allegiance? A study of commitment in the United Kingdom electronics industry', *British Journal of Industrial Relations*, 29(1): 75–96.

Guest, D. and Hoque, K. (1993) 'Are greenfield sites better at human resource management?'. CEP Working Paper No. 435. London: LSE.

Involvement and Participation Association (1992) *Towards Industrial Partnership: A New Approach to Management–Union Relations*. London: IPA.

Kochan, T., Katz, H. and McKersie, R. (1986) *The Transformation of American Industrial Relations*. New York: Basic Books.

Marchington, M., Goodman, J., Wilkinson, A. and Ackers, P. (1992) *New Developments in Employee Involvement*. Research Series No. 2. London: Employment Department.

Marginson, P., Armstrong, P., Edwards, P. and Purcell, J. (1993) 'Decentralization, collectivism and individualism: evidence on industrial relations in transition from the 1992 company level industrial relations survey'. Paper presented to the BUIRA Conference, York, July.

Metcalf, D. (1993) 'Industrial relations and economic performance', *British Journal of Industrial Relations*, 31(2): 255–83.

Millward, N. (1993) 'Industrial relations in transition: the findings of the third workplace industrial relations survey'. Paper presented to BUIRA, York, July.

Millward, N., Stevens, M., Smart, D. and Hawes, W. (1992) *Workplace Industrial Relations in Transition*. Aldershot: Dartmouth.

Mowday, R., Porter, L. and Steers, R. (1982) *Employee–Organization Linkages: The Psychology of Commitment, Absenteeism and Turnover*. London: Academic Press.

Reichers, A. (1985) 'A review and reconceptualization of organizational commitment', *Academy of Management Review*, 10: 465–76.

Reichers, A. (1986) 'Conflict and organizational commitments', *Journal of Applied Psychology*, 71: 508–14.

Smith, P. and Morton, G. (1993) 'Union exclusion and decollectivization of industrial relations in contemporary Britain', *British Journal of Industrial Relations*, 31(1): 97–114.

Storey, J. (1992) *Developments in the Management of Human Resources*. Oxford: Blackwell.

Trevor, M. (1988) *Toshiba's New British Company*. London: PSI.

Turnbull, P. and Weston, S. (1993) 'Cooperation or control? Capital restructuring and labour relations on the docks', *British Journal of Industrial Relations*, 31(1): 115–34.

Walton, R. (1985) 'From control to commitment in the workplace', *Harvard Business Review*, 63 (March–April): 76–84.

Wickens, P. (1987) *The Road to Nissan*. London: Macmillan.

Wickens, P. (1993) 'Lean production and beyond: the system, the critics and the future', *Human Resource Management Journal*, 3(4): 75–90.

12

Missionary Management

Madeleine Bunting

In the early sixties an American psychologist, Abraham Maslow, left his university post and headed west to a company in Del Mar, in southern California, in a radical new departure in his career. He had pioneered concepts such as self-actualisation and the hierarchy of needs, and radically redrawn a framework of human motivation and human potential. Now he would turn his mind to a totally new territory – business and management. He kept a journal of his summer in the Californian factory, and eventually it was published under the unpronounceable title of *Eupsychian Management*. Not surprisingly with a title like that, it never reached any bestseller list, nor did it make for Maslow the millions acquired by subsequent business gurus who have adopted and popularised his ideas, which are now commonplace in corporate boardrooms all over the United States and Britain. But it was Maslow, in a hot Californian summer in 1962, who first dreamt of a new way to manage people which would make them into a 'better type of human being'. He set a grand and glorious goal: 'Proper management of the work lives of human beings, of the way in which they earn their living, can improve them and improve the world and in this sense be a utopian or revolutionary technique.'[1] It was through the properly managed company, Maslow argued, that the individual could find personal growth and achieve the ultimate aim of human existence – 'self-actualisation'. The 'only real path [to personal salvation is] via hard work and total commitment to doing well the job that fate or personal destiny calls you to do, or any important job that "calls for" doing'. Work was, Maslow continued, the route to happiness: 'This business of self-actualisation via a commitment to an important job and to worthwhile work could also be said, then, to be the path to human happiness.'[2]

Source: Madeleine Bunting (2004) *Willing Slaves: How the Overwork Culture is Ruling our Lives*. London: HarperCollins Publishers. Edited version.

This was a way of recasting the work ethic by fusing it with the growing preoccupation of the sixties' New Age movement with self-development and personal potential; put simply, it was through work that one 'found oneself'. It reformulated the concept of commitment; it was no longer enough to do a good job – nothing short of total dedication, of setting oneself to achieve the impossible and to exceed every expectation, was enough. The task for management was to nurture and stimulate this kind of heroic self-realisation. That required devising a company culture 'so that the goals of the individual merge with the goals of the organisation'.

In one of Maslow's essays in *Eupsychian Management* he listed thirty-six assumptions which should underlie 'enlightened management' (the very use of the word 'assumption' rather than 'principle' or 'rule' shows how this method of management would mask potential conflict by claiming to be implicit). Here are some of them:

Assume in all your people the impulse to achieve.
Assume there is no dominance–subordination hierarchy.
Assume that everyone will have the same managerial objectives and will identify with them.
Assume that everyone can enjoy good teamwork – not enough attention has been given to the pleasures of being in a love community with which one can identify.
Assume that people can take it … the strain should not be constant but people can benefit from being stretched and strained and challenged.
Assume that people are improvable.
Assume that everyone prefers to feel important, needed, useful.
Assume that everyone prefers or even needs to love their boss.
Assume that everyone wants responsibility, prefers to be a prime mover rather than a passive helper.
Assume that we all prefer meaningful work, a system of values, of understanding the world and of making sense of it.
Assume that no matter how menial the chore it can become meaningful by participation in a meaningful or important or loved goal.
Assume that the person is courageous enough for enlightened processes, i.e. he has stress-tolerance, knows creative insecurity and can endure anxiety.[3]

Maslow's challenge to management was astonishingly ahead of its time; only in the late eighties and early nineties did his ideas begin to take form as organisations sought to reformulate the 'psychological contract' with their workforce. In the new contract they no longer offered security, there was no such thing as a 'job for life', nor could they ask employees for loyalty; but they wanted harder work than ever. What companies were increasingly aware of was that employees' commitment made a significant difference to the bottom line. For knowledge-based companies, their biggest asset is their employees; it used to be that companies had about 80 per cent of their assets in buildings, plant, land and stock, and 20 per cent in employees; now the proportions have reversed. It's not just a cliché that a company is its people: increasingly, a company's value lies in immaterial assets such as employees and how the organisation works. As John Micklethwait and Adrian Woolridge put in their 1997 book *The Witch Doctors: What the Management Gurus are Saying, Why it Matters and How to Make Sense of it*: 'Now firms realise that their most important asset is knowledge, [which] is so much more difficult to manage than capital: fixed in the heads of pesky employees rather than stored in the bank and infuriatingly volatile and short-lived to boot.' Never has 'the ghost in the machine', as early management theorists described motivation, been so critical to a company's performance and valuation.

Over the last couple of decades the aim in many companies seeking to motivate their staff has been to devise a work culture which people would *like*, would find fun, and which offered the kind of personal development and individual affirmation people needed. The result was the emergence in the early nineties of the 'employer brand', as the marketing department was pulled into human resources meetings to assist in the task of 'selling' the brand to the 'internal customer'. Employees were no longer expected to be loyal to the boss, but *committed to the brand values* (the shift of wording from 'loyalty' to 'commitment' underlines the end of reciprocity). The brand values, of course, were devised with an eye on what would go down well with the prospective audience, the workforce. The aim was to 'align the employees with the brand', which meant recruiting people who reflected, or could be moulded to reflect, the brand values. As one human resources director put it, he wanted the company's brand values in his employees' heads at all times and in everything they did at work. The organisation wanted the right 'psychological fit' between employee and company culture. As a psychologist put it in the Chartered Institute of Personnel and Development's magazine, *People Management*, 'The organisation and the human resources function in particular needs to articulate not just how it wants people to act differently, but how it wants them to think and feel differently too. Then it needs to set about finding people who will do, think and feel those things. It needs to change those who don't, and it needs to focus on the power, influence and obstacles that smooth or roughen the path of change.'[4]

What this can amount to is an unprecedented invasiveness as management practices reach after parts of the employee's personality which have hitherto been considered private in order to unlock the required commitment, high performance and overwork. Richard Barrett of the World Bank says: 'The only way to develop long-lasting commitment is to tap into an individual's mental and spiritual motivations. Our mental needs are met in the realm of personal and professional growth. Our spiritual needs are met when we find meaning in our work; when what we do actually makes a difference; and when we are able to be of service. This is the realm of spiritual growth.'

Depending on your point of view, either this reformulation of the psychological contract licenses a re-engineering of human personality to suit the ends of the corporation, or the company is simply taking on the roles of other declining social institutions by meeting employees' need for purpose, identification and personal affirmation. In one survey 46 per cent of men and 37 per cent of women said they were looking for a job which would provide meaning;[5] David Boyle in his book *Authenticity: Brands, Fakes, Spin and the Lust for Real Life* (2003) comments that 'Most people can't bear to devote their lives to companies whose only purpose is to make a profit. They need a higher purpose.'

To try to resolve where the balance lay between these two views, I visited three companies, all well known for their strong 'brand cultures'. Two of them – Microsoft and Asda – are past winners of the *Sunday Times* Best Company to Work For title, and their own employees rated them highly. The third, Orange, developed a distinctive brand culture in its pioneering days; in the course of two visits, two years apart, I gathered some idea of how it had weathered the vicissitudes of a turbulent market. Microsoft and Asda (which is owned by the American Wal-Mart chain) have been influenced strongly by their US parent companies, though both stoutly insist on key elements being home-grown: they represent the British version of the American 'absorptive corporation'. In all three, the brand culture is regarded as critical to motivate the kind of commitment, emotional labour and hard work considered essential to the companies' commercial success.

Picture of perfection

The bus ride from Reading station to the computer giant Microsoft's UK headquarters is only twenty minutes, but it seems like a passage to another world from the shabby terraced streets of Reading to the swathes of landscaped lawn of the Thames Valley Business Park. In front of Microsoft there's a nature reserve bordering a lake on which a fountain plays, and on summer afternoons the company offers free ice creams and picnic rugs to its employees. Inside the airy atrium of the American corporation's most successful subsidiary (an annual turnover of £17 billion) is one of four cafés in the complex. Employees – including the chief executive – sit in armchairs in open-neck shirts for meetings, and waiters stroll over to offer drinks. There's a quiet, purposeful hum more akin to a café than an office. Microsoft workers have little reason to leave the office during daylight hours: there's a dry cleaner's, a crèche, a financial adviser, and a well-being centre with qualified nurses on hand. Groceries are delivered to your car, and the canteen offers such good breakfasts that employees plan their team meetings at 8.30 a.m. to take place there.

Perhaps this is the sort of utopia Abe Maslow had in mind. Certainly, Microsoft UK is proud of having put a great deal of effort into providing exactly the right conditions in which to cultivate the most commitment. Kay Winsper, a senior human resources manager, even has the job title 'Head of Great Companies', and is responsible for nothing less than the 'physical, emotional and intellectual well-being' of employees. It probably helps that Microsoft is a young company – founded in 1990 – so there has been no gear-grinding adaptation of an old corporate culture: it's had a green-field site both literally and metaphorically. In 2003 Microsoft was awarded the *Sunday Times* title 'Best UK Company to Work For', and such is the level of interest from other companies that it is holding open days to spread the word. According to the *Sunday Times'* survey, 93 per cent of Microsoft UK's employees are proud to come to work, and as Kay Winsper adds, 'They put phenomenal energy into their jobs.'

One of the first things Kay wants to talk about is Microsoft's 'strength finder' programme. This assesses employees' personalities to find their top five strengths, so they can focus on them. She shows me a wall chart which illustrates how identifying your strengths leads to good work, which in turn leads to customer satisfaction, which leads to profit increases, and finally stock-price increases. It is a perfect illustration of the merging of individual and organisational goals. Employees' personal development at Microsoft UK is perfectly attuned to raising the company's share price.

The problem is that Microsoft UK just can't find the staff, complains Steve Harvey, Director of People and Culture, over a delicious lunch in the company canteen. He explains: 'We've had 13,000 applications for jobs in the last nine months, and we hired fourteen. We're having to target individuals now – sniping to pick out the good ones. We look for change agents, the best and the brightest.'

Everything that can be outsourced at Microsoft UK has been; what's left is a hard-core team of 1,595 'change agents'. Fifty-five per cent of employees are under thirty-five, and fewer than 1 per cent are over fifty-five; the ratio of men to women is 74:26. People work there for an average of seven years at senior levels, and only three and a half years at junior levels. When I challenge Mr Harvey that the company is creaming off the years of peak energy and drive of the top talent, he agrees: 'These are people who are doing what they love,' adding, 'There has to be "clear contracting", and the employee and employer have to understand each other. It's implicit in the culture that there is no job for life.'

He refers several times to 'clear contracting', and insists it is about 'putting people back in control of their lives': 'So many people in the technology sector come in and hand over their soul. You could work all day long here … I want people here to know why they are here. If you hand over your soul, any corporation will use it. I don't want it, I don't want to take over their lives.'

What he does want is exemplary dedication for a short period of time; any longer and it's probably not sustainable, as employees lose momentum, or family commitments compete for their time. Microsoft's culture of 'all or nothing' doesn't really work part-time – there are only twenty-three part-timers amongst the Reading workforce. Mr Harvey becomes emphatic over the question of work–life balance: 'What a stupid question! We hire very driven people who try to balance work–life over a life. They take the long-term picture. The difficulties come when you try to balance work–life on a daily or weekly basis.'

I ask how that fits in with being a parent, and he responds by referring me to the company's two-day 'Personal Excellence Programme', which inculcates a form of corporate philosophy in employees: 'We try to teach choices and consequences – if you choose to have a family or play golf, you have to be honest about what kind of job you can do and what responsibilities you can manage. We're educating people to make those choices, and loads of jobs are very demanding and very challenging. Women look at how big those big jobs are, and take a choice.' That explains the 80:20 per cent split of men to women at the senior levels, he argues, but insists that the 'senior ladies are getting through'. The average age of employees is thirty-four, and significantly, most of those I met had no children.

According to Mr Harvey, it's good two-way deal: employees know the score, and are paid handsomely (average salary is around £65,000, and there are stock-option schemes and flexible pensions), and in return the company gets their hard work. But he knows what the critics say; he muses that a temp working for him had accused him of exploiting his employees, saying that Microsoft's was a culture in which 'no one ever took their foot off the gas'. His comment was: 'We challenge people to make choices.'

The 'change agents' Microsoft UK wants to employ are not just clever – in fact cleverness is quite secondary, insists Harvey. Far more important is the right kind of personality. He sums this up as 'very driven, very adaptable, and passionate'. I suspect it's the combination of drive and adaptability that is the most tricky to find in prospective employees: one is a characteristic of focus, determination and single-mindedness, the other is more commonly associated with flexibility, compromise and pragmatism. Add a requirement for unbridled enthusiasm to the mix, and one begins to see why Mr Harvey has a recruitment problem. 'If you aren't adaptable, it'll kill you here,' he admits.

The problem is the 're-orgs', or re-organisations, which seem to be going on almost continuously. In the past five months, three hundred positions in the company have been 'touched' (as Harvey puts it), and 16 per cent of employees have moved jobs. Management is 'always keeping an eye on the bottom 5 per cent – constantly testing them and asking, is it time for them to move on?' he explained, adding, 'If you're a great Microsoft employee, it shouldn't bother you. If you're talented, there's always opportunities coming up.' Harvey smiled, leaned back in his chair and added happily, 'It's lovely. There's constant pressure to perform. You know where you're going in life, it's up to you how hard you push yourself.'

The most striking characteristic of Microsoft's work culture is the emphasis on the individual. A poster on the wall sums it up: a motorbike boot standing next to a clog stamped with the Microsoft logo. Underneath are the words: 'All Microsoft employees are different, the one thing they do have in common is their individuality'. Harvey said he wanted to know what made each employee tick. This focus on the individual and how he or she negotiates the 'choices' offered by Microsoft is reinforced not only by the Personal Excellence Programme, but also by their extensive mentoring scheme. Everyone in Microsoft can choose an internal 'mentor', and meet them as frequently or infrequently as they like. At more senior levels, employees are entitled to the services of both an external and an internal mentor. Around 65 per cent of the workforce is involved in the mentoring at any one time.

Given the level of constant restructuring, many employees are almost permanently thinking about what job they might like or might be able to do next. The mentor can help them plot their career, at the same time reinforcing Microsoft's values: the company handbook says one of the qualities needed by a mentor is to 'overtly aim to live the values in day-to-day concrete behaviours'. Among the duties of being a mentor is 'passing on corporate wisdom and knowledge and to equip people to become more self-managing, a crucial skill in the future world of work ... the mentor's role is to help the mentee reach their *picture of perfection* – for their role, their career, their team or Microsoft as a whole' (my italics).

According to the handbook, people want three things from work: money, meaning and magic. It draws a distinction between 'salary work' and 'soul work', and states that, through the mentoring scheme, Microsoft aims to increase the latter: 'Talented people are crying out to spend time with individuals who can help them focus on their purpose in their private and professional lives.' From the comments of mentees included in the handbook, the connection to hard work is evident:

> 'Having the opportunity to have a mentor ... makes me feel like I'm a valuable asset to the company and ensure that I work hard to maintain that perception.'

> 'After a mentoring session I feel focused and driven to achieve my personal and professional goals.'

> 'With the re-org coming up, I want to ensure I am making my best possible contribution to Microsoft and playing to my strengths.'

Making claims to recognise employees' individuality is an effective tool of human resources: it pre-empts the potential formation of any countervailing collective identity, such as that of a trade union. It goes without saying that the individuality Microsoft celebrates is within strict, corporate-defined limits: you can wear clogs to work, play snooker for three hours a day and eat all the ice creams you like, but woe betide anyone who fails to show the right degree of enthusiasm – *passion* is the ubiquitous word – for technology and for Microsoft, or who fails to put in the hard work which is regarded as standard in Themes Valley.

A lot is expected of employees, and none of those I interviewed was in any doubt that that meant hard work. 'It takes three to four months to get your head around the culture. People are so busy, I thought they were unfriendly – they are constantly trying to cram more and more into their day, and rushing around. They've always got full diaries. It's great. We are a busy organisation, there's always a lot of pull on our time. But because it's fun and rewarding, you don't mind doing more. You want to see it through to completion', said twenty-nine-year-old Chris Bartlett, a Business Productivity Advisor. He joked: 'People do say it's like the Moonies at Microsoft.'

He smiled, then resumed his earlier train of thought. 'The reward is that we're making a positive difference to how people live their lives and do their work … We're helping people to do things better, faster and more efficiently – if we aren't, we might as well pack up and go home.' It's not the money which keeps him at Microsoft: he says he could get better-paid jobs elsewhere. 'I made a conscious decision that I wanted to be on the bus and that I wanted to be near the driver. I have a passion for technology and all those brand values.'

Bartlett says his mentor has been helping him to find his 'soul work' – the job which will make him jump out of bed in the morning – because 'If work doesn't make you feel really good, why do it?' His mentor helps him work out 'what I'm about as a person, making myself feel better and making others feel better. I want people around here to enjoy their jobs at Microsoft.'

Kathy Isherwood is forty, and sees things a little differently. She manages a busy team on a customer technical support desk. It's pressured, demanding work, and Microsoft expects high standards: the customer must be made to 'feel delighted and that we've been waiting for their call'. Kathy is hugely enthusiastic about the degree of autonomy she has in her job, and praises the Microsoft culture. She's clearly very dedicated; as she talks, I notice that whenever I ask her a question she thinks not of her own situation, but of her team's. She tells me how she took on a team which 'had lost its ways', and how she 'healed them'; she says several times, 'My people come first,' and when I press her, she explains, 'I need to be there for my people.' She commented fondly that they were all so different they were like 'dolly mixtures', and with some satisfaction concluded that, during re-orgs, 'I've been the point of stability for my team'. Probably a very good manager, she reminded me of a proud mother talking of her large brood of thriving children.

But one thing she was very clear about was that, although while she was in the office Microsoft of course came first, it was most definitely 'part of my life, not the whole of my life'. This was not the case for some of her colleagues, she added, suddenly becoming animated: 'There's a lot of people here who get into trouble. They are addicted to Microsoft. They're in denial, but they live, eat and breathe Microsoft. It's their world. The thing is, they choose to throw themselves into something. They *need* to be addicted. If it wasn't Microsoft, it would be something else: they need to prove themselves. They are so absorbed by what they're doing – like Rembrandt – there's no start, no end to what they're doing.'

Is that Microsoft's fault?

'Sometimes Microsoft could be more responsible and help that person to understand they are addicted. I make my team take lunch, but a lot of people here work and work. It's a bit lame when Microsoft says it's their choice. If you have an alcoholic in the house, you don't put a bottle of gin by the bed.'

But she took a very clear-eyed view of the labour market: 'There's no job for life, it's hard out there. You need to have the right skills, and people work very hard. We're a commodity, and they'll get everything out of you. If you offer Microsoft your soul and your life – and people here want to please, they need to feel valued, because Microsoft employs high achievers who want to be the top of the tree – they'll take everything that's offered. I've found people in the loo sobbing, exhausted and overstretched. People are frightened of getting a bad review. You're only as good as your last project. There's tremendous pressure to perform, but that's because of today's business environment, there's nothing Microsoft can do about that.'

Kathy's exoneration of Microsoft from responsibility was echoed by other employees. The frequent internal communication reinforces the sense of a market environment where the wolves are baying for blood. There is never a let-up in the competitive pressures. If that is the case for Microsoft, the world's biggest multi-national, how much more true is it for the lesser fry? Microsoft has created a utopia available to an elite for a short period of their lives. It's an extremely clever, utterly internally coherent sealed community, divorced from its geographical context and, it would seem, from any other social context.

Microsoft UK is exceptional on one particular point: it is very successfully doing what many other British companies are increasingly attempting to do. Its model of the high-performance, high-commitment workforce is the goal towards which hundreds of other highly skilled, so-called knowledge companies are fumbling. You can see why – it works (very hard), and it's immensely profitable. Microsoft UK is at the bleeding edge of technology, motivating highly skilled workers in a competitive labour market. But how does a company succeed in motivating the lowest skilled?

Miles of smiles

From the staff canteen at Asda on the York ringroad, one has a superb bird's-eye view of the entire store: a vast emporium of neatly stacked shelves beneath a ceiling of brightly coloured banners announcing special offers. On the corridor on the way to the canteen is a detailed breakdown of the store's key performance indicators over the previous week, giving sales measured against targets, profitability and staff absences, in pages and pages of statistics, including a category called 'Go the Extra Mile', under which the York store had failed to score any points in the previous week. (At least these indicators weren't pasted on the inside of the toilet door, as a researcher discovered in another supermarket.)

Like all Asda stores, the one at York is continually monitored by mystery shoppers on every aspect of its performance, from points as mundane as whether the tins are stacked correctly on the shelves to whether the checkout girl smiled throughout her three-and-a-half-hour shift, and whether the shopper felt the warmth of the greeter. The manager receives these audit figures every day, with the store ranked against other stores in its geographical region as well as nationally. The smile above the 'Happy to Help' badge can't slip for a moment without it being tracked on Asda's computer systems. The corridor from the staff changing rooms to the shopfloor passes these noticeboards, and on the staircase there's a full-length mirror and above it a big sign reading: 'Are you ready for the Asda stage?'

David Smith, head of HR at Asda's headquarters in Leeds, promised me I would feel the warmth immediately I entered the store: 'Our store is a community. Staff are encouraged to chat to each other, and the managers to get to know the staff. How can you treat people with respect unless you understand them? You can feel the warmth in our stores. We have regular customer focus groups, and stringent mystery shoppers providing quality information to measure what it feels like.'

The mystery shoppers measure the friendliness of each interaction with staff, the eye contact, and the use of the customer's name at the checkout. The 'colleagues', as staff are known, are exhorted to exhibit 'miles of smiles'. 'It's got to be a *real* smile,' says Smith. 'We don't just take anyone – a degree of gregariousness, that's the most important recruitment characteristic. You can make people more gregarious – we can draw out the gregarious side. We do have a sense that people in the Asda family live the values – it's gregarious, off the wall, a bit wacky, flexible, family-minded, genuinely interested in people, respect for the individual, informal. That's what makes the business go – we've gone into personality, a family and a community feel. Society is more isolationist – solitary lives, single households – so people look for interactions in a retailer. We have elderly people who come to our store every day, and we set out to meet that need.'

I asked him if that meant he employed more staff. He quickly rejected that. 'It's not that we employ more people. We have to be efficient. It's the quality of the interaction.' He pauses. He's wearing the same 'Happy to Help' name badge as a shelf-stacker. 'Life is much more than what people get paid day to day. Instead, it's "What does the boss think of me? And what do the colleagues think of me?" Maslow was an absolute genius. Once people are warm and fed, they want to be fulfilled.'

Asda has taken this last point very seriously; it (rather complacently) admits it doesn't pay its 133,000 UK workforce particularly well – a basic

£5.07 per hour – but it lavishes them with 'Bursting with Pride' and 'Thank You' certificates. There are 'listening groups' and 'huddles' and 'colleagues circles' to hear their views and tell them about how the store is doing and to encourage a sense of 'ownership', as Smith puts it. There are so many forms of competition within Asda, from Oscars awarded to colleagues for work 'above and beyond the call of duty' to various leagues such as the 'Fantasy Store' and the 'Horror Store', that I lost track.

Back at York, Owen Hickley has just arrived as the new general manager from the store he set up in Dewsbury. He's been at the company for twenty-three years, and has worked his way up from storeman to running the six hundred staff at York. He's a true believer, full of sincerity and devotion to Asda and his colleagues. He didn't flinch from pulling everyone into line when he started out in Dewsbury: 'We took on three to four hundred people, and we recruited people purely on attitude. I took a dozen of the management to a lovely hotel and put them through their paces and we watched them doing the Wal-Mart Chant – if they couldn't throw themselves into something like that, how could they serve? I wanted people who were not just good, but great. It's a bit American, and I was a bit sceptical at first, but I find it quite natural now. It's a good leveller. It's the way you measure whether people are with you.'

He was proud of the larks they'd had at Dewsbury, and the fundraising they'd done. He described a breast cancer awareness day which the store had got involved in; every member of staff either dyed their hair pink or wore some pink clothing: 'Everyone joined in, it was a great cause. But there were two dissenters who forgot. I told them to go home. I told them, "You're not in the team." They knew what was the right or wrong behaviour, and they went off, bought pink shirts and came back.'

Hickley had gained a reputation in Asda for the number of schemes he'd invented to reward staff, from free cinema tickets to a week of free 'Stuff your Face' lunches in the canteen. 'We're trained to look for what people are doing right. Asda is the best possible company in the world to work for – there's a wow factor. It makes you feel ten feet tall. There's a contract: you'll never walk on my shopfloor unless you're dressed properly and shaved properly. I'll send you home because you're not one of the team. We want it inch perfect, every tin facing in the right direction, and that's really hard. It's much harder managing like this than by "tell and do". One manager I hired was excellent on the figures, but he was cold, and I pulled him in and said, "I'm going to have to let you go unless you change. You're not taking the people with you. You have to be observant, intuitive and pick up on how they feel. Do they feel a million dollars?" I ask employees to choose their attitude. You can do that, you know. You can choose to feel happy or sad. All these initiatives and incentives don't work unless you believe in them passionately and buy into the vision.' Hickley was a huge success in Dewsbury: his absence levels were the lowest in the country, and the store rated highly in the national audits. Teams from Wal-Mart, Asda's American owner, even visited to hear how he did it. He's a rising star in Asda management.

But talking to some 'colleagues' late on a Thursday afternoon in the York store canteen, I heard a different story. Did I just chance upon some rare grumpy dissidents, or was it a truer picture? Maggie, Kath and Jean (not their real names) had little to say about Asda's culture. What they wanted to talk about was the pay: it was terrible. 'I might as well be a cleaner for this money. For what we do, balancing all the till receipts, we'd get £3 more an hour at other places,' said Kath, her face tired and strained. 'I should have gone a long time ago.'

Kath is on what she calls an 'old-world contract' of a lower than usual hourly rate, but which pays double time for her regular Sunday shift. Her biggest complaint is that she was paid better in the past, before the company phased out supervisors. She's still doing the same job, with some managerial duties, but she's no longer paid for the level of responsibility she has. She's doing a forty-three-hour week for about £185 take-home pay. She's taken on a second job in a pub six evenings a week to keep up with the payments on a new car and the mortgage – giving her a working week of about sixty-seven hours.

But Kath is still there at Asda after more than twenty years, despite all her complaints. There must be something about the place, I say, if she's stayed so long? 'I've made quite a lot of money on the shares, and I'd lose some of that,' she concedes. 'I like my job, I'm left to get on with it. The managers do actually speak to you now – before, they didn't. It's a much more comfortable atmosphere. The quarterly meetings, when they tell you how the store is doing and what's going on in the next three months, are good fun. You come out with a positive attitude.' Then she remember another thing which irks her: 'They've cut the number of staff in our office, so I have to work harder to get through all the work'.

Jean's story was similar. 'I've worked here for more than ten years, and we're so understaffed. It's much worse than it used to be – we're rushed off our feet. You do make an effort. They've cut back on the staff, down to a minimum, and I go home really stressed.' What had kept her – and Maggie – at Asda was the flexible hours; they both work part-time, which fits in with the rest of their lives. But Jean admitted she'd finally had enough, and was looking for another job.

As for Asda's prided distinctive culture, it has made little impression on these three employees: 'All the league tables – there are so many scores, I don't bother, but there's a lot of goodwill to charities and social events, things like that.'

'They tried the Wal-Mart Chant once here.'

'The "Asda stage" notice above the mirror is a bit cheesy, I just check my eyeliner.'

'You cringe when you watch the videos at quarterly meetings.'

Jean, Maggie and Kath had a much more clear-eyed attitude to their employer than did either their store manager or Asda's head of human resources. They saw right through the claims of 'Respecting the Individual' (emblazoned in the atrium of the company headquarters), and wanted to know why that didn't translate into better pay. On the other hand, Asda must be doing something right, or such long-term employees in a tight labour market like York would have moved on; Asda claims its staff turnover rates are 10 per cent below the retail industry average of around 35 per cent. Offering very flexible part-time work accounts for some of this, but another is in the culture: Asda offers its staff more autonomy than some of its competitors, and they appreciate the lack of formality and the approachability of the management. While Jean, Maggie and Kath may have been diffident about it with me, some of the morale-raising has evidently worked. Asda's achievement is consider-able: it doesn't pay its shopfloor staff particularly well, and is working them harder than ever, with constant demands to perform – yet it succeeds in keeping them.

Living and breathing the brand

Take another brand, the mobile telephone company Orange. I first visited and interviewed Orange employees in 2001, and returned two years later after the company had gone through a rocky time in a fiercely competitive market. In 2001 it was still riding high as one of the most successful brands of the late nineties. Its advertising was beautiful and humorous: it associated technology with being human, funky and warm-hearted. Its human resources policies were a combination of high tech and New Age: *feng shui* call centres, aromatherapy and headsets. It even produced aromatherapy sprays named after its brand values, so employees could spray on some 'Integrity', some 'Fun' or some 'Honesty'. A bag labelled 'Boost' containing all the fragrances had been given to each employee in the North Shields call centre (they were not, however, allowed to take them home).

In 2001 Nicole Louis, Orange's former head of brand communications, summed up the commitment of employees as something that 'can't be bought with bonuses, it can't be incentivised. They fall in love with the brand. I did. It's like a relationship.' For Sharon Young, then head of call centres on North Tyneside, the brand means a different type of call centre altogether: 'We asked [employees] how they wanted to sit, and we try to create a community envi-ronment with units of twelve people. Call centres are traditionally open-plan, vast and impersonal, but our teams go for lunch and breaks together to build up rapport. It's a big challenge in a call centre – staff don't feel important. But we don't hot desk, and we encourage a sense of belonging so that people feel, "I'm not just a number, this is my home."' The response from employees in 2001 was enthusiastic. They liked the sociability of the job and the approachability of the management. One told me that people changed after working for a while in Orange: they became more friendly and relaxed. As at Asda, the pay has never been good, and in August 2002 it had to be increased to match the industry average in the region.

Some of the old enthusiasm was still there in 2003, even after a bout of redundancies and restructuring which had made everyone in the call centre feel insecure. Julie, a supervisor, commented, 'In previous call centres where I've worked it was like pigs in a pen, but here the team is all together in a community. Some of these people have worked together for quite a while. It's like a little family: if someone's stuck, someone else is happy to help out.'

In spite of the knocks, people were still being won over: 'On Valentine's Day, there was a heart-shaped chocolate on everyone's desk. I thought, no one has ever done that before. It sounds very small and trivial, until you come in and find it there,' said one employee. Little gestures make people feel appreciated, but as the same employee brusquely commented, 'No one is that naive to take on all the brand stuff.'

That's not what the management think, either at the cell centre or in the London headquarters. As at Asda, my impression was that the people to whom the brand values and culture really matter are management. Simon Cartwright is Orange's head of human resources, and readily admits to working long hours and at weekends. In fact, he takes his mobile phone away on holiday with him, and jokes that his wife sometimes resorts to hiding it. But, he insists, it's all fun. 'I passionately believe it should be fun to work here. People tend to work long hours at Orange, but the relationships and the atmosphere can be fun. We're in a sector where there's immense competitive pressure, and our culture is hard-working and driven. Hans Snook [the departed founder of Orange] left this legacy that "Being good is not good enough." Once we achieve a goal we set the bar higher, and people are driven by that.'

He said he wanted employees to 'live and breathe the brand'. Did he, I asked. 'I feel proud to work at Orange. I'm proud of what Orange stands for in the marketplace. I'm passionate about the business, and I care about the people and what we do. I get frustrated when I see us behaving in a way that isn't Orange.' Later, he added, 'I see my values as aligned with Orange values. I don't hold myself up to being a saint, but I try to incorporate the brand values into everything I do.' Then he laughed. 'It's beginning to sound like a cult.'

I pressed him on how he 'incorporated the brand values' (one of which is specifically about trust, after all) into making people redundant. 'It doesn't undermine my faith in the brand, because I rationalise it. You can deal with the employees you're losing in a way that's consistent with the brand values. You have to be open and empathetic, and don't keep people waiting. If we have to let someone go, it's our mistake. I'd do more than say sorry. I'd take them through the rationale: "We not only feel sorry, we feel concerned. We built this [the organisation], the world has changed, we weren't flexible enough. Orange was at fault, not uniquely so." It's very difficult – the economic cycles of the world are sharper and shorter, and to avoid those, societies and individuals have to be more flexible.'

What's in the new psychological contract?

Jack Welch, the legendary Chief Executive of the US corporation General Electric, said that 'Any company trying to compete … must figure out a way to engage the mind of every employee'. His words are up on the walls of Microsoft's office, and it's a lesson that all these three companies are trying to implement.

In earlier stages of industrialisation, employers could rely on a combination of material need and discipline to exact hard work. That kind of command-and-control labour relations doesn't work with the highly skilled who want autonomy and whose work is such that their contribution cannot be specified and ordered; for example, a manager of a computer programming team won't know as much of the technical detail as will those who work under him. Nor can the kind of emotional labour expected at Asda or Orange be ordered: you can't yell at someone to put warmth into their smile, or personality into their telephone voice. As one researcher put it, 'You need their [the employees'] commitment, not their obedience.'[6] Competitive pressures drive the need to raise the quality of the service or increase productivity; both require employees' discretionary effort.

In return for wanting more from employees, the company offers more – not more money, and no longer much job security of course. Instead it offers to meet a range of emotional needs. This was summed up in a working paper by two consultants from Hay Group:

> Getting engaged performance is not just about investing financially in employees through pay and benefit increases. It is about striking a new contract in which the organisation invests *emotionally* in its workforce. In exchange, employees make a similar emotional investment, pouring their 'discretionary effort' into their work and delivering superior performance. The new contract says, 'We'll make your job (and life) more meaningful. You give us your hearts and minds'.[7]

The paper goes on to quote the comment of an American corporate executive: 'It's imperative that leaders give people meaning in their work because passionate employees get better results. If leaders can't give people passion about their work, employees will find it somewhere else.'

A well-developed brand culture firstly offers to meet the employee's need to be recognised as an individual – the anonymity of the factory-floor assembly line won't deliver high discretionary effort. It requires emotional investment: if you want people to work hard, you have to spend a lot of management time on them, coaching them, singling them out for praise, encouraging them, appraising them in 'one to one's', and then devise all manner of recognition events to 'celebrate the successes'. Management is required to do a lot of stroking, which makes the job of middle managers more complex and more emotionally demanding, as both Kathy Isherwood at Microsoft and Owen Hickley at Asda indicated. Tom Peters pointed it out in his 1982 business best-seller *In Search of Excellence*: 'We like to think of ourselves as winners. The lesson that the excellent companies have to teach is that there is no reason why we can't design systems that continually reinforce this notion; most of their people are made to feel that they are winners.' He was articulating a long tradition of American management theory going back to Elton Mayo in the 1930s, who argued that social rewards such as consultation and recognition were more important than economic incentives in winning the co-operation of the workforce.

Secondly, the company's brand culture offers to meet the need to partici-pate in a purpose greater than the pursuit of one's own interest. Companies put great effort into identifying and exalting their 'mission' and encouraging staff to subscribe to it. One phrase which employees and companies alike frequently come up with is 'making a difference'; behind its banality lies an appeal to a sense of agency, of personal impact on the world. Meeting this need is one of the main drivers behind the corporate social responsibility agenda: employees need to feel their labour is doing more good than just increasing the company's share price, and employers cater for that need by setting up voluntary schemes for their staffs, such as helping out in local schools.

This spills over into the third need the brand culture offers to meet: the need for meaning. This marks another development in the expansion of the work ethic. Work has always provided identity and belonging; what's new is that it now also offers to provide purpose and meaning. It used to be religious institutions, political parties and the state which met such needs; now, *faute de mieux*, they are channelled into work. Gurnek Bains, a business psycholo-gist at the London-based YCS Ltd consultancy, refers to Abraham Maslow and his famous hierarchy of needs to explain this corporate philosophising: 'At the bottom are the most basic such as the need for food and security, but as these are fulfilled, we seek other needs and the top need is the need for mean-ing. In a wealthy society, most people's material needs have been met, and the need for meaning becomes the most important; rather than work being a transactional relationship for money, more and more people are looking for emotional engagement in work and a sense of purpose. Companies have always been about the generation of profit, but people can't get excited about that. One way to give meaning is to make the brand important, and try to get people to buy in emotionally. In large urban societies, work is the only way to connect you to society in a meaningful way and recognisable brands meet a basic need to connect.'

American sociologist Joanne Ciulla is critical of how employers are expanding the work ethic, and comments in her book *The Working Life* (2000) how one 'consequence of this loaded meaning of work is that we put our happiness in the hands of the market and our employers ... earning a decent living is not enough, we want something more ... and this challenges employers to find ways to motivate people to satisfy a variety of abstract desires and needs such as self-development and self-fulfilment. Managers are charged with the task of "making meaning" and have tried new ways of persuading employees to invest more of themselves in their work than the job required ... words such as "quality", "commitment" and "teamwork" all attempt to control and change the meaning of work in an organisation.'

Three companies hardly amounts to a representative sample, but what was striking in Microsoft, Asda and Orange was that the higher they were in the pecking order, the more excited the managers were about their brand. After all, it was probably they who had spent a lot of time devising it and thinking about how to communicate it, and they are certainly expected to subscribe passionately to it. The brand business – because it *is* a multi-million-pound business, with innumerable consultancies – belongs to a generation that grew up in the sixties and seventies believing they had to fight for a great cause, and found by the eighties and nineties nothing but disillusionment after Vietnam and the failure of communism. Business gurus from Tom Peters to Gary Hamel, with some help from Charles Handy, spotted an opening for the corporation: there was a vacuum of spiritual purpose amongst the 'hungry spirits' and 'empty raincoats', as Handy called them in the titles of two of his books. A huge reserve of energy and commitment could be tapped by a corporation which offered its management a chance to make, as Peters put it in *In Search of Excellence*, not just money, but *meaning* for people, because 'We desperately need meaning in our lives and will sacrifice a great deal to institutions that will provide meaning for us.'

'Meaning-making' was exactly what that generation had experienced in the protest movements of the sixties and seventies; they simply applied that experience and that reforming energy to corporate life. They used their egalitarianism to flatten corporate hierarchies and put everyone on first-name terms, while doing little to alter the bigger picture of dramatically-increasing inequality through the last decades of the twentieth century. Gary Hamel, another business guru to capitalise on this baby-boomer generation's angst, melds the language of sixties protest and corporate capitalism, and offered companies such as the doomed American energy corporation Enron a blueprint for the 'business activist' to 'lead the revolution', urging them to 'first break all the rules'.

While the brand cultures which managers devise may or may not have a positive effect on their workforce, they are significant for their own levels of motivation. Those institutions which offer them the opportunity to 'make meaning' get a lot of time and energy in return, as Peters had promised. This goes a long way towards explaining why the harried senior executive willingly forgoes the freedom of his own time, and accepts the trade-off of invasive work for the pleasures of being needed, and involved in something meaningful. The trade-off can be punitive, argues André Gorz in a passionate description of how the corporate brand culture entraps the willing slave in a self-reinforcing logic:

> In a disintegrating society, in which the quest for identity and the pursuit of social integration are continually being frustrated, the corporate culture and the corporate loyalty inculcated by the firm offer the young workers a substitute for membership of the wider society, a refuge from the sense of insecurity. The firm offers them the kind of security [which] monastic orders, sects and work communities provide. It asks them to give up everything – to give up any other form of allegiance, personal interests and even their personal lives – in order to give themselves body and soul to the company, which in exchange will provide them with an identity, a place, a personality and a job they can be proud of. They become members of a 'big family', and the relationship to the company and to the corporate work collective becomes the only social bond; it absorbs all their energy and mobilises their whole person, thus storing up the danger for them of a total loss of self-worth … if they lose the confidence of the company and that is earned by indefinitely improving their performance.[8]

Gorz's analogy with monasticism – it's one which the business guru Charles Handy also uses for the managerial elite – echoes the re-emergence of a spiritual language in people's everyday lives. It isn't in the church they never visit, but in the office and on the shopfloor that they hear of 'soul work', 'vocation' and the 'corporate soul'. Jack Welch said people 'wanted to be rewarded in their pocket and their soul'. Work is where we now most often hear of sacrifice. Books with titles like *Corporate Religion* and *Leading with Soul* are no longer on the wacky fringes of business literature, but are symptomatic of an American-driven phenomenon which recognises that the 'super-performance' companies require from employees involves a process of transformation of potential, of self-discovery and self-realisation and transcendence of limitations, which springs directly from the New Age spiritual experiences of the sixties. Doing a job well is no longer enough; 'stretch targets' deliberately push the boundaries of the possible; there are no limits to the expectations. 'The giant within' must be awakened, claims Anthony Robbins, one of the business gurus, along with Stephen Covey, who has made millions out of this genre of business spirituality.

Simultaneously, the corporation speaks the language of a religious institution – 'meaning' – and, confusingly, the language of love. 'Passion' has slipped from bedroom to boardroom, and spread like a contagion throughout management-speak; the word carries connotations of both emotional intimacy and strength of purpose. The language used to articulate brand values is elastically stretched to accommodate contradictions and confusions in evocative phrases intended to obfuscate – to window-dress – the sometimes brutal workings of the organisation, as well as to inspire. Employees are subjected to mission statements, vision statements, brand values, all of which are designed to capture their hearts, minds and souls. Employees, in a deceptively egalitarian spirit (not borne out by the pay structure) are known as 'colleagues' in Asda, or 'partners' in Starbucks; 'human resources' – itself a comparatively recent replacement for the earlier 'personnel department' – has taken on pleasantly democratic overtones as the 'people department'; and companies are very fond indeed of instituting 'communities' in place of departments, while 'positions', not people, are made redundant. Two of the most ubiquitous and fraudulent words are 'empowerment' and 'ownership'; companies claim they want their employees to be 'empowered' and to 'own' their jobs; as the currency of these words has spread in the United States, American companies have been down-sised, and inequalities over pay have grown. You may 'own' your job, but you're unlikely to own much else on some of the wages low-paid Americans earn; they may not own their home or most of their belongings (bought on credit), but they are expected to lavish on 'their' job all the time, energy and responsibility which ownership requires.

Is this an Orwellian, ideologically motivated use of words to conceal the truth, asked Deborah Cameron, Professor of Languages at the University of London, in an elegant analysis in the *New Statesman* in 2001: 'The problem ... is not so much that it represents reality inaccurately or dishonestly, but that it does not set out to be a representation of anything at all. When organisations proclaim they are "pursuing excellence" ... they want us not to believe the words, but to applaud the sentiments behind them. Their claims are not primarily "veracity claims" ("What I am telling you is a fact") but "sincerity claims" ("What I am telling you comes from the heart").'[9]

There are large swathes of the British workforce which are impervious to, or even downright cynical about, the brands for which they work. They have a pragmatic view of their job and what it requires of them, and realise that this may on occasion include their paying lip service to the brand values. To Lucy Kellaway, a seasoned observer of management fads in her column in the *Financial Times*, brand cultures are not to be taken too seriously, they are simply a set of conforming principles in the organisation, a way of measuring enthusiasm. The reason management imbibes them particularly deeply is because they become enmeshed in office politics: everyone wants to outdo each other in their admiration of the imperial new clothes. Believing in the brand becomes part of your tool kit for climbing the greasy pole. One manager admitted to me that at her company 'everyone had become paranoid about being off-brand'.

It's possible to see how much the brand culture rubs off on even the most sceptical employee. Joanne Ciulla sums up the dangers of these management practices: 'First, scientific management sought to capture the body, then human relations sought to capture the heart, now consultants want to tap into the soul ... what they offer is therapy and spirituality lite ... [which] makes you feel good, but does not address problems of power, conflict and autonomy.'[10] The greatest success of the 'employer brand' concept has been to mask the declining power of workers, for whom pay inequality has increased, job security evaporated and pensions are increasingly precarious. Yet employees, seduced by a culture of approachable, friendly managers, told me they didn't need a union – they could always go and talk to their boss.

At the same time, workers are encouraged to channel more of their lives through work – not just their time and energy during working hours, but their social life and their volunteering and fundraising. Work is taking on the roles once played by other institutions in our lives, and the potential for abuse is clear. A company designs ever more exacting performance targets, with the tantalising carrot of accolades and pay increases to manipulate ever more feverish commitment. The core workforce finds itself hooked into a self-reinforcing cycle of emotional dependency: the increasing demands of their jobs deprive them of the possibility of developing the relationships and interests which would enable them to break their dependency. The greater the dependency, the greater the fear of going cold turkey – through losing the job or even changing the lifestyle. 'Of all the institutions in society, why let one of the more precarious ones supply our social, spiritual and psychological needs? It doesn't make sense to put such a large portion of our lives into the unsteady hands of employers,' concludes Ciulla.

Life is work, work is life for the willing slaves who hand over such large chunks of themselves to their employer in return for the paycheque. The price is heavy in the loss of privacy, the loss of autonomy over the innermost workings of one's emotions, and the compromising of authenticity. The logical conclusion, unless challenged, is capitalism at its most inhuman – the commodification of human beings.

Notes

1   Abraham Maslow (1998) *Maslow on Management*, John Wiley & Sons.
2   Ibid., p. 8.
3   Ibid., pp. 20–42.
4   Karen Moloney (2003) *People Management*, 5 May.
5   Cited in Jayne Buxton (1998) *Ending the Mother War, Starting the Workplace Revolution*, Macmillan.
6   Marek Korczynski (2002) *Human Resource Management in Service Work*, Palgrave/Macmillan.
7   Helen Murlis and Peggy Schubert (2002) 'Engage employees and boast performance', Hay Group working paper, www.haygroup.com.
8   André Gorz (1999) *Reclaiming Work*, Polity Press.
9   *New Statesman*, 5 November 2001.
10 Joanne Ciulla (2000) *The Working Life: The Promise and Betrayal of Modern Work*, Random House.

Part 4

Strategic Human Resource Management in Practice

Part 4 consists of chapters with a practical focus. SHRM is based on knowledge and theories and these require analysis and critique, which was the concern of Part 1. But is also entails action: evaluating and designing systems, structures, processes and ultimately individuals, making decisions, offering recommendations, helping to build the capacity of the organization and its staff. So it is the role of those who study and analyse organizations and SHRM to contribute to this decision-making. Some prefer to offer solutions; others prefer to assist the evaluation of proposals. Part 4 consists of examples from both types.

Chapter 13 by Treviño and Brown offers a refreshing overview of some major ethical issues. There has long been a problem with ethics in organizational life and analysis. The problem is not simply or primarily that organizations occasionally deviate – sometimes dramatically and appallingly – from ethical standards and commitments. The problem is the problem of explaining the gap between discussions of ethical principles and actual organizational behaviour. Invoking greed or megalomania or CEO vanity, although often appropriate, is not enough. Ethical deviance by organizations remains ultimately an organizational issue. So it needs to be explained in terms of organizational dynamics, as an unusual outcome of normal dynamics. And this is what Chapter 13 offers.

Chapter 14 by Binney and Williams addresses one of the most significant issues faced by HR professionals: designing, implementing or dealing with the consequences of change. These are pressing and practical issues. And they are also difficult issues: change programmes routinely fail to deliver their promises. These authors argue that a major reason for the disappointing success of change programmes may be a result of the *model of change* inherent in the change projects. Their argument is simple, but important and far-reaching: that organizations may not only need to change their structures, systems, values and processes, but they may also need to change the way they approach and design change. Organizations probably tend to approach the design of change in the same way they do everything else, which is highly organized, top-down, and heavily controlled. This approach to change may reflect a type of organization they actually are trying to move away from. But they try to escape from centralization through centralized change programmes. These authors suggest that those designing change start by considering the design of the process of change and the values, principles, and assumptions it implicitly carries.

The final chapter by Clark achieves two objectives at once. On the one hand it is a comprehensive overview of the elements and processes associated with performance management. This is useful in itself since Clark plots the options available and their assumptions and implications. But he does much more than this. He also demonstrates a core paradox of organization – and of SHRM – and this is a paradox that we have met before: many of the problems organizations face are not accidental or incidental but are systemic; they are design problems that arise from the core structures and values of the organization. Performance management is such an issue. Knowledge management is another. When organizations are poor at managing performance this is not usually because they lack a formal performance management system. Rather, it is because a whole series of features of the structure and functioning and history of the organization – including its patterns of relationships – obstruct or divert a focus on performance. Simply fixing a formal performance management system in such an organization is not going to work until it addresses or surfaces the more fundamental obstacles to performance management.

Managing to be Ethical: Debunking Five Business Ethics Myths

Linda Klebe Treviño and Michael E. Brown

The twenty-first century has brought corporate ethics scandals that have harmed millions of employees and investors, and sent shock waves throughout the business world. The scandals have produced 'perp walks' and regulatory backlash, and business ethics is once again a hot topic. Academics and managers are asking: What caused the recent rash of corporate wrongdoing, and what can we do, if anything, to prevent similar transgressions in the future? Perhaps because everyone has opinions about ethics and personal reactions to the scandals, a number of pat answers have circulated that perpetuate a mythology of business ethics management. In this article, we identify several of these myths and respond to them based upon knowledge grounded in research and practice.

Myth 1: It's easy to be ethical

A 2002 newspaper article was entitled, 'Corporate ethics is simple: If something stinks, don't do it.' The article went on to suggest 'the smell test' or 'If you don't want to tell your mom what you're really doing ... or read about it in the press, don't do it.'[1] The obvious suggestion is that being ethical in business is easy if one wants to be ethical. A further implication is that if it's easy, it doesn't need to be managed. But that suggestion disregards the complexity surrounding ethical decision-making, especially in the context of business organizations.

Source: Linda Klebe Treviño and Michael E. Brown (2004) 'Managing to be ethical: debunking five business ethics myths', *Academy of Management Executive*, 18(2): 69–81. Edited version.

Ethical decisions are complex

First, ethical decisions aren't simple. They're complex by definition. As they have for centuries, philosophers argue about the best approaches to making the right ethical decision. Students of business ethics are taught to apply multiple normative frameworks to tough dilemmas where values conflict. These include consequentialist frameworks that consider the benefits and harms to society of a potential decision or action, deontological frameworks that emphasize the application of ethical principles such as justice and rights, and virtue ethics with its emphasis on the integrity of the moral actor, among other approaches.[2] But, in the most challenging ethical dilemma situations, the solutions provided by these approaches conflict with each other, and the decision maker is left with little clear guidance. For example, multinational businesses with manufacturing facilities in developing countries struggle with employment practice issues. Most Americans believe that it is harmful and contrary to their rights to employ children. But children routinely contribute to family income in many cultures. If corporations simply refuse to hire them or fire those who are working, these children may resort to begging or even more dangerous employment such as prostitution. Or they and their families may risk starvation. What if respecting the rights of children in such situations produces the greater harm? Such business decisions are more complex than most media reports suggest, and deciding on the most ethical action is far from simple.

Moral awareness is required

Second, the notion that 'it's easy to be ethical' assumes that individuals automatically know that they are facing an ethical dilemma and that they should simply choose to do the right thing. But decision makers may not always recognize that they are facing a moral issue. Rarely do decisions come with waving red flags that say, 'Hey, I'm an ethical issue. Think about me in moral terms!'[3] Dennis Gioia was recall coordinator at Ford Motor Company in the early 1970s when the company decided not to recall the Pinto despite dangerous fires that were killing the occupants of vehicles involved in low-impact rear-end collisions. In his information-overloaded recall coordinator role, Gioia saw thousands of accident reports, and he followed a cognitive 'script' that helped him decide which situations represented strong recall candidates and which did not. The incoming information about the Pinto fires did not penetrate a script designed to surface other issues, and it did not initially raise ethical concerns. He and his colleagues in the recall office didn't recognize the recall issue as an ethical issue. In other examples, students who download their favorite music from the Internet may not think about the ethical implications of 'stealing' someone else's copyrighted work. Or, a worker asked to sign a document for her boss may not recognize this as a request to 'forge' legal documents.

Researchers have begun to study this phenomenon, and they refer to it as moral awareness, ethical recognition, or ethical sensitivity. The idea is that moral judgment processes are not initiated unless the decision-maker recognizes the ethical nature of an issue. So, recognition of an issue as an 'ethical' issue triggers the moral judgment process, and understanding this initial step is key to understanding ethical decision-making more generally.

T.M. Jones proposed that the moral intensity of an issue influences moral issue recognition,[4] and this relationship has been supported in research. Two dimensions of moral intensity – magnitude of consequences and social consensus – have been found in multiple studies to influence moral awareness.[5] An individual is more likely to identify an issue as an ethical issue to the extent that a particular decision or action is expected to produce harmful consequences and to the extent that relevant others in the social context view the issue as ethically problematic. Further, the use of moral language has been found to influence moral awareness.[6] For example, in the above cases, if the words 'stealing' music (rather than downloading) or 'forging' documents (rather than signing) were used, the individual would be more likely to think about these issues in ethical terms.

Ethical decision-making is a complex, multi-stage process

Moral awareness represents just the first stage in a complex, multiple-stage decision-making process[7] that moves from moral awareness to moral judgment (deciding that a specific action is morally justifiable), to moral motivation (the commitment or intention to take the moral action), and finally to moral character (persistence or follow-through to take the action despite challenges).

The second stage, moral judgment, has been studied within and outside the management literature.[8] Lawrence Kohlberg's well-known theory of cognitive moral development has guided most of the empirical research in this area for the past thirty years.[9] Kohlberg found that people develop from childhood to adulthood through a sequential and hierarchical series of cognitive stages that characterize the way they think about ethical dilemmas. Moral reasoning processes become more complex and sophisticated with development. Higher stages rely upon cognitive operations that are not available to individuals at lower stages, and higher stages are thought to be 'morally better' because they are consistent with philosophical theories of justice and rights.

At the lowest levels, termed 'preconventional,' individuals decide what is right based upon punishment avoidance (at stage 1) and getting a fair deal for oneself in exchange relationships (at stage 2). Next, the conventional level of cognitive moral development includes stages 3 and 4. At stage 3, the individual is concerned with conforming to the expectations of significant others, and at stage 4 the perspective broadens to include society's rules and laws as a key influence in deciding what's right. Finally, at the highest 'principled' level, stage 5, individuals' ethical decisions are guided by principles of justice and rights.

Perhaps most important for our purposes is the fact that most adults in industrialized societies are at the 'conventional' level of cognitive moral development, and less than twenty per cent of adults ever reach the 'principled' level where thinking is more autonomous and principle-based. In practical terms, this means that most adults are looking outside themselves for guidance in ethical dilemma situations, either to significant others in the relevant environment (e.g., peers, leaders) or to society's rules and laws. It also means that most people need to be led when it comes to ethics.

The organizational context creates additional pressures and complexity

Moral judgment focuses on *deciding* what's right – not necessarily *doing* what is right. Even when people make the right decision, they may find it difficult to follow through and do what is right because of pressures from the work environment. Research has found that principled individuals are more likely to behave in a manner consistent with their moral judgments, and they are more likely to resist pressures to behave unethically.[10] However, most people never reach the principled level. So, the notion that being ethical is simple also ignores the pressures of the organizational context that influence the relationship between moral judgment and action.

Consider the following ethical-dilemma situation. You find yourself in the parking lot, having just dented the car next to you. The ethical decision is relatively simple. It's about you and your behavior. No one else is really involved. You have harmed someone else's property, you're responsible, and you or your insurance company should pay for the repairs. It's pretty clear that you should leave a note identifying yourself and your insurance company. Certainly, there may be negative consequences if you leave that note. Your insurance rates may go up. But doing the right thing in this situation is fairly straightforward.

Contrast that to business-context situations. It is much harder to 'just say no' to a boss who demands making the numbers at all costs. Or to go above the boss's head to someone in senior management with suspicions that 'managing earnings' has somehow morphed into 'cooking the books.' Or to walk away from millions of dollars in business because of concerns about crossing an ethical line. Or to tell colleagues that the way they do business seems to have crossed that line. In these situations, the individual is operating within the context of the organization's authority structure and culture – and would likely be concerned about the consequences of disobeying a boss's order, walking away from millions of dollars in business, or blowing the whistle on a peer or superior. What would peers think? How would the leadership react? Would management retaliate? Is one's job at risk?

It may seem curious that people often worry about whether others will think of them as too ethical. But all of us recognize that 'snitches' rarely fit in, on the playground or in life, and whistleblowers are frequently ostracized or worse.[11] The reasons for their ostracism are not fully understood, but they may have to do with humans' social nature and the importance of social group maintenance. Research suggests that people who take principled stands, such as those who are willing to report a peer for unethical behavior, are seen as highly ethical while, at the same time, they are thought to be highly unlikable.[12] Nearly a third of respondents to the 2003 National Business Ethics Survey[13] said 'their coworkers condone questionable ethics practices by showing respect for those who achieve success using them.' Further, about forty per cent of respondents said that they would not report misconduct they observed because of fear of retaliation from management. Almost a third said they would not report misconduct because they feared retaliation from coworkers.

If you think this applies only to the playground or the factory floor, ask yourself why we haven't seen more CEOs proclaiming how appalled they are at the behavior of some of their peers after recent ethics scandals. Yes, we heard from a few retired CEOs. But very few active senior executives have spoken up. Why not? They're probably uncomfortable passing moral judgment on others or holding themselves up as somehow ethically better than their peers. So, social context is important because people, including senior executives, look to others for approval of their thinking and behavior.

In sum, being ethical is not simple. Ethical decisions are ambiguous, and the ethical decision-making process involves multiple stages that are fraught with complications and contextual pressures. Individuals may not have the cognitive sophistication to make the right decision. And most people will be influenced by peers' and leaders' words and actions, and by concerns about the consequences of their behavior in the work environment.

Myth 2: Unethical behavior in business is simply the result of 'bad apples'

A recent headline was 'How to Spot Bad Apples in the Corporate Bushel.'[14] The bad-apple theory is pervasive in the media and has been around a long time. In the 1980s, during a segment of the McNeil Lehrer Report on PBS television, the host was interviewing guests about insider trading scandals. The CEO of a major investment firm and a business school dean agreed that the problems with insider trading resulted from bad apples. They said that educational institutions and businesses could do little except to find and discard those bad apples after the fact. So, the first reaction to ethical problems in organizations is generally to look for a culprit who can be punished and removed. The idea is that if we rid the organization of one or more bad apples, all will be well because the organization will have been cleansed of the perpetrator.

Certainly there are bad actors who will hurt others or feather their own nests at others' expense – and they do need to be identified and removed. But, as suggested above, most people are the product of the context they find themselves in. They tend to 'look up and look around,' and they do what others around them do or expect them to do.[15] They look outside themselves for guidance when thinking about what is right. What that means is that most unethical behavior in business is supported by the context in which it occurs – either through direct reinforcement of unethical behavior or through benign neglect.

An example of how much people are influenced by those around them was in the newspaper in November, 2002. Police in New Britain, Connecticut confiscated a 50-ft. long pile of stolen items, the result of a scavenger hunt held by the 'Canettes,' New Britain high school's all-girl drill team. According to the Hartford Courant, police, parents, and school personnel were astonished that 42 normally law-abiding girls could steal so many items in a single evening. But the girls had a hard time believing that they had done anything wrong. One girl said: 'I just thought it was a custom … kind of like a camaraderie thing, [and] if the seniors said it was OK and they were in charge, then it was OK!' In another incident in May 2003, suburban Chicago high school girls engaged in an aggressive and brutal 'hazing ritual' that landed five girls in the hospital.[16] We might say that these are teenagers, and that adults are different. But many of these teenagers are about to start jobs, and there are only a few years between these high school students and young people graduating from college. Most adults are more like these teens than most of us think or would prefer. The influence of peers is powerful in both cases.

When asked why they engaged in unethical conduct, employees will often say, 'I had no choice,' or 'My boss told me to do it.' Stanley Milgram's obedience-to-authority experiments, probably the most famous social psychology experiments ever conducted, support the notion that people obey authority figures even if that means harming another person.[17] Milgram, a Yale psychologist, conducted his obedience-to-authority experiments in the Hartford community on normal adults. These experiments demonstrated that nearly two-thirds of normal adults will harm another human being (give them alleged electric shocks of increasing intensity) if asked to do so by an authority figure as part of what was billed as a learning experiment. Were these people bad apples? We don't think so. Most of them were not at all comfortable doing what they were being asked to do, and they expressed sincere concern for the victim's fate. But in the end most of them continued to harm the learner because the authority figure in a lab coat told them to do so.

How does this apply to work settings? Consider the junior member of an audit team who discovers something problematic when sampling a firm's financials and asks the senior person on the audit team for advice. When the leader suggests putting the problematic example back and picking another one, the young auditor is likely to do just that. The leader may add words such as the following: 'You don't understand the big picture' or 'Don't worry, this is my responsibility.' In this auditing example, the harm being done is much less obvious than in the learning experiment and the junior auditor's responsibility even less clear, so the unethical conduct is probably easier to carry out and more likely to occur.

The bottom line here is that most people, including most adults, are followers when it comes to ethics. When asked or told to do something unethical, most will do so. This means that they must be led toward ethical behavior or be left to flounder. Bad behavior doesn't always result from flawed individuals. Instead, it may result from a system that encourages or supports flawed behavior.

A corollary of the bad-apples argument is that ethics can't be taught or even influenced in adults because adults are autonomous moral agents whose ethics are fully formed by the time they join work organizations, and they can't be changed. This is simply not true. We know from many empirical studies[18] that the large majority of adults are not fully formed when it comes to ethics, and they are not autonomous moral agents. They look outside themselves for guidance in ethical-dilemma situations, and they behave based to a large extent upon what those around them – leaders and peers – expect of them. So, we have to look at the very powerful signals that are being sent about what is expected. We also know that the development of moral reasoning continues into adulthood. Those who are challenged to wrestle with ethical dilemmas in their work will develop more sophisticated ways of thinking about such issues, and their behavior will change as a result.

Myth 3: Ethics can be managed through formal ethics codes and programs

If people in organizations need ethical guidance and structural support, how can organizations best provide it? Most large organizations now have formal ethics or legal compliance programs. In 1991 the U.S. Sentencing Commission created sentencing guidelines for organizations convicted of federal crimes (see *www.ussc.gov* for information). The guidelines removed judicial discretion and required convicted organizations to pay restitution and substantial fines depending upon whether the organization turns itself in, cooperates with authorities, and whether it has established a legal compliance program that meets seven requirements for due diligence and effectiveness. These formal programs generally include the following key elements: written standards of conduct that are communicated and disseminated to all employees, ethics training, ethics advice lines and offices, and systems for anonymous reporting of misconduct. The Sarbanes-Oxley law, passed during the summer of 2002, requires corporations to set up an anonymous system for employees to report fraud and other unethical activities. Therefore, companies that did not previously have such reporting systems are busy establishing them.

Research suggests that formal ethics and legal compliance programs can have a positive impact. For example, the Ethics Resource Center's National Business Ethics Survey[19] revealed that in organizations with all four program elements (standards, training, advice lines, and reporting systems) there was a greater likelihood (78 per cent) that employees would report observed misconduct to management. The likelihood of reporting declined with fewer program elements. Only half as many people in organizations with no formal program said that they would report misconduct to management.

Yet, creating a formal program, by itself, does not guarantee effective ethics management. Recall that Enron had an ethics code, and the board voted to bypass its conflict-of-interest policy.[20] Not surprisingly, research suggests that actions speak louder than words. Employees must perceive that formal policies go beyond mere window dressing to represent the real ethical culture of the organization. For example, the National Business Ethics Survey reports that when executives and supervisors emphasize ethics, keep promises, and model ethical conduct, misconduct is much lower than when employees perceive that the 'ethics walk' is not consistent with the 'ethics talk.'[21] In another study[22] formal program characteristics were found to be relatively unimportant compared with more informal cultural characteristics such as messages from leadership at both the executive and supervisory levels. In addition, perceived ethics program follow-through was found to be essential. Organizations demonstrate follow-through by working hard to detect rule violators, by following up on ethical concerns raised by employees, and by demonstrating consistency between ethics and compliance policies and actual organizational practices. Further, the perception that ethics is actually talked about in day-to-day organizational activities and incorporated into decision-making was found to be important.

So, for formal systems to influence behavior, they must be part of a larger, coordinated cultural system that supports ethical conduct every day. Ethical culture provides informal systems, along with formal systems, to support ethical conduct.[23] For example, the research cited above found that ethics-related outcomes (e.g., employee awareness of ethical issues, amount of observed misconduct, willingness to report misconduct) were much more positive to the extent that employees perceived that ethical conduct was rewarded and unethical conduct was punished in the organization. Further, a culture that demands unquestioning obedience to authority was found to be particularly harmful while a culture in which employees feel fairly treated was especially helpful.

The fall of Arthur Andersen

Barbara Toffler's book *Final Accounting: Ambition, Greed, and the Fall of Arthur Andersen* (2003)[24] can help us understand this notion of ethical (or unethical) organizational culture. Andersen transformed over a number of years from having a solid ethical culture to having a strong unethical culture. The company's complete demise is a rather dramatic example of the potential results of such a transformation.

In the mid-1990s, Arthur Andersen did not have a formal ethics office, but it did have formal ethical standards and ethics training. Ironically, it also established a consulting group whose practice was aimed at helping other businesses manage their ethics. Barbara Toffler was hired to run that practice in 1995 after spending time on the Harvard Business School faculty and in her own ethics consulting business. After joining Andersen, Toffler learned quickly that the firm's own ethical culture was slipping badly, and she chronicles that slippage in her book.

The book opens with the following statement 'The day Arthur Andersen loses the public's trust is the day we are out of business.' Steve Samek, country managing partner, made that statement on a CD-ROM concerning the firm's Independence and Ethical Standards in 1999. It was reminiscent of the old Arthur Andersen. Andersen's traditional management approach had been a top-down, 'one firm' concept. Arthur Andersen had built a strong ethical culture over the years where all of the pieces fit together into a seamless whole that supported ethical conduct. No matter where they were in the world, if customers were dealing with Andersen employees, they knew that they could count on the same high-quality work and the same integrity. Employees were trained in the 'Andersen Way,' and that way included strong ethics. Training at their St. Charles, Illinois training facility was sacred. It created a cadre of professionals who spoke the same language and shared the same 'Android' values.

Founders create culture and Arthur Andersen was no exception. Toffler says that in the firm's early days, the messages from the top about ethical conduct were strong and clear. Andersen himself said, 'My own mother told me, "Think straight – talk straight." … This challenge will never fail anyone in a time of trial and temptation.' 'Think straight, talk straight' became a mantra for decades at Arthur Andersen. Partners said with pride that integrity mattered more than fees. And stories about the founder's ethics became part of the firm's lore. At the young age of 28, Andersen faced down a railway executive who demanded that his books be approved – or else. Andersen said, 'There's not enough money in the city of Chicago to induce me to change that report.' Andersen lost the business, but later the railway company filed for bankruptcy, and Arthur Andersen became known as a firm one could trust. In the 1930s Andersen talked about the special responsibility of accountants to the public and the importance of their independence of judgment and action. Arthur Andersen died in 1947 but was followed by leaders with similar convictions who ran the firm in the 1950s and 1960s, and the ethical culture continued for many years. Pretty much through the 1980s, Andersen was considered a stable and prestigious place to work. People didn't expect to get rich – rather they wanted 'a good career at a firm with a good reputation.'

But, the ethical culture eventually began to unravel, and Toffler attributes much of this to the fact that the firm's profits increasingly came from management consulting rather than auditing. The leadership's earlier commitment to ethics came to be drowned out by the firm's increasing laser-like focus on revenues. Auditing and consulting are very different, and the cultural standards that worked so well in auditing didn't fit the needs of the consulting side of the business. But this mismatch was never addressed, and the resulting mixed signals helped precipitate a downward spiral into unethical practices. Serving the client began to be defined as keeping the client happy and getting return business. And tradition became translated into unquestioning obedience to the partner, no matter what one was asked to do. For example, managers and partners were expected to pad their prices. Reasonable estimates for consulting work were simply doubled or more as consultants were told to back into the numbers.

The training also began falling apart when it came to hiring experienced people from outside the firm – something that happened more and more as consulting took over. New employees had always been required to attend a three-day session designed to indoctrinate them into the culture of the firm, but new consultants were told not to forego lucrative client work to attend. So, Toffler never made it to the training, and many other consultants didn't either.

By the time Toffler arrived at Andersen, the firm still had a huge maroon ethics binder, but no one bothered to refer to it. Ethics was never talked about. And, she says, 'when I brought up the subject of internal ethics, I was looked at as if I had teleported in from another world.' The assumption, left over from the old days in auditing, was that 'we're ethical people; we recruit people who are screened for good judgment and values. We don't need to worry about this stuff.' But, as we all learned, their failure to worry about ethics led to the demise of the firm.

Could a formal ethics office have helped Arthur Andersen? Probably not, unless that office addressed the shift toward consulting, identified the unique ethical issues faced in the consulting side of the business, developed ethical guidelines for consulting, and so on. It is easy for formal ethics offices and their programs to be marginalized if they don't have the complete support of the organization's leadership and if they are inconsistent with the broader culture. In fact, Andersen still had ethics policies and they still talked about ethics in formal documents. But the business had changed along with the culture that guided employee actions every day, while the approach to ethics management had not kept pace.

Myth 4: Ethical leadership is mostly about leader integrity

In our discussion of Arthur Andersen, we suggested the importance of leadership. But what is executive ethical leadership? The mythology of ethical leadership focuses attention narrowly on individual character and qualities such as integrity, honesty, and fairness. The *Wall Street Journal* recently ran a story on its website entitled 'Plain Talk: CEOs Need to Restore Character in Companies.' It said, 'The chief problem affecting corporate America right now is not the regulatory environment or snoozing board directors. It's character.'[25] But as Arthur Andersen demonstrated, leaders must be more than individuals of high character. They must 'lead' others to behave ethically.

Recent research has found that certain individual characteristics are necessary but not sufficient for effective ethical leadership. Such leadership at the executive level is a reputational phenomenon. In most large organizations, employees have few face-to-face interactions with senior executives. So, most of what they know about a leader is gleaned from afar. In order to develop a reputation for ethical leadership, an executive must be perceived as both a 'moral person' and a 'moral manager.'[26]

Being perceived as a 'moral person' is related to good character. It depends upon employee perceptions of the leader's traits, behaviors, and decision-making processes. Ethical leaders are thought to be honest and trustworthy. They show concern for people and are open to employee input. Ethical leaders build relationships that are characterized by trust, respect and support for their employees. In terms of decision-making, ethical leaders are seen as fair. They take into account the ethical impact of their decisions, both short term and long term, on multiple stakeholders. They also make decisions based upon ethical values and decision rules, such as the golden rule.

But being perceived as a 'moral person' is not enough. Being a 'moral person' tells followers what the leader will do. It doesn't tell them what the leader expects *them* to do. Therefore, a reputation for ethical leadership also depends upon being perceived as a 'moral manager,' one who leads others on the ethical dimension, lets them know what is expected, and holds them accountable. Moral managers set ethical standards, communicate ethics messages, role model ethical conduct, and use rewards and punishments to guide ethical behavior in the organization.

Combining the 'moral person' and 'moral manager' dimensions creates a two-by-two matrix (see Figure 13.1). A leader who is strong on both dimensions is perceived to be an *ethical leader*. We can point to Arthur Andersen as an exemplar of ethical leadership. He was known as a strong ethical person who also clearly led his organization on ethics and values. People knew what they could expect of him, and they knew what he expected of them from an ethics perspective. Another example of ethical leadership is James Burke, CEO

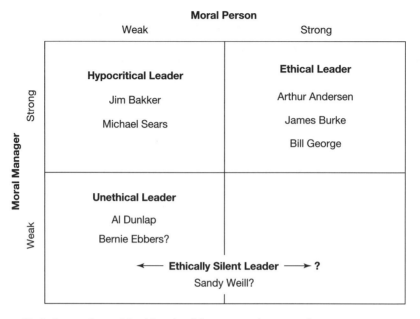

Figure 13.1 *Executive ethical leadership reputation matrix*

Figure adapted with permission from Treviño, L.K., Hartman, L.P., Brown, M. 2000. Moral person and moral manager: How executives develop a reputation for ethical leadership. *California Management Review*, 42(4): 128–142.

of Johnson & Johnson during the early 1980s Tylenol crisis (when Tylenol was laced with cyanide in the Chicago area). Burke handled that crisis masterfully, recalling all Tylenol at a huge financial cost to the firm. But his ethical leadership had begun much earlier when he first took the CEO helm. He focused the organization's attention on the company's longstanding credo and its values. He demanded that senior executives either subscribe to the credo or remove it from the wall. He didn't want to run a hypocritical organization. He also launched the credo survey, an annual survey that asks employees how the company is doing relative to each of the credo values. Bill George, recently retired CEO of Medtronic, is a more current example of an ethical leader. In his book *Authentic Leadership*, George calls for responsible ethical leadership in corporate America while recounting his own struggles to stay true to the company's mission and to himself.[27]

A leader who is neither a moral person nor a moral manager is an *unethical leader*. In our research, Al Dunlap was frequently identified as an unethical leader. Subject of a book entitled *Chainsaw*,[28] Dunlap was known as an expert turnaround manager. But while at Sunbeam, he also became known for 'emotional abuse' of employees. As a result of his demands to make the numbers at all costs, employees felt pressure to use questionable accounting and sales techniques, and they did. Dunlap also lied to Wall Street, assuring them that the firm would reach its financial projections. In the end, Dunlap could no longer cover up the sorry state of affairs, and he left a crippled company when the board fired him in 1998. In 2002, he paid a $500,000 fine for financial fraud and agreed never to serve as an officer or director of a public corporation. Unfortunately, there are many candidates for a more current example of unethical leadership: Dennis Kozlowski from Tyco, Bernie Ebbers from WorldCom, and Richard Scrushy from Health-South are just a few executive names attached to recent business scandals.

Leaders who communicate a strong ethics/values message (who are moral managers), but who are not perceived to be ethical themselves (they are not moral persons) can be thought of as *hypocritical leaders*. Nothing makes people more cynical than a leader who talks incessantly about integrity, but then engages in unethical conduct himself and encourages others to do so, either explicitly or implicitly. Hypocritical leadership is all about ethical pretense. The problem is that by spotlighting integrity, the leader raises expectations and awareness of ethical issues. At the same time, employees realize that they can't trust the leader.

Jim Bakker, the founder of PTL Ministries, is our favorite example of a hypocritical leader. At its peak, his television ministry had 2000 employees and reached more than ten million homes. Bakker preached about doing the Lord's work while raising funds for his Heritage USA Christian theme park. The problem was that he sold more memberships than could ever be honored. He tapped millions of dollars donated by his followers to support PTL operating expenses including huge salaries and bonuses for his family and high ranking PTL officials. PTL filed for bankruptcy in 1987, and Bakker spent eight years in prison.[29]

Michael Sears, recently fired from Boeing for offering a job to an Air Force procurement specialist while she was overseeing negotiations with Boeing, represents a more recent example of a hypocritical leader. Sears had played a significant role at the Boeing Leadership Center which is known for its programs related to ethics. Also, shortly before his firing, Sears released advance copies of his book *Soaring Through Turbulence* which included a section on maintaining high ethical standards.[30]

We call the final combination *ethically silent leadership*. It applies to executives who are neither strong ethical nor strong unethical leaders. They fall into what employees perceive to be an ethically neutral leadership zone. They may be ethical persons, but they don't provide leadership in the crucial area of ethics, and employees aren't sure where the leaders stand on ethics or if they care. The ethically silent leader is not perceived to be unethical but is seen as focusing intently on the bottom line without setting complementary ethical goals. There is little or no ethics message coming from the top. But silence represents an important message. In the context of all the other messages being sent in a highly competitive business environment, employees are likely to interpret silence to mean that the top executive really doesn't care how business goals are met, only that they are met, so employees act on that message. Business leaders don't like to think that their employees perceive them as ethically silent. But given the current climate of cynicism, unless leaders make an effort to stand out and lead on ethics, they are likely to be viewed that way.

Sandy Weill, CEO of Citigroup, may fit the ethically silent leader category. The company has been playing defense with the media, responding to ugly headlines about ethics scandals, especially at its Smith Barney unit where stock analysts were accused of essentially 'selling' their stock recommendations for banking business. Weill's management style is to hire competent people to run Citigroup's units and to let them do their jobs. That may work well for other aspects of the business, but ethics must be managed from the top and center of the organization. According to *Fortune* magazine, Weill has now 'gotten religion,' if a bit late. Weill has 'told his board that he feels his most important job from now on is to be sure that Citigroup operates at the highest level of ethics and with the utmost integrity.' New procedures and business standards are being developed at corporate headquarters, and a new CEO was appointed at Smith Barney. However, *Fortune* also cites cynicism about this recent turnabout, noting that Weill is often 'tone deaf' on ethical issues.[31]

So, developing a reputation for ethical leadership requires more than strong personal character. Employees must be 'led' from the top on ethics just as they must be led on quality, competitiveness, and a host of other expected behaviors. In order to be effective ethical leaders, executives must demonstrate that they are ethical themselves, they must make their expectations of others' ethical conduct explicit, and they must hold all of their followers accountable for ethical conduct every day.

■ Myth 5: People are less ethical than they used to be

In the opening to this article, we said that business ethics has once again become a hot topic. The media have bombarded us with information about ethics scandals, feeding the perception that morals are declining in business and in society more generally.

According to a poll released by the PR Newswire in summer 2002, sixty-eight per cent of those surveyed believe that senior corporate executives are less honest and trustworthy today than they were a decade ago.[32] But unethical conduct has been with us as long as human beings have been on the earth, and business ethics scandals are as old as business itself. The Talmud, a 1500-year-old text, includes about 2 million words and 613 direct commandments designed to guide Jewish conduct and culture. More than one hundred of these concern business and economics. Why? Because 'transacting business, more than any other human activity, tests our moral mettle and reveals our character' and because 'working, money, and commerce offer … the best opportunities to do good deeds such as … providing employment and building prosperity for our communities and the world.'[33]

So, unethical behavior is nothing new. It's difficult to find solid empirical evidence of changes over time. But studies of student cheating have found that the percentage of college students who admit to cheating has not changed much during the last thirty years.[34] Some types of cheating have increased (e.g., test cheating, collaboration on individual assignments). Other types of cheating have declined (e.g., plagiarism, turning in another student's work). Certainly, given new technologies and learning approaches, students have discovered some clever new ways to cheat, and professors have their work cut out for them keeping up with the new methods. But the amount of overall cheating hasn't increased that much. Further, when employees were asked about their own work organizations, the 2003 National Business Ethics Survey found that employee perceptions of ethics are generally quite positive. Interestingly, key indicators have actually improved since the last survey conducted in 2000.[35]

Alan Greenspan said it well on July 16, 2002: 'It is not that humans have become any more greedy than in generations past. It is that the avenues to express greed [have] grown so enormously.' So, unethical behavior is nothing new, and people are probably not less ethical than they used to be. But the environment has become quite complex and is rapidly changing, providing all sorts of ethical challenges and opportunities to express greed.

If ethical misconduct is an ongoing concern, then organizations must respond with lasting solutions that embed support for ethics into their cultures rather than short-term solutions that can easily be undone or dismissed as fads. The risk is that the current media focus on unethical conduct will result in 'faddish' responses that offer overly simplistic solutions and that result inevitably in disillusionment and abandonment. Faddish solutions often result from external pressures to 'do something' or at least look like you're doing something. The current focus on scandal certainly includes such pressures.[36] But the recognition that unethical conduct is a continuing organizational problem may help to convince managers that solutions should be designed that will outlast the current intense media focus.

What executives can do: guidelines for effective ethics management

Building upon what we have learned, we offer guidelines for effective ethics management. The overarching goal should be to create a strong ethical culture supported by strong ethical leadership. Why culture? Because we've seen that being ethical is not simple, and that people in organizations need ethical guidance and support for doing the right thing. Effective leaders must provide that structure and ethical guidance, and they can do that best by harnessing multiple formal and informal cultural systems.[37] People should respond positively to the kind of structure that aims to help them do the right thing. If management says, 'We want you to do the right thing, the ethical thing, and we're going to try to create a culture that helps you to do that,' employee response should be quite positive so long as employees believe that management is sincere and they observe consistency between words and actions.

First: Understand the existing ethical culture

Leaders are responsible for transmitting culture in their organizations, and the ethical dimension of organizational culture is no exception. According to Schein, the most powerful mechanisms for embedding and reinforcing culture are: (1) what leaders pay attention to, measure, and control; (2) leader reactions to critical incidents and organizational crises; deliberate role modeling, teaching, and coaching by leaders; (3) criteria for allocation of rewards and status; and (4) criteria for recruitment, selection, promotion, retirement, and excommunication.[38]

If leaders wish to create a strong ethical culture, the first step is to understand the current state: What are the key cultural messages being sent about ethics? It's a rare executive who really understands the ethical culture in an organization. And the higher you go in the organization, the rosier the perception of the ethical culture is likely to be.[39] Why? Because information often gets stuck at lower organizational levels, and executives are often insulated from 'bad news,' especially if employees perceive that the organization 'shoots the messenger.' Executives need anonymous surveys, focus groups, and reporting lines, and people need to believe that the senior leaders really want to know, if they are to report honestly on the current state of the ethical culture.

In surveys, ask for employee perceptions of supervisory and executive leadership and the messages they send by their communications and behavior. And listen to what employees say. Ask employees whether they perceive that they are treated fairly, and whether they perceive that they are treated fairly, and whether the company acts as if it cares about them, its customers, and other stakeholders. Find out what messages the reward system is sending. Do employees believe that ethical 'good guys' are rewarded and unethical 'bad guys' are punished in the organization? What do employees think is required in order to succeed or to be fired? Follow the kinds of calls coming in to ethics telephone lines. Learn whether employees are asking questions and reporting problems. Use this information to identify needs for training and other interventions. In focus groups, find out who the organizational heroes are (is it the sales representative who steps on peers in order to get ahead or a manager who is known for the highest integrity?). Ask what stories veterans would tell a new hire about ethics in your organization.

Second: Communicate the importance of ethical standards

Employees need clear and consistent messages that ethics is essential to the business model, not just a poster or a website. Most businesses send countless messages about competition and financial performance, and these easily drown out other messages. In order to compete with this constant drumbeat about the short-term bottom line, the messages about ethical conduct must be just as strong or stronger and as frequent. Simply telling people to do the right thing, is not enough. They must be prepared for the types of issues that arise in their particular business and position, and they must know what to do when ethics and the bottom line appear to be in conflict. Executives should tie ethics to the long-term success of the business by providing examples from their own experience or the experiences of other successful employees.

Make sure that messages coming from executive and supervisory leaders are clear and consistent. Train employees to recognize the kinds of ethical issues that are likely to arise in their work. Demand discussion of ethics and values as part of routine business decision-making. When making important decisions, ask, 'Are we doing the "right" (i.e., ethical) thing? Who could be hurt by this decision? How could this affect our relationships with stakeholders and our long-term reputation?' Share those deliberations with employees. Finally, be sure to let employees know about exemplary ethical conduct. For example, the famous story about Arthur Andersen losing the railway business because he refused to alter the books was recounted over and over again in the firm and made it absolutely clear that 'think straight, talk straight' actually meant something in the firm.

Third: Focus on the reward system

The reward system may be the single most important way to deliver a message about what behaviors are expected. B.F. Skinner knew what he was talking about. People do what's rewarded, and they avoid doing what's punished.[40] Let's look at the positive side first – can we really reward ethical behavior? In the short term, we probably cannot. For the most part, ethical behavior is simply expected, and people don't expect or want to be rewarded for doing their jobs the right way.[41] But in the longer term, ethical behavior can be rewarded by promoting and compensating people who are not only good at what they do, but who have also developed a reputation with customers, peers, subordinates, and managers as being of the highest integrity. The best way to hold employees accountable for ethical conduct is to incorporate evaluation of it into 360 degree performance management systems and to make this evaluation an explicit part of compensation and promotion decisions. The idea is that the bottom line and ethical performance both count; unless individuals have both, they should not advance in the organization.

Also, exemplary behavior can be rewarded. At Lockheed Martin, at the annual Chairman's meeting, a 'Chairman's Award' goes to an employee who exhibited exemplary ethical conduct in the previous year. All senior corporate leaders are expected to expend effort each year to find examples of exemplary ethical conduct in their own business units and make nominations. The award ceremony, attended by all 250 senior executives, is exactly the kind of 'ritual' that helps to create an ethical culture. Stories are shared, they become part of the organization's lore, the potential impact growing as the stories accumulate over time.[42]

Perhaps even more important than rewarding ethical conduct is taking care not to reward unethical conduct. That's what began to happen at Arthur Andersen as generating revenue became the only rewarded behavior, and it didn't matter how you did it. For example, consultants were rewarded for making a project last by finding reasons (legitimate or not) to stay on. Toffler says, 'Like the famous Roach Motel, consultants were taught to check in, but never check out.'[43] So, clients were overcharged, consulting jobs were dragged out, and colleagues were 'screwed' along the way because the rewards supported such unethical conduct.

And what about discipline? Unethical conduct should be disciplined swiftly and fairly when it occurs at any level in the organization. The higher the level of the person disciplined, the stronger the message that management takes ethics seriously. That's what is behind the 'perp walks' we have observed in the media. The public wants to see that fraudulent conduct among America's executives will not be tolerated. Similarly, inside organizations, employees want to see misconduct disciplined, and disciplined harshly.[44] Overall, employees must perceive that good guys get ahead and bad guys don't – they get punished. But, remember, it's often not enough to punish or remove a bad guy or a bad apple. The system should be checked to see if the existing reward system or other messages contributed to the bad behavior.

Fourth: Promote ethical leadership throughout the firm

Recall that being a 'moral person' who is characterized by integrity and fairness, treats people well, and makes ethical decisions is important. But those elements deal only with the 'ethical' part of ethical leadership. To be ethical leaders, executives have to think about the 'leadership' part of the term. Providing ethical 'leadership' means making ethical values visible – communicating about not just the bottom-line goals (the ends) but also the acceptable and unacceptable means of getting there (the means). Being an ethical leader also means asking very publicly how important decisions will affect multiple stakeholders – shareholders, employees, customers, society – and making transparent the struggles about how to balance competing interests. It means using the reward system to clearly communicate what is expected and what is accepted. That means rewarding ethical conduct and disciplining unethical conduct, even if the rule violator is a senior person or a top producer. Find a way to let employees know that the unethical conduct was taken seriously and the employee disciplined.

Ethical cultures and ethical leaders go hand in hand. Building an ethical culture can't be delegated. The CEO must be the Chief Ethics Officer of his or her organization.[45] Many CEOs may feel that they would rather pass on this challenge – that they don't really know how to do it – or they may prefer to believe that everyone in their organization is already ethical. But ethics is being 'managed' in their organizations with or without their attention to it. Benign neglect of the ethical culture simply leads to employees reaching the conclusion, rightly or wrongly, that leaders don't care as much about ethics as they do about other things. Leaders develop a reputation in this arena. Chances are that if the leader hasn't thought much about this reputation or hasn't been very proactive about it, people in the organization will likely label him or her as an ethically neutral leader. That doesn't mean that the leader *is* ethically neutral or doesn't take ethics into account in decision-making. It does mean that people aren't sure where the leader stands on the frequent conflicts between ethics and the bottom line. Without explicit guidance, they assume that the bottom-line messages are the most important.

As we've said, senior executives are extremely important. They set the tone at the top and oversee the ethical culture. But from an everyday implementation perspective, front-line supervisors are equally important because of their daily interactions with their direct reports. An ethical culture ultimately depends upon how supervisors treat employees, customers, and other stakeholders, and how they make decisions. Do they treat everyone honestly, fairly and with care? Do supervisors point out when their group is facing a decision with ethical overtones? Do they consider multiple stakeholder interests and the long-term reputation of the organization in decision-making? Do they hold themselves and their people accountable for ethical conduct? Or, do they focus only on short-term bottom-line results?

Ethics isn't easy

Unethical conduct in business has been with us as long as business transactions have occurred. People are not necessarily more unethical today, but gray areas abound along with many opportunities to cross into unethical territory. Much unethical conduct is the result not just of bad apples but of neglectful leadership and organizational cultures that send mixed messages about what is important and what is expected. It isn't easy to be ethical. Employees must recognize ethical issues in their work, develop the cognitive tools to make the right choices, and then be supported in those choices by the organizational environment. Executives must manage the ethical conduct of their employees as proactively as they manage any important behavior. And the complexity of the management system should match the complexity of the behavior being managed.

The best way to manage ethical conduct is by aligning the multiple formal and informal cultural systems in support of doing the right thing. Cultural messages about the importance of trust and long-term relationships with multiple stakeholders must get at least as much attention as messages about the short-term bottom line, and employees must be held accountable for ethical conduct through performance management and reward systems.

Notes

1   St. Anthony, N. Corporate ethics is simple: If something stinks, don't do it. *Star Tribune (Minneapolis-Saint Paul) Newspaper of the Twin Cities.* 28 June 2002.

2   For a simple overview of these theories, see Treviño, L.K. and Nelson, K. 2003. *Managing business ethics; Straight talk about how to do it right.* 3d ed. New York: Wiley.

3   Gioia, D. 1992. Pinto fires and personal ethics: A script analysis of missed opportunities. *Journal of Business Ethics,* 11(5,6): 379–389; Gioia, D.A. 2003. Personal reflections on the Pinto Fires case. In Treviño and Nelson.

4   Jones, T.M. 1991. Ethical decision making by individuals in organizations: An issue-contingent model. *Academy of Management Review,* 16: 366–395.

5   May, D.R. and Pauli, K.P. 2000. The role of moral intensity in ethical decision making: A review and investigation of moral recognition, evaluation, and intention. Manuscript presented at the meeting of the National Academy of Management, Toronto, August, 2000.

6   Butterfield, K., Treviño, L.K. and Weaver, G. 2000. Moral awareness in business organizations: Influences of issue-related and social context factors. *Human Relations,* 53(7): 981–1018.

7   Rest, M. 1986. *Moral development: Advances in research and theory.* New Jersey: Praeger.

8   Weber, J. 1990. Managers' moral reasoning: Assessing their responses to three moral dilemmas. *Human Relations,* 43: 687–702; Weber, J. and Wasieleski, 2001. Investigating influences on managers' moral reasoning: The impact of context, personal, and organizational factors. *Business and Society,* 40(1): 79–111; Treviño, L.K. 1986. Ethical decision making in organizations: A person-situation interactionist model. *Academy of Management Review,* 11(3): 601–617; Treviño, L.K. 1992. Moral reasoning and business ethics. *Journal of Business Ethics,* 11: 445–459.

9   Kohlberg, L. 1969. Stage and sequence: The cognitive-developmental approach to socialization. In *Handbook of socialization theory and research.* D.A. Goslin, ed., Rand McNally, 347–380.

10 Thoma, S.J. 1994. Moral judgment and moral action. In J. Rest and D. Narvaez (ed.), *Moral development in the professions: Psychology and applied ethics.* Hillsdale, NJ: Erlbaum: 199–211.

11 Miceli, M. and Near, J. 1992. *Blowing the whistle.* New York: Lexington Books.

12 Treviño, L.K. and Victor, B. 2004. Peer reporting of unethical behavior: A social context perspective. *Academy of Management Journal*, 353: 38–64.

13 Ethics Resource Center. 2003. *National Business Ethics Survey; How employees view ethics in their organizations.* Washington, DC.

14 PR Newswire. How to spot bad apples in the corporate bushel. 13 January 2003. Ithaca, NY.

15 Treviño and Nelson; Jackall, R. 1988. *Moral mazes: The world of corporate managers.* New York: Oxford University Press.

16 Drill team benched after scavenger incident, Sleepover busted. *Hartford Courant*, 15 November 2002; Paulson, A. Hazing case highlights girl violence. *Christian Science Monitor*, 9 May 2003.

17 Milgram, S. 1974. *Obedience to authority; An experimental view.* New York: Harper and Row.

18 Rest, J.S. (ed.). 1986. *Moral development: Advances in research and theory.* New York: Praeger. Rest, J.S. et al. 1999. *Postconventional moral thinking: A neo-Kohlbergian approach.* Mahwah, NJ: Erlbaum.

19 Ethics Resource Center, 2003. op. cit.

20 Schmitt, R.B. Companies add ethics training: Will it work? *Wall Street Journal* (Eastern edition), 4 November 2002: B1.

21 Ethics Resource Center, 2003. op. cit.

22 Treviño, L.K. et al: 1999. Managing ethics and legal compliance: What works and what hurts. *California Management Review*, 41(2): 131–151.

23 Treviño and Nelson.

24 Toffler, B.L., with J. Reingold. 2003. *Final accounting: Ambition, greed, and the fall of Arthur Andersen.* New York: Broadway Books. All of the following material on Toffler's experience at Arthur Andersen is from this source.

25 Kansas, D. Plain talk: CEOs need to restore character in companies. *WSJ.COM*. Dow Jones & Company, Inc., 7 July 2002.

26 Treviño, L.K., Hartman, L.P. and Brown, M. 2000. Moral person and moral manager: How executives develop a reputation for ethical leadership. *California Management Review*, 42(4): 128–142; Treviño, L.K., Brown, M. and Pincus-Hartman. 2003. A qualitative investigation of perceived executive ethical leadership: Perceptions from inside and outside the executive suite. *Human Relations*, 56(1): 5–37.

27 George, B. 2003. *Authentic leadership: Rediscovering the secrets to creating lasting value.* San Francisco: Jossey-Bass.

28 Byrne, J. 1999. *Chainsaw: The notorious career of Al Dunlap in the era of profit-at-any-price.* New York: HarperBusiness.

29 Tidwell, G. 1993. Accounting for the PTL scandal. *Today's CPA*. July/August: 29–32.

30 Frieswick, K. Boing. *CFO Magazine*, (1 January 2004) *www.cfo.com*.

31 Treviño and Nelson; Loomis, C. Whatever it takes. *Fortune*, 25 November 2002: 76.

32 PR Newswire. Big majority believes tough new laws needed to address corporate fraud; modest majority at least somewhat confident that Bush will support such laws. 27 July 2002.

33 Kahaner, L. 2003. *Values, prosperity and the Talmud. Business lessons from the ancient rabbis.* New York: Wiley.

34 McCabe, D. and Treviño, L.K. 1996. What we know about cheating in college. *Change: The Magazine of Higher Learning.* January/February: 28–33; McCabe, D.L., Treviño, L.K. and Butterfield, K. 2001. Cheating in academic institutions: A decade of research. *Ethics and Behavior*, 11(3): 219–232.

35 Ethics Resource Center, 2003. op cit.

36 Abrahamson, E. 1991. Managerial fads and fashions. *Academy of Management Review*, 16: 586–612; Carson, 1999; Gibson, J.W. and Tesone, D.V. 2001. Management fads: Emergence, evolution, and implications for managers. *The Academy of Management Executive*, 15: 122–133.

37 Treviño and Nelson, K.

38 Schein, E.H. 1985. *Organizational culture and leadership.* San Francisco, CA: Jossey-Bass.

39   Treviño, L.K., Weaver, G.A. and Brown, M. 2000. Lovely at the top. Paper presented at the Academy of Management meeting, Toronto, August.

40   Skinner, B.F. 1972. *Beyond freedom and dignity*. New York: Bantam Books.

41   Treviño, L.K. and Youngblood, S.A. 1990. Bad apples in bad barrels: A causal analysis of ethical decision-making behavior. *Journal of Applied Psychology*, 75: 376–385.

42   Treviño and Nelson.

43   Toffler, p. 123.

44   Treviño, L.K. 1992. The social implications of punishment in organizations; A justice perspective. *Academy of Management Review*, 17: 647–676; Treviño, L.K. and Ball, G.A. 1992. The social implications of punishing unethical behavior: Observers' cognitive and affective reactions. *Journal of Management*, 18: 751–768.

45   Treviño, Hartman and Brown.

14

The Myth of Managing Change

George Binney and Colin Williams

'Managing change!' The phrase rings out like a clarion call across organizations far and wide. It sounds like the secret of success, the elixir which will enable managers to steer their organisations to survival and growth. It is a tantalising proposition. What a weight would be taken off the minds of leaders if they could discover the formula, understand the recipe and create this magic.

Many different organisations have sought to transform some aspect of the way they work in order to adapt when circumstances change. They have wanted to change the 'code' of their organisations: the often unwritten rules that govern how people behave.

[...]

What is characteristic of these transformations is that they involve a radical shift in thinking as well as behaviour. Underlying the patterns of behaviour that define organisations are the mental models that people have, the assumptions and frameworks that enable them to make sense of the world. For example, does a company exist to make money, to exploit a technology or expertise, to serve customers, to have fun? Or a mix of these and other purposes? What beliefs do people have about 'what business are we in?', 'what does it take to succeed in this business?', 'what sort of people do we need?', 'how do you manage people to get results?'

It is these mental models or paradigms that ultimately organisations have sought to change. And that, of course, is why change is often difficult. It is very difficult to let go of these mental models. To give them up is to let go of part of ourselves, part of our identity, the part that allows us to understand the world and stops it being a terrifying mass of confusion. Again and again people in organisations have held on to patterns of thinking and behaviour long after the world that gave rise to them has changed. Twenty years ago

Source: Chapters 2 and 3 in G. Binney and C. Williams (1995) *Leaning into the Future: Changing the Way People Change Organizations*. London: Nicholas Brealey Publishing Ltd. Edited version.

Andrew Pettigrew showed how companies often hold on to flagrantly faulty assumptions about their world for as long as a decade, despite overwhelming evidence that the world has changed. But how can you bring about this change in mental models? How can individuals help their company or organisation adapt to changing circumstances?

▌ The characteristics of change programmes

The most commonly used approach in recent years has been some form of 'top-down' change programme. There are many varieties of this, but all have five key characteristics in common:

- vision
- telling people what that vision is
- top management determination
- planning and programming
- adopting best practice.

One of many exponents of this approach – and one whom we respect very much – is John Kotter of Harvard Business School. He explains why change programmes put vision at centre stage:

> In every successful transformation effort that I have seen, the guiding coalition develops a picture of the future that is relatively easy to communicate and appeals to customers, stockholders, and employees … in failed transformations, on the other hand, you find plenty of plans and directives and programs, but no vision … A vision goes beyond the numbers that are typically found in five-year plans … It says something that helps clarify the direction in which an organisation needs to move. (Kotter, 1995)

What is needed is to knit together the change efforts in different parts of an organisation and to motivate participants in the change efforts. Kotter suggests a rule of thumb: 'If you can't communicate the vision to someone in five minutes or less and get a reaction that signifies both understanding and interest, you are not done with this phase of the transformation process.'

Whose vision is this? Generally that of the person at the top of the organisation, sometimes that of a small group of senior managers. That's the job of a chief executive: to create and communicate the vision of the future of the organisation.

Once developed, the vision has to be communicated effectively. Top managers must tell people what future they are trying to create. Kotter puts the case:

> Transformation is impossible unless hundreds or thousands of people are
> willing to help, often to the point of making short term sacrifices. Employees
> will not make sacrifices, even if they are unhappy with the status quo, unless
> they believe useful change is possible. Without credible communication, and
> a lot of it, the hearts and minds of the troops are never captured.

That's the phrase that crops up again and again in change programmes:
'hearts and minds'. The task is to win them and the means are to market, to
sell the vision, to persuade. Kotter continues: 'In successful transformation
efforts, executives use all existing communication channels to broadcast
the vision.'

They probably also create new channels to get the message across. It is
recognised that executives who communicate well incorporate messages into
their hour-by-hour activities and in the famous phrase that they must 'walk
the talk', consciously seeking to become living symbols of the new corporate
culture. 'Communication comes in both words and deeds and the latter are
often the most powerful form,' says Kotter.

In communicating the vision another characteristic of change management
thinking becomes apparent: determination and drive.

[...]

One reason sheer willpower is so important is that there are likely to be
many in every organisation who will, it is said, 'resist change'. The change
management literature abounds with discussion of the possible causes of
resistance and how to overcome them. [...]

Change in recent years has, of course, often entailed reductions in employee
numbers, closures, redundancies, loss of position and loss of benefits. So it's
not surprising that groups are seen as 'resistors of change'. In the sights are
often middle managers, sometimes front-line staff, sometimes senior managers who are said to be fearful of change and slow to shift in the ways the
organisation requires: different people make different assessments of where
the blockages lie.

To overcome resistance careful planning and preparation are needed. Change
programme approaches may vary, but they all contain this emphasis on thinking through what change you want to bring about and preparing implementation in a logical, sequential way. [...]

Often the planning centres on 'gap analysis': measuring the gap between
where the organisation is now and the vision and then planning how to fill
it. To oversee and coordinate the necessary steps, the advocates of change
programmes typically recommend that a steering group is formed. This is a
group of senior managers and others eager for change which has the responsibility of ensuring that the steps are made in the correct sequence, that the
organisation does not rush to the later stages of change before the early ones
are complete; also that change processes and actions are 'aligned', that is

consistent one with another. Has the vision, for example, been well enough communicated for everyone to understand it and be willing to act on it? Does the style of management and leadership practised in the organisation support the vision?

The team has to consider the 'obstacles' to change and how to overcome or avoid them. Perhaps overly narrow job descriptions prevent staff thinking about improvement or customers. Reward and incentive schemes may cause people to think about selfish and departmental concerns in preference to corporate interests. Or perhaps key individuals are only paying lip-service to the need for change and must be persuaded to give genuine support or to be moved to another part of the organisation.

Also important is applying best practice from other organisations. There are, so the gurus and consultants would have us believe, patterns and approaches that work, that have transformed well know companies and that now can do the same for your organisation. You are not alone: the challenges you face are ones others have faced before, so it makes sense to distil their experience and draw the necessary lessons.

This is how change management thinking has developed in the last 30 years. The approach has considerable strengths. It has focused management attention on the issues of change. For many organisations 'more of the same' has ceased to be an option. Order of magnitude improvements in performance have been needed and have demanded radical upheavals in structures, systems, working processes, skills and strategy. Change programmes have helped management understand the scale of the task and the interlocking nature of the different factors in play. They have encouraged managers to stand back from the familiar operational and strategic issues and think about management in a new light: how to bring about long-term shifts in the nature of their organisations.

They have helped management see the degree of will and determination often needed in processes of change. Those who want to shape the future must be prepared to keep pressing on when others are discouraged or ambivalent.

Change programmes have helped managers see the importance of focus and clarity, pushing them to think through what they want to change and how. Many management teams have been encouraged to develop a shared understanding of what they are trying to achieve. The attention paid to communication has pushed managers into talking to people throughout the organisation about goals and direction and, sometimes, to do more listening. The emphasis on planning and programming has encouraged managers to anticipate problems, to prepare what can be prepared and to consider the best sequence for change activities. The reference to best practice elsewhere has challenged the belief that 'our organisation is different' and pushed managers to look outside their own organisation and industry to see what can be learnt from very different organisations.

▋ The problems with change programmes

Yet in real life there are nagging problems, problems we see in one organisation after another. Most change efforts we have observed are neither complete successes nor abject failures. They are somewhere in the middle of the range: some clear gains, some disappointments but with a strong tinge of frustration, a sense that despite enormous investments of time, energy and money the efforts have not paid off as hoped. We meet many managers who are exhausted and frustrated, bruised and battered by the endless new projects and initiatives designed to 'bring about' change, yet who are never quite happy with the results. They often say that 'managing change' is the essence of their jobs: yet the business of how to 'manage change' remains mysterious in many ways. Let's look at what these problems are.

Unintended consequences

The first problem is how often unintended consequences accompany and sometimes displace the intended consequences of change. We worked with the chief executive of one international manufacturing group who was determined to restore the fortunes of his group, once the technological leader in its field but now finding its profitability under pressure as competitors eroded its quality and product edge. To encourage divisions to improve their performance, each year he selected an area on which he required them to focus and improve. One year it was manufacturing, another it was distribution, another it was human resource management. Demanding objectives were agreed for each division in the required area of focus. The chief executive's logic about the need for focus and rapid improvement in the chosen areas was impeccable, as were his awareness and understanding of best thinking and practice in each area.

Yet the unintended consequences of the approach was that increasingly divisional executives found it difficult to have an honest discussion with the group chief executive about their priorities or progress. They felt obliged to produce plans for the year's area of focus, even if they actually felt other issues were more important to the success of their division. Once an area had been 'done', they found it hard to admit to their continuing shortcomings in that area. […] Increasingly, reviews with the chief executive became ordeals and it was difficult to share hopes and concerns for the business openly.
[…]

The gap in perception between leaders and followers

In change efforts we have often met a gap in perception between those who initiate change and those who respond. The word 'change' itself is interpreted in very different ways. Senior managers often talk about the imperatives of change in the sense of responding to changed customers, markets and stakeholders. For the people they manage, 'change' can seem like another piece of management speak, a mantra that is muttered from time to time to justify confusing and exhausting reorganisations and new initiatives. [...]

Change is 'messy'

Transformation efforts have an uncomfortable habit of not working out as intended. Shifts in the way people think and work do not happen in a neat, orderly, programmed fashion. The 'Five Stages of Corporate Renewal' or the 'Fourteen Steps to Nirvana', so often advocated by consultants and academics, break down in practice. While their frameworks may illustrate certain points, they make change too neat. They understate the sheer contrariness of people and organisations.

The reality of organisational change is not tidy. As experienced managers know, the path is confused and uncertain, strewn with obstacles and unexpected difficulties. It is not something that can be planned and predicted. It is a process which evolves. Successful managers start with a strong sense of the direction in which they want to move but unsure of how to get there or how fast they can go. They are constantly adjusting their course to hold on to their chosen direction. Indeed, sometimes as they proceed they change their view of where they want to get to.

One reason they have to keep adjusting course is that the world moves on: just when a company has improved its performance it finds its competitors have as well and the hoped-for competitive advantage has crumbled to dust.

Vision – one step from hallucination

The unintended consequences of change programmes are much in evidence when companies seek to vision their way to the future. We are struck by how often visions simply don't work: they don't inspire, they don't encourage, they are viewed with cynicism by many or most within an organisation. They often become part of 'management speak', phrases and words which the ambitious become adept at using but which have lost any meaning they may once have had for the majority.

We can think of one insurance company where the management team locked itself away for a day to consider the objectives of the recently appointed chief executive and to formulate a new vision for the organisation. The session was compelling: people seemed to talk frankly about past disappointments and frustrations and spoke in a personal way about their aspirations for the company. After some initial hesitation, but driven on by the chief executive, a vision statement was formulated. It wasn't easy: participants found it difficult not to use management 'buzzwords' like excellence and quality, which it was agreed were too vague and didn't express specifically enough what the team wanted to achieve. Nevertheless, by the end a statement had been drafted. It wasn't perfect, people said, and would need reworking, but it was a creditable first draft and seemed to command a good deal of support from around the table.

What happened next – or rather what didn't – was what was most interesting. Instead of being seen as a rallying point for all those in the organisation who wanted change, the impact of the vision statement as it was shared around the organisation was either blank or negative. For some the vision was just another management exercise, something you had to live with but with no effect on the way work was done in practice.

Others reacted with hostility. How dare a new chief executive come in from another company and start talking about quality and customer service? What did he think managers and staff had been doing in the past? Did he have no understanding of their efforts to maintain quality in the face of intense pressure? And what was now stopping them from providing quality, except the new output targets and staff reductions imposed by this same chief executive?

It emerged that what was valuable about preparing the vision statement was the process the management team had been through. They had learnt about each other and, while formulating the vision, come closer together and understood more of their common aspirations. Those who had not partici-pated in developing the vision were left cold by it: to them the words sounded like worthy, generalised aspirations, not a guide to conduct and action in the here and now. It was not something they had helped shape so they felt no 'ownership' of it.

We have seen these same problems in many organisations. First there is the difficulty of developing distinctive visions with some bite to them. So many vision statements sound generalised, exhortative, too ill defined and undeni-able to be effective. If you say you are in favour of quality and customer service, so what? Who isn't? So many management words have become devalued, robbed of all meaning.

Isn't it curious that so many visions are the same? How do so many organ-isations, despite all their differences of history, environment and culture, come to the same words about quality, customer service, valuing people and the rest of it? What chance does a company have of competing successfully if its objectives mirror those of its competitors?

In some cases the visions, however banal, are printed on plastic cards, included in videos, stuck on the wall in reception areas, put up around facto-ries and offices and included in the annual report. Employees can come to feel a sense of embarrassment about the vision statement and pretend it doesn't exist – a bit like the member of the family with anti-social habits whom you hope no one will notice!

Often the vision seems overwhelming to people within the organisation. Instead of being energised, people are left feeling depressed: knowing the dif-ficulties and frustrations of day-to-day operations, they sense that the vision, with its idealised picture of the future, is unattainable. 'How can we ever turn the organisation we know into the paragon described in the vision?' they ask.

What frequently happens is that the vision is developed and communicated (at least to some extent) but then not followed up. It is supposed to guide strategy and operations but somehow is lost sight of under the pressure of day-to-day priorities. Employees nod intelligently but gain no clear picture of what change is intended. The key step of testing the aspirations against reality is often ignored: 'What does this vision mean to you? What difference will it make? How will you act differently?'

Very often employees contrast the beliefs espoused in the vision with the management behaviour and decisions they experience. Vision then becomes a stick with which to beat management. The gap that is sure to exist between the intention set out in the vision and the current behaviour and decisions of managers is bound to be noticed and thrown in managers' faces. Employees ask: 'How can you expect us to take this vision seriously when you, the managers, are not living up to it?'

Repeated rescues

One of the strongest images of managing change is of heroic chief executives riding to the rescue of ailing companies. They arrive from outside, determined to bring to an end a period of decline and to renew the organisation. They carry the answer to the company's problems in their knapsack: even before appointment they were able to identify the key problems and with a little first-hand experience they are able in the first 100 days to see what has to be done. Thereafter it is mainly a question of effective implementation: communicating incessantly their vision of renewal and pushing through the changes needed. They act swiftly, often moving people, bringing in their own team, making key symbolic changes in the critical first period in the post and acting with a decisiveness and energy that were lacking in the old regime. If they are true heroes, their formula is right and after months or even years of struggle they win through, transforming companies and gaining the reputations to go on to even larger responsibilities in the future.

It's a beguiling picture. But how often is it true? Even when chief executives succeed in turning around companies, is it more than a caricature of what has happened? How is it that only a few years after a triumphant turnaround some companies are back in deep trouble?
[...]

Mistaking structure for organisation

Another real-life problem with change programmes is managers acting as if structural change – changing roles and responsibilities on the organisation chart – is the key to transformation. It's an old fallacy in a new guise. [...]

Yet still the pattern persists of managers changing structures and expecting transformation to follow. When one reorganisation does not deliver the expected benefits, it's on to the next one. In the 1970s it was divisionalisation, for a while strategic business units ruled supreme, now there is process-based organisation – no more functional directors, no more turf battles, no more interdepartmental fighting, just smooth, effective cross-business processes. The passion for cross-functional organisation is no more than the latest stage in this evolution. Already managers are finding that this type of organisation is easy to draw but much more difficult to create in reality.

Frequently reorganisations get in the way of change rather then enabling it. While reorganisation is pending, managers turn inwards, looking to see how they can protect their current position or carve out a larger one. They focus on the internal politics of the organisation, on whom to please and how. They often lose sight of the external objectives that are meant to be the purpose of the change. We meet many managers sagging under the pressure of constant reorganisations, unsure what their current role is, exhausted by the internal battles, fearful for their futures. We meet others who are immobilised by fear, traumatised by one reorganisation after another and incapable for the moment of doing anything but react to events.

[...]

Navel gazing

A tendency to become internally absorbed is another paradox of efforts aimed at improving the external effectiveness of the organisation.

[...]

Strangely the more inward the focus, often the more frenetic the activity. In order to measure and control the change efforts, senior managers ask for reports of how many groups have met, how many suggestions made, how many newsletters issued. The change initiative becomes an industry in its own right, and the focus slips from business results to change activities. As a Roman general is reported to have said: 'Having lost sight of our goals, we redoubled our efforts.'

Programmitis

[...]

The pattern of frenetic change activity – and disappointing results – has reached its zenith with the current passion for change programmes, particularly in large organisations. There is a continuing interest in magic solutions to organisational problems. Just when you thought total quality management was dying away, along comes business process reengineering. Whatever the cynicism about the formulas, the conferences continue to be full, the books keep selling. The idea that someone somewhere already has the answer to your problem, that you take it and plug it into your organisation like a domestic appliance, continues to be attractive.

[...]

The phenomenon of programmes does not stop with just one effort. As one programme reaches its plateau – and often before it has – managers launch other programmes. In recent years large organisations in both the private and public sectors have been through a succession of change initiatives. In the most extreme cases this becomes the scourge of 'programmitis', an ever-increasing number of programmes and initiatives. One company we worked with had 19 initiatives going at once. In their anxiety to push through change, senior managers try harder with more exhortation and more demands for staff to shift their thinking and behaviour. They search around for new mechanisms to push through what they want and new banners to work under. The less the programmes work, the more senior managers pile on new initiatives.

The consequences

Frustration and exhaustion

The result of this plethora of change programmes is corporate – and individual – exhaustion. People in an organisation become bewildered by the range of change initiatives, unsure about the priorities they are supposed to work to. The different change initiatives often seem inconsistent. There is a sense of imposition – 'we're doing this because we've been told to' – and a corresponding reduction in the energy and commitment that go into achieving the desired changes.

In the most serious cases, the pattern of increasing 'change' activities and mounting frustration is fuelled by managers' sense of insecurity. [...]

The pattern of insecurity and relentless activity is sometimes mirrored at different levels of an organisation. Managers who are the victims of change initiatives imposed from above become persecutors of staff below them. [...]

And the less the change programmes work, the more managers try to control developments. They ask for more and more measurement and reporting – often of the change activities, not of the substance of change they are seeking. This leads to a contradiction. Change initiatives come to rely heavily on control, which defeats their supposed objectives of empowering people and encouraging learning.

Ironically, change programmes often place an impossible burden on senior managers. They have to supply the energy for change. They have to find the formula for success. They have to be latter-day Churchills inspiring people to transform their behaviour. And the less it works the harder they try. No wonder some managers describe managing change as pushing water uphill! And it's no surprise they are exhausted.

Ultimately change programmes implies an *instrumental* view of change. They are based on the belief that change is *done to* organisations, that people at the top can know the answer and then apply it to the organisation. But what if fundamental change – the transformation that occurs when people change their mental maps of the world – cannot be predicted? What if it is inherently uncertain and the mental models of those seeking to lead change are as much subject to change as those who follow? What if transformation *cannot* be managed – what can be put in the place of change programmes? [...]

Flawed assumptions about change

It would be tempting to say that the problems we described earlier are the result of faulty implementation: that it is not change programmes which are wrong but the way they are handled. We think not. The problems are too common, they form too much of a pattern for that to be a satisfactory answer. Instead it is the thinking on which change programmes are based which needs to be reexamined, not in fact because it is wrong, but because it does not take account of the whole picture of people and organisations. It is a partial view, one that works for a time but ultimately leads to frustration.

Comparing two different models of change

We now look in turn at the critical assumptions which underpin two very different ways of considering change. First we look at the assumptions made if organisations are seen as machines, as happens with the change programmes described earlier. Then we look at the assumptions made if organisations are viewed as living systems: self-organising, dynamic and with a natural capacity to make the most of the environments they are in. In this second view, individuals cannot 'manage' change. Trying to achieve shifts in thinking and behaviour is too subtle, too unpredictable a process for it to be possible to manage it. The best individuals can do is 'work with' change, responding to it and seeking to influence it.

Finally we suggest how to move beyond the black and white choices involved in these two sets of assumptions to explore another way of working with change. This is what we call 'leaning into the future' – a combination of leading *and* learning.

Organisations as machines

'Change needs to be driven'

The first assumption we very often hear when organisations are seen as machines is that change in the patterns of an organisation needs to be made to happen. Without some push, some injection of energy, nothing will shift. The words that are used are telling: managers talk of 'forcing', 'driving through', 'bringing about' change. Many of the metaphors are ones of violence and force. There is a clear assumption that the energy needs to come from outside the mass of the organisation, usually from top management, sometimes from outsiders such as shareholders or the government.

[...]

The assumption is that change has to be made to happen. There is, it is said, a natural inertia in people and organisations. People are inherently conservative, it is asserted. They prefer what they are familiar with: they also have vested interests and positions to defend. They are naturally fearful that any change will leave them worse off than before. In addition, there are some people in every organisation who will block change or try to sabotage it. These are the 'resistors' of change: they must be managed, minimised and, if necessary, removed from their jobs if the change process is to be successful.

It is also often said that we live in an era of unprecedented change. The pace of technological developments, the speed of communications, the removal of barriers to the global economy mean that managers must act fast to change their companies before they are overwhelmed by events. [...]

Against this background there is always more for managers to do: more initiatives to launch, more to communicate, more difficult decisions to take. Managers can never relax. One of the most popular images we hear is that of change as a journey, with no fixed departure point and no definite arrival. When you have climbed one mountain, there looming in front of you is the next summit. Always, it seems, there is a new mountain to conquer.

'Change starts with visioning'

Earlier we discussed the central role that visioning plays in change programmes. It is assumed that the challenge is for leaders to develop and communicate clear and coherent visions of the future which can then provide a beacon for the efforts of others. Effective visions are said to inspire: they enable staff to see where the organisation is going and how their efforts fit with those of others. They provide 'the context for designing and managing the change goals and the effort needed to bridge the gap to meet those goals.' In particular, vision provides the template against which plans and programmes can be measured. Do proposals 'align' with the vision? Without visioning, it is said, organisations will not change in the ways needed, will not adapt and prosper in changing environments.

'The answer is out there'

If managers feel under pressure to drive change through and to create effective visions, help is at hand in the further assumption that the answer, the way in which your organisation needs to change and how, is already available. There are a limited number of situations and challenges you can face. If you look long enough and hard enough, some 'excellent company', some guru or consultant, can tell you how to handle it. We mentioned the previous chapter how extraordinarily popular business process reengineering has become. If you don't like reengineering, there are programmes to reduce cost, improve quality, develop continuous improvement, 'delayer' and 'downsise', improve customer service, empower employees, change culture, develop vision and values, 'delight' customers. And while cynicism about the 'magic bullet' answers grows, still the business books sell as never before, the consultancies continue to expand, the conferences continue to be well attended. Coming next: the impact of complexity theory?

[...]

'You have to start afresh'

The essence of this assumption is that each of the answers is new, radical, transcends all that went before it. The logic is clear: if people are to change the way they view their work and organisation, a clean break with the past is needed. [...]

Reengineering – sweeping away the past

The belief that the past needs to be uprooted has reached a peak with the current craze for reengineering. In its rhetoric at least – much less in its practice – reengineering demands that companies reinvent themselves. Reengineering, say Hammer and Champy, is 'starting over. It is about beginning again with a clean sheet of paper. It is about rejecting conventional wisdom and received assumptions of the past ... it is about reversing the industrial revolution ... tradition counts for nothing. Reengineering is a new beginning.' Its key words are 'fundamental', 'radical', 'dramatic' and 'process'.

The last person to use language like this was China's Chairman Mao in the Cultural Revolution. He too insisted on sweeping away the past. Priceless artifacts, codes of conduct, norms of human behaviour developed over centuries: all had to be smashed before he could create his perfect society. 'Destroy to build' was his motto. The ways of the past were utterly wrong. There had to be an uprooting, a tearing away from the past before the future could be created.

This was, after all, the logic of communism taken to its extreme: the idea that the future could be rationally planned and that the past was of no account. It's ironic that when communism has almost died, its thought process should reappear inside Western companies. What is reengineering but the 'planned economy' reappearing on a smaller scale?

Our view is that successful organisations do not deny or seek to destroy the inheritance of the past. Instead, they seek to build on it. They attempt to understand in depth why they have been successful and they try to do more of it. They are respectful of the learning accumulated from experience, much of which they recognise is not made explicit at the top of the organisation. They acknowledge their faults but try to see them in balance with their good qualities. Their desire to change is based on self-confidence and self-belief, not denigration of what they have been.

'Everyone is for change – for others'

The terms of the requests for help we receive are often the same: how to sell, market, put new energy into the change managers want to do *to* the organisation. Senior managers see a need for *other people* to care more about customers, work harder, control costs better, change their ways of working. The assumption is that top managers have the answer. They're OK. The challenge is to get the others – sometimes other senior managers, often middle managers and shopfloor workers – to adopt the change.

[...]

Often the assumptions of those further down the hierarchy mirror those of senior managers. They too see change as an issue for others; they also see others as the blockage. In the case of middle managers it can be front-line staff and senior managers themselves; in the case of front-line workers, all managers, particularly first-level supervisors.

'Change can be planned and predicted'

The multi-step approaches, the gap analysis, the 'change management' steering groups, the emphasis on aligning activities with the vision, the careful monitoring and control [...] are all indicative of the assumption that change can be planned and predicted. If the answer – the pattern of priorities and actions that will enable an organisation to succeed – is known, then the rest is merely a matter of implementation. It needs to be planned carefully, the requisite responsibilities and resources have to be assigned, progress must be monitored: essentially 'change management' becomes a huge project. The scale of the task and of the issues involved may seem intimidating, but senior executives can look to the well-understood disciplines of project management to help them achieve the desired results.

Organisations as machines

Taken together, the assumptions we have examined – that change is done *to* organisations by those with vision, that it needs to be driven, that the answer is 'out there', that the past needs to be swept away, that others need to change and that transformation processes can be planned and predicted – are characteristic of a mechanical view of organisations. This is a metaphor which keeps reappearing. More than 30 years after Burns and Stalker identified the limitations of the machine metaphor for organisations, that analogy proves astonishingly persistent. It still underlies much current practice of 'change management'. The signals are the words people use: managers and consultants talk about 'pushing' or 'driving through' change, they describe 'barriers' and 'obstacles' and identify the 'resistance' to change and how they must be 'overcome'. They identify 'levers for change' and talk about the need to 'generate momentum'. They draw pictures of motor cars and flywheels.

The idea is of a machine which can be designed and built, driven and controlled. And now, of course, 'reengineered'.

Yet the mechanical analogy is inadequate. Organisations are living things with personalities and histories. They contain people with all their richness and complexity. They are subtle systems. Cause and effect are not linear. If you make a change in one place, unintended consequences may arise at some remove, both in distance and in time. If you focus on one element in isolation, you are likely to be frustrated. The only way to try and understand is to look at the whole. Fortunately, that is what the intuition in all of us does naturally – provided we are prepared to use it.

Organisations as living systems

An alternative view is to see organisations as living systems. Instead of the mechanical metaphor, what would it mean if organisations were regarded as organisms which live and die, grow and decline and whose species evolve? What if the latest thinking in biology and ecology were considered? What implications would this have?

It would suggest that organisations were *adaptive*. Living systems are not passive; they try to turn events to their advantage. Thus species in the natural world have an innate capacity to evolve to make the most of the changing environment. This view suggests that patterns of behaviour and thinking shift of their own accord, sometimes slowly, sometimes quickly, under the pressure of events.

Adopting this view would encourage us to look at the *self-organising* properties of organisations: elements within a system adapt to each other and acquire collective properties without anyone willing it to happen. Thus the millions of cells in a person's skin maintain an equilibrium, develop and age without anyone being in charge or consciously organising it.

It would suggest that organisations were *interdependent* with their environment, interacting with it in complex ways, being influenced by it and shaping it.

And it would draw attention to the *dynamic* nature of organisations. They are obviously alive. They are constantly balancing the need for order and coherence (which taken too far leads to rigidity) and for flexibility (which taken too far leads to anarchy).

Given this alternative model, let's look at what it would imply for managers seeking to transform their organisations.

'Change is natural, but not easy!'

In living systems change occurs as a natural phenomenon all the time. The environment changes, individuals age, change in patterns of behaviour and thinking is happening all the time without anyone necessarily willing it to occur. [...] In the case of changes in the norms of thinking and behaviour in organisations, the change may sometimes seem very slow, particularly to those involved, conscious of the patterns day to day. To an outsider, able to step back and look at shifts over months and years, the change in attitudes and behaviour can seem very rapid.

The living systems view would acknowledge that adjusting to change is often painful. Change may be happening all the time but adapting to it is still difficult. It is not easy to give up familiar ways of thinking and acting. People who have had to let go of failed relationships, those who have had to find new ways of working when made redundant, people who have given up the expectations of parents and learnt to work to their own goals, know how hard this letting go can be.

The same applies to organisations. One of the problems with many large organisations is that they take on new priorities and initiatives but do not let go of the old. They do not make space, both physical and psychological, for the new initiatives. One company we worked in had built success on product quality markedly superior to that of its competitors. Over the years its product edge had eroded as competitors caught up. Yet managers found it very hard to see their product as a commodity and shift to other priorities of cost reduction or service improvement. For them there had to be some way of recapturing the golden age when customers had flocked to buy their product, despite higher prices and poor service.

The living systems thinking suggests there is a potential appetite for change in all organisations. What if workers wanted to improve and have been prevented by blocks which the organisation has put in their way? How many of us are happy to do a poor job, to know that customers are dissatisfied, that we are not giving of our best?
[...]
The living systems view is that the challenge is not to *drive* change but to *release* the potential for change, leading and encouraging it in the directions that will help the organisation to flourish. It suggests that there are few organisations that do not already have energy to change. Some of it is in people's hopes and aspirations, some in their frustrations and concerns, but it is there. The issue for leaders becomes one of removing the constraints to innovation and adaptation and of channelling and connecting the desire for change. Understanding exactly what the constraints are and why they have arisen

is the key to 'unsticking' the organisation and releasing latent energy for change.

'Don't be anxious about change'

The living systems view challenges the widely held belief that we live in an era of unprecedented change. Change is inherent in the growth and decline, evolution and death of living systems. The anxiety about unprecedented rates of change helps no one except the consultants and gurus. It suggests that the enormous pressure to change being placed on organisations by books, conferences and consultants is artificial and the activity they generate does not help organisations. Henry Mintzberg in his book *The Rise and Fall of Strategic Planning* asks: 'Why does every generation have to think that it lives in the period with the greatest turbulence?'

The living systems thinking suggests that much of the 'change' which organisations are undergoing is self-inflicted: the result of managers desperate to force change through instead of working with the natural capacity of people and organisations to develop. It suggests that by working against the grain of organisations managers waste time and energy. If they could find ways to tap the natural potential of people to develop, they would save themselves a lot of frustration and avoid unnecessary pain and anger among the recipients of the 'change initiatives'.

[...]

The living systems view says that the pressure for incessant change also overlooks the need for stability. No organisation and no individual can cope with complete uncertainty, having all their key beliefs and norms forever open to question. We need periods of relative stability and we need areas of certainty. We need to be clear about what we know as well as what we don't know. And that's the natural pattern of transformation. Periods of rapid change are interspersed with long periods of relative stability. To suggest, as some management writers like Tom Peters appear to, that everything needs to be up for grabs, all the time, is a recipe for madness.

'Awareness of current reality'

The living systems view shifts attention from looking at aspirations for the future to becoming clearer about current reality. A problem with visions is indeed that they often seem disconnected from the reality staff see around them. Employees feel that the vision denigrates the present and the past of the organisation. By talking about the idealised future the vision seems to ignore the pressures and difficulties people have faced. Staff who have made their career with the organisation derive part of their sense of self-worth from its achievements and their identity with it. They now feel undermined and angry: their work appears not to be valued. They often also feel both depressed and guilty because they cannot live up to the lofty aspirations set out in the vision.

And the only people who really take responsibility for the vision and its implementation are those few who developed it.

Most disturbingly, the living systems perspective challenges the idea that change is a process of activity aimed at a particular outcome. Instead, it suggests that organisations are too subtle, the interdependencies within an organisation and between the organisation and its environment are too involved for managers to be able to shape the future in this way. 'Shaping the future' is a fantasy of control. Managers need to let go of the idea that they can control the future: instead they should be as true as they can to their own convictions and seek to live in harmony with the world around them.

Advocates of this view even deny that intention exists apart from action. They see managers as expressing their true intention in the actions they take; if their intention shifts their actions also will. What is important, therefore, is not any statement of vision but the pattern of actions and behaviour: these reveal what managers really believe.

Instead of developing unreal wish lists in the form of visions, managers should consider the capacity of their organisation to respond to change. They should work to remove the obstacles or constraints that reduce an organisation's capacity to respond. Species and organisations do not develop independently: they evolve together, turning to advantage the opportunities created by others' development. The health of an organisation is closely related to the health of its environment: in attending to its environment, an organisation is attending to itself. If leaders are keenly aware of changes in the environment and in other companies or organisations, they can anticipate the opportunities that may arise. It is important to ask: 'How can we gain advantage from the developments of others? What could we do that might be mutually beneficial?'

'The answer is within'

As living systems, organisations have their own personalities and histories. Every organisation is different and has particular reasons for developing as it has. There is no one right way forward – it depends on the context of each system and environment. What one company or organisation may find a good solution in one context may not work for another.

There are no excellent companies. Organisations need to let go of the idea that there are paragons out there which they can copy. Just like individuals, organisations need to find their own reasons to change. Being told to change – by a guru, consultant or chief executive – is a fruitless exercise. Trying to emulate another organisation is as foolish as an individual seeking to copy another person's way of living.

'Reinforce emerging patterns'

Because each organisation is different, it is important to look carefully at the reasons for an organisation's past success and its current distinctive competences or capabilities. The patterns of thinking and behaviour in an organisation have developed for a reason. Systems have found a way to flourish in the environment they are in. Those that didn't no longer survive. There is a richness and subtlety in what has evolved, what has stood the test of time, which it may be difficult for any one actor to see. If you want to lead change, it is vital to understand in depth why the system has been successful. Starting by understanding the past and the present is the best way to prepare for the future.

So it is with other changes in behaviour and thinking. Often they are not willed to happen so much as *emerge*. The skill of leaders is not pathfinding in isolation but seeing the new pattern and directing attention to it.
[...]

'We need to change'

In a living system all the elements are changing together. The shift one element makes has a knock-on effect on others. The patterns of behaviour in one part of the system reflect the patterns in other parts and in the system as a whole.

Thus this view suggests that something else is needed for effective leadership of transformation: leaders strong enough to admit that they too are learning, that maybe they are part of – perhaps they *are* – the problem. We have often been asked by managements to help change their employees (so they care more about customers, are more cost conscious, take responsibility for improvement), only to find that a precondition of change in the organisation is that the management team itself changes.

Very often the attitudes that top managers complain about are merely the reflection of their own behaviour and thinking. One chief executive complained that his people never had any ideas and that all initiative had to come from him. What was his behaviour when people did occasionally put their heads above the parapet and offer a suggestion? He always had an answer: it couldn't be done for this reason or that; or he had already looked into it and it was impractical. The chief executive was right to think his style was open and accessible. What he did not appreciate was that people felt browbeaten by him. He was brighter than most of his managers and better informed. Why should anyone else take the initiative with such a boss?

The same is true for other people in organisations. Just as it is usually vital that senior managers see that they need to change, so also middle managers and front-line workers need to see that they have a part in change and that blaming problems on others leads nowhere.

If the living systems view is accurate, it would also suggest that management and business are not separate from the rest of the world, with their own norms and characteristics. The insights people learn in the rest of their lives are just as applicable to organisations. The wisdom we all accumulate through our adult lives, as we grow up, as we learn about ourselves and about others, as we bring up children, as we learn to cope with disasters and tragedies, opportunities and success, should be made available in the world of work. Instead of seeing our life in organisations as in a separate compartment, subject to different rules and assumptions and surrounded by the strange language of management and business, we should bring to bear our experience of life, apply the same rules and assumptions that work for us elsewhere.

'Live with uncertainty'

The evolution of living systems is inherently unpredictable; there are too many variables and too much interdependence to be sure about cause and effect. The future is shaped by actions and reactions, of which only a percentage can be predicted, a limited distance into the future. People must be prepared to work with the known *and* to respond to emerging opportunities.

In a process of radical organisational change the future is unknowable. The environment or markets in which the organisation will have to live in the future are unpredictable. It's an old saying that 'the only thing you can be sure about a forecast is that it is wrong'. The value of a forecast is not what it tells you about the future, but the light it sheds on where the organisation is now and the choices open to it.

The future is unknowable because the patterns of behaviour and thinking that will enable the organisation to thrive in that future environment have yet to be discovered.

[...]

'Feelings and emotion are important'

Living systems thinking pushes us to see people as a whole: to consider their emotional and subconscious as well as their rational side.

Often people get stuck because their conscious need and wants are in conflict with unconscious forces and motivations. We are all aware that we are not always rational beings: at times our actions are driven by emotions and feelings and sometimes we don't know where these feelings come from.

The importance of this for change is, of course, that people do things for the strangest reasons. Rationality is often a poor guide. [...]

Intuition is important. Often people know what to do but can't articulate why. They have an instinct, a feeling that they ought to do something or behave in a certain way. So also with change. In our experience managers have a great deal of instinct and intuition about what works and what doesn't. If they feel it is OK to discuss openly what their instinct tells them, there is a huge well of insights to be drawn from.

'Managers should try less hard'

The optimistic conclusion from applying the living systems thinking is that managers should try *less* hard when handling change. Most organisations, it is suggested, are full of energy for change. The problem is that most of it lacks a constructive outlet and therefore assumes negative forms: bitching, cynicism, defensiveness, territorial battles. Once some of it is converted to help the organisation rather than hinder it, the potential for change is great.

[...]

Leaning into the future

We have drawn two sharply contrasting pictures of change and of what individuals can do. In the mechanical metaphor, managers push through transformation, applying known answers in a logical, sequenced way. In the living systems view, managers work with the forces that are already there and with patterns that emerge. They do not bring about change at all; they encourage responsiveness and learning.

Both pictures illuminate and have their limitations. They remain metaphors: they are not the whole truth, simply one way of understanding reality. A way of seeing is also a way of not seeing. The mechanical metaphor assumes that change is 'done to' organisations, that important shifts in thinking and behaviour can be planned and predicted, that logic alone is enough.

The living systems metaphor also has its limitations: it underplays the importance of intention. Organisations do not just respond to natural forces; they are made up of people who make choices and consciously decide what future they want for themselves. As Gareth Morgan points out, the living systems metaphor rests on the assumption of functional unity: each element of the system supporting and aiding the others, as in the human body. In organisations elements often do not support each other and can indeed conflict or break away from one another.

The two pictures do not come ideology free. The mechanical model is linked to the view that control is paramount and that senior managers do the thinking while others implement; the living systems thinking is associated with the assumption that organisations flourish as they allow their people to develop their potential to the full.

For us the challenge is not to adjudicate between these two conflicting pictures, nor to decide one is right and the other wrong, but rather to try and go deeper, to consider what each model offers, and then to integrate an approach to change which goes beyond both pictures while combining the best from both metaphors.

An example of this process of thinking is the business of quality. When quality was equated with luxury, people in business felt there was a choice: base your strategy on lower cost *or* higher quality. To add features to a product or service was to add cost. To lower cost would (usually) reduce the quality. Then along came the Japanese, redefining quality as reliability, consistency, products and services that kept their promise, whatever that was. Now a small car could be as much a quality product as a Rolls Royce. And suddenly lower costs went hand in hand with higher quality. Less waste in the factory meant lower production costs and greater product consistency. Increased cooperation between departments and reduced product development times meant lower costs and increased responsiveness to the customer.

The trick is in finding how to achieve the *ands:* how to combine the positive sides of apparently very different perspectives. By this we do not mean a compromise between the two views or a middle point. Rather we mean reframing the issues in a way that goes beyond the original perspectives, incorporating their benefits and finding a more rewarding picture of reality.

This is what we seek [...]: to go beyond the mechanical and living systems views of change and develop a practical guide for people in organisations. Both metaphors are very influential and widely used: people have found that they help them make sense of change. Our purpose therefore is not to knock them down, but to learn from them and to reframe the way we all consider change.

Leading *and* learning

The key value of the mechanical metaphor is the emphasis it places on *leading*. Effective leaders have a strong sense of intention and are clear, emotionally and logically, about what they want to change. They are true to their convictions and determined to see certain objectives and standards attained.

The key value of the living systems model is its focus on *learning*. It is not possible to prescribe in advance or in detail how people in an organisation will change and what shifts in thinking and behaviour will be required. The unpredictable always happens, so flexibility is essential. Leaders are learning along with everyone else in the organisation.

'Leaning into the future' recognises that effective leadership of change involves bringing together apparently contradictory qualities (see Figure 14.1). Successful leaders shape the future *and* they adapt to the world as it is. They are clear about what they want to change *and* they are responsive to others' views and concerns. They are passionate about the direction in which they want the organisation to go *and* they understand and value the current reality of the organisation, why it has been successful and what its people are good at. They lead *and* they learn.

The image of a person leaning forward captures our view. To lean as far forward as you can requires you to have both feet firmly on the ground – stand on tip toe and you topple over.

What is intriguing is the power of the combination, of the *ands*. Far from being contradictory, the firm grasp on reality and the clear vision go hand in hand. The visions of leaders are clearer and more powerful if they have a firm grasp on reality. The clearer they are about what they want, the more they are able to get in touch with current reality.

Similarly and paradoxically, by recognising the limits of what they can do, they become more effective. They don't challenge the impossible but focus their efforts where they can succeed.

[...]

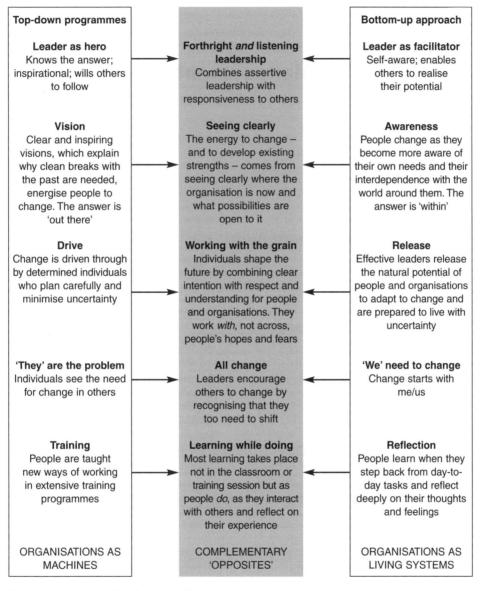

Figure 14.1 *Leaning into the future*

Reference

Kotter, J. (1995) 'Leading change: why transformation efforts fail'. *Harvard Business Review*, March–April.

15

Performance Management Strategies

Greg Clark

Performance management: underlying theory

Performance management is not new, despite the fact that the use of the term has grown popular recently. Managers have always devised ways, formally or otherwise, to set tasks, see that they are carried out well, and make modifications designed to secure further improvements. Models of performance management may seem to be 'an apparently obvious invention' as Jevons (1883) described performance-related pay, one type of performance management system but nevertheless are founded on well developed theoretical foundations. Or rather it may be fairer to say, since the economist Alfred Marshall described the theoretical case for performance-related pay as 'a formalization of existing practice', that a substantial body of theory has grown up around models of performance management in use. All too often, however, the theory is forgotten in favour of searches for instant solutions to empirical problems, whereas referring to underlying theory provides a solid base for understanding and criticizing applications of performance measurement.

The essence of performance management is establishing a framework in which performance by human resources can be directed, monitored, motivated and refined; and that the links in the cycle can be audited. Unsurprisingly, given this, the principal theoretical foundation of performance management is social psychology, with its detailed consideration of the ways in which *people* are *motivated to perform*. Two theories are particularly pertinent to discussions of performance management: goal-setting theory (e.g. Locke et al., 1981), and expectancy theory (Vroom, 1964).

Source: Greg Clark (1998) 'Performance management strategies', in C. Mabey, G. Salaman and J. Storey (eds), *Human Resource Management: A Strategic Introduction*, pp. 123–52. Edited version.

Goal-setting theory

Goal-setting theory was established by Edwin Locke in a paper published in 1968, in which he argued that goals pursued by employees can play an important role in motivating superior performance. In following these goals people examine the consequences of their behaviour. If they surmise that their goals will not be achieved by their current behaviour, they will either modify their behaviour, or choose more realizable goals.

SHRM involves integrating the wider objectives of the organization with the behaviour of its employees. Accordingly, if managers can intervene to establish the organization's goals (or translations of them for the group or individual) as being worthwhile for employees to accept, they can harness a source of motivation to perform, and direct it to securing strategic outcomes.

Subsequent empirical research into goal-setting (cf. Mento et al., 1987) has specified more precisely the conditions necessary for organizational goals to be motivating to employees; these are that:

■ goals should be specific, rather than vague or excessively general;
■ goals should be demanding, but also attainable;
■ feedback of performance information should be made; and
■ goals need to be accepted by employees as desirable.

Goal-setting theory has been subject to a great deal of theoretical and empirical scrutiny since it was first advanced. The resulting body of evidence now provides a set of rigorously tested principles which offer clear guidance to designers of performance management systems. Later in the chapter we will be applying each of these lessons to performance management.

Expectancy theory

A book published by Victor Vroom in 1964, *Work and Motivation*, stimulated a flurry of research interest in *expectancy theory* as a framework for understanding motivation at work. Expectancy theory hypothesizes that it is the anticipated satisfaction of valued goals which causes an individual to adjust his behaviour in a way which is most likely to lead to his attaining them.

In fact, while the popularity of expectancy theory is relatively recent, it draws on a tradition which can be traced back to the early Utilitarians. Mill and Bentham described an ethical system in which people determined their actions by a conscious calculation of the consequences which they expected the actions to bring about. In the twentieth century psychologists such as Tolman (1932) and Lewin (1938), as advocates of theories of performance by people which held that performance is governed by expectations concerning future events, turned a normative theory of how people *should* base their actions, into a positive theory of how people *do* behave. [...]

Expectancy theory has been developed from Vroom's early specifications to be expressed very clearly (e.g. Galbraith and Cummings, 1967) as a combination of three factors:

■ The person's own assessment of whether performing in a certain way will result in a measurable result. This factor is labelled the *expectancy*.
■ The perceived likelihood that such a result will lead to attaining a given reward. This factor is known as *instrumentality*.
■ The person's assessment of the likely satisfaction, or *valence*, associated with the reward.

These factors can be expressed in diagrammatic form as in Figure 15.1. In practice, if a person sees it as being clear that performing in a certain way will bring about a reward which he or she values, then this individual is more likely to attempt to perform in that way than if the relationship between effort and measured performance, or measured performance and rewards, is slight or uncertain.

Like goal-setting theory, expectancy theory highlights some of the key design principles which practitioners face in establishing systems of performance management.

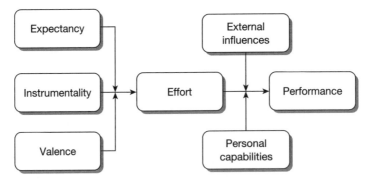

Figure 15.1 *A simple expectancy model*

Designing performance management systems: lessons from theory

We have seen that both expectancy theory and goal-setting theory underpin the concept of a performance management system. In this section we will draw on the contributions of each of these models to add depth and complexity to

The Performance Management Cycle

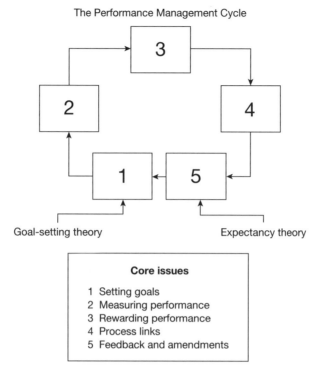

Figure 15.2 *Performance management: lessons from theory*

the schematic model of performance management advanced at the beginning of this chapter.

Figure 15.2 summarizes a number of core issues, common, in varying degrees, to both expectancy theory and goal-setting theory. They represent the key factors which must be addressed in designing a system of performance management. We review the contribution of theory to each of these issues in turn.

Setting goals

As an instrument of strategic human resource management, a system of performance management is predicated on the need to take the wide, strategic goals of the organization, and translate them into goals for smaller groups and individuals.

Tests of both goal-setting theory and expectancy theory have demonstrated the importance of specifying, few, relatively concrete goals. Yet in practice, designing a performance management system which is in keeping with these principles may prove problematical, for three reasons: the organization may be unable to identify and articulate clear strategic objectives; objectives may be more diverse and numerous than are consistent with theory; and the strategic goals of the organization may be inherently unstable.

Identifying clear strategic objectives for itself is a precondition for an organization to be able to translate them into performance goals. You may be familiar, from studying business strategy (e.g. Mintzberg, 1992), with the view that many organizations acquire and follow strategies not as a result of conscious, rational planning process but rather that strategies 'emerge' in response to time and events. Further, the organization may have a number of objectives at any one time, some of which may be potentially contradictory or competing (for example, a commitment to investing in people at the same time as a need to 'downsize'). If the organization is unable to set out explicitly its strategy (which is defined (Johnson and Scholes, 1984) as summarizing its objectives and goals) it is unlikely to be able to carry out the next step from this, which is to identify particular dimensions of performance that are most likely to achieve its strategic goals. Case study research of the shifting psychological contract in three UK organizations, found that operationalizing the link between the strategy and values of companies concerned and the objective-setting process was problematic for three reasons: the short-term focus of the companies; the degree of change the companies were experiencing; the perception that objectives were imposed, not jointly negotiated (Stiles et al., 1997).

A second source of criticism is the exhortation of both expectancy and goal-setting models to choose a limited number of performance dimensions to measure and reward. People in organizations, whatever the terms of their written contract, can be said to have a 'psychological contract' with their employer, which is a rich and nuanced collection of shared understandings built up over time. Often, to choose and emphasize a limited number of performance dimensions is to fail to appreciate the subtlety of organizational life, and to risk shattering subtle structures of tacit but critical employee commitment by substituting a simplistic set of objectives. It carries the danger that if the system does 'work', in the sense that people focus on those elements of performance which have been selected and highlighted by the organization, the results may be not at all desirable: a preexisting pride in skill and work may be replaced by a contractual focus on the rules. The following real-life example (Box 15.1) illustrates this point.

A third problem concerns timing. Identifying desirable aspects of individual performance, which will be measured and rewarded, may be possible in an organization that enjoys a relatively stable internal and external environment, but where greater turbulence is experienced it is possible that objectives and hence performance dimensions targeted today may be inapplicable tomorrow. [...] Companies must be careful to diagnose the appropriateness of the *time interval* within which their objectives are set.

Box 15.1   When performance targets backfire

A performance management system was introduced into a major continental European telecommunications utility in 1993. An overall corporate strategic objective of improved productivity was set, and cascaded down the organization. For the directory assistance division this objective was translated into a goal of reducing the time spent by operators in dealing with each enquiry. Performance against the goal was measured by a system-generated measure of the average length of call.

Managers scrutinizing the early results of the system found that the average length of each call had declined markedly, but operators seemed still to be continuously busy: apparently improved productivity did not seem to be translated into spare capacity. Closer investigation revealed that operators felt that the pressure to keep calls short conflicted with what they saw as an important personal desire to establish a rapport with callers, which they felt could not be done under time pressure. It turned out that operators had discovered that they could reduce the average time per call by immediately disconnecting one call in three, while continuing to spend the usual length of time in small-talk with the remainder of their callers.

Measuring performance

Assuming the organization has been able to identify which dimensions of performance it will choose to include in a performance management system, it faces another set of issues concerning how the dimensions will be measured. In practice, choosing objectives and setting performance measures is often linked, although not necessarily desirably: Fowler (1990) has suggested that performance dimensions are sometimes chosen not because they are most valued by the organization, but because they are the most easily measured.

Quantitative measures

Most organizations will use at least some quantitative (i.e. numerical) indicators of their performance to assess whether they are achieving the goals they have set for themselves. For example, many organizations will have financial health as one of their objectives, explicit or otherwise, and so monitor their financial performance regularly, and are quite likely to cascade this objective down through the organization. In doing so they may monitor financial performance against budgets for groups and individuals. Moreover, organizations typically generate, or can access, a whole range of quantified data such as sales figures, output, productivity, absenteeism. Two types of problem can arise in choosing quantitative measures in a system of performance management. The first concerns their sufficiency, and the second their quality.

A performance management system which has genuinely distilled dimensions of performance to be applied to groups and individuals from its wider strategy, may find that some of the dimensions are not measured by existing indicators, and may not be available from the current management information system. It is possible, for example, that increasing customer satisfaction is identified as an outcome to be rewarded and encouraged, but that no adequate measure exists to report this. In this case the organization must do one of two things: either remove the objective from the set which a performance management system will concentrate on (which would undermine the rigour of the system), or develop a means to measure the dimension.

The second problem which must be addressed with quantitative measures is that of their quality. Although so-called quantitative measures often have an aura of robustness and objectivity surrounding them, a closer analysis reveals that they may be rather more arbitrary and subjective than supposed (cf. Walsh, 1992). Profitability would seem to be a tried and tested performance measure, for example, yet financial managers or accountants will confirm that profits are highly subject to decisions made by managers on how to treat costs and revenues, and when paper gains should be released onto the profit and loss account.

Qualitative measures

Not all aspects of performance can be easily measured and quantified. You may be able to judge whether someone is competent or not, but find it difficult to put a precise figure on how competent they are. Many aspects of performance identified for inclusion in a performance management system may, if they are to be assessed at all, rely not on quantitative measures, but on qualitative judgements. Although quantitative measures have traditionally enjoyed a higher status, it is clear that many instances of hard data, such as accounting information, are actually more mutable than is commonly supposed. On the other hand, if qualitative assessments of performance are well designed, and thoroughly audited, their outcomes may be a more valid and accurate reflection of reality than many quantitative measures.

In general, the quality of any measure of performance or performance indicator will depend whether it is both valid and reliable. Validity refers to whether the indicator actually measures what it is supposed to measure. For example, profitability of a particular unit or group might be taken as an indicator of managerial effectiveness. However, it is possible that factors outside the manager's control could have a greater effect on profitability, and thus it is not a valid indicator of managerial effectiveness. Reliability is a simpler criterion. It means that similar results will be discovered if the measure is used on the same object or person by different people and/or at different times. So, reliability reflects repeatability, whereas validity describes whether you are measuring what you intend to measure. In addition, for practical reasons, a good measure needs to be straight-forward to understand and inexpensive to collect. To the extent that these conditions are not met, a performance management system will include flaws which make it depart from the expectancy theory ideal.

Judgements about performance are made all the time in organizations. Most people will have a clear, and for that matter complex, picture of the ability and performance of a colleague with whom they work closely. Usually, this view will rely only in part on formal quantitative measures, but also on a variety of qualitative judgements. Inevitably, whatever measures are used there will be an element of subjective judgement. Promotions, for example – a possible element of a performance management system – are often made on the basis of subjective assessments of a person's performance and suitability for a new job. The challenge for a performance management system is that its procedures should be *auditable*, so that it can be verified that any measures are being used fairly and effectively. This tends to result in a move to formalize the process of subjective performance measurement. The most common way in which this is carried out is via a system of appraisal.

Appraisal systems

Appraisal systems can take many forms, from annual verbal discussions between an employee and their superior, to systems which may include written reviews from peers and subordinates, as well as superiors and the use of various quantitative performance indicators. The common characteristic of each, however, is that on a regular basis a subjective assessment of an employee's performance is recorded.

Some question the extent to which appraisals can ever be an adequate means of assessing employees' performance because they inevitably involve subjective judgements. One school of thought emphasizes the social processes which underlie performance appraisals. It argues that because ratings are given by people to other people it is impossible to disentangle the social influences which are present: do the appraiser and appraisee enjoy a social rapport? Do non-relevant aspects of the appraisee influence the perception which the appraiser has of his performance? An example of this latter point is US research (e.g. Kraiger and Ford, 1985), which demonstrates that employees receive significantly higher ratings from appraisers of their own race. Other studies have indicated that female success at traditionally male tasks is often ascribed to luck, ease of the task, or 'connections' rather than to superior performance. More generally, appraisers may feel socially uncomfortable about giving appraisal ratings which may be relatively poor. The reaction to this may be to cluster ratings artificially around the mean, or to give way to a general 'rating creep' by awarding more marks above a suggested mean than below.

An increasing number of organizations are using 360 degree feedback to support decisions about resourcing, appraisal and rewards (as against personal development); the concern here is that employees would be likely – in these circumstances – to manipulate the process for their own purposes.

Another perspective on appraisal comes from the analysis of power. Far from being a neutral exercise in seeking out the truth, appraisal may be a highly political process, with the parties involved pursuing their own power strategems through it. For example, appraisal may represent an ideal vehicle for a boss to consolidate his or her power over a subordinate. [...]

One type of solution which has been applied to overcome these problems with appraisal is to expand the number of appraisers who contribute to the subjective assessment of an employee. This would tend to even out any 'rater bias' in response that was related to particular appraisers, though of course it would not address the problem of group bias against racial or gender groups, for example. Increasing the number of contributors to an appraisal might also dilute the social pressure on the appraiser, resulting in allocating too high ratings. Another solution to this specific problem, which has been used by some organizations, is to 'force' appraisals to be non-neutral by specifying, for example, that a certain proportion of top grades must be allocated as well as a certain proportion of low grades. This can also be done statistically by forcing a certain desired distribution of ratings onto the actual ratings given by appraisers (Box 15.2).

Box 15.2   Incorporating peer reviews in appraisals

Performance management at the investment bank JP Morgan has at its heart an unusual appraisal system. Each employee of the rank of 'officer' (a term which covers the majority of employees) is required to ask up to five colleagues who have worked with him during the past year to submit confidential appraisals of his performance. In addition, anyone else in the company is entitled to submit an unsolicited appraisal on any other individual they have worked with, and it may be positive, negative or a mixture of both. Such unsolicited appraisals cannot be given anonymously: the person co-ordinating the assessment has the right to discuss their views further with them, but the identity of the unsolicited appraiser is not revealed to the subject of the appraisal. The manager of the appraisee's department collates the feedback, and summarizes it in a document which also contributes his own assessment. This document is discussed with the employee, and forms the basis of a performance ranking on which promotions, pay rises and bonuses will be made.

The solutions to the problems of bias in subjective appraisals can be one cause, however, of another problem frequently encountered by organizations making use of an appraisal system. This is that the process of appraisal becomes bureaucratic and unwieldy. This can lead to it consuming undesired resources in the organization, and being seen as an administrative nuisance and consequently not taken seriously by either appraisers or appraisees. More fundamentally, the practical implications of this aspect of performance management, in terms of bureaucracy and formalism, may be in direct opposition to other moves in the organization towards delegation, empowerment, team-work and devolution of previously centralized policies.

Rewarding performance

A system of performance management will not succeed in bringing about high performance against objectives unless employees consciously act in ways seen as being most likely to achieve the objectives. Expectancy theory and goal-setting theory both emphasize the importance of ensuring that employees make this decision, but each takes a different route in describing what causes this to be made. Expectancy theory specifies the need to tie performance outcomes to *rewards* which are valued by employees. Goal-setting theory lays stress on the need for acceptance by employees of the goals per se, so that motivation is more intrinsically based.

At one level, expectancy theory is almost tautological. It seems to suggest that people will perform in order to attain outcomes which they value, without specifying what it is that people value. This shortcoming has roots in the principles of hedonism, on which utilitarianism, and ultimately expectancy theory, is based. In claiming that all human actions are motivated by the desire to seek pleasure and avoid pain, the philosopher Hobbes proposed, in effect, a theory of psychological hedonism but failed to specify what *constitutes* pleasure and pain. If expectancy theory is to be applied usefully it requires a complementary theory of *what* motivates people; for the designer of a performance management system this carries the clear implication that a judgement must be made of what rewards will be valued by employees.

The concept of valence in expectancy theory establishes the notion that successful performance will only result to the extent that rewards on offer are valued by employees. There exists a myriad of rewards which firms can offer employees, of which money is just one. Others include power, autonomy, praise, status, and fringe benefits. A choice must be made by companies as to what rewards are to be granted in response to performance, and the choice must reflect the importance of that reward to individuals, as well as what the organization can feasibly offer.

Rewards which can be offered can be thought of as *intrinsic* or *extrinsic*. Intrinsic rewards arise from within the system itself. For example, the sense of achievement of meeting performance targets may be reward enough for some employees to cause them to strive for certain performance outcomes. Extrinsic rewards are added separately to the system and may be pecuniary (e.g. a cash bonus) or non-pecuniary (e.g. time off from work).

Pay is one possible means of rewarding employees in a system of performance management. Although performance-related pay is widespread, it need not be assumed that performance management is money driven. From early days, psychological research has argued consistently that pay is variable in its attractiveness to employees (e.g. Brayfield and Crockett, 1955). In this regard, goal-setting theory is a useful complement to expectancy theory for designers of performance management systems. This is because goal-setting theory places particular emphasis on the *intrinsic* motivation associated with achieving performance goals which have been set. This becomes particularly important for organizations in the voluntary sector (see Box 15.3).

Box 15.3 Managing the performance of volunteers

'Many people working for voluntary organizations feel that they are not primarily in it for the money. Good senior managers recognize this and are aware of the desire of their staff to be recognized for their achievements. At the same time, the organization needs to make sure that poor performance is identified and corrected. The most positive aspects of performance management are (1) managers and supervisors are obliged to think through in detail what they expect of their staff or volunteers, who then have a clear framework for their work, and (2) it sends a clear message that performance matters, and allows the organization to set corporate goals and align individual personal objectives to those goals. The gains from the introduction of such a system can be considerable in terms of improved performance and morale.

On the down side, experience in both the private and voluntary sectors has shown that the personal biases of managers assessing performance can skew results. This is the fear most commonly voiced by opponents of such systems. To some extent, this can be corrected by training and by involving other managers in cross-checking their peers' performance appraisals.

The value system in voluntary organizations tends to emphasize personal worth, the development of the individual, and the removal of barriers to advancement. The reality of working in voluntary organizations can contrast sharply with this rhetoric, with the 'caring' values of the organization seeming to get lost under high work loads and inadequate people management skills. In this situation, providing support to individuals' personal development can be an important step in valuing individuals. People respond positively when they feel that their managers are taking a personal interest in their future, within and beyond their current job.'

Lawry-White (1997)

The problem for practitioners is twofold. First, how to find out which goals or rewards will be valued by employees. A solution to this would seem to be preliminary research among employees to discover their preferences. A second problem arises from individual differences. Within an organization, different employees may have markedly different preferences for rewards, or views regarding which goals are valuable. While the ideal would be to tailor these to meet the preferences of individual employees, in practice this is likely to introduce excessive complexity into a performance management system, already subject to the risk of being overly bureaucratic. As a result companies should recognize they will be constrained to offer a 'second best' system.

All this assumes that, while preferences between people might vary, they are constant within a given person. That is to say, a person who values pay, or autonomy, highly will do so consistently, other factors being equal. There is, however a *marginal valence problem*. This problem is that the value (or valence) of a particular reward is likely to be subject to diminishing marginal returns, as is the case for most other valued goods and services. The value which a person places on autonomy, say, depends in part on how much autonomy he or she has currently. As more autonomy is granted, the value placed on further increase in autonomy is likely to fall (and may even become negative). Equally, goals which are committed to on one occasion, may be less motivating when repeated time after time. For managers designing a system of performance management the marginal valence problem means that it is not sufficient to choose and incorporate rewards, or goals, which are *currently* valued by employees. If the system is to be on-going, both must be reviewed regularly to assess whether they continue to be highly valued by employees, and if not, they should be replaced with others. This makes the point very clearly that a system of performance management may not be designed and left unchanged during its period of operation, but must be the subject of continuous review.

Process links

Expectancy theory and goal-setting theory make it clear that for a performance management system to succeed in securing high performance, it is not sufficient to get the content issues (discussed above) right. Attention must be paid to the linkages within the system: in other words *how* the system works.

Expectancy theory in particular maintains that it is of crucial importance that employees perceive a close link between their efforts and what is measured as the chosen dimensions of performance. It is equally important that they perceive there to be strong ties between performance as measured and the rewards which may result. Goal-setting theory takes a different emphasis, which makes it not entirely commensurable with expectancy theory. Empirical tests of goal-setting theory have established that if they are to bring about high performance, goals should be demanding, but not unattainable. To this extent the theory shares expectancy theory's concern with the design of the links between objectives and the ability to attain them. However, whereas expectancy theory predicts that performance objectives which are easily met will prompt high performance (providing that they are closely associated with a valued reward), goal-setting theory contends that an easily met objective will fail to produce motivation to perform.

Two principal process links are to be found in models of performance management, the link between effort and measured performance, and the link between performance and rewards. We consider each of these links in turn.

Linking effort and measured performance

Expectancy theory carries the clear implication that if a system is to promote effort leading to superior performance, people must feel confident that by adjusting their behaviour they will be able to affect the performance measures which have been established. Ensuring that this is the case will involve both design work and communication by the organization.

It is not automatically the case that an individual will be able to affect a given performance measure. Two reasons account for this. The first, as the expectancy model in Figure 15.1 shows, is that individual effort and application are unlikely to be exclusive determinants of performance on a given dimension. The tools, either in the sense of physical equipment, or in the sense of skills and abilities, which someone is equipped with will play an important role in determining outcomes. If these are not supplied by the organization, the employee will justifiably feel a reduced ability to influence the performance measures, and, expectancy theory predicts, will not engage in an attempt to improve performance. It could also be the case that achieving performance standards which have been set is beyond the personal capabilities of the employee. Try as he or she might, a person may simply not have the interpersonal skills required, say, to meet an assessment criterion of being seen as a departmental leader by colleagues: such objectives, which appear unachievable, will neutralize any attempt to improve performance.

Another way in which people may feel that they are unable, through their own efforts, to influence performance measures significantly has to do with the size of groups whose performance is measured. An important debate in the economics literature (e.g. Alchian and Demsetz, 1972) concerns the question of 'shirking' or 'free-riding' by individuals in groups. This is the idea that if it is the performance of the whole team which is measured, and which determines rewards, then any individual worker can choose to work less hard than their colleagues, to 'take it easy', confident in the knowledge that they will benefit anyway from their team-mates' effort. But of course if everyone in the team thinks in a similar way, then no one will work hard with the result that the performance of the whole team will be poor. The expectancy theory interpretation of the problem is that any individual will see his or her own efforts as having sufficiently little individual effect on performance to justify supplying much.

Some writers (e.g. Alchian and Demsetz, 1972) conclude that team-based performance management systems are flawed because of this problem. Others (e.g. Kanter, 1989) suggest that the problem can be resolved internally by the social processes within groups and teams. Members of a team will monitor how well their colleagues are working, and exert 'peer pressure' on them not to let their performance fall, thereby letting the side down. It is easy to imagine such an atmosphere prevailing in a sports team, for example. Kanter reports that in a group-based performance management system at the Lincoln Electric Company in the USA 'peer pressure can be so high that the first two years of employment are called "purgatory"' (1989: 264).

The issue raises important questions for the design of performance measurement systems. In many circumstances it may not be feasible to separate out the contribution to performance of individual members of a group or team, and the performance of the group as a whole is measured as part of the system. On other cases it might be administratively more straightforward to measure team performance. Either way, this way be a weak link in the performance management cycle.

Expectancy theory emphasizes the link between effort and measured performance as *perceived* by the employee. To accept the argument that the organization is not so much a rational set of clear structures and policies as a socially determined environment is to allow the possibility that people's perceptions may not be objective pictures of actuality. People may be convinced that their efforts will not be noticed, even if the designers of a system of performance management have in fact addressed the potential problems with the links between effort and performance. It may therefore be necessary for a communications policy to be used to reinforce the message of the design of the system if perceptions are to be accurate. The type of communications policy that may prove effective could vary: in some organizations only seeing a performance management system piloted may be sufficient to persuade doubters of its validity.

Linking measured performance and rewards

Expectancy theory, used as a framework for analysing performance management systems, also draws attention to the links which an employee perceives between measured performance and rewards, if the system is to succeed in encouraging maximum performance. As in the case of the links between effort and measured performance, it is the *perception* of the link which will determine the success of the system, although in an on-going system the most important determinant of this is likely to be the objective mechanisms in place.

There are two broad ways in which the measured performance-reward contingency can be structured: a formula-based determination, or a more informally determined approach. The advantage of the former is that it provides an objective basis for encouraging the perception that rewards are linked to performance, but suffers the drawback of inflexibility. A less rigidly determined contingency allows for a variety of unforeseen factors which may have affected performance (either positively or negatively) to be taken into account, but runs the risk of appearing arbitrary or political, thereby weakening the degree to which employees consider that rewards reflect actual performance.

Some organizations operating performance management systems, especially those which use financial rewards, rather than intrinsic factors, as motivators, specify precisely in advance the relationship which will prevail between achieved levels of measured performance and the rewards which they will trigger. This may be in the form of a policy which states, for example, that each grade above the average in an appraisal will earn the individual a financial bonus. Another form of this approach is to pay out to employees a proportion of the value of something allied to the stated performance objectives, such as increased sales. Gainsharing, a performance management system popular in the United States in recent years (cf. McKersie, 1986), pays out to employees a pre-determined proportion of labour cost savings achieved during a specified period. The principal problem with such a mechanistic approach to linking performance and rewards stems from the problem of 'noise'. Performance measures even in a well-designed system may be unable to avoid being subject to the influence of factors other than employees' personal endeavours. External economic conditions, unforeseen incidents and other 'random' variation may still affect measures such as sales or production performance. At a time when these noise elements turn out to have been especially significant in determining measured performance, a closely defined system may distribute rewards unfairly. If an unexpected currency appreciation has severely affected export sales, for example, it may be unfair to penalize a salesforce which did relatively better than the competition, but whose rewards were tied to sales volume. Equally there are companies who reward their executives through bonuses related to their share price, who have found themselves paying out more than they intended following a general rise in the stockmarket, or after takeover interest in the company, unrelated to superior performance, has caused an increase in the share price. To some extent these problems could be overcome by better design of measures (using share price *relative* to comparable companies, for example, or sales *relative* to those of competitors), but in practice it may be impossible to specify the whole range of contingencies in a performance measure without overcomplicating the design and transparency of the system (Box 15.4).

Box 15.4   Direct line: a case of excessive PRP?

The question of the precise relationship between performance and rewards, it should be specified, is a perennial, and intractable one. The case of Direct Line, the motor insurer subsidiary of the Royal Bank of Scotland, illustrates the dilemma.

Peter Wood founded the Direct Line insurance company in 1985. As a new entrant to a UK insurance market dominated by large, household-name insurance groups, it was uncertain whether Direct Line's strategy of offering low-cost motor insurance by telephone would result in a viable business. Peter Wood sold his stake in the company to the Royal Bank of Scotland in 1988, agreeing to stay on to manage the business. In exchange for his shareholding, Wood negotiated an incentive pay package with RBS which would reward him through a fixed formula tied to the growth of assets of the insurance business.

As it turned out, Direct Line proved a phenomenal success, far exceeding expectations of its performance. Much of the success is certainly attributable to Wood, both for conceiving the strategy, and for proving a shrewd manager of the business. Direct Line's profits reached £50.2 million in the year ending 1993, and by 1994 the company had become Britain's biggest motor insurer. Peter Wood's performance related pay skyrocketed in line with the success. Wood earned £1.6 million in 1991, £6 million in 1992 and £18.2 million in the year to September 1993.

The Royal Bank of Scotland and Peter Wood became embarrassed by the remuneration figures, which were the subject of increasing public attention. In November 1993 the Royal Bank bought itself out of its contractual obligation by making a one-off payment to the Direct Line chief of £24 million.

The question which was exercising public opinion is unresolved today: is it appropriate for performance which is significantly better than envisaged to trigger rewards which are significantly more generous than envisaged?

Links between performance and rewards which are not tied to a specific formula may avoid some of these difficulties. Rather than knowing precisely how much, in terms of reward, a given level of performance might bring, managers may be granted discretion over a certain sum or other pool (e.g. a number of days of time off) which they can allocate to staff on the basis of performance against agreed objectives. For a large organization, this may be the only practical way to run a performance management system: it is likely to be difficult and complex enough to cascade the organization's strategic objectives down to the level of individuals' objectives, without having to specify in detail what the consequences of an individual attaining his or her goals will be. The obvious downside to this greater flexibility, however, is that it may weaken the *perceived* link between measured performance and rewards, and so undermine the system of performance measurement. The extent to which this does occur will be closely related to the level of trust within the organization, and experience of the system in practice. In a context of antagonistic relations within the company, the suspicion that the managers of the system could entice high performance through the promise of rewards which never materialize to the extent envisaged may be enough to prevent that performance from being made in the first place.

Feedback and amendments

Two aspects of feedback and amendment are relevant to the design of systems of performance management: the feedback, and discussion of individuals' performance, to assist them in continuous improvement; and the review of functioning of the system as a whole.

Reviewing individual goals and behaviour

Goal-setting theory places great emphasis on the need for the feedback of information on performance if employees are to be motivated to perform well, and most applications of the theory go further to specify the need for coaching on how performance can be improved. This reflects the role of performance management as a *communications process,* serving a number of information-flow functions from establishing strategic objectives in the minds of employees, to offering advice on how performance can be improved. It is obviously the case that, whatever the motivation of a person to perform, if they genuinely cannot see how their behaviour should be altered, then they will be unable to achieve any performance improvements. Performance management, and specifically the appraisal process, should therefore provide a platform for practical advice on ways in which behaviour should be changed to contribute the organization's strategic objectives.

The difficulty with this aspect of the performance management approach is that it brings together two aspects of communication between which there may be a tension. When an appraisal process determines rewards, expectancy theory itself would predict that employee behaviour within the process will be directed instrumentally towards securing the rewards on offer. This may conflict with the openness and candour needed for a sensitive discussion of ways to improve performance. For example, employees may feel the need to present a façade of confidence and competence to their appraiser which masks difficulties they are experiencing, and which could possibly be addressed if brought to the attention of the organization. Moreover, from a strategic point of view, the process could encourage a 'groupthink' by which employees feel the need to express commitment to the strategic objectives of the organization (since it is performance against these which is rewarded), with the result that no critical appraisal of the objectives themselves is made, or at least expressed. This carries the great risk that strategies which are proving unworkable, or damaging, persist without amendment thereby handicapping the organization.

Reviewing the performance of the performance management systems

The second element of feedback and review concerns evaluation of the performance management process itself. Whereas we have characterized performance management as a cycle, expectancy theory is more often presented as a linear chain, without an internal feedback mechanism. To adapt the analysis of expectancy theory to the particular application of performance management we therefore need to build in a reflexivity into the process.

There are three reasons why continuous review of the operation of performance management needs to be conducted. First, the need for such reflexivity is fundamental to the strategic role of performance management. In the first section of this chapter we described one of the purposes of performance management as being to provide a framework for internally auditing the means by which the organization delivers wider strategic goals, with a view to continuously improving them. Secondly, as we have already pointed out, strategic goals themselves may be far from fixed, but rather constantly evolving. The likelihood is that some unknown contingencies will reveal themselves only in application, so that the system must be capable of reforming itself to take account of lessons from practice.

Table 15.1 summarizes the elements of continuous scrutiny to which a performance management system should be subject. Performing the tasks implied is a mechanical process, but requires investigative, diagnostic and design skills on the part of those responsible for the system.

Methodological criticisms

In the first section we argued that the performance management approach rests on a set of essentially rationalist assumptions. Expectancy theory, and to some extent goal-setting theory, are themselves founded on the premise that people – managers (the designers and operators of performance management systems) and employees (the people to whom they are applied) – think in a way which is optimizing, calculative and individualistic. This set of assumptions has been labelled variously *rational economic man* (Hollis and Nell, 1975), *neo-classical rationality* (Etzioni, 1988), or simply as *rationality* (Leibenstein, 1976).

Table 15.1 *Feedback loops in performance management*

Step	Review questions	Modifications
1 Identifying objectives	Are organizational objectives still appropriate?	Update objectives
	Are they adequately translated to group or individual level?	Amend cascade of objectives
2 Choosing measures	To what extent were measures • noise free? • objective? • simple to understand? • inexpensive to collect? • relevant to objectives?	Design and specify different sets of measures
3 Defining links between effort and measured performance	Is training adequate for objectives to be met?	Provide appropriate training if justified
	Is equipment adequate for objectives to be met?	Provide appropriate equipment if justified
	Is support adequate for objectives to be met? (including time available)	Reconfigure support (time allocation, assistance, organization)
	Are persons' capabilities adequate for objectives to be met?	Consider substitution of person or less demanding objectives
	Does team size encourage perception of weak link between effort and performance?	Redesign link between measures and rewards
	Do employees perceive link between effort and measured performance?	Design and implement communications strategy
4 Selecting rewards	Are rewards valued by employees?	Specify different rewards
5 Defining links between performance and rewards	Do employees perceive link between performance and rewards?	Design and implement communications strategy
	Are extraneous factors affecting performance or rewards?	Redesign link between measures and rewards

These assumptions are rarely made explicit, still less criticized, with the result that often little thought is given to questions such as whether they are correct at all times, and in all circumstances. Yet a growing body of theory and evidence suggests that human decision-making does not approximate to that assumed under this conception of rationality at all times and in all places. Mitchell (1980), for example, notes that the essential question is shifting from *does expectancy theory work?* to *where does it work?*

Take the question of national setting, for example. For many years researchers (such as Tonnies, 1922) have identified important and consistent differences in the *values* of different national cultures. Hofstede (1980) has argued that the value of individualism forms an axis by which countries can be categorized: in the United States a strongly individualistic value system suggests that policies which rely on enlightened self-interest may succeed; whereas in Sweden, whose dominant value system emphasizes more collective interests, such policies may fail.

> An Eastern approach might call for holism and generalisation, while a Western approach calls for analysis and specialisation. Latins might emphasise in-tuition and flexibility, and the German cultures might prefer self-control and structure [...] To a Dutchman, whose heroes are quiet men, empowering is a perfectly normal practice; to a Frenchman it would mean abandonment. (Hoecklin, 1995: 132)

Etzioni (1975) found that individualism went hand in hand with a *calculative* decision-making process, such as that assumed under expectancy theory, and so the success of policies such as performance-related pay which are based on this way of thinking will be contingent on an appropriate national setting. It is significant that while performance-related pay is widespread in the United States, it is much less common in continental Europe. Yet this is too often ignored by those who peddle prescriptions: as Hofstede notes 'the silent assumption of universal validity of culturally restricted findings is frequent. The empirical basis for American management theories is American organizations, and we should not assume without proof that they apply elsewhere' (Hofstede, 1980: 373).

It is not only nations which have values, governing ways of thinking and behaving, which may not be consistent with that assumed by expectancy theory and performance management. Particular organizations have their own traditions and cultures which may or may not be consistent with the successful use of performance management systems. For instance, research found that reactions to the introduction of performance-related pay were different across the 15 divisions of an Irish multi-divisional organization. The objectives of the HR Director who introduced the performance-related pay (PRP) scheme were often at variance with the managers involved, leading to difficulties with the scheme, as Box 15.5 shows.

Box 15.5   Contrasting views of PRP in an Irish multi-divisional company

'The managers did not share the same set of perceptions of the scheme, nor did they share the same value system: for some the most important element in their jobs was pay and PRP did have a strong effect on performance, for others the reverse was the case. These differences could not be explained by factors such as age, length of service, trade union membership or gender, but had to be sought in the companies within which these managers worked.

   This company comprised 15 subsidiaries, each with its own history and culture. Some were fairly new organizations, others were long established, yet the same PRP scheme had been implemented in each. From the HR Director's perspective, one of the objectives of the scheme was to reinforce and reward the changes involved in moving the company from a bureaucratic, public sector organization to one which would embrace a performance driven, enterprise way of thinking. However, given the diversity of companies operating within the group, it is not surprising to find that a uniform reward scheme was unable to achieve this purpose.' Kelly and Monks (1998: 216)

Another example might be companies with an entrenched culture of collective bargaining who find that the introduction of a performance-related pay system militates against the way employees think about their performance, and so prove unsuccessful. However, Guest (1993: 222) notes that 'attempts to use individualised PRP to drive a wedge through trade union membership have sometimes backfired.' At the very least, policies should diagnose at what level performance management should be applied: in an organization with a strong teamwork culture, individual incentives may be resisted as incompatible [...]; equally, group bonuses applied to a sales-force may violate passionately-held attachment to individual autonomy.

The importance of contextual factors, such as culture, in the success of performance management systems highlight a potential hidden agenda behind some organizations' adoption of the approach. Clark (1995) has argued that while performance-related pay is often claimed to be introduced in order to create an incentive for improved performance, it is sometimes chosen by managers wishing to instigate' *cultural change* rather than to achieve the vaunted improvements in individual performance. This may not be a misplaced strategy: Hofstede (1980) argues that changing first the behaviour of individuals, such as by forcing them to take part in a performance-related pay system, is one of the most effective ways of changing value systems, which are in turn (Schein, 1984) a principal component of organizational culture. If cultural change is the real objective of introducing performance management systems, their success cannot be gauged on whether the systems improve individuals' performance, because they are quite likely to depress it initially if introduced into an 'inappropriate' context, but must be judged on whether they ultimately bring about changes in attitudes and values.

Conclusions and summary

Performance management is an approach to managing human resources which is designed to tie HR policies securely into a framework of achieving the strategic goals of the business. To do so it advocates the formation of a system for managing human resources which generates personal goals from wider strategic objectives, provides information on the extent to which contributions are being made to these objectives, and supplies a means of auditing the process links which deliver the contributions. Rather than comprising a blueprint set of policies, performance management is an approach which can be implemented through a variety of linked policies, including objective-setting, performance appraisal and performance related pay.

The performance management approach draws on a number of theoretical models, of which expectancy theory and goal-setting theory are the most prominent. Applying the models to performance management highlights a set of critical factors which the designers and practitioners of performance management systems must address. These are associated with the feasibility of setting goals, measuring performance, rewarding performance, the design of the process links within the system, and procedures for feedback and amendment. What emerges is a complexity of issues which a precipitous move to implement a performance management system may overlook. Empirical studies, including those applied to performance-related pay, tend to confirm the importance of getting these factors right. In many cases organizations fail to do so, with the result that the effect of performance management systems on performance has not been strong in practice, and is sometimes negative.

The performance management approach can be criticized for relying on a model of management which is more rational than is achievable in practice. In particular, prescriptions are often couched in universalist terms, which take no account of the contextual factors which play a large part in determining success. The contextual factors include cross-cultural differences between nations, as well as different corporate environments and traditions.

In addition, by contrast with the social systems which link people in the organization, performance management may imply a relatively simplistic model by which to achieve enhanced performance in line with strategic objectives. It carries the danger that it may substitute a crude set of mechanisms for a subtle psychological contract linking the organization and its employees.

The overwhelming lesson from theory and practice is that the complex, and sometimes contradictory, set of issues which performance management comprises requires a critical approach to the design of systems. A performance management system, if it is to succeed, must reflect an appreciation of the particular characteristics of the organization, and have included within it a strong element of continuous review. An off-the-shelf approach to choosing a performance management system is highly unlikely to achieve its aim of contributing to the achievement of strategic objectives.

Key points

■ Performance management has become a popular vehicle for attempts to integrate the management of human resources with the organization's wider strategy.

■ Performance management refers to an approach, rather than a particular package of policies. The approach involves linking five policy elements: setting objectives, measuring performance, feeding back results, setting rewards, and amending objectives and activities.

■ Performance management is based on a rationalist conception of the organization and management, which may not reflect the subtlety, complexity and ambiguity of the actual world in which managers operate. In particular it has little to say about the social processes and power systems in which it will operate.

■ Principles of goal-setting theory and expectancy theory underpin the performance management approach. They offer a set of lessons for the design and implementation of performance management systems.

■ A host of crucial issues of design and implementation mean that operating a performance management system is a complex endeavour, requiring rigorous prior, and on-going analysis.

■ Empirical studies confirm that performance management systems are successful in improving performance only where fundamental design principles are followed.

■ The underlying assumptions of performance measurement tend to be universalist: they do not consider the importance of context. Yet the values of countries, organizations and people may depart from what is assumed, making models of performance management limited in their application.

References

Alchian, A.A. and Demsetz, H. (1972) 'Production, information cost and economic organization', *American Economic Review*, vol. 62, 777.

Clark, G. (1995) *Performance Related Pay in the Public Sector*, London: Social Market Foundation.

Etzioni, A. (1975) *A Comparative Analysis of Complex Organisations*, New York: Free Press.

Etzioni, A (1988) *The Moral Dimension*, New York: Free Press.

Fowler, A. (1990) 'Performance management: The MBO of the 1990s', *Personnel Management* vol. 22, 75–80.

Galbraith, J. and Cummings, L.L. (1967) 'An empirical investigation of the motivational determination of task performance', *Organizational Behaviour and Human Performance*, vol. 2, 237–57.

Guest, D. (1993) 'Current perspectives on human resource management in the United Kingdom', In A. Hegewisch and C. Brewster (eds), *European Developments in Human Resource Management*, London: Kogan Page.

Hoecklin, L. (1995) *Managing Cultural Differences: Strategies for Competitive Advantage*, Wokingham: Addison-Wesley.

Hofstede, G. (1980) *Culture's Consequences*, Beverley Hills, CA: Sage.

Hollis, M. and Nell, E.J. (1975) *Rational Economic Man: A Philosophical Critique of Neo-classical Economics*, London: Cambridge University Press.

Jevons, W.S. (1883) *Methods of Social Reform*, London: Macmillan.

Johnson, G. and Scholes, K. (1984) *Exploring Corporate Strategy*, London: Prentice-Hall.

Kanter, R.M. (1989) *When Giants Learn to Dance*, London: Unwin.

Kelly, A. and Monks, K. (1998) 'A view from the bridge and life on deck: Contrasts and contradictions in performance related pay', in C. Mabey, D. Skinner and T. Clark (eds), *Experiencing Human Resource Management*, London: Sage.

Kraiger, K. and Ford, J. (1985) 'A meta-analysis of rat race effects in performance ratings, *Journal of Applied Psychology*, vol. 70, 56–65.

Lawry-White, S. (1997) 'Management issues facing voluntary organisations', Briefing Paper, Swindon: Vine Management Consulting.

Leibenstein, H. (1976) *Beyond Economic Man*, Cambridge, MA: Harvard University Press.

Lewin, K. (1938) *Conceptual Representation*, Durham, NC: Duke University Press.

Locke, E.A., Shaw, K.N., Saari, L.M. and Latham, G.P. (1981) 'Goal setting and task performance 1969–1980', *Psychological Bulletin*, vol. 90, 125–52.

McKersie, R.B. (1986) 'The promise of gain-sharing', *ILR Report*, 7–11.

Mento, A.J., Steel, R.P. and Karren, R.J. (1987) 'A meta-analytic study of task performance: 1966–1984', *Organizational Behavior and Human Decision Processes*, vol. 39, 52–83.

Mintzberg, H. (1992) 'Five Ps for strategy' in H. Mintzberg and J. Quinn (eds), *The Strategy Process*, Englewood Hills, NJ: Prentice-Hall.

Mitchell, T. (1980) 'Motivation: New directions for theory and practice', *Academy of Management Review*, vol. 7, 80–8.

Schein, E. (1984) 'Coming to a new awareness of organizational culture', *Sloan Management Review*, Winter, 3–16.

Stiles, P., Gratton, L., Truss, C., Hope-Hailey, V. and McGovern, P. (1997) 'Performance Management and the psychological contract', *Human Resource Management Journal*, vol. 7, no. 1, 57–66.

Tolman, E.C. (1932) *Purposive Behaviour in Animals and Men*, New York: Century.

Tonnies, F. (1922) *Gemeinschaft and Gesellschaft*, Berlin: Curtins.

Vroom, V. (1964) *Work and Motivation*, New York: Wiley.

Walsh, E. (1992) 'Management accounting and the measurement of business performance: some dilemmas', in K. Bradley (ed.), *Human Resource Management: People and Performance*, Aldershot: Dartmouth.

Index

360 degree feedback, 51, 326

ACAS, 182, 183
accounting profits, 130
alliances, 199–201
 and employment relations, 208–36
alternative work practices, 149
analogy and metaphor, in strategic
  decision-making, 79, 83–5, 86, 87, 88
Andersen, Arthur, 281–2, 290
Appelbaum, E., 154
appraisal, 51, 67, 69, 325–6, 334
architectural approach, 20–1, 24
Argyris, C., 32
Arthur, J.B., 26
Asda, 259–63
Ashkenas, R., 205
availability heuristic, 80–1, 86, 88
avowal, 73
Axelrod, R., 82

bad-apple theory, 277–9
Bailey, T., 126, 157–8
Bains, Gurnek, 266
Baird, L., 124
Bakker, Jim, 285
Baldamus, W., 63
Barker, J.R., 154
Barling, J., 241
Barney, J., 18–19, 25
Baron, R.M., 140
Barrett, Richard, 253
Barton, Leonard, 95
BBC, 200–1
Becker, G., 153
behavioural decision theory, 80
Benetton, 201
'best practice' HRM, 221, 222
body, control of actions of, 68
Bougon, M., 82
boundaryless organization, 205
Boxall, P., 4–5, 20, 24, 26
Boyatzis, R., 48–9
Boyle, David, 254
Boyne, G.A., 230
Brading, E., 177–8
brand values and cultures, 253–70
Brown, W., 180, 247
BT, 198
Burchell, B., 211

Burchell, Graham, 44, 54
bureaucracy, 189
 bureaucratic control system, 190–1
 dual potential of, 205
 reform of, 191–3
 vs. enterprise, 8
 vs. excellence, 43
Burke, James, 283–4
Burns, T., 108
business ethics, 273–94
 bad-apple theory, 277–9
 and CEO, 291
 complexity of decisions, 273–7
 ethical culture, 280–2, 287–9
 ethical leadership, 283–6, 288, 290–1
 ethically silent leadership, 285–6
 ethics management guidelines, 287–91
  communicate importance of ethical
   standards, 289
  focus on reward system, 289–90
  promote ethical leadership, 290–1
  understand existing ethical
   culture, 288–9
 and faddish solutions, 287
 fall of Arthur Andersen, 281–2
 formal codes and programmes, 279–82
 hypocritical leaders, 285
 leader as moral person and moral
  manager, 283–6
 and moral development, 275–6
 myths about, 273–87
 need for moral awareness, 274–5
 and organizational context, 276–7
 and peer influence, 277, 278
 and supervisors, 291
 unethical behaviour not new, 286–7
 unethical leaders, 284–5
business performance, 117–83
Business Process Re-engineering,
  6, 194–7
business spirituality, 268

'cafeteria principle', 181
call centres, 228, 263–5
Cameron, Deborah, 269
capitalization of time, 69–70
Cappelli, P., 19, 151, 157, 223
car industry, 157, 244
centres of excellence, 196
Champy, J., 6, 47, 196, 307

change, management of, 7, 295–317
  characteristics of change
      programmes, 296–8
    adoption of best practice, 298
    communication of vision, 296–7
    management determination, 297
    planning and preparation, 297–8
    vision, 296
  consequences of change
      programmes, 304–5
  flawed assumptions about change, 305
  and gap analysis, 297
  and 'hearts and minds', 297
  instrumental view of change, 304–5
  and leading and learning, 316
  and leaning into future, 315–17
  and mental models, 295–6
  and organizations as living
      systems, 309–15
    anxiety about change, 311
    awareness of current reality, 311–12
    change as natural but difficult, 310–11
    change as self-inflicted, 311
    importance of feelings and
        emotions, 314
    living with uncertainty, 314
    managers should try less hard, 314–15
    need for change at all levels, 313–14
    need for stability, 311
    organizations as adaptive, 309
    organizations as dynamic, 309
    organizations as interdependent
        with environment, 309
    organizations as self-organizing, 309
    reinforcement of emerging
        patterns, 312–13
    uniqueness of organizations, 312
  and organizations as machines, 305–9
    change as driven, 305–6
    change as issue for others, 308
    magic bullet answers, 306–7
    need to plan and predict change, 308
    reengineering, 307–8
    visioning, 306
  problems with change
      programmes, 299–304
    change as 'messy', 300
    inward focus, 303
    mistaking structure for
        organization, 302–3
    perceptual gap between leaders and
        followers, 299–300
    programmitis, 303–4
    reorganizations, 303
    repeated rescues, 302
    unintended consequences, 299
    vision, 300–2

change, management of, cont.
    and resistance, 297
    and steering group, 297–8
    'top-down' change programmes, 296
    two models of change compared, 305–15
'change agents', 255, 256
child labour, 274
Chittipeddi, K., 83
Ciulla, Joanne, 267, 269–70
Clark, G., 338
classification schemes, 67
Coff, R., 222
cognition
    and innovation, 95–6
    and strategic decision-making, 78–90
cognitive heuristics and biases, 79–81,
        85–6, 87, 88
cognitive maps, 82–3, 85–6, 87
cognitive moral development, 275–6
cognitive simplification, 79, 86
Coleman, J.S., 32
Collins, M., 180
competence(s)/competency(ies)
    and actual performance, 49
    behavioural model of, 48–9
    competence principle, 49
    competency approach, 50–3
        criticism of, 52, 53, 55
    competency audit, 50–1
    constitution of 'competent' manager, 40–57
    definitions of, 49
    identification of, 50
    implementation of, 50
    and job analysis, 69
    measurement of, 50–1
    portfolio of, 29–30
    'soft', 52, 53
    turn to, 40, 48–50
competitive advantage, 18–20, 21, 22,
        28, 91
competitive strategy, 124, 125, 129–30
concertive control, 154, 156
confession, the, 73–4
contingent approaches to HRM, 221–2
contingent workers, 218
contract(s), 210–11
    articulation of, 67–70
    indeterminacy of, 63–4
    and managers, 46
    and multi-employer relationships, 229–30
    and performance-related pay, 179–80
    short-term, 2, 3
contractualization, 44
Coombs, J.G., 217–18
Coombs, R., 96
Cooper, R., 92
core competencies, 27–8, 29–30, 34, 95, 198

core organization, and networks, 204
corporate financial performance, impact of
        HRM practices on, 121–46, 150–4
    and competitive strategy, 124, 125, 129–30
    employee motivation factor, 126
    employee skills and organizational
        structures factor, 126
    and fit concept, 123–4
    fit vs. 'best practices', 124–5
    and HR policy consistency, 128
    limitations of prior empirical work,
        122–4, 151–2
    measurement of High Performance Work
        Practices, 126
    measurement of internal and external
        fit, 128–30
    and productivity, 130, 135–7, 140–1
    sources of gains, 140–1
    and systems of HRM practices, 123–4
    theoretical background, 122–5
    and turnover, 130, 132–5, 140–1
Crocker, J., 83
culture change programmes, 6–7
Curme, M.A., 131
customer value, 197
Cyert, R.M., 96

Davidow, W.H., 201–2
Deakin, S., 228
decentralization, 192
decision-making
    ethical, 273–7
    strategic, see strategic decision-making
Delaney, J., 148
Delbridge, R., 155
Delery, J., 26
Devanna, M.A., 17, 144
developmental appraisals, 73–4
Dewe, P., 241
Direct Line, 333
disciplinary practices, and knowledge
        and power, 64–75
disciplinary procedures, 74, 224, 227, 290
discipline, 60–1
discourse concept, 42
discretionary behaviour, 21–2, 265–6
Disney, R., 248
disposable workplaces, 157, 166
dividing practices, 64–7
Dougherty, D., 95
downsizing, 192
Drago, R., 157
Dreyfus, H., 59
DTI, 91
dual commitment, 238, 240–2
du Gay, P., 8
Dunlap, Al, 284–5

Dutton, J., 79
dynamic capabilities, 30–1, 34, 96

economic profits, 130
Edwards, R., 190
Eisenhardt, K.M., 30
Ellwood, D., 162
emotional investment, 265–6
employee, defined, 210
employee behaviour, 21–2
employee compensation, 137
employer brand, 253
employment protection, 210–11
Employment Relations Act
        1999, 211
employment relationship
    and changing organizational
        forms, 208–36
    and Foucault's work, 63–4
    legal definition broadened, 210–16
    in liberal market economies, 164–8
empowerment, 269
enclosure, 64, 65
enterprise, 8
enterprise form, 44, 53
'entrepreneur of the self', 45, 54
entrepreneurial governance and
        managers, 43–7, 54–5
equal pay legislation, 226
Eribon D., 60
ethics, see business ethics
Etzioni, A., 337
examination, the, 71–3
excellence, 6, 43
expectancy theory, 319–20, 325–7,
        329–31, 335, 337
external pay relationships, 181
extrinsic rewards, 327–8

Fiorito, A., 160
fit, 123–4, 143
    external, 124, 125, 129–30, 141–2
    internal, 124–5, 128–9, 141
    and managers' theories of
        innovation, 91–115
    as matching, 128, 129, 141, 142
    measurement of, 128–30
    as moderation, 128–9, 141
    vs. 'best practices', 124–5
Flamholtz, E., 70
Fombrun, C.J., 17
Forth, J., 158
Foucault, Michel, 48, 58–77
Fowler, A., 323
franchises, 225, 227
Freeman, R., 82, 151, 155, 160
Fullager, C., 241

Gabriel, Y., 189
gainsharing, 332
Gardner, T.M., 26
Garland, D., 71
George, Bill, 284
Gerhart, B., 26
Gibbons, M., 97
Gilovich, T., 84–5
Gioia, D., 83
Gittell, J.H., 223
Gittleman, M., 157, 162
goal-setting theory, 319, 327, 328,
    329–30, 334
Godard, J., 148, 151, 153, 159, 163, 167
Godfrey, P.C., 26
Gordon, C., 44–5, 60
Gorz, André, 268
governmentality, 60, 66
Grant, R.M., 31
Greenspan, Alan, 287
Gronhaug, K., 29–30
group performance pay, 182
groups, strategic decision-making in, 79
Guest, D., 6, 151, 156, 221, 222, 239,
    241, 338

Hambrick, D., 78
Hamel, G., 29, 48, 192, 205, 267
Hammer, M., 6, 195, 196–7, 307
Handel, M., 157
Handy, C., 42, 267
Harley, B., 155
Herzberg, F., 180
heuristics and biases, in strategic
    decision-making, 79–81, 85–6, 87, 88
high commitment management, 221
high-performance practices (HPPs),
    118, 147–76
    alternative work practices, 149
    complementarities thesis, 150, 151, 152–3
    and co-ordinated market economies, 168
    costs of, 153, 165–7
    and economic performance, 121–46, 150–4
    high-commitment employment
        practices, 149
    high-performance paradigm, 148–9, 161–4
    implications for public policy-makers, 170
    implications for unions, 147, 159–61
    implications for workers, 154–8, 166–7
    intensification approach, 149, 157, 165–6
    involvement approach, 149, 157, 165
    'lean' vs. 'team' systems, 149
    levels of adoption of, 152, 162, 166
    and liberal market economies, 164–8
    and managerial failures, 162–3
    and market failures, 163–4, 168
    matching thesis, 150, 151, 153

high-performance practices (HPPs), cont.
    measurement of, 126
    and pay, 157–8
    political economy approach to
        limitations of, 164–8
    and structural variables, 167
Hill, C.W.L., 26, 218
Hill, S., 53
Hochschild, A., 74
Hoecklin, L., 337
Hofstede, G., 337, 338
Hoque, K., 223
Huber, G.P., 231–2
Huff, A., 85
Hull, R., 96
human asset accounting, 70
human capital, 25, 27–8, 32, 33
human capital advantage, 20
human capital pool, 19–20, 21, 22, 24–5
human process advantage, 20
human resource advantage, 20
human resource management (HRM)
    as construction and production of
        knowledge, 64
    Foucault's implications for, 63–75
    impact on corporate financial
        performance, 121–46
    and power/knowledge, 58–77
    'soft' and 'hard' versions, 221–2
    and trade unions and industrial
        relations, 237–50
human resources
    and new organizational forms, 189–207
    and resource-based view of firm, 17–39
    vs. human resource practices, 19–20
Hunter, L., 209
Huselid, M.A., 23, 26, 150–1, 153, 159
Hutchinson, S., 223

Ichniowski, C., 152–3
Iles, P., 52
illusion of control, 81, 86, 87, 88
individual
    concept of, 61–2
    constitution of, 70–5
    focus on, 257
    'knowability' of, 62, 71
individualism, and performance
    management, 337
individualization, 72
individuation, 72
industrial relations, 1–2, 237–50
    and 'black hole' option, 243, 248–9
    and commitment, 239–42
    and individualized HRM option,
        243, 247–8
    and 'new realism' option, 243, 244–6

industrial relations, *cont.*
  and policy options, 242–9
  and traditional collectivism option,
      243, 246–7
industrial subject, creation of, 70–5
information technology, 217
inimitability, and HR practices, 19–20
Innes, P., 192
innovation
  and 'ambidexterity', 95, 109
  cognitive approach to, 95–6
  as desirable or threat, 100–1, 107–13
  enablers and barriers, 94–6
  gap between theory and practice, 92
  importance of, 91–2
  incremental, 94, 98
  innovation management
      systems, 103, 111
  and leadership, 109, 111
  and loose/tight polarity, 105, 108
  managers' theories of, 91–115
  meanings and definitions of, 93, 98–9
  and organizational cultures, 105–7, 111
  and perceptions of chief executives, 95
  process innovation, 194–5
  and product businesses, 104
  radical, 94, 98, 111
  and size of organization, 94–5
  and structures, 102–5, 111
  underlying attitude towards, 112
intellectual capital, 28, 33, 205
internal labour markets, 190–1
internal pay relationships, 180–1
interpersonal skills training, 69
intrinsic rewards, 327
Isenberg, D., 83–4

job analysis, 68–9
job evaluation, 66, 180–1
job-related knowledge, 31
joint ventures, 199–201, 217, 219
Jones, T.M., 275

Kahneman, D., 80
Kanter, R., 52, 331
Katz, H., 244
keitsu, 203
Kelly, A., 338
Kelly, J., 160
Kenney, J., 69
Kenny, D.A., 140
Kessler, I., 177, 178, 179, 182
Ketchen, D.J., 217–18
King, A.W., 26
Kirkman, B.L., 202
Klein, K., 95
Kleinschmidt, E., 92

knowledge
  as asset, 252–3
  firm-specific, 217–18
  HRM as construction and production
      of, 64
  mode 2 production, 97
  and new organizational forms, 217–18, 219
  and power, 15–16, 58–77
  SHRM and, 13–115
knowledge-based companies, 252–3, 259
knowledge-based theories of firm, 31–2
knowledge management behaviour, 33
knowledge repositories, 32
Koch, M.J., 23–4
Kochan, T., 160, 244
Kohlberg, Lawrence, 275
Kotter, John, 296–7

labour
  as asset, 1
  gendered division of, 65
  paid vs. unpaid, 65
labour process, articulation of, 67–70
Lado, A.A., 20
Langer, E.J., 81, 87
language, use of, 268–9
Lawler, E., 50
Lawry-White, S., 328
leadership, 7
  and business ethics, 283–6, 287–91
  and innovation, 109, 111
  and managing change, 299–300, 306,
      313, 316–17
Lefebvre, L., 95
Leonard-Barton, D., 32
Lepak, D.P., 20–1, 24, 30
Liebeskind, J.P., 31
Likert scales, 66–7
Littler, C.R., 192
Locke, Edwin, 319
Lyles, M., 79

McCormick, B., 26
MacDuffie, J.P., 21–2
McGrath, R.G., 23–4
McGregor, D., 73
McKersie, R., 244
McMahan, G.C., 19–20, 24, 26
McWilliams, A., 19–20
'making a difference', 266
Malone, M.S., 201–2
management, redefinition of, 46
management by objectives (MBO)
      systems, 69–70
manager(s), 40–57
  character of, 42
  competence of, 47–53, 69

manager(s), *cont.*
  contemporary managerial discourse and
    conduct of management, 42–3
  contract with employer, 46
  enhanced role for, 48
  and entrepreneurial governance and
    personal conduct, 43–7
  ethics management guidelines for, 287–91
  and high-performance practices, 162–3
  'making up' of, 41–2, 48, 54
  mobilization of subjectivity of, 53–5
  moral, 283–4, 285
  and performance-related pay, 179
  role of theorizing by, 9
  self-improvement of, 51
  theories of innovation, 91–115
managing change, *see* change,
  management of
Mangham, I., 47–8
manual and non-manual workers, division
  between, 181–2
March, J., 22, 96
Marginson, P., 249
Marglin, S., 217
market-relevant knowledge, 31
Markides, C., 95
Martin, J.A., 30
Maslow, Abraham, 251, 252, 266
Mason, P., 78
Mason, R.O., 79, 82
mathesis, 65, 66, 67
Matusik, S.F., 218
May, E., 84
meaning, employees' need for, 266–8
mechanical view of organizations, 308–9,
  315, 316
mentoring, 74, 257
Merck, 200
mergers, 199–201
Meshoulam, I., 124
Metcalf, D., 247
Micklethwait, John, 253
Microsoft, 254–9
Miles, R.E., 17
Milgram, Stanley, 278
Miller, P., 48, 54
Millward, N., 158, 249
Mintzberg, H., 78, 85, 311
missionary management, 251–70
Mitchell, T., 337
Mitroff, I.I., 79, 82
mode 2 knowledge production, 97
Monks, K., 338
moral awareness, 274–5
moral development, 275–6
moral judgement, 275
moral managers, 283–4, 285

Morgan, G., 43
Morgan, JP, 327
Moynihan, L.M., 26
multi-employer relationships, 208–36
  and areas of ambiguity, 214–16
  conflicts and contradictions in, 224–9
  and conflicts of interest, 215–16
  and contract or status, 229–30
  and discipline, 215, 227
  and grievances, 215
  legal definition of, 210–16
  and loyalty and confidentiality,
    215–16, 218
  and motivation, 218
  and organizational commitment, 222–4,
    228–9, 232
  and pay and conditions, 224–6
  and performance management, 226–8
  and skilled labour, 218–19
  and supervision and control issues, 215
mystery shoppers, 260

networks, 201–4
  and employment relations, 208–36
Neumark, D., 151, 157
'new managerial work', 40, 52, 53
Nissan, 244
Nonaka, I., 205
non-union firms, 249
Nordhaug, O., 29–30
Nortel, 102–4, 109

obedience-to-authority experiments, 278
oil industry, 248
Orange, 263–5
O'Reilly, C.A., 96
organizational capital, 25, 27–8, 32
organizational change, 7, 295–317
organizational commitment, 2
  definition, 240
  and industrial relations, 238, 239–42
  and multi-employer relationships, 222–4,
    228–9, 232
organizational culture
  change programmes, 6–7
  and ethics, 280, 281–2, 287–9
  and innovation, 105–7, 111
  and performance management, 337–9
organizational forms and relationships,
  new, 185–270
  and employment relationship, 208–36
  'hard' and 'soft' aspects, 190
  and learning and knowledge acquisition,
    217–18, 219
  links with human resources, 189–207
  and resource-based view of firm, 217
  and transaction costs, 216–17

organizational governance, entrepreneurial, 43–7, 54
organizational learning, 32, 231–2
organizational process advantage, 20
Osterman, P., 157, 162, 163, 164
outsourcing, 197–9, 204–5
    and employment relations, 213, 217, 219, 225–6, 227–8
ownership, 269

Park, H., 26
partitioning, 64, 65, 66
partnerships, and employment relations, 208–36
passion, 268–9
pay and conditions, and multi-employer relationships, 224–6
pay structure, 180–1
people management systems, 22, 27, 33, 34
performance management, 318–41
    as communications process, 334
    and expectancy theory, 319–20, 325–7, 329–31, 335, 337
    and goal-setting theory, 319, 327, 328, 329–30, 334
    and individualism, 337
    methodological criticisms of approach, 335–9
    and multi-employer relationships, 226–8
    and national setting, 337
    and organizational culture, 337–9
    and rationality, 335–7
    and responsibilization, 46
    systems design, 320–35
        appraisal systems, 67, 69, 325–6, 334
        and audit, 325
        and communications policy, 331
        feedback and amendments, 334–5
        and individual differences, 329
        linking effort and measured performance, 330–1
        linking measured performance and rewards, 331–4
        marginal valence problem, 329
        noise elements and performance measures, 332
        performance measurement, 323–6
        process links, 329–34
        and psychological contract, 322
        qualitative measures, 324–5
        quantitative measures, 323–4
        rater bias problems, 326
        rewarding performance, 327–9
        setting goals, 321–2
        and subjective judgements, 325
        team-based systems, 331

performance management, cont.
    validity and reliability of measures, 324–5
    theory, 318–20
    and voluntary organizations, 328
performance-related pay (PRP), 118–19, 177–83
    contingency approach, 179
    and contract, 179–80
    and fairness, 180
    and groups, 182
    ideological reasons for, 179
    and intrinsic motivation, 178
    and managers' choices of pay systems, 179
    merit rating, 177
    and national setting, 337
    and organizational culture, 337–9
    and pay structure, 180–1
    and performance assessment process, 178
    and profit sharing, 182–3
    and reward management issues, 180–3, 328, 333
    and rewards as 'motivator' or 'hygiene' factor, 180
    and self-development, 45–6
    and status differences, 181–2
    types of, 177
personality testing, 72
Peters, T., 6, 49, 266, 267
Philip, M., 59
Pisano, G., 96
Pollard, S., 41
Porter, M.E., 17, 129
post bureaucracy thesis, 189
power
    and appraisal, 326
    creative element of, 61
    'how' of, 60
    and knowledge, 15–16, 58–77
    relational aspect, 59–60
Prahalad, C.K., 29, 48, 192, 205
prescreening inventories, 73
process-centred organization, 195, 196
process innovation, 194–5
process management, 193–7
process performer, 196
process re-engineering, 194–7
product development capabilities, 27
productivity, impact of HRM practices on, 121–46
productivity bargaining, 2
productivity rating index, 70
profit sharing, 182–3
psychological contract
    new, 252, 254, 265–70
    and performance management, 322
Purcell, J., 4–5

quality issue, 315–16
Quinn, J.B., 198, 205

Rabinow, P., 59
racial diversity, 24–5
Ramsay, H., 155, 156
ranking, 64, 65–7
Rau, B.L., 159
re-engineering, 6, 194–7, 307–8
Reichers, A., 240
resource-based view of firm (RBV),
    14–15, 17–39
  application to SHRM, 18–19
  and changing organizational forms, 217
  convergence with SHRM, 28–32
  and core competencies, 29–30
  and dynamic capabilities, 30–1
  and empirical SHRM research, 23–8
  integration of strategy and SHRM
    within, 32–5
  and knowledge-based theories of
    firm, 31–2
  and macro perspective, 28
  and SHRM theory, 19–23
responsibilization of self, 46, 47
reward management
  and ethical behaviour, 289–90
  and performance management,
    326–9, 331–4
  and performance-related pay, 180–3
Richard, O.C., 24–5
Roche, W., 159, 160
Rorty, A., 41
Rose, N., 47, 48, 71, 72, 74
Rosen, B., 202

Salaman, G., 52
Sapienza, A.M., 84
Scarbrough, H., 209, 225
Schein, E.H., 288
schemata, strategic, 79, 83, 85–8
Schon, D.A., 32
Schroder, H.M., 49
Schwenk, C., 81
scientific discourse, 61
scientific management, 68
Sears, Michael, 285
selection interviews, 73
selection testing, 66, 71–2
self-actualization, 251–2
self-employment, 211
Senge, P., 205
Shared Service Centre (SSC), 200–1
Sherman, W.S., 26
short-term contracts, 2, 3
Shrivastava, P., 82
Silver, M., 47–8

Simon, H., 22, 79, 86
Singh, H., 19
skills
  and multi-employer relationships, 218–19,
    223, 226
  and resource-based view of firm, 20, 21,
    22, 33
Smart, D.L., 24
Snell, S.A., 20–1, 24, 25, 26, 30
Snow, C.C., 17
social capital, 25, 27–8, 32
social rewards, 266
Sorra, J., 95
'soul work', 257, 258, 268
Stalker, G.M., 108
status approach, and multi-employer
    relationships, 229–30
status divide, 181–2
Steeneveld, M., 24, 26
Steinbruner, J.D., 84
Storey, J., 4, 7, 239, 245
strategic decision-making and
    cognitions, 78–90
  analogy and metaphor, 79, 83–5, 86,
    87, 88
  cognitive maps, 82–3, 85–6, 87
  cognitive simplification, 79, 86
  complexity of problems, 79
  decision aids, 89
  heuristics and biases, 79–81, 85–6, 87, 88
  integrative model of, 85–8
  interaction of biases, 81
  and personal/industry experiences,
    87, 88
  and recent successful decisions, 87, 88
  research on, 79–85
  schemata, 79, 83, 85–8
  and stakeholders, 82
  strategic assumptions, 79–80, 82, 87
Strategic Human Resource
    Management (SHRM)
  and business performance, 117–83
  categories of, 3–5
  definition, 3–9
  elements of, 13
  and knowledge, 13–115
  model of basic components, 21–2, 23
  in practice, 271–341
  significance of, 1–3
  and societal/political discourses,
    6, 7–8, 9
  and underlying forces, 5–9
Strategic Human Resources Management
    Index, 144
strategic objectives, and performance
    goals, 322
strategic outsourcing, 197–9, 204–5

strategic problems
    solutions to, 85
    understanding of, 85
strategy and HR, resource-based view of
    firm as link, 17–39
Streeck, W., 229, 230
'strength finder' programme, 255
subjectivity, 59, 61–2, 70–5
supply chain management, 193–7
    and employment relationship, 212–13

taxinomia, 65–6
Taylor, C., 72
Taylor, S., 83
team involvement system, 149
technologies of self, 71
Teece, D.J., 31, 91, 96, 113
temporal regulation, 68
temporary workers, 215, 225
Thompson, J.D., 206
360 degree feedback, 51, 326
Tichy, N.M., 17
time compression diseconomies, 22, 27
Toffler, Barbara, 281, 282
Tolman, E., 82
trade unions, see unions
training, 69, 229
Transfer of Undertakings (Protection of
    Employment) 'TUPE' Regulations
    1981, 213, 226
trust relationships, 230
Turner, S., 58, 59
turnover, impact of HRM practices
    on, 121–46
Tushman, M.L., 96
Tversky, A., 80

unions, 237–50
    and 'beauty contest', 244
    decline in significance of, 237, 248–9
    and developments in industrial
        relations and HRM, 242–9
    and dual commitment, 240–2
    and high-performance practices,
        147, 159–61
    and status differences, 182

valence, and rewards, 320,
    327, 329
Valentin, E.K., 96
value chain, 203, 204
Venkatraman, N., 128
virtual organizations, 201–4,
    205, 217
virtual teams, 202
vision statements, 301
voluntary organizations, 328
von Hippel, E., 96
Vroom, Victor, 319

Wade, B., 241
Walker, J., 17
Walsh, K., 228
Walton, R., 239, 244
Waterman, R., 6
Waters, J., 78
Weick, K., 82
Weill, Sandy, 286
Welch, Jack, 265, 268
Wells, D., 161
Wernerfelt, B., 18
whistleblowers, 277
White, H., 74
White, M., 156–7
Whitfield, K., 155
Williamson, O., 63
Wilson, M.C., 20
Wood, S., 152
Woodruffe, C., 49
Woolridge, Adrian, 253
workers
    definition and use of term, 208,
        211, 223–4
    enterprise among, 47
    implications of high-performance
        practices for, 154–8, 166–7
Wright, P.M., 19–20, 24, 26
Wright, V., 177–8

Youndt, M.A., 25
Young, A., 160

Zeithaml, C.P., 26